San Francisco Autumn 2004

Dear Mary

Happy birthday to you
from Tapper Buffett,
Susie. Anne and me.
Fondly,   Michèle

Life in the
FRENCH
COUNTRY
HOUSE

Life in the FRENCH COUNTRY HOUSE

Mark Girouard

ALFRED A. KNOPF
NEW YORK 2000

This is a Borzoi Book

Published by Alfred A. Knopf

Copyright © 2000 by Mark Girouard

All rights reserved under International and Pan-American
Copyright Conventions.

Published in the United States by Alfred A. Knopf, a division of
Random House, Inc., New York, and published in Canada by
Random House of Canada Limited, Toronto.

Distributed by Random House, Inc., New York.
www.randomhouse.com

Originally published in Great Britain by Cassell & Co, London.

Library of Congress Cataloging-in-Publication Data

Girouard, Mark.
   Life in the French country house / Mark Girouard.
     p. cm.
   Includes index.
   ISBN 0-679-42711-2 (alk. paper)
   1. Country homes–France–Social life and customs–Pictorial works. 2. Upper
class–Dwellings–France–Pictorial works. 3. Home economics–France–Pictorial works.
4. Architecture, Domestic–France–Pictorial works. I. Title.

DC33 G53 2000
944–dc21

Knopf, Borzoi Books, and the colophon are registered
trademarks of Random House, Inc.

Designed by Nigel Soper
Typeset in Bembo
Manufactured in Italy

First American Edition

(ENDPAPERS) *The grand salon of the château of Montgeoffroy.*

(PREVIOUS PAGE) *A jovial dinner given by the Prince of Salm in eastern France in
about 1770. Coats have been left at a table by the entry to the salle à manger, and
bottles are kept cool in water-filled containers strategically disposed around the table.*

*Family and friends dressed for theatricals posing in front of the château at Boisset-les-
Prévanches – c. 1900.*

(NEXT PAGE) *French eighteenth-century châteaux were designed to accommodate
large house-parties, and even the smaller bedrooms were fitted up with elegantly
appointed beds and chairs, as at the château of Montgeoffroy, which preserves much of
its original furniture and fittings.*

TO MY SISTERS

CONTENTS

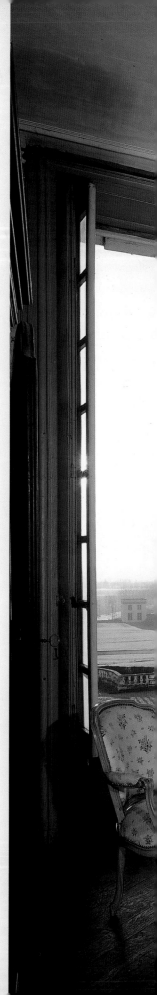

FOREWORD

THIS BOOK IS CONCERNED with how French châteaux and seigneurial residences were lived in from the fourteenth to the twentieth centuries, and how the way in which they were used was reflected in their planning and architecture. To keep the subject within manageable dimensions I deal only marginally with royal residences or town houses, scarcely at all with parks or gardens, and have not concerned myself with the details of furnishing and decoration which have been so richly covered in Jean Feray's *Architecture intérieur et décoration en France* (1988). Even so the field remains an enormous one and stimulating though it has been to explore the richness and complexities of French châteaux through the centuries I am only too aware of the shortcomings of what is essentially a pioneering work.

I am grateful for all the help and hospitality I have had from the very many owners or curators of châteaux, private and public, which I visited, often arriving out of the blue and being more kindly received than I deserved. A full list would be wearisome, but for their generosity in giving me access to archival material, as well as help in other ways, I would especially like to thank the Baron d'Aligny, Monsieur Emmanuel Arnauld d'Andilly, Vicomtesse Jean-Pierre de Baritault du Carpia, the Marquis de Puget de Barbentane, the Marquis de Brissac, Comte Laurent de Beaumont de Repaire, the Comtesse de La Loge d'Ausson, the Comtesse de l'Espinasse de Bournazel, Comte Albert Pasquier de Franclieu, the Marquise and Marquis de Lastic, the Vicomte de La Panouse, Monsieur Alain Delom de Mézerac, the Marquis de Quinsonas-Oudinot, the Vicomte de Rohan, the Duc de Rohan, the Marquis de Rosanbo, Comte Louis de Vogüé, the Baron de Watteville-Berckheim, Comte Raymond de Nicolay and Comte Hugues de Bonardi du Mesnil. The last two have been especially generous with their time and help.

I have warm memories of the courtesy and kindness of Prince and Princesse Jean-Charles de Ligne La Tremoille, and of the stimulating company of Madame Marie Mallet. I would also like to thank the Marquis de Contades, Baronne Élie de Rothschild, the Princesses Charles-Louis and George-Henri de la Tour d'Auvergne Lauraguais, the Princesse de Beauvau-Craon, Comtesse Hubert de Commarque-Pinet de Senailhac, Comtesse Antoine de Dreux-Brézé, Comte Christian de Pourtalès-Schickler, Madame Emmanuel de Margerie, Comte Pierre de Bizemont, Monsieur Jean-Jacques Journet, Baron and Baronne de Rochetaillé, Monsieur Pierre Salmon-Legagneur, Prince Carlos d'Arenberg, Odile Rosetti-Balanesco, Christiane de

Nicolay-Mazery, Beatrice de Boisanger, Louis Decazes, Howard Adams and Philip and Patricia Hawkes for help, interest, advice, or especial kindness. Comte and Comtesse Henri Méhérenc de Saint Pierre have been unfailingly supportive from the beginning of my researches.

It is sad that a work that has occupied me for several years inevitably has an obituary element. Three friends, old and new, who took an especial interest in the progress of my book, and did much to help me, died while I was in the course of its preparation: Jean-Charles (Bobby) de Saint Victor, Jean de Selancy and Isabel de Watteville. A grievous loss was the death, in a car accident early this year, of Jean Feray, to whose unrivalled knowledge and infectious enthusiasm the châteaux and monuments of France owed so much, and who had been unfailingly helpful. Another sad death was that of Alain Nazare-Aga, always generous with suggestions based on his extensive knowledge of châteaux and their contents. I am grateful to the Leverhulme Trust for a Research Fellowship that helped fund my first two years of research.

Among fellow historians who have generously shared knowledge and ideas, I must especially thank Monique Chatenet, Jean Guillaume, Claude Mignot, Mary Whiteley, Olivier Meslay, Thierry Crépin-Leblond, John Whitehead, Philippe Seydoux, Claude d'Anthenaise, Bernard Toulier, Jean-Jacques Rioult, Christophe Amiot, Guy Le Goff, Vincent Bouvet, Alexandre Pradere, Annie Regond, John Rosselli, Charles Coulson, Dominique Letellier, Pauline Prevost-Marcilhacy and Bruno Tollon. I owe much to the efficiency and helpfulness of the staff of the Archives Nationales, the library of the Institut de France, and departmental archives and libraries throughout France. Perhaps this is also the place to lament the passing of the old reading room of the Bibliothèque Nationale, where I spent many fruitful hours, and to hope that the new library is emerging from the troubles which plagued the last months of my researches. I must thank Elise Archambault for her work on the illustrations, Claire Colreavy for her editorial help and patience, and Elizabeth Manners for her invaluable assistance on this as on others of my books.

Finally, I am more than grateful to my friends Dominique de Grunne, Charlotte Ellis, Martin Meade and Sylvia Couturié, for keeping up my spirits, in Paris and elsewhere.

MARK GIROUARD

LONDON 2000

1

A QUICK RUN ROUND THE FRENCH NOBLESSE

The château of Haroué was rebuilt to the designs of Germain Boffrand in 1720–32, but Boffrand's corner towers recall the memory of the old château and underline the feudal dignity of the Prince de Beauveau-Craon for whom the château was built.

ON 13 APRIL 1789 a picturesque figure rode into the courtyard of the château of Rambouillet, as he and his predecessors had been doing for centuries past. He was booted and spurred; his sword clanked by his side; he wore white gloves, a white scarf, and a chaplet and garland of periwinkles; his horse had white fetlocks, and a white flash on its forehead; he held on his saddle tree a bottle of wine in a wickerwork pannier and a cake decorated with more periwinkles. He called out three times, 'Monsieur de Montorgueil, are you or your representative there?', and when his representative appeared presented him with cake, wine and gloves, as vassal to overlord.[1]

The ceremony had originated 700 years ago, as the required form in which the Prior of Saint-Thomas d'Épernon rendered homage to the Seigneur de Montorgueil. By 1789 Montorgueil no longer existed: it had been absorbed into the Seigneurie of Rambouillet, Rambouillet had become a royal residence, there was no longer a prior at Épernon, the bailiff at Rambouillet stood proxy for the king, and what had been a dignified ceremony became a picturesque survival carried out, perhaps rather perfunctorily, by minor officials. Nevertheless it survived. All over France in 1789 vassals were still swearing fealty to their overlords by the thousand, often by proxy and without picturesque feudal adjuncts; but they were still doing it. A complete feudal structure, such as had virtually disappeared in England in

the sixteenth century, if not before, still existed in France, radiating from the king downwards. It was only the husk of a structure; many of the strengths and much of the meaning had been drained out of it; alternative systems had developed alongside it; at the start of the French Revolution the husk crumbled away, and was heading for dissolution anyway, even without the onset of revolutionary flames. Even so, by its survival it still conditioned the way people thought, believed and built; and the ghost or memory of it was to continue to influence attitudes, after the Revolution and up to the present day.[2]

The system, from similar beginnings, developed differently from the system in England. Few Englishmen (and not all that many Frenchmen) know or knew how the French system worked. Words that mean or meant one thing in England mean or meant something quite different in France. Castle and château are etymologically the same, but their connotations are quite different. 'Noble' means one thing in England and another thing in France. The French parlements bore little relation to the English Parliament. Titles had different connotations too: a French marquis was and is a different creature from an English marquis, and the functions and status of titles generally was quite different in the two countries. But if one is to understand the meaning and function of châteaux, one needs to know something about the system which they existed to serve.

Its beginnings were straightforward. The leaders of the warrior bands which flooded into France in the fifth, ninth and tenth centuries carved out domains for themselves, which they ruled by force of arms. They acquired their own castle or castles, and their own bands of armed and mounted companions who rode round with them and fought with and for them. They rewarded these companions by carving smaller domains out of their own big ones, and giving them to their followers. On these smaller domains were built smaller castles. These domains were not outright gifts; they were held in return for oaths of service; they were fiefs held 'en foi', as the French put it. The seigneurs of the fiefs had to fight for, and attend on, their overlord when needed; they held their castles on his behalf, and one of the functions of the smaller castle was to police that portion of his domains.

This is an over-tidy account of a process made complex and messy by a continuous alternation between joining together and splitting apart: unity and the idea of a crowned and anointed king imposed under Charlemagne, the subsequent breaking away of the great seigneurs from the crown, and smaller seigneurs from great ones, the reimposition of authority as lesser people gave up their independence and acknowledged suzerainty, impelled by force or self-interest – and another continuous process of accretion or dispersion as a result of marriages or death without children.

By the fourteenth century France was covered with a network of seigneuries, interlinked with incredible complexity, but based on a comprehensible hierarchy. At the head of this was the King of France, and a group of great nobles who in theory acknowledged his overlordship, but who in fact were virtually independent rulers at some periods: more powerful and richer than the king – among them the ducs of Brittany and Lorraine, the counts of Champagne, Toulouse and Foix, the ducs of Aquitaine (who happened also to be kings of England), the ducs of Anjou, who acquired a claim to the Kingdom of Sicily and for a time called themselves kings on the strength of it; and the ducs of Burgundy, who were also counts of Flanders, and as a result enormously rich. Each of these had their own conglomeration of castles, and a claim of overlordship over many more castles appertaining to the fiefs which depended on them. Side by side with these secular lords was a network of ecclesiastic domains belonging to archbishops, bishops and abbots, all with secular fiefs depending on them, and at the centre of it, the Pope, with his own little principality in and around Avignon.

Who was whose overlord could be full of complexities. The simplest situation was that of the seigneur of a single seigneurie, with a single overlord. Great nobles who owned many seigneuries could have many overlords. In the thirteenth century, for instance, the Count of Champagne held his various territories as vassal of the Holy Roman Emperor, the King of France, the Duc of Burgundy, the archbishops of Reims and Sens, the bishops of Autun, Auxerre and Langres, and the Abbot of Saint-Denis. Kings could be, and usually were, kings in one place and vassals in another. When a direct line died out, or ended in daughters, the problems of succession produced feuds and wars all over medieval Europe; the claim of the kings of England to the throne of France, following on the death of Charles IV without sons in 1328, led to the Hundred Years War between France and England.

*At the château of
Louye the upper half
of the Salle des Cerfs
on the ground floor is
decorated with a
cavalcade of stags
(detail, left), basically
early sixteenth century
although with later
background and
embellishments.*

From a small seigneur (the equivalent of an English squire), up to the great man who was the overlord of the small seigneur's overlord, all the members of this network acquired one element in common. They, all their children, and all their descendants, not just the bearers of titles, were noble, and conscious of being creatures of a different make from the mass of the inhabitants of France, who were not noble. They formed the second estate, legally distinct from the clergy of the first estate, and the commons of the third estate. The status that in England was confined to members of the House of Lords was legally enjoyed by many thousands in France. The numbers are disputed, and will never be established with accuracy: estimates of the noble population in 1789, for instance, vary wildly between 135,000 and 340,000; but whatever the exact figure, all these thousands of people enjoyed privileges similar to, or greater than, those confined in England to holders of peerages, which was 57 people in 1487, 121 in 1641, and 250 in 1780.[3]

Owing to their origins as a warrior aristocracy, who served the king by fighting for him, they paid no taxes. They had a privileged position in the legal system, and could be tried only by other nobles. Numerous offices and functions were reserved to them. They, and only they, could become knights. They carried swords, and wore distinctive clothes.

Their recreations were those of a warrior class: mimic fighting in tourneys and hunting on horseback (hunting was forbidden to those who were not noble). The importance of hunting, as a noble recreation and a sign of nobility, can scarcely be exaggerated in France. English fox-hunting is an eighteenth- or nineteenth-century sport in origin and language. The French hunt the boar or the stag, and never (except in imitation of the English) the fox, and use a quite different and more ancient language (which English hunters cannot understand, and even find ridiculous), that goes back to the Middle Ages. The image of the stag haunts the French château, inside and out, closely followed by the image of the horse: the naïf, chunky, life-sized wooden stags which now greet visitors as they come into the 'salle

The pleasures of hunting the stag have drawn the French noblesse to their châteaux since the Middle Ages, and stags and hunting scenes feature prominently in their decoration, as in a chimney-piece in the sixteenth-century château of Filain (left). Arcades along the forecourt of Raray (below) are surmounted by a continuous sequence of stags and hounds.

Life-size seventeenth-century wooden sculptures of stags in the grande salle at the château of Meillant (left) were originally accompanied by bawdy inscriptions about cuckolded husbands.

basse' at Meillant; the life-sized stone stag which bursts out of the sixteenth-century overmantel at Filain; the row of alternating stags and dogs that process along the top of the courtyard wall at Raray; the stag heads that march like a frieze around the salle basse at Louye.

The legal status of the French noblesse developed gradually: in effect a *de facto* situation developed into a *de jure* one, and finally solidified in the fourteenth and fifteenth centuries. A key moment was in 1404, when members of the noblesse were powerful enough to claim and obtain exemption from the main tax, the taille, on the grounds that they served the king by fighting for him, and should not be expected to pay taxes as well. Tax-exemption remained perhaps the main and most highly valued privilege of the noblesse up to the Revolution, long after any direct connection between noblesse and military service had disappeared.

Although all the noblesse had the same legal status and basic privileges, the importance of an individual noble was conditioned by the number, size and privileges of the seigneurie or seigneuries which he owned. All seigneuries, however small, had rights and revenues attached to them. The peasants who farmed the land paid rent to the seigneur in money or service. The seigneur (and only the seigneur) had the right to erect a dovecot, and fill it with pigeons who grew fat by eating the corn of the peasants, and the right to hunt over the land and kill game, which his peasants were not allowed to touch. But seigneuries were graded, not only in size, but in privileges and judicial powers, attached to some but not to others. A seigneur held his own courts, in which according to his importance, he had the right of the high, the middle and the low justice, or just the middle and the low, or just the low. The high justice included the power of condemning to death; the low justice was limited to imposing fines and short terms of imprisonment. A seigneurie to which the high justice was attached usually had other privileges as well, including the right of building a market. In architectural terms a seigneur with the high justice had the right to a fully fortified residence, complete with towers, moats, battlements, drawbridge, gatehouse, and windvanes enriched with his coat of arms at the top of the steep roofs which crowned each tower. The lesser seigneurs (who became known as 'écuyers' – squires or esquires) had to get permission to fortify their residences, and normally had to content themselves with a moat, a wall and some form of crenellation. By the fourteenth century 'château' (or in Latin *castrum* or *castellum*), which had previously been loosely applied to any fortified structure, including a walled town, began to be confined to such fully fortified residences; modest ones became known as 'maisons-forts', or 'maisons seigneuriales'.

The language of fortification had become, in fact, not just a language of military strength but a symbol both of nobility and of the judicial and economic status attached to the more important seigneuries; and to them the écuyers in the surrounding constellation of more modest maisons-forts would resort for a certain period of each year to serve their overlord, and feel pride in doing so, just as the overlords were proud to serve in the entourage and even bigger castles of the kings or great noblemen who were their overlords.

If one moves from the fourteenth to the seventeenth century, one finds the whole system still in existence, the nobility still with all their privileges, the hierarchy of seigneuries still in existence, vassals still kneeling yearly before their overlords and swearing fealty to them. But in fact important changes had taken place.

The power of the monarch had been on the increase since the fifteenth century, and by the seventeenth, as a result of conquest or marriage, it extended over virtually the whole of France: there were no great independent nobles, apart from a few, such as the Prince of Orange in Orange, the Papacy in Avignon or the ducs of Lorraine in Lorraine, and Richelieu and Louis XIV in succession greatly reduced the power of all the richer and more ancient noble families.

By the seventeenth century not all seigneurs were noble, and not all nobles were seigneurs. The change had started when seigneuries began being bought and sold. If a rich merchant or official bought a seigneurie, did he become noble by virtue of owning it? For some centuries he did; buying a seigneurie became the first way of buying nobility. The old nobility and the king himself found it distasteful that a rich, self-made merchant could join their number and acquire their privileges by a simple cash transaction. In 1579 Henri III issued an edict explicitly blocking this route to nobility. In fact families owning a reputable seigneurie and a château or handsome maison seigneuriale to go with it, after they had lived there in style for two or three generations, could usually assume nobility and get away with it.

At the same time new and officially recognized routes into the nobility had opened. The French kings, and the great territorial magnates in their independent dukedoms or counties, had built up a civil service and a judiciary which became increasingly powerful and important. The most eminent elements were the courts in Paris: the Parlement, which acted as a supreme legal court and registered new laws, and the Cour des Comptes, which audited the accounts of royal servants. These courts had been created as early as the thirteenth century, and by the end of the sixteenth century they had won the privilege of nobility for their members, after three generations of service for the 'conseillers' who filled the lower ranks, and immediate for their presidents. The ducs of, for instance, Brittany and Aquitaine had created their own courts at Nantes and Bordeaux, which had been absorbed into France, and also conferred nobility. By the end of the seventeenth century a complex structure of parlements, Cours des Aides, Chambres des Comptes, Bureaux des Finances and a limited number of municipal offices had grown up which, in one way or another, conferred nobility. So did the job of 'Secrétaire du Roi', which had automatically conveyed nobility since the fifteenth century, when the secrétaires actually had a function, one that by the end of the seventeenth century they had largely lost.

In short, the old correlation between nobility and fighting had gone and a new class of nobility had been created, the 'noblesse de robe', so-called from the distinctive gowns which they wore as a sign of their office, as opposed to the 'noblesse d'épée', the nobility of the sword. Legally, however, there was no difference between them; both types were equally noble, and equally members of the Second Estate.

For the new nobles nobility had two attractions: privilege and status. They had entered the upper class, and they had joined the non-tax-paying class. For the king, the creation of more and more new nobles was partly a result of the increasing importance of this judicial and administrative class, but it also acquired a simple and straightforward function: it brought him more money. The income of the French kings, enormous though it was as compared to the income of all other European potentates, was never large enough to pay for the wars they waged, the style in which they lived, the buildings they built, and the favourites, male and female, whom they rewarded. By the early seventeenth century, and frequently before, all the offices which conferred nobility were for sale.

To begin with the old noblesse d'épée despised the new noblesse de robe – the 'robins', as they called them. It was difficult to do so for very long. The robe families were usually better educated than the sword families. They acquired nobility, but they also acquired seigneuries, châteaux, and titles to go with it. They resided, by the nature of their positions, for most of the year in Paris or the bigger provincial towns, where they bought or built handsome houses, and lived and entertained with sophistication and style. They became rich, sometimes very rich. For a sword family, particularly one which had run up a load of debts, as many of them had, marriage to a rich daughter of the new robe nobility could bring a useful injection of cash and property, and also, not infrequently, a level-headed organizer who would instil order into a run-down property. Such alliances became more and more common; and the new nobility further blurred the distinction by sending, not infrequently, their sons into the army or navy, the hereditary domain of the old nobility, which their own rank now opened up to them. By the time of the Revolution the links between the two groups were many. Even so, they remained distinct; the two types remained very conscious of their origins: the sword families continued to feel superior, and the robe families to recognize their superiority. They still do so today.

Acquiring a seigneurie no longer automatically brought nobility, but anyone who had acquired nobility by other means almost always bought a seigneurie or seigneuries as well. A seigneurie brought a stake in the most prestigious and paying form of property, it brought status, and, not least, it brought a change of name. Monsieur Le Fevre, noble or on the way to it, as a conseiller of the Paris Parlement, had his property at Ormesson elevated to a seigneurie, became the Seigneur d'Ormesson, and was addressed as Monsieur d'Ormesson, and no longer as Monsieur Le Fevre: his

The Parlement of Paris was the supreme court of the realm and all laws were registered in it. Membership led to nobility, and the parlementary families, known as the noblesse of the robe as opposed to the more ancient noblesse of the sword, built grand houses in Paris and châteaux outside it. An engraving by Sebastien Le Clerc of about 1664 shows a Président of the Parlement in his robes.

children and all his descendants became Le Fevre d'Ormesson. The pages of French history – and of the *Bottin Mondain*, the snob's guide of today – are littered with this combination of a plebeian surname joined by a 'particule' to a seigneurial one: Le Tonnelier de Breteuil, Le Peletier de Rosanbo, Hérault de Gourville, Riquet de Caraman, and so on. The emphasis is always on the seigneurial half of the combination, and the plebeian beginning has a way of quietly disappearing.

The next step up was to acquire a title. To become a seigneur, one simply had to buy a seigneurie; to become a baron, a count, a marquis or a duc needed (in theory, at any rate) an act of creation by the king.

French titles are quite distinct from English ones. An English title conferred nobility and carried a seat in the House of Lords; a French title (before the Revolution) could only be given to someone who was already noble and, with one exception, entailed no legislative function. An English title, after the early Middle Ages, had no necessary connection with a particular property. The dukes of Devonshire owned property in almost every county except Devon; the dukes of Marlborough had never had any connection with Marlborough; the Marquess of Bath did not own a stick of land in Bath. In France they would have been the Duke of Chatsworth and Blenheim and the Marquess of Longleat, for French titles were tied to property owned by the bearer of the title. The accepted procedure was for a group of seigneuries belonging to one owner to be 'erected' by the king into a barony, a county, a marquisate or a dukedom, depending on the size of the group, and be given the name of the most important seigneurie – usually the one which contained the château where the bearer of the title lived. The owner of a new marquisate became a marquis on the strength of the grant and the ownership; if he sold the land, in theory he lost the title.

In theory the French system might seem clearer and more logical than the English one; one knew where one was: the carrier of a French title was not only, by definition, noble, but the certified owner of substantial seigneurial property in a named place; the higher the title, the bigger the property. In fact it did not work out like that. Because an English title brought a seat in the House of Lords, and the power and privileges that came with that, it was carefully regulated and supervised. A French title conferred honour and status but very little else, with one exception: the 'ducs-pairs' had a role to play in the Parlement, and as a result the ducs-pairs (which by no means included all the ducs) had a particular prestige. Other titles were in fact little regulated, treated with remarkable casualness and not used in normal social life. The Marquis de Breteuil, for instance, was (and still is) normally referred to as Monsieur de Breteuil by everyone except tradesmen and servants; and the same applied to all titles. It would be inconceivable for a socially aware Englishman to address the Marquess of Bath as Mr Bath or even 'Mr of Bath'.

One curious consequence of this laid-back attitude was that the members of the eighteenth-century noblesse started to award themselves titles, and nobody, least of all the king, seems to have bothered about it. The most respectable form of self-appointed titles were the ones assumed by those who enjoyed what were known as the 'honours of the court'. These much-prized honours were awarded by the king, almost always to members of sword families of ancient extraction, and gave them the right to attend court balls and receptions, to travel in the king's carriages and to accompany him when he went hunting. It became an accepted convention, recognized or at least tolerated by the king, for such people to assume a title (anything but duc or prince) which they chose themselves from one of their own properties.

Less reputable self-elevations are revealed by Monsieur Le Tourneur, in the War Ministry, voicing his worries in 1748 to his superior M. de Clairambault. A Monsieur de Brehon had assumed the title of marquis, with no justification. Should anything be done about it? Clairambault thought not. Unjustified marquises, counts and barons were becoming as common in the army as unjustified 'abbés' without an abbey among the clergy. He admitted it was against all the rules, along with the coronets which such people were putting on their coats of arms 'in consequence of these imaginary titles'. But he did not think it was worth bothering about. The assumption of titles had become too common, it had been going on for too long and it would cause too much offence to try to stop it; after all, these phoney titles were used only in addressing letters, and by servants and inferiors talking to or about their titled superiors. Clairambault contented himself with a funny story. A phoney marquis had a quarrel with someone and threatened to dig him out wherever he hid himself. The man replied that there was one place where he would not be able to find him. 'Where?' asked the marquis. 'In your marquisate,' he replied.[4]

What really mattered was how long a family had been noble, rather than the titles which it had picked up on the way. One can reasonably wonder why, if titles were so relatively unimportant, men of standing bothered to assume them? It is all, perhaps, a matter of myth and reality: a mythical image and a group of real people. The mythical image was that of the members of the nobility as they would like to be (and as writers like Boulainvilliers[5] assured them that they were), a race set apart from common men, descended from warrior ancestors, untainted in blood, unswerving in honour, inspired by the deeds of their ancestors and their inherited genes to carry on a real tradition, living in feudal dignity in their towered and moated châteaux, on their ancient demesnes, but always ready to leave them to serve or fight for their king. This was the myth. The reality was the nobility as it actually and legally was, a miscellany ranging from impressively old to glaringly new families, 140,000 people or more by 1789, one third of whom, at the time of the Revolution, belonged to families which had only become noble since 1700, two thirds of whom had only become noble since 1600 – over half of whom had acquired nobility by straightforwardly buying it, with the proceeds of trade or the law, or finance, dubious or otherwise, or who had been given it by the king as a reward for sexual services, or for making a suitably oleaginous speech when he visited a city, or laid a foundation stone. To this add a new arrival of the 1770s and 1780s, the product of a new idealism, as a result of which Louis XVI started to confer nobility – extraordinary idea – as a reward for merit. The nobility of genuine medieval origin was at best a third of the nobility as a whole, and a sizeable proportion of this minority had long ago lost all their money and lived in pathetic poverty with only a rusty sword and a roll of parchment to demonstrate their rank.[6]

But there was an inner group within the nobility as a whole, a core made up of families of substance, noble for at least several generations, owners of one or more sizeable châteaux, and seigneuries to go with them, and also a handsome town house in Paris or one of the provincial capitals. There were all sorts of variations within this inner group; some families were immensely rich, some only comfortably off; some were of ancient blood and very conscious and proud of it, some of more recent origin, and still living it down; there were court families and Parlement families and army families, provincial families and metropolitan families. But it was still a group, the members of which accepted each other, despised the brand-new nobility on the one hand (even if prepared to marry its daughters), and ignored the penniless old nobility on the other.

What is interesting is that both new and old nobility accepted the myth. Just by being noble they felt a race apart, and a superior one at that. A man of modest origin, who had made a fortune big enough to buy the post of Secrétaire du Roi, and acquire nobility, immediately felt himself translated to a different sphere, and altered his lifestyle and his attitudes accordingly. The older families knew they were different anyway; and both types accepted the medieval symbols as outward and visible signs of their spiritual grace. The symbols were titles, coronets and coats of arms on the one hand, and a residence called a château, with a moat, towers and spires, and perhaps a donjon – at least the square, high-roofed pavilions which were the sixteenth-century development on round medieval towers – all adding up to a recognizable and valued silhouette, with feudal resonances even if without feudal details.

All over France one finds châteaux comfortably rebuilt in the seventeenth or eighteenth century, but in which the medieval towers, or at least one or two of them, have been retained along with the moat, or even had new towers built, as the sign of a seigneurial residence. There were, to be sure, cases where the glamour of Italy or the prestige of Versailles, or a desire to be enlightened or progressive, inspired a quite different model, towerless flat- or flattish-roofed classical villas, that in some cases replaced an older château which had been entirely demolished; and in the case of a 'maison de plaisance' or 'maison de campagne' – a house with no seigneurial connotations, built for enjoyment alone – seigneurial symbols were unnecessary and inappropriate anyway. But what is remarkable is how rare mini-Versailles were, and how common and all-prevailing the other model was, in all its variations, through all the centuries.

In the mid sixteenth century, when the château of La Tour d'Aigues in the south of France was rebuilt in the latest Renaissance style, the huge looming medieval donjon was preserved, and made its central feature – covered with a new classical skin, it is true, but still preserved. When Jules Hardouin Mansart moved from Versailles to design a new château for the Duc de Luynes nearby, on the foundations of an old one which was completely demolished, far from producing

a scaled-down version of Versailles, he kept the moat, crowned his classical façades with high roofs, and built two new round towers on the foundations of the old ones. When the Prince de Craon employed Boffrand, a highly sophisticated Parisian architect working in the rococo style, to rebuild his château at Haroué in Lorraine, it was erected on the moated site of the old château, and four brand-new round towers rose up on the foundations of the old ones, to frame the rococo façades. In Burgundy one finds a Président of the Dijon Parlement doing much the same in a more modest way at the château he acquired at Missery, except here he actually kept the old towers and rebuilt the rest; the Maréchal de Contades, coming from a different and grander background, did the same at Montgeoffroy in Anjou in 1771. Just before the Revolution, when the Président of the Besançon Parlement built himself a very grand neoclassical château at Moncley, he still attached two brand-new little towers to the corners of the whole complex, in complement to his own nobility and the seigneurial background of the château. These are random examples, taken from literally hundreds of others.

In addition to the noblesse, it is worth taking a brief look at the would-be noblesse. Nobility was the haven in which virtually all French families with ambitions were hoping to end up, but many never acquired the money, the connections, the offices or the good luck to get them there. But there was a kind of halfway house, which was worth getting to, even if it did not lead any further. If a local tax-collector, Monsieur Brun, bought a little property held in fealty called Boisrolin, he could call himself the Seigneur or at least the Sieur de Boisrolin[7] and his family became Brun de Boisrolin: it had acquired the modest prestige of a particule, the French equivalent of a double-barrelled name. Such families would usually hope to do sufficiently well to move on and buy an office conferring nobility, but in the

The château of La Tour d'Aigues (above) was largely rebuilt in the 1570s, but its superb classical gatehouse was lined up with the medieval donjon, which was embellished but carefully preserved as the symbolic centre of the château.

Bird's eye views of the château of Missery as it was in the seventeenth century (right) and as it is today (below). The main body of the château was rebuilt in about 1760, but the moat and four corner towers were retained.

majority of cases they never managed to make this crucial second step. There were thousands of these non-noble sub-seigneurial families all over France in the seventeenth and eighteenth centuries. They were lawyers, tax-collectors, officials in the big seigneuries, minor officials in royal or noble households or in the lower echelons of the parlements or the financial courts. Occasionally they became well known – like the son of M. Arouet, a prosperous Parisian notary, whose aquisition of a little seigneurial property enabled him to develop into Monsieur Arouet de Voltaire and finally just into Monsieur de Voltaire. In about 1760 a Lorraine lawyer, Antoine Huot, bought the little seigneurie of Goncourt: as a result all his descendants could style themselves Huot de Goncourt, and his great-grandchildren Edmond and Jules quietly dropped the Huot. But most of these families remained small fry.

The essence of a seigneurial property was that it was held by swearing annual fealty to an overlord (in addition to paying a straightforward commercial price). Swearing fealty was still, in the eighteenth century, a business of kneeling in front of the overlord, placing one's hands between his and swearing the relevant oath. A degree of resentment could grow up between a man of an old noble family and the new commoners to whom he was selling off chunks of his property; the former could console himself by telling funny stories about scoring off the pretentious new men – like the noble landowner near Bordeaux to whom two local worthies came to swear fealty, accompanied by servants carrying velvet cushions for them to kneel on; the landowner got his secretary to read out the conditions of tenure, and finding no mention of velvet cushions ordered them to be taken away, saying that he did not want to have 'more than was due to him'.[8]

These little properties were often no more than a few fields and a farmhouse, with no proper seigneurial residence, and their owners did not bother to build one because what they wanted was the title of seigneur or sieur and the particule, not a residence. But sometimes they built one, or there was one there already, always of a modest nature. These houses did not usually rate towers and a moat; often a decent symmetry, a dovecot, and a coat of arms over the door was all they had to lift them above the common level; sometimes they only had one main storey, and belonged to the agreeable type of residence which is known today as a 'chartreuse' – a term which seems first to have appeared in the late eighteenth century. Such houses could also be inhabited by modest families who actually were noble, but without title or ownership of a seigneurie with more than the 'low justice'. Very charming, and, for the needs of today, desirable they can be, the French equivalent, perhaps, of the 'Old Rectories' of England.

The Revolution abolished nobility as a privileged status and swept away the whole system of seigneurial rights. Neither were ever to be revived in France. But titles came back with the Empire. Napoleon created his own hierarchy of titles. Louis XVIII brought back the titles of the Ancien Régime, recognized the Napoleonic ones, and created new titles, as did his successor Charles X. Louis XVIII also created a Chamber of Hereditary Peers, as a legislative body, modelled on the English House of Lords, and made up of a mixture of Ancien Régime,

The modest single-storey châteaux or gentilhommeries known as 'chartreuses' are one of the most attractive products of eighteenth-century France. At the château or chartreuse of Monbrun (right), built in about 1760, the main building backs at the rear (below) onto what was originally a farmyard, complete with well-house, barns, cow-house and stables.

Napoleonic and new titles. Louis-Philippe accepted old titles, created new ones and continued the Chamber of Peers, but abolished its hereditary nature. Napoleon III accepted old titles, and created still further new ones, but did not revive the Chamber of Peers, which had disappeared under the Second Republic.

With the fall of the Second Empire, and the rise of the Third Republic, French titles lost all official status and have never recovered it. Titles continue to be used, however, and indeed have proliferated, for the convention arose in the nineteenth century that all members of a titled family, however remote their relationship to the head of their family, were addressed by a title, followed by their forename, to mark their junior status (Comte Jean de Blanche, as opposed to the Comte de Blanche). This had not normally been the case under the Ancien Régime. If one adds these honorary titles to the different layers of Bourbon or Napoleonic titles, to old papal or Holy Roman Empire titles acquired by French families, up to the Second Empire, and to new papal titles acquired since the fall of Napoleon III (as a result of which the Vatican became almost the only source of titles available to Frenchmen), and if one realizes that there is now no effective official regulatory body or publication to act as a deterrent to the assumption of phoney titles, it is not surprising that to bemused foreigners it may seem that everyone they meet in polite society is at least a marquis, a count, a viscount or a baron.

Making fun of the bogus or dubious titles or claims to noblesse of others is, in fact, an agreeable occupation among the French upper classes, and a whole literature of pamphlets and articles showing up the fraudulent or listing the genuine has grown up, specimens of which are to be seen casually lying on the coffee-tables of those who feature favourably in them.[9]

Of the two pre-Revolutionary groups already described, the first, the nobility as a separate Estate, has ceased to exist, at least in legal terms. But a successor to the 'core nobility', in the sense of a cohesive social class, continued to be of importance in the nineteenth century and up to the present day.

The immediate effect of the Revolution on the nobility has been much exaggerated in the popular imagination; far more serious, in the long term, was the abolition of primogeniture by the Code Napoléon, and the resultant compulsory dividing up of property for every generation. Those gallant but doomed aristocrats who went to the guillotine in the terrible years of 1793 and 1794 formed, in fact, a small percentage of the nobility. Only 1200 or so of the 160,000 guillotined or otherwise executed in this period were noble; perhaps if the numbers of those who died in prison or who were killed without trial were added the figure might be doubled, but it still needs to be set against the total noble population of 140,000 or more. Many châteaux were sacked or burnt; the property of nobles who were guillotined or who had fled the country was confiscated, and the châteaux and their contents put up for sale. But many noble families who kept a low profile were left undisturbed; other families avoided confiscation by transfer of ownership or other legal devices. In 1800–1802 property which had been confiscated but not actually sold was returned to the owners, and some owners were able to buy back land on the cheap from purchasers who were afraid that there might be a general restoration of confiscated property; in 1825 emigré families were indemnified in part for their losses, and were able to buy back property, or acquire new property, as a result. The losses of the nobility varied, anyway, very much from area to area, but one estimate is that the old nobility lost, on average, about one fifth of their land, and (adding on the loss of feudal rights) about one third of their income as a result of the Revolution; and they were able to make this up to some extent by raising rents to compensate for loss of rights. In 1800 one third of the thousand richest landowners in France were former nobles.[10]

Dented and shaken by the Revolution but very far from destroyed, the old noble families survived into the nineteenth century to form the nucleus of an upper class still living in their châteaux, which they often rebuilt or enlarged, still owning substantial property, still using titles, regardless of whether France was or was not a Republic. As under the Ancien Régime, their numbers were gradually supplemented by new families, now not necessarily noble or titled but acceptable because they too had acquired châteaux by purchase, inheritance or marriage, and shared the same values as their longer-established neighbours.

These values were to some extent conditioned by a reaction against what were seen as the faults of their forebears in the decades before the Revolution. They had been, it seemed to their descendants, too frivolous, too irreligious, too urban, too neglectful of their estates and their peasantry, and they had suffered for it. The nineteenth-century upper classes saw themselves as bastions of religion and tradition against the forces of republicanism and anti-clericalism. A chapel in the château, the bishop to stay once a year, and the curé to dinner once a week, six months in the country and six months in an appartement, or, if they were rich enough, a house in Paris, good works in the village, care of their woods, and the pigs, ducks and prize cattle of their home farms, stables and a resplendent harness-room for the hunt, kennels for their shooting dogs, marriage with their own kind, but occasionally with a carefully selected heiress from outside, a trip to Trouville or one of the other seaside resorts in the summer, and perhaps a house there – a pattern emerged, even if one with endless variations, and enjoyable tensions within the basic unity. As a class they had lost their privileges – their direct links with the government and their virtual monopoly of certain aspects of it – but they were still powerful in diplomacy, the church and the armed forces. On the whole they kept out of politics, local and national, though in a conservative neighbourhood they sometimes served as mayor of their local town or village. They remained a force to be reckoned with because of their wealth, their cohesion, their social and historic status, and the prestige of the châteaux in which they lived.

A château was a basic element of their image; the word 'château', because of its connotations, was applied to houses which would not have been thought worthy of the name before the Revolution (though families of lesser social pretensions were content with the term 'manoir', which was revived for their more modest residences). An old historic château retained unbeatable prestige, and because the class stood for tradition, new châteaux always evoked the past in one form or another. Which period of the past was recalled depended on the taste of the builder and the fashion of the moment: the Middle Ages, or buildings that in one way or another suggested the age of accepted heroes such as François I, Henri IV, Louis XIII and (less often) Louis XIV, were all acceptable, but until the late nineteenth century, Louis XV and Louis XVI were avoided as a little dangerous or frivolous; although, as the trauma of the Revolution receded, they, and sometimes the frivolity to go with them, came back into fashion, and commodes, 'fauteuils', elegant grey-painted 'boiseries', Watteau and Fragonard began to drive out carved oak cupboards, ponderous velvet chairs, heavy Louis XIII cabinets, stencilled walls and heraldic chimney-pieces.

In spite of all the pressures it has been put under, this world is still recognizable in France today. Many châteaux have been demolished, or sold to foreigners, or passed into public ownership, or been converted into hotels or clubs, or for institutional use, but perhaps even more remain in the possession of the families which have owned them at least for several generations, if not for centuries. The Code

The rich late-Gothic detailing of the château of Bournel built in the 1860s for the Marquis Leonel de Moustier, sumptuously expresses the desire of the post-Revolution noblesse to go back to its roots.

Napoléon may have depleted the contents and reduced the land round the château to a handful of hectares; ownership may be shared among several people, all feuding together from different wings; the owners may have ceased to be men of leisure and keep going by working in a bank or industry in Paris or Lyon; he and his family may live in the stables and let out the château for weddings (or the other way round), they may open it to the public, install a museum in it, or run it themselves as a hotel or a conference centre; their visits may be reduced to a month or two in the summer, and to weekends, made possible from Paris by autoroutes and the TGV; they will tell one that their world can't survive their generation, but they keep going. They are still marrying each other, to a far greater degree than their

English equivalents; their children go around together in the curious social groups known as 'rallyes' in Paris, or in huge house-parties for holidays, dances and weddings in the summer; the fact that they are amiable and unassuming and keep a low profile, and look exactly like everybody else, doesn't mean that they are not conscious of their ancestry and their separate identity; those of noble descent are intensely aware of it, they belong to the Association de l'Entraide de la Noblesse Française, and sport the initials ANF after their name in the *Bottin Mondain*, the social handbook of France; and in the same publication a little symbol of a castle printed in the address after the name shows the tenacity with which, against all the odds, they hold on to their châteaux and continue to live in them.

2
THE
LANGUAGE
OF CHIVALRY

THE CHÂTEAU, OR FRAGMENT OF A CHÂTEAU, in the village of Saint-Floret is one of those agreeable buildings, common enough in France, which belong to the village, and into which, once the door is opened in the morning, the visitor can wander on his or her own, with no interposing barrier of ticket kiosk, postcard stall or attendants. It consists, today, of little more than the remains of a fourteenth-century tower with a vaulted salle on the ground floor. It is not much visited, and is often empty. Up in the vault, lit by circular traceried windows, are extensive fragments of frescoes depicting the romance of Tristan and Iseult. Against a background landscape of formalized trees, knights fight on cavorting steeds or protect mounted damsels; up on high, a much effaced fragment shows Tristan and his lover Iseult together. Passages of text in between or below the pictures fill out the story.

The vaulted salle of the fourteenth-century château of Saint-Floret is frescoed with scenes from the romance of Tristan, one of the many stories of chivalry which filled the lives of dwellers in châteaux in the Middle Ages.

The fragments at Saint-Floret are a rare survival of paintings which must have existed on the walls of many medieval châteaux. They were one form in which medieval romances soaked into the lives of their occupants, whether depicted on walls, told in illustrated manuscripts read to them in the evening or recited by minstrels as an accompaniment to feasts. Some of these romances were set in the past, often in what we would call the mythical times of King Arthur, which were then accepted as historical; some were given a contemporary or near-contemporary setting. But whatever the ostensible setting, the buildings and way of life were described in terms that were comprehensible to the audience, and related to what they knew. Reading a romance can help put the modern reader into the skin of the people who first listened to it, and not only to see the spaces being used as they saw them but to some extent to savour their emotions.

After the first sight of a castle and its cluster of towers, sometimes with the endlessly curious occupants hanging out of the windows or peering from the top of a tower to see who is coming, the arrival is always into the hall. Over and over again the romances describe the going – usually up – into the salle, the welcome in the salle from king, count or seigneur or their wives, or alternatively the discovery of them seated at table for a meal. Sometimes only knights and squires are to be found eating in the salle, but at special festivities their ladies are there too; they go off with the châtelaine or countess to her chambre when the meal is over, and sing and tell stories with her while the tables are being cleared, but then they come back for the dancing, the juggling and the minstrels:

When the court was all assembled
There was not one minstrel in the country
Whatever was his skill
Who was not present there.
Great was the joy in the salle.
One of them leapt, another turned somersaults,
    another conjured.
One told stories, another sang,
One whistled, others played instruments:
One on the harp, others on the rote,
On the viol and the hurdy-gurdy,
On the flute and the pipe,
While the young girls formed rings and danced.[1]

And the narrators seldom fail to relate what magnificent presents the performers were given after the feast.

Not infrequently there is a bed in the salle, and the hero of the romance is put to sleep there. More often he or she is given their own chambre; in the *Roman de Jaufre* it is the heroine's maidservants who sleep in the salle.[2] At night the salle acts as an overspill for those for whom there is no room elsewhere. Chambres are frequently shared: two sisters sleep there together; the mistress sleeps there with her demoiselles; Tristan, who was the 'écuyer' (gentleman servant) of Iseult's husband King Mark, sleeps in the same chambre as Iseult and her husband.

Salle, chambre, stairs and tower provide a scaffolding, up and down which took place the action of the romance, and the drama of real life. Iseult's husband suspects Tristan of having an affair with his wife in his absence, and spreads sand between the two beds to take Tristan's footprints; Tristan, even though handicapped by a barely healed wound, jumps from one bed to the other in a mighty leap. Another jealous husband, convinced that his wife is being unfaithful, shuts her up in a tower with two of her ladies for company and walls up the door, leaving an aperture for food to be carried over the courtyard from the kitchen which is opposite it. Yet another locks his wife in a room at the top of a tower. She lowers a rope each night, up which her lover climbs. The husband discovers this, and from a lower room in the tower cuts the rope as the lover is climbing up it, and he falls to his death.[3]

In another romance, the 'châtelaine' (the wife of the châtelain or captain of the castle) is having a love-affair with a knight or squire with whom a duchess is also in love. The duchess, sitting with her ladies in her chambre, reveals to the châtelaine that she knows all about the affair; the châtelaine thinks that her lover has betrayed

her, because he loves the duchess, not her. The duchess and her ladies go off to dance in the hall, all but the châtelaine. She retires into a garderobe, the little room for the storage of clothes often used too as a room of privacy or retreat, and after a long lament dies of a broken heart. Her lover, who is dancing in the hall, goes to look for her, finds her dead and kills himself. The duke discovers what has happened, and kills the duchess.[4]

Château-dwellers tended to see their own lives in similar terms, as dramatic sequences of heroic combats, marvellous happenings, extravagant vows, magnificent feasts and the pursuit of honour or love – lives in which knights, that is to say nobles, and their wives or ladies are what matter, and lower mortals scarcely exist. It is in these terms that chronicles describe contemporary history, so that the modern historian has to read behind their accounts to guess at the other forces at work beneath the surface.

Gaston-Phébus, Comte de Foix, was nicknamed 'Phébus' after the sun-god Phoebus Apollo because his glorious golden hair spread like an aureole around his head. 'All my life', he claimed, 'I have delighted in three things – fighting, love and hunting.'[5] His four principal bastards, whose four mothers were ensconced in four different corners of his castles, were a product of the second interest; his famous *Treatise on Hunting* came from the third. His military power was based on his four main castles: at Foix itself, and at Orthez, Pau and Montaner in Béarn.

Phébus was renowned for the lavishness of his hospitality, and his patronage of troubadours and minstrels who came in crowds to his castles to sing and play at his feasts. The chronicler Jean Froissart visited him at Orthez in 1388, and like all his

This manuscript illustration evokes a grand dinner in the fifteenth century. The hostess, and two ladies of similar rank, are being served by a gentleman servant carrying a short sword to show his rank. Inferior swordless servants look after lesser guests at the second table.

contemporaries was impressed by his glamour and style of living. 'There was seen', he wrote

> in his hall, chambre and court knights and squires of honour going up and down, and talking of arms and of amours; all honour there was found, all manner of tidings of every realm and country there might be heard, for out of every country there was resort, for valiantness of this earl.

Froissart describes Phébus's routine at supper-time.[6] His schedule, all his life, was to get up at midday and have supper at midnight. The way from his chambre to the hall was lit for him by twelve servants carrying twelve torches; they held these before his table all through supper, filling the hall with light. The hall was crowded with knights and squires; supper was provided for any of these who turned up. Phébus ate, on the whole, in silence at his table; no-one talked to him unless he spoke first. He loved to have songs and rounds sung to him as he ate. He drank very little, fond of breast and wing of chicken, but was also intrigued by foreign dishes and would pass these to the tables of his knights and squires after he had tasted them. He normally sat at table for two hours.

Christmas dinner in 1388 lasted four hours, for it was a special occasion, with many extra guests. Froissart lists who was there. At his own table Gaston-Phébus had four bishops on one side of him, and three viscounts and a visiting English knight on the other. At a second table there were four abbots and two Spanish knights; at a third table twelve knights and squires from Gascony and Bigorne; at other tables a great many knights of Béarn. A chief 'maître de la salle' directed the service, assisted by four 'maîtres d'hôtel'; all five were knights. The top table was served by Phébus's two bastard brothers and his two bastard sons. Both his own and visiting minstrels were there in crowds; he gave 500 francs to them, 500 francs to the heralds, and spent 200 francs on outfits of cloth-of-gold trimmed with miniver as presents for the minstrels of the Duke of Touraine.

It was the custom of Gaston-Phébus to go with a selection of his knights after dinner and walk up and down in the galleries which he had at all four châteaux, chatting and joking. There was a fireplace in at least one of these galleries, which was lit when it was cold: only a small fire, because he disliked a big one. On one unusually cold day, however, he remarked that the fire was too small. A visiting Spanish knight looked through the window into the courtyard and saw a troop of donkeys entering, loaded with bundles of firewood. He ran down the flight of steps which led from the gallery into the courtyard, picked up one of the donkeys along with its load, ran up the stairs again, pushed his way through the crowd of knights and squires all round the fireplace, and held the donkey upside-down over the fire so that the firewood fell into it.[7] It was the kind of gesture which went down well with Gaston-Phébus and his entourage.

Gaston-Phébus's lifestyle, and the buildings which it produced, all had a purpose. They were conditioned by the society in which he lived, but he skilfully used the

resources of that society to aggrandize himself. Like all feudal lords of any importance, he presided over a complex structure. He owed two hereditary domains, the county of Foix, which he held as a vassal of the kings of France, and the bigger and richer seigneurie of Béarn, for which he claimed he owed fealty to no-one. His aim was to link the two by establishing lordship over the intervening territory – a complex of seigneuries large and small, including the county of Bigorre – and by doing so assemble an independent or semi-independent territory running 240 kilometres or so along the Pyrenees. In building up his own power he made greater lords anxious for his support – including, above all, the two greatest competing powers in France at this time, the kings of France and England. He played, in fact, a skilful balancing act, by supporting first one and then the other.

His various underlords from Béarn, as they feasted in his hall, were strengthened in their loyalty; the visiting knights and squires from Gascony and Bigorre were tempted to come in with him. Public relations were as important to Gaston-Phébus as to any modern politician. To be talked of as successful was one way towards becoming successful. His lavish gifts to visiting troubadours, his hospitality to a chronicler like Froissart, helped ensure that stories of his greatness would be spread abroad; his carefully cultivated idiosyncrasies gave them something to talk, write or

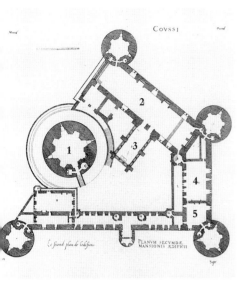

sing about. Lifestyle and image were supported by buildings: by the fortifications which enclosed his castles, by the halls in which he feasted, by the slender, many-storeyed towers in which he had his own quarters, and which rose like beacons on the hill-tops above the main bulk of his castles.

All too little remains of his buildings; they have suffered either from wholesale demolition as at Montaner and Orthez, or large-scale remodelling, as at Pau. The appearance of Montaner is to some extent preserved in Gaignières' seventeenth-century drawing of it, but today only the slender tower survives untouched, rising from the shattered foundations of the rest of the castle. One can get a more vivid feeling of the manner in which buildings contributed to the image of a grand seigneur from the earlier château of Coucy, in the north of France, where another great lord, Enguerrand

de Coucy, lived as ambitiously as and even more splendidly than Gaston-Phébus. Although it is only a heap of ruins today, the photographs of its great central tower, taken before the German army blew it up in 1918, combine with du Cerceau's sixteenth-century plan of it, to speak vividly of magnificence and power: a huge hall, for festivities, justice and ceremony; a chapel letting off the hall; a massive round tower, for the seigneur and his family; four smaller towers at the corners, for his fifty castle knights; a perimeter wall joining the towers to form a mighty fortification; and down the hill to one side, an enormous outer courtyard or 'basse-cour'.[8]

These great castles were not just fortified strongholds: they were legal, judicial, economic and family units, as well as military ones. They presided over a complex sovereignty fuelled by goods, money and services, from a combination of which the power of the seigneur derived. The basse-cour stood for one element of their power and wealth; it was crowded with peasants, servants and merchants coming to and fro, its barns and stabling were filled with grain, hay and livestock, deriving either from the seigneurial lands which the seigneur farmed directly, often with the help of compulsory labour from his peasants, or from the compulsory payments in kind which were made to him.

The wealth and manpower encapsulated in the basse-cour played an essential role in the importance of a seigneurie, but the power and the glory were all in the main castle building, into which many of the people in the basse-cour never penetrated. Here lived, served or were entertained the mounted and armoured soldiers who formed the other half of a seigneur's power. Here, surrounded by ladies of her own rank and often of her own blood, lived the seigneur's wife, whose inheritance and connections were usually an essential element in his power. Here the wealth in coin, precious stones and metals – progressively more important as payment in coin gradually replaced payment in goods and services, and fighting men were increasingly hired rather than attending as part of feudal duty – were stored in a vaulted room in one of the strongest towers, as were the deeds and charters which encapsulated the seigneur's power over his vassals or his relationships with his overlord or his fellow seigneurs.

Until the fifteenth century the main castle was likely to be a complex of freestanding buildings within a circuit of towers linked by an outer wall. Separate elements included a chapel and sometimes a kitchen standing alone, which could be an impressive structure, ventilated through a lofty roof in the centre with high chimney-pieces on the periphery, as in the surviving example at the château of Montreuil-Bellay. But the kitchen was sometimes incorporated in the lower storey of a tower or even removed to the basse-cour, with food carried from it into the main castle building. The chapel, although sometimes an impressive building, was often modest and not very large. The dominant buildings were the principal tower, and, in the larger châteaux, a free-standing or largely free-standing grande salle.[9]

Such grandes salles derived from the halls built in the principal towns in the time of Charlemagne, in what were known as 'palaces'. All through the Middle Ages the term continued to be applied to the places of residence of kings, grands seigneurs or bishops

The grande salle of the Palais des Comtes at Poitiers was built by Eleanor of Aquitaine, heiress of the Counts of Aquitaine and successively married to Louis VII of France and Henry II of England. The hall was used for great feasts, but also as a meeting-hall and court of justice.

situated within the fortifications of towns and therefore not in need of any but minor fortification themselves. But free-standing halls, perhaps in imitation of these, also began to be built in the more important castles, as at Coucy and many other examples.

In the eleventh and twelfth centuries the main castle was likely to be lived in by the seigneur and his 'castle knights', who formed his armed and mounted band, and occupied the lesser of the towers around the castle periphery. In the course of the centuries these, or their descendants, tended to move off to smaller castles or fortified houses of their own, either on land which they held in fealty from the seigneur, or on independent seigneuries which they had carved out for themselves.

By the fourteenth century the extensive noble clientele of a grand seigneur could be drawn from a wide area, and made up of descendants of the original castle knight, and other lesser seigneurs who had become his vassals as a result of conquest or because they had voluntarily placed themselves under his protection. This hard core could be extended by alliances formed or mercenaries hired on a straightforward financial basis. Feudal vassals normally, as part of their oath of allegiance, bound themselves to serve their overlord with a stipulated number of supporters for an agreed number of days a year, and did duty at his castle or in the field with him, in this period. But this obligation was increasingly commuted for a cash payment.

The resident noble population in a big castle now contained two quite separate elements. The first consisted of the squires, knights and ladies of the seigneur's own personal household, often related to him or from families which had served him for several generations, often also his vassals, but not necessarily so; they were paid an annual wage, but usually served for only half the year, to give them time to look after their own seigneuries, and moved round as upper servants from castle to castle of their overlord, who almost invariably owned more than one castle and travelled between them. The second element was the castle garrison, under the command of a capitaine. Its members were straightforward mercenaries, with no close personal links with the seigneur; they lived permanently in the château, often in the towers of the gatehouse.

The garrison might include unmounted non-noble soldiers armed with crossbows, but the fighting men who counted in contemporary French consideration, both in the garrison and a seigneur's personal entourage, were the mounted and armoured knights, and the mounted écuyers or squires who hoped to become knights – the class of men who by the end of the fourteenth century were firmly established as noble. Unmounted soldiers were held of small account – too small, as the English victories in the Hundred Years War were to make clear. In contemporary manuscripts they, like the servants of lower rank who were allowed into the main castle building to serve the nobles, were depicted, if they were depicted at all, half the size of their superiors!

It is tempting to think of medieval châteaux as bristling with soldiers and crowded with people of all types. Sometimes, indeed, they were, but by no means always. A seigneur who owned many châteaux could not live in all of them; usually he made three or four his principal places of residence, and travelled round between these with his household. In the intervals a château was left to a handful of people, and a garrison, if there was one. The seigneur sometimes installed a brother or other relative in the other châteaux, but often they were occupied only by a garrison. The function of these châteaux could be mainly a military one, especially in the unsettled times of the Hundred Years War.

A garrison could vary very much in size. The historical novel *Le Jouvencel*, which is in fact a roman-à-clef of the life of the renowned fifteenth-century warrior Jean de Bueil, describes the life of the fifteen or so mounted garrison in the château of Lue (synonym for l'Hermitage in the Sarthe).[10] They are of all ages, all noble and all hungry, as they are living off a countryside already ravaged by war; young

Jouvencel's capture of the cow belonging to the captain of a neighbouring rival castle, and grazing outside it, is considered a real coup. But when, a little later, Jouvencel captures the town and castle of Grathor (synonym for Sablé), the Duc d'Anjou sets him up there in command of 126 men-at-arms.

It was likely that the basse-cour was always full of people coming and going, but the main château, if without a garrison and with no family in residence, or the seigneur and his entourage away, could be all but empty. In the late fourteenth century the formidable freebooting warrior Aymerigot Marchès evolved a plan to capture the château of Nonette, the main seat of the Duc de Berry in Auvergne. He and his men were to creep at night into the basse-cour, which was not guarded, and hide in the barrels stored in it – not unlike Ali Baba and his forty thieves. When the porter opened the gates of the main château in the morning and let out the night-watchmen, they would emerge from the barrels, overpower him and occupy the castle. There would be no difficulty in doing this, because in Aymerigot's own words, 'This castle is inhabited by few or no people to guard it.'[11]

Around 1400 the château of Saint-Flour in Auvergne was occupied by a capi-taine with a garrison so small that he went to his seigneur, the Bishop of Clermont, to ask for more men. In his absence a party of freebooters was riding along the other side of the valley. The porter, thinking that they were at a safe distance, came out to have a look at them; a skilful crossbowman was able to pick him off, in spite of the distance, and the freebooters then occupied the château without difficulty.[12]

But a big château with the seigneur in residence was inevitably crowded with people, especially on the occasions – a marriage, a funeral, a feast-day, the swearing of fealty by vassals – when a major dinner was given in the grande salle. Such enter-tainments, in addition to marking a particular event, served to advertise the power, wealth and connections of the seigneur, and encourage others to come in on his side, or ally themselves with his family.

In the twelfth century, according to the verse romance *Joufrois*, 700 knights were entertained in the grande salle of the Palais of the Comtes de Poitou at Poitiers, the predecessor of the huge hall built about 1200 by Eleanor of Aquitaine, which is still there today.[13] In 1377 at least a thousand are said to have been seated in the grande salle of the Palais de la Cité in Paris. This was the biggest grande salle of medieval France, bigger, perhaps deliberately so, than Westminster Hall in London; its great size was made feasible by being divided into two by an arcade, as was the case with Westminster Hall, before triumphant medieval technology threw the present great roof across it in a remodelling of the 1390s. The occasion of the Paris dinner was the visit of the Emperor Charles IV to Charles V of France, and in spite of the number of tables, and the crush of spectators, the meal was so well organized that all the tables, high and low, were equally well served – according to Charles V's biographer, Christine de Pisan.[14]

In the *Roman du Comte d'Anjou*, written in 1316 by Jean Maillart, possibly an official of that name in the household of the Duke of Burgundy, the count, after a long sojourn abroad, is welcomed on his return by a splendid dinner, followed by

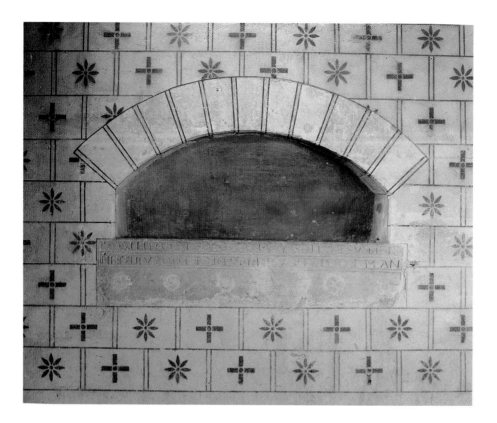

the usual washing of hands and entertainment by minstrels; while the older knights
talk of battles they have fought in, and the young nobles talk about love-affairs, dogs
and falcons, the servants – the 'serviteurs' – go off quietly to eat elsewhere.[15] Where
they went off to was likely to have been a salle underneath the grande salle. France
was different from England. In England the concept developed of the great hall
where the whole household ate together – the lord, his family and his guests of equal
status, on a raised dais at one end, the rest in the body of the hall down below. Except
in a few local variants (in Brittany, for instance), there was no such tradition in
France. The grande salle was for nobles and clerics. The raised dais, if there was one
– and it was a comparatively rare feature – was there to separate a king, bishop or
duke from the lesser nobles and clergy. The nature of a grande salle is made clear
in the twelfth-century Bishop's Palace in Angers. Here, the grande salle was
originally T-shaped, and in it each bishop gave a dinner to celebrate his inauguration, sitting himself with the more important guests in the cross-arm of the T. At
the other end of the hall, at its entry, the long stone lavabo in which guests washed
their hands as they entered is still in position. On it is the following inscription:
'Clericus et miles pergant, ad cetera viles. Nam locus hos primas decet, illos vilis et
imus.' (Clergy and knights can enter, the lower classes go elsewhere. The superior
place is appropriate for the former, the latter go humbly down below.) In other
words, 'third estate keep out', and for them was reserved the long vaulted 'salle basse'
or undercroft below the great hall.

The inaugural feast at Angers went on into the sixteenth century, and there is a surviving description of it in 1542: the bishop was carried into the cathedral for the actual inauguration on the shoulders of four barons, all his vassals, and afterwards 464 people were feasted in the salles.[16] There is no record of the numbers attending in earlier centuries, but evidence survives for the number at a somewhat similar event, the dinner given in the Archbishop's Palace in Reims after the funeral of Archbishop Richard Picque in 1369. A gathering of 320 were entertained, exclusive of those who were fed with the leftovers. The Bishop of Soissons, Simon de Bucy, rode over in a party of twenty to say the funeral mass, and stayed for three

nights. Others who came included the Abbots of Saint Rémy and Saint Thierry, and 'many' seigneurs, all of whom would have arrived with an escort, the burghers of Reims, who had carried the coffin, and 'the officers, bailiffs, provosts and captains' who had served the Archbishop. The food eaten is given in one of those overpowering lists which the scribes of the Middle Ages must have enjoyed putting together: 3960 rolls (or 'petits pains'), 15 sheep, 2 entire cattle, 7 pigs, 501 chickens, 140 rabbits, 34 partridges, 300 eggs, and so on.[17] A washerwoman and a kitchen help were brought in for three days, to supplement the kitchen staff. The guests were probably separated by status in the salle haute and the salle basse, as in the bishops' feasts at Angers; their successors exist today, rebuilt in the fifteenth century, with a grande salle that was to accommodate the inaugural banquet after the king was crowned for the next 400 years. It survives as an evocative example of a later medieval grande salle – even if its appearance is largely due to sensitive reconstruction and redecoration in post-war years. As at Angers, there is a much lower salle basse beneath it.

The biggest of these free-standing grandes salles are unlikely to have been in regular daily use: they were for special occasions, and a smaller salle, such as certainly existed at Angers, served for everyday meals. But more modest-sized ones probably doubled up for everyday and great events, as was the case in Gaston-Phébus's castles, if Froissart is to be relied on.

The two-tier arrangement became a common one, but was not invariable, and salles did not have to be free-standing. They could rest on the ground, or be built over a cellar, or, if not too large, be incorporated into one storey of a tower. Chrétien de Troyes, in his *Percival*, makes his hero, when still a naïf boy from a lonely manor in the forest, ride straight from the courtyard of King Arthur's palace into the hall, and up to the king seated at his table, so that his horse inquisitively nuzzles off the hat of the king.[18] The hall at Poitiers is built on the ground; so is the much smaller hall at Bricquebec; the halls at Coucy and Blois are built above cellars. Bricquebec and Blois are both built with two naves, like the hall in the Palais de la Cité, and perhaps in imitation of it.[19]

But there are many examples of two-tier halls, at both palaces and at châteaux outside a large town, or next to a small one. A drawing by du Cerceau vividly presents such a hall in the royal château of Montargis; and judging from the results, it was in a two-tier hall that a famous disaster took place at the feast held in the château of Sury-le-Comtal in 1313. This was given by the Comte de Forez before his departure on pilgrimage to the Holy Land. Feasting in the grande salle was followed by dancing, in the usual fashion; the floor collapsed and the whole company, or the greater part of it, was killed. 'Une danse de Forez' became, as a result, a proverbial expression for any great disaster.[20]

Some salles were used for judicial business, the reception of delegations and possibly the swearing of fealty. The king in Paris, and the counts of Aquitaine in Poitiers, originally sat with their council in their grande salle, and adjudicated themselves, but they increasingly delegated their judicial authority.[21] The Parisian

In the grande salle of the Palais of the Archbishop of Reims, known as the Palais de Tau, the inaugural dinners after the coronations of the kings of France in the Cathedral were held from the time it was built in the fifteenth century to the coronation banquet of Charles X in 1824.

Parlement developed out of this delegation, and ultimately took over the royal palace on the Île de la Cité, and the kings removed to the Louvre; a similar development took place on a lesser scale in Poitiers. In both cities the site of the palais is now the Palais de Justice, though in Poitiers the grande salle survives, and in Paris it was destroyed by fire in the seventeenth century.

In the château of La Clayette, as late as 1742, all those who held property by fealty appeared on the appointed occasion before the seigneur, who was 'seated in a chair with arms in the grande salle', and swore fealty to him 'bare-headed, without sword or spurs, kneeling with hands joined between his'.[22] Presumably a similar ceremony had taken place in the salle ever since the château was built in the late fourteenth century.

Seigneurial courts may have been held in the salles of the less important seigneuries, but there is little evidence for this. The courts, except in very early days, were not presided over by the seigneur himself, but by an official appointed by him, who was never noble. These officials were mainly adjudicating in cases involving peasants in the seigneurie, and the courts had none of the prestige of those held in the city palaces. At Châteaudun a court-room separate from the salles still exists, and although the existing fittings date from the eighteenth century, courts may have been held in this room from much earlier times. At Anjony in 1469 seigneurial courts were held in the market-place of the village.[23]

All salles, on the other hand, were used as places of general reception, and for dancing. The latter normally, and perhaps invariably, took place after a meal, and in the same salle. Conversion from one use to the other was easy, because in all salles

Du Cerceau's engraving of the grande salle of the royal château of Montargis gives a vivid impression of the nature of a great two-tier salle of the fourteenth century, with an impressive salle haute above a lower and less prestigious salle basse.

up until well on in the sixteenth century, the tables consisted of boards on trestles, which could be put up for the meal, and then dismantled to clear the floor.

A wedding feast in the vanished grande salle of the château of Lallaing, near Douai, is described in Georges Chastellain's contemporary life of Jacques de Lallaing. The wedding was that of Jacques's father, Guillaume de Lallaing, and took place in about 1420. After the marriage service, the bride, with her mother, her two young brothers, and a crowd of knights and squires, was escorted to the château and received by her father and mother-in-law

> accompanied by a great number of knights, squires, ladies young and old, their relatives and neighbours, who with much joy and merriment received the noble bride and led her up into the grande salle, and then to the chambre which had been prepared for her; and when supper-time was coming up the young lady was led into the hall, richly clothed and adorned and escorted on either side by her two brothers-in-law, tall, handsome and shapely young squires. Then merriment and festivity broke out in the grande salle of the château of Lallaing. As soon as supper was ready and the tables had been put in place and covered, water was brought; everyone washed their hands and sat down at the tables. I don't want to go into the details of how they were seated and fed, you can be sure enough that nothing could have been richer or more splendid. Then when dessert had been served and the tables removed dancing and carol-singing started in the grande salle of the château of Lallaing, and trumpeters and minstrels set to work to show their skills. Music was made on many melodious instruments; everyone did of their best. After all the dancing and revelling was finished, the time came for the company to go off to bed. The young bride was led into her chambre, in which she lay that night with her lord and husband, to such good effect that a little while after they produced a very fine son.[24]

This was Jacques de Lallaing, who grew up to become a famous warrior.

The free-standing, two-tier grande salle was by no means an invariable feature of medieval châteaux. Often the salle was incorporated into one of the towers, bigger and more important than the others, at first usually called the 'grosse tour' and ultimately known as the donjon. This was the older arrangement; the free-standing hall, as suggested above, was probably an importation from the urban palais.

The history of the tower in French châteaux starts with single towers. Such single fortified towers, prominently raised on hill-tops or artificial mounds, had first begun to rise out of the French countryside in the eleventh century, if not before. The early ones were often built of wood; later ones were of stone and to begin with were square or rectangular in plan, but from the twelfth century increasingly round.

At first their function was essentially military: they were the fortified strongholds of armed men, who dominated and sometimes terrorized the surrounding countryside. Inevitably, however, their striking silhouettes, visible, often, for miles around, became symbols of the power and lordship which they supported. And as fortification grew more elaborate, and the big single towers were supplemented by smaller ones, and by stronger perimeter walls, their military importance diminished and sometimes largely disappeared.

They became, literally, status symbols: the status they symbolized was that of the seigneuries in which they stood, and of the seigneur who held the seigneurie. It was the donjon, rather than the château as a whole, which was sometimes listed in legal documents as the seat of the power of the seigneur. In Paris the fiefs of the kings derived from the great circular donjon built by Philippe-Auguste in the courtyard of the Louvre, until this was demolished by François I in the early sixteenth century. The fiefs of the comtes de Poitou and their royal successors derived from the great tower next to the grande salle in the palais, known as the Tour Maubergue, from the name of the mistress of Comte Guillaume VII of Poitou; it continued to be the seat of all the dependent fiefs up to the Revolution.[25]

At Sully-sur-Loire, the vanished donjon or 'grosse tour ronde' built by Philippe-Auguste around 1200 became known as the 'tour des fiefs' in the time of the ducs de Sully who later owned it, and the archives of the dependent fiefs were stored in it.[26] In a more modest context the little donjon in the château of Bressieux in the Dauphiné was never residential, and by the eighteenth century was being used as an archives tower, as may always have been its use.[27] Archives were similarly stored in the donjon of the château of Goulaine, which survived the rebuilding of the rest of the château in the early sixteenth century; and the donjon incorporated into the château of Le Touvet near Grenoble is still an archive tower today.

In such cases the status of donjons as the centres of their seigneuries was legally defined, or demonstrated by their use for legal purposes. More often it came from the visual power and distinctiveness of their shape and silhouette, and not necessarily from the status of the use to which they were put. They were by no means always the residence of the seigneur himself; some were not residential at all. Their uses tended, however, to be appropriate to his power or wealth. At Provins the great octagonal donjon which looms above the town, and was built by the comtes de Blois in the late twelfth century, had become the count's prison by at least 1250.[28] Other donjons contained treasure. The long-vanished five-storey tower at the château of Cornillon in Provence, as described in an inventory of 1379, was crammed to bursting with treasure, valuables and manuscripts: swords and crosses on the ground floor; tapestries and cushions for benches and footstools on the first floor, the tapestries adorned with parrots, a stag hunt, a girl surrounded by birds, and the story of David, the cushions embroidered with coats of arms; gold and silver plate, both secular and religious, on the second floor; robes, altar fittings, reliquaries and religious books and pictures on the third floor; manuscripts on the fourth floor, and 'in various places' over 20,000 gold and silver coins of various denominations.[29]

Only the top floor of the massively bleak, circular donjon at Châtillon Coligny was residential, probably for the use of the seigneur; the rest was without chimney-

In the late fourteenth
century one end of the
grande salle of the
Palais des Comtes at
Poitiers was remodelled
for the Duc de Berry,
uncle of Charles VI,
to provide a setting in
which the duke could
feast or preside over
meetings or courts on a
raised dais against a
background of a triple
chimney piece and
magnificent sculpture
and architecture.

pieces or latrines, and its original use is not known; the tower is only very summarily fortified, and its military function cannot have been significant. But at Coucy all four floors of the donjon were supplied with a chimney-piece and a two-seater latrine hollowed out in the enormous thickness of the walls; the bottom floor contains an oven and well, and must have functioned as a kitchen, though not the main kitchen of the castle. Many donjons were, like Coucy, completely residential, and almost certainly occupied by the seigneur himself. The individual function of their rooms is not always clear; some donjons certainly contained a salle, referred to as 'du la turris' in contemporary documents. Some, like the enormous rectangular donjon at Crest, had complex building histories, expanding in layers around the original core.

In fact the distinction between salle (a room of general resort) and chambre (a room assigned to a particular person or a small group of persons) was, to begin with, probably not a hard and fast one; in early châteaux, containing relatively few rooms, many rooms used as salles also contained beds, where guests or part of the household bedded down every night. Chambres, as they developed, were often shared. In 1312, for instance, the seigneur of the château of Génat, down by the Pyrenees, was occupying one chambre with his two sons; the women in the family seem to have been sleeping separately from the men, but probably together themselves.[30] In 1322 Beatrix de Béziers, seigneuresse of Cesseras and Belvèze, was sharing both her chambre and her bed with her two daughters. She was living in her château of Cesseras

with a small household, but apparently no garrison. At any rate, a party of sixteen men had no difficulty in breaking in at night: they forced their way into the chambre where Beatrix was sleeping with her daughters, 'pierced the bed with their swords and lances, and carried off many of their possessions'.[31] The episode gives a feeling of the simplicity of life as lived in a château of this date, even by the seigneurial family, as well as of its potential violence.

By the end of the fourteenth century life had grown considerably less simple, at least in the households of richer and more powerful seigneurs. If one stands halfway along the grande salle in the Palais des Comtes at Poitiers and looks towards the entrance, one sees a hall not all that different from the form in which Eleanor of Aquitaine built it around 1200, in all its rather bleak magnificence. If one swivels round 180 degrees, and looks in the other direction, one moves into a different world. This end of the salle was remodelled by the Duc de Berry at the end of the fourteenth century. It is an architecture of luxury and fantasy. A flight of steps leads up to the dais. All along the back of it ran a triple fireplace, richly carved and surmounted by three shields of the duke's coats of arms, each supported by flying angels. Up above the wall is hidden by a coruscating veil of open tracery, carved in front of the windows; little open staircases rise up on delicate stone frameworks to either side. A painting by the Pol de Limbourg brothers shows the duke eating in splendour in another of his residences, but the painting helps to bring the grande

salle at Poitiers to life. The duke sits before the fireplace, protected from its heat by a large circular fire-screen; a golden salt cellar floats like a ship on the table; to one side a buffet is piled with three tiers of gold plate. The whole scene is enriched by a wealth of textiles: the patterned robe of the duke himself, sweeping under the table; the rich dress of his courtiers and the young nobles who are serving him; the great tapestry of warriors which hangs on the wall behind him; and the canopy, embroidered with his arms and crest of lilies and swans, which projects over his head.

The external version of this kind of feudalism made fantastic took its most extreme form in the Duc de Berry's château at Mehun-sur-Yèvre – again, as depicted by Limbourg, but enough of it survives to show that he was not romancing. The old formula, so frequently grim – round towers, massive walls, crenellations, a moat – has been transformed. A chapel, like a miniature version of the Sainte-Chapelle in Paris, bursts out from one side; the towers dissolve at their summits into slender cages of stone and glass; even the crenellations (as one knows from those that survive) were carved with trefoils and foliage.

In the last decades of the fourteenth century a new richness appeared, and along with it a new feeling for comfort and intimacy. A magnate as powerful as the Duc de Berry could indulge in this to the full, but the development was by no means confined to him. It was stimulated, perhaps, by the twenty years of virtual peace between the two halves of the Hundred Years War. Its most remarkable manifestation was the way in which the personal accommodation of great people became more elaborate. Monarchs, bishops and grands seigneurs set in train a development that then started to percolate down the social scale.

This improved accommodation involved several rooms, collectively known as the 'logis' of whoever occupied them (their English equivalent was similarly known as 'lodgings'). A great person's logis contained at least two chambres as well as a garderobe, generous provision of latrines, and sometimes a private oratory and a study, or 'estude'.

This illustration from a fifteenth-century manuscript of the Dream of Roi René gives a vivid impression of a luxurious chambre of the period, with canopies over the beds, carpets and matting on the floor, and a smaller bed for a servant. René of Anjou, heir to one of the greatest feudal families of France, claimed the crown of Sicily, but was never able to establish his claim.

The outer (or sometimes lower) of the two chambres was known as the chambre 'de parement', 'd'apparat' or 'à parer', the inner or upper one as the chambre 'de retrait' or 'de gîte', and sometimes just as the chambre, because it was the room in which the occupant of the lodgings actually slept. In a few cases – at the Louvre, for instance, as occupied by Charles V – there were three chambres: the chambre de parement, chambre de retrait and chambre.[32]

'Parer', 'parement' and 'apparat' can best be translated as 'state', and the room was so-called because it contained the 'lit de parement'. The point of this was that it was a state bed, magnificently appointed, in which nobody slept; its one function, other than to look good, seems to have been to lay out the body of the occupant of the logis after his death. Indeed, just before Charles V died in 1380, he was moved from his sick bed in his chambre in the Château de Beauté outside Paris to his adjacent chambre de parement, so that he could die in a suitably dignified setting.[33]

What had happened was that a chambre had hived off a more private inner chambre, so that the chambre de parement became a reception room or ante-room, leading to the chambre, but with a fossilized – or rather formalized – bed remaining in it. The occupant of the logis sometimes ate in the chambre de parement, as did his or her gentlemen or ladies, when they wished to eat more privately than in the salle; but if they wanted the maximum of privacy, they still continued to eat in their chambre.

In later decades the chambre de parement tended to increase in size and because of its uses and ambiguous status – a bedroom that was not a bedroom – was sometimes known as the 'salle de parement'. It was so called in Roi René's great château at Angers in 1471, but there was still a 'grand charlit de parement' (wooden structure of a bed) in it, protected by a wooden trellis 'so that the dogs do not lie on it'. The room was clearly used for eating and recreation, and contained three tables, six benches and a big dresser, and also a board for playing the game of 'quills' – a kind of miniature ninepins.[34]

At Brussels in 1456, towards the end of the vogue for such chambres, the bed in the chambre de parement of Isabelle de Bourbon, wife of Charles le Téméraire, was described as follows:

> a large bed, which was hung all round with crimson satin, with a cover of
> the same material, and another cover hung above it as a canopy, each piece
> of material finely and richly embroidered with a big sun, as large as a carpet
> … the bed made up and covered like a bed in which no-one sleeps; and at
> the head of it was a big square of crimson and cloth of gold …[35]

At the Louvre, which was built around a courtyard, the logis of Charles and his wife filled the first and second floors of the north range, one above the other. In the 1380s Enguerrand VIII de Coucy, the great-great-grandson of the Enguerrand de Coucy who had built the original château of Coucy in the early thirteenth century, deserted the donjon and rehoused himself in the same style as the king, and probably in imitation of him. One can see why: his huge vaulted chambre in the donjon, with a little light filtering into it through the thickness of the walls, splendid though it was in its way, must have been uncomfortable and painfully out of date. It survived as a status symbol, and he moved to new rooms built on the first and second floors along the inside of the north-west perimeter wall, at the north end of the grande salle. Enguerrand's own logis was on the second floor. It consisted, as can be deduced from the building accounts, of a garderobe next to the grande salle, followed by a large 'chambre à parer de Monseigneur', and a smaller 'chambre de Monseigneur'. Both chambres were well lit through much thinner walls than those of the donjon; the chambre à parer had a row of five windows looking over the courtyard to the donjon in its abandoned grandeur. Enguerrand's chambre de parement had an additional sophistication, a tiny vaulted closet or study, with one window and a fireplace, hollowed out of the wall, and letting off the middle of the chambre. In the time of Duke Louis d'Orléans, who acquired the château and seigneurie in 1399, this was described as 'a secret place, in which, without anyone knowing about it, the prince could have a consultation with his chief courtiers, or could write if he felt so inclined, and do whatever he wanted to do secretly and apart'.[36]

There was an identical arrangement of rooms, including the little closet, on the floor below. These probably served as the logis of Enguerrand VII's wife, and of the duchesses of Orléans who succeeded her. The chambre de parement was originally known as the 'poêle', because instead of being heated by an open fireplace it had the unusual luxury of a poêle or stove – a rare, though certainly not unique feature at the time. This was later replaced by the dukes of Orléans with a large open fireplace carved with a frieze of the nine Women Worthies (heroines of medieval chivalry), a less common complement to the nine Male Worthies, and one which was suitable for the chambre de parement of a great noblewoman (at the same time sculptures of the Male Worthies were placed in alcoves all along the grande salle).

The logis in horizontal ranges at the Louvre and Coucy were important prototypes for future developments in the planning of châteaux. But more often in the fourteenth century these improved logis were fitted into a tower, a sophisticated fourteenth-century

An illustration (below), showing the king talking with Pierre Salmon in about 1412, is probably an accurate representation of the king in his chambre, and makes clear the supreme importance of textiles in accommodation at this level of luxury.

The grosse tour or donjon of the château of Vincennes (above), as built by Charles V in about 1360–80, provided a model for the personal tower of a great man, and was imitated all over France. His private kitchen was in the basement, his chambres de parement, chambre de gîte and chambre on the next three floors, successively more exclusive and hard of access; the turrets contained staircases, studies, garderobes, privies and oratories.

version of the great towers of earlier châteaux. The most remarkable surviving example is the donjon at Vincennes, where Charles V, on succeeding as king in 1364, heightened and enlarged the tower which he had started to build as Dauphin. The donjon had its own fortified 'enceinte', a wall on one side of a huge rectangular enclosure, the periphery of which was studded by nine lower but still lofty towers, lodgings for royal officials and other members of the royal family. This amazing epitome of feudalism and chivalry was brilliantly depicted by de Limbourg in the *Très Riches Heures du Duc de Berry*; but in fact the arrangement survived virtually intact until Napoleon chopped off the upper storeys of the subsidiary towers in the early nineteenth century.

The donjon at Vincennes takes the form of a square of four main storeys, each vaulted from a central pillar, with four round turrets at the corners, one of them containing the staircase. There was a privy kitchen on the ground floor; the king's chambre de parer and his own chambre and chambre de retrait were on the first, second and third floors; and there were chapels and garderobes in the turrets and a stack of latrines on every floor, along with an estude built out on the second floor, in an extension to one side.[37]

The king's chambre, as Mary Whiteley established in her seminal article on the donjon, is almost certainly the room depicted in a miniature of about 1412. This vividly suggests the clothing of textiles which brought colour and comfort to these rooms when the king was in residence; but even without the textiles the richly carved or moulded columns, vaulting, chimney-pieces and doorways, as they have lasted to this day, still preserve a savour of intimate luxury, which has survived the donjon's centuries of use as a prison.

The king's tower at Vincennes was, as might be expected, the most luxurious of these late-fourteenth-century towers, but there is no shortage of other examples, both simple and complex. The simplest type is represented by the towers built by Gaston de Foix at Montaner and Pau: that at Montaner is seven storeys high and impressive from its height, but basic, not to say bleak, in its planning – just plain square rooms, with no smaller rooms off them, no latrines even, suggesting that for Gaston-Phébus comfort was less important than show.

Bishops seem to have had a greater feeling for comfort. A group of towers built by them in the late fourteenth or early fifteenth centuries includes two which still exist: at Bassoues, not far from Montaner in the foothills of the Pyrenees, built by Arnaud Aubert, Archbishop of Auch, and all but completed at his death in 1371, and at Septmonts, built by Simon de Bucy, Bishop of Soissons, as a country residence a few kilometres from his cathedral, sometime between his installation as bishop in 1362 and his death in 1404. No inventories are known to survive to

The six-storey donjon of the château of Bassoues (left), built in about 1370, accommodated the personal quarters of the Archbishop of Auch, whose country residence it was. His vaulted chambre de parement and his own personal chambre filled the first and second floors. At the highest level was a vaulted strong-room and a roof-top walk with superb views.

document the arrangements of either tower, but these can be surmised from the surviving inventories of 1389, for towers built by the Archbishop of Reims at the château of Porte Mars in Reims itself, and at the château of Courville, his main seat in the country. At Courville the sequence of rooms runs: 'chambre de parement en la tour', 'chambre de retrait' and 'garderobe au dessus'.[38]

The slender tower at Bassoues dominates the village, and is a beacon for miles in the surrounding countryside. In contrast to the unadorned rectangularity of Montaner, it is given distinction and elegance by what appear to be square buttresses set diagonally at each corner, but are in fact big enough to be hollowed out and to contain the staircase and latrines. The tower is six storeys high, with one room to a floor, two of them vaulted. The vaulted room on the second floor can be surmised

to have been the Archbishop's chambre de parement, and the room above, which has a flat ceiling of timber beams, to have been his chambre or chambre de retrait. By the late fourteenth century ceilinged rooms were clearly felt to be more comfortable than vaulted ones; building accounts show that at this period vaults were being taken out and replaced by timber ceilings in both the palais at Poitiers and the château just outside it.

Both the two chambres at Bassoues are elegantly finished, with hooded and carved chimney-pieces, stone seats in the windows, and washbasins set in the walls under elegantly cusped arches. The room on the floor above the chambre may have been a garderobe, and above it, on the summit of the tower, is a smaller octagonal strong-room, without windows. Around this runs a battlemented walk above the crenellations, with access to the little pepper-pots which surmount the buttresses; as often in the later Middle Ages one is not certain whether this lovely cloud-high walk, with a panoramic view over the surrounding countryside, was designed for pleasure, or defence, or both.

The planning of Simon de Bucy's donjon at Septmonts[39] is reminiscent of that of Bassoues, but it is more elaborate, inside and out. It is eight storeys high, including the cellar, with one room to a floor, except on the two main floors, where there are two minor rooms in addition. The plan of each floor is substantially different, and throughout there is generous accommodation for privies. All this is expressed externally by elaborate corbelling, so that the tower swells out here and there and finally recedes, and rises to the slender turret of the last stages of the staircase, leading to a look-out room under a spirelet. All in all the result is so complex that

The château of Septmonts (below right) was the main country residence of the Bishops of Soissons. Between 1362 and 1404 Bishop Simon de Bucy built the largest and most luxurious of its sequence of towers (above). His chambre de parement and oratory were on the first floor (B on plan below), his personal chambre and small study on the second floor (C), and a strong-room on the third floor (D). The upper floors were probably occupied by chaplains and secretaries, and corridors wrapped round the staircase gave access to privies.

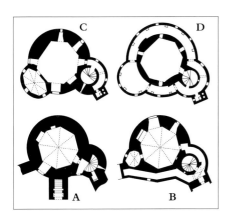

one finds it hard to believe what one is seeing when one first enters the castle court-yard. The castle must have seemed even more extraordinary when the donjon was one of a constellation of three towers, rising above the moat, as shown in an early engraving. The middle one of the three was based on a tower of the thirteenth century, of which the ground-floor room remains, elegantly vaulted round a central capital. Simon de Bucy preserved this tower, though he heightened it. The existing free-standing block of the sixteenth century, with a grande salle on the first floor, may be a replacement of a medieval two-tier salle.

Although much has disappeared, a visit to Septmonts is still a remarkable experience. It belongs to the commune: gates and tower are normally open, and one can wander in and around, with no interposition of tickets or guides. On weekdays it is often deserted. Simon de Bucy's donjon is completely empty, but in such good condition that it seems as though the Bishop had just moved out, taking his hangings, his coffers and his beds with him. It feels like a desirable and luxurious residence. The vaulted ground floor, which has a later fireplace of the fifteenth century, leads to the staircase, and up to the handsome vaulted octagon on the first floor, with its carved chimney-piece. This was the Bishop's chambre d'apparat, and off it is his little vaulted oratory. Up the staircase again to his chambre de retrait. As its nature required, this is a more genial room than the chambre d'apparat; it is better

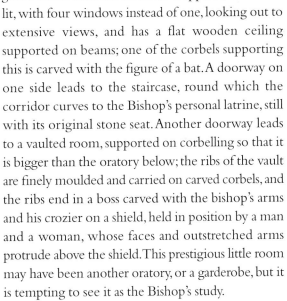

lit, with four windows instead of one, looking out to extensive views, and has a flat wooden ceiling supported on beams; one of the corbels supporting this is carved with the figure of a bat. A doorway on one side leads to the staircase, round which the corridor curves to the Bishop's personal latrine, still with its original stone seat. Another doorway leads to a vaulted room, supported on corbelling so that it is bigger than the oratory below; the ribs of the vault are finely moulded and carried on carved corbels, and the ribs end in a boss carved with the bishop's arms and his crozier on a shield, held in position by a man and a woman, whose faces and outstretched arms protrude above the shield. This prestigious little room may have been another oratory, or a garderobe, but it is tempting to see it as the Bishop's study.

The floor above has a wide walk, originally covered in, corbelled out and crenellated for defence, so that the room on this floor, which is a low one, has no fireplace and no external windows, just small barrel openings, looking out on to the walk; above this are three more rooms, each with a fireplace, the highest one originally up in the roof, which no longer exists. The conventional interpretation is that

The vaulted chambre de parement on the first floor of the great tower at Septmonts (left) would have been used by the Bishop of Soissons as a room for receptions and private eating: a little vaulted oratory was immediately adjacent. His own chambre on the floor above (below) was more domestic, with flat ceiling, bigger windows, and an adjacent study.

the 'garrison' was up here, occupying the habitable chambres and storing arms and munitions in the barred room. But while in cases of need the tower is clearly defensible, it is architecturally so prestigious, but also so comfortable, not to say domestic in feel, that it seems more convincing to assign it to the Bishop's personal staff and use, and to visualize him walking for exercise round and round the spacious circuit, and enjoying the thought of his treasures behind bars in the inner room, and to make the upper space a garderobe, and perhaps rooms occupied by his chaplain and secretaries. (In one of them Victor Hugo scribbled his name, and the name of his companion and mistress Juliette, and the date.)

Bishops had no family, and fitted easily enough into a tower with one room to a storey. Seigneurial families, if they were to occupy a single tower, were likely to need something more complex. The finest surviving example of how this was provided is the donjon at Largoet in Brittany.[40] It was built, probably between 1375 and 1390, by the powerful Malestroit family; Henry Tudor was put up there from 1474 to 1476, before he left Brittany for England and the campaign which made him Henry VII. The tower contains five main floors, and a smaller sixth floor. A list of repairs to be made to what is called the 'grosse tour' in 1481 gives the uses of some of the rooms on each floor, and shows how it was occupied in that year; the uses probably had not greatly changed since it was built. It was a family tower, with lodgings

On each floor at Largoet (right above) a large salle or chambre de parement is supported by nests of smaller rooms cunningly fitted into the smooth octagon of the tower. Each room, even the smallest (right), has its own fireplace.

KEY
A. GROUND FLOOR
B. FIRST FLOOR
C. SECOND FLOOR
D. THIRD FLOOR

The great château at Largoet (left), sometimes known as the Tours d'Elven, was the main residence of the powerful Malestroit family. The biggest of its two principal towers provided accommodation for different members of the family rather than for a single great person, as at Vincennes, Bassoues and Septmonts. The future English king Henry VII spent some years here before his successful campaign to wrest the crown from Richard III.

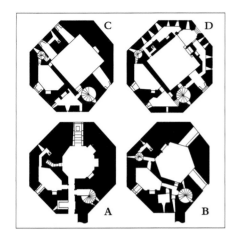

for different members of the family on each floor. These consisted for the most part of a sizeable 'salle', probably a salle de parement, a chambre and a garderobe. The tower was at the opposite extreme to Septmonts, where the complexity of the interior is reflected and even exaggerated by that of the exterior. At Largoet the smooth octagon, almost as simple as the great cylinder at Coucy, contains, unlike Coucy, an amazing complexity of large and small rooms, corridors and galleries, two staircases and a great bundle of shafts for latrines, fitted together like the drawers in a jewellery-box, with as much ingenuity as the architects of the eighteenth century were to fit the entresols and petits appartements around their

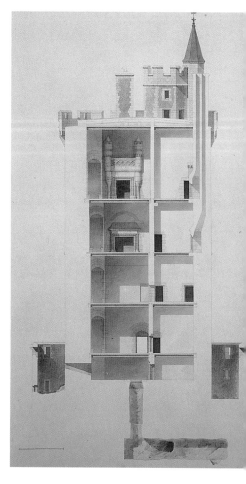

chambres de coucher behind their smoothly elegant, classical façades. There are at least twenty-three rooms in the donjon, almost all of them with a fireplace; a chapel on the third floor had separate seigneurial closets hollowed out in the thickness of the wall, each with a view on to the altar at one end, plenty of windows and a little fireplace.

At Oudon, 200 kilometres or so from Largoet, the same family built another octagonal tower at much the same time. It is smaller, its plan simpler, and as a result it is slimmer: a slender shaft of great elegance rising out of and above the little town. There are two rooms on each of its six floors, and extra closets and privies hollowed out here and there in the thickness of the wall. On the analogy of Largoet, it was probably a family tower, less elaborate because it was for more occasional use, with, on most of the floors, the two rooms used as a chambre or salle de parement and a smaller chambre, but with perhaps one floor given over to garderobes. The main logis was up on the top floor; it rose higher than the others, and had a two-tier chimney-piece, embellished with turrets like a miniature castle.

Other late-fourteenth-century donjons with two or more rooms to a floor include the Duke of Brittany's tower at Dinan, built as a gatehouse leading into the

The Malestroit family of Largoet had a smaller château at Oudon also with a family tower (above left), five storeys high. There are two rooms on each floor, as shown in the section (above right). On the three upper floors these probably served as chambre de parement and chambre for different members of the family; the top floor was the grandest, with an especially magnificent fireplace.

town, and made up of two round towers elided together like Siamese twins, and what must have been a splendid and influential example, the five-storey family tower built as part of his great castle of Pierrefonds by Duc Louis d'Orléans, at much the same time as he was embellishing the château at Coucy. It had three rooms to a floor, probably a chambre de parement, chambre and garderobe; the main rooms all had sumptuous chimney-pieces.[41] Sumptuous it all still is, but only after reconstruction by Viollet-le-Duc as what would have been the private appartements of Napoleon III and the Empress Eugénie, if the Franco-Prussian War had not intervened.

Not all these later donjons were built by great families: the formula was widely imitated by nobles all over France. A nice example is the donjon of Chevenon, built by Guillaume de Chevenon between 1382 and 1406. He served under Charles V as 'capitaine des châteaux et tours de Vincennes', that is to say, he was in charge of security and the garrison there. He and his soldiers were probably lodged in the Tour du Village, the gatehouse tower by which the château of Vincennes is entered from the town. His own house was, as it were, an expanded version of this, with some echoes of the Vincennes donjon as well; it was built as a gatehouse over the entrance to the courtyard, but with two rooms, one large and one small, to a floor, and round towers at the corner on two of the façades.

The château of Sarzay (right) is one of many that carried on the fourteenth-century formula of rectangular tower with corner turrets into the fifteenth century.

What can be called donjons continued to be built all through the fifteenth century, most commonly with two or three rooms to a floor, sometimes embellished with corner towers, as at Sarzay, sometimes formidable square masses with or without a staircase tower, as at Rosières and Fourchaud-Besson.

At Anjony, however, in the remote uplands of the Massif Central, Louis d'Anjony, a tough professional soldier in the royal army, built himself a scaled-down version of the donjon of Vincennes in about 1435. His descendants continued to serve as professional soldiers into the twentieth century, and are still in their tower at Anjony. It neither became a ruin, nor an empty appendage to a bigger and later château; a very modest wing was added in the eighteenth century, but unlike most medieval towers, it is still fully lived in.

It is four storeys high, exclusive of a floor for defence in the roof. There is one main room to a floor, and round corner turrets, one of them containing a staircase, as at Vincennes. Unlike Vincennes, only the top-floor room is vaulted. There are no early inventories from which to establish the original use of the rooms, and no remains of any other buildings of the same date, though these may have existed. The walls of the second-storey room, known today as the Salle des Preux, were decorated in about 1560 with paintings of the Nine Worthies and portraits of Louis's descendant Michel d'Anjony and his wife Germaine de Foix. In 1760, according to an inventory of that year, Claude d'Anjony, the then seigneur, occupied this room as his bedroom, and had his cabinet de toilette in one of the turrets. It is possible that it was always the chambre of the seigneur, and that the vaulted room above was his chambre or salle de parement.[42]

The romantic little château of Anjony (above), lost in the mountains of the Massif Central, was built in about 1435 by Louis d'Anjony in imitation of his royal master as a simplified version of the donjon at Vincennes.

The château of Martainville (above), built in the late fifteenth and early sixteenth centuries, is an expanded version of the residential towers of the previous two centuries, but follows the same pattern.

One can see the influence of these donjons in a group of compact châteaux built all through the sixteenth century, slightly expanded in plan and usually lower in height than the fifteenth-century towers; the plan-type proved a useful one for families of middling status. The château of Martainville near Rouen is a good early example, a luxurious and elaborately decorated little château, started in 1485 but embellished in the early sixteenth century by Jacques Lepelletier, a rich merchant of Rouen who bought his way into the nobility. Its four towers give it something of a castle air, but almost all elements of fortification have been abandoned. The château at Chenonceau, built in the 1520s by Jean Bohier, of similar extraction to Lepelletier but for a time even more successful, is in the same tradition, brilliantly sited both for security and pleasure on an artificial island in the Loire. But interesting though this group is, the main line of châteaux in France was to take a different direction.

3
'GRACIOUS HOMES FOR NOBLE SEIGNEURS'

The great staircase tower built by the Duc de Longueville in about 1510–18 is the larger of the two magnificent open staircases at the château of Châteaudun. It gave access to the apartments of the duke and duchess on the ground and first floors. These towers became one of the main status symbols of the sixteenth- and seventeenth-century noblesse.

I
T IS INTERESTING TO LEAVE TRISTAN and the Knights of the Round Table, as painted in the fourteenth century in the vaulted salle of Saint-Floret, and move ten kilometres over the hills to the frescoes in the gallery or cloister of the château of Villeneuve-Lembron, painted 150 years or so later. One has come into a different world: instead of high romance, battling knights and prancing chargers, we find salty, not to say crude humour, alternating with sober domestic dignity.

At either end of the gallery are depictions of two fabulous beasts, Bigorne and Chiche-fache. They are of a different make from the fabulous beasts that roamed the forests of the romances. Bigorne is sleek and well fed because his staple diet is hen-pecked husbands, and they queue up to ask him to eat them in order to get away from their wives. He is depicted in the course of eating one, and a second is waiting for his turn. Chiche-fache is skeleton-thin and ravenous. She lives off wives who obey their husbands, and although she has one in her jaws, it is her first meal for ten thousand years.[1]

Further along the gallery is a depiction of Rigault d'Oureille, who built Villeneuve-Lembron, probably in the decade before his death in 1517. He is seated in a handsomely carved chair, dressed in cap and gown, and holding his staff of office as maître d'hôtel to four successive monarchs. The picture suggests a way to honour and respect other than fighting. The dignified figure in his chair is reminiscent in dress and position of the seigneur in one of a sequence of miniatures of the late fifteenth century, showing the four ages of man. He too is seated in a richly carved chair, but it is a two-seater one; he is sharing it with his wife, and their two children stand or kneel next to them. A dresser in the background, with two shelves groaning with plate, underlines his seigneurial dignity, but he is depicted in a domestic rather than a military role. In spite of its four towers, defensive ditch and modest provision of loopholes for guns, the château of Villeneuve-Lembron is essentially domestic, low and friendly, with gardens round it, and a spacious courtyard open on

Rigault d'Oureille (right), maître d'hôtel to four successive kings of France, though a professional soldier by origin, is depicted at one end of the open ground floor gallery of his château of Villeneuve-Lembron as a dignified secular worthy.

In the same gallery is a fresco of Bigorne (below), the legendary monster who grows fat on eating hen-pecked husbands. The salty humour of the depiction is in striking contrast to the chivalrous heroics of decorations in fourteenth- or fifteenth-century châteaux.

Villeneuve-Lembron (right) is an evocative example of the way in which the clusters of lofty towers typical of medieval chivalry were brought down to earth in the sixteenth century.

Chiche-fache (below) pairs with Bigorne as a beast who feeds off faithful wives and is emaciated because there are so few of them. She is depicted in the gallery at Villeneuve-Lembron, but this example comes from a ceiling at the contemporary château of Le Plessis-Bourré.

one side to welcome the sun. Its feel is close enough to the feel of the imaginary house described in 1539 by Gilles Corrozet in his charming book *Blasons Domestiques*, in which the house and all its parts and contents are celebrated in a series of verses, very much as a 'maison' rather than as a 'château'.

I begin by talking about the house:
A place of outstanding invention.
Peaceful house, in which are to be found in abundance
A high proportion of the pleasures of this world.
House strongly built and crafted
On a good and firm foundation.
House constructed in a pleasant climate,
Where there is no trouble from bad winds.
House with its look and aspect
Towards the east, so that when the sun
Gets up, it lights up and makes glad
This outstanding and illustrious house.
House of value, well decorated in the classical manner,
House built of dressed ashlar,
Of liass, marble, and other kinds
Entered by a capacious gate.
House where one finds cellars, vaults and stables,
House where there are delicious gardens,
Rooms, attics, stables, galleries,
Gracious setting for noble seigneurs.
Oh beautiful house, pleasant and secure,
Worthy of an honourable owner
To set off your beauty even more.
House in which storey is set on storey
With spacious staircases easy to climb.
Well made dwelling, even more rich and prosperous
Than the house of Psyche, so richly decorated
As described in the Golden Ass.
Noble house filled with great wealth.
Rich house furnished with every kind of furniture.
Your deviser deserves all praise
For bringing such great fruitfulness to mankind.[2]

The good life as lived in a house of this kind, and the kind of man who lived it, was extolled sixty years later in the funeral panegyric of the Maréchal de Retz, and of the life he lived in the château of Noisy. The panegyrist describes him as a civilized man, rather than as a great soldier. Every aspect of his life – his library, his table, his gardens, his servants – is so well ordered that everything moves smoothly, and nothing is ever discomposed, with the result that it is a pleasure for friends and guests to visit him. At his table there is good food and good conversation, full of information; if there is argument or discussion, it is always good-tempered, 'so that his table is a veritable school of philosophy'. After meals he walks in the gardens 'in the delightful mazes of Noisy', accompanied by learned men, discoursing on agriculture, the seasons, the right time to plant and sow, the right kind of feeding and grazing, and such-like matters of country interest. Then back to his room, a little business, some religious reading, a sober supper, discussion of the news of the day, some letter-writing to friends, prayers and bed.[3]

Villeneuve represents a new type of château that had developed in the course of the fifteenth century. The prototype had appeared in the later fourteenth century, when Charles V had remodelled the Louvre to an alternative formula to that which reached its culmination at Vincennes.[4] Accommodation, instead of mounting up vertically in separate towers, was laid out horizontally in two main layers around a courtyard. The towers, rather than taking off from the ground, served to anchor the château to it. In terms of accommodation, rather than each tower being a self-contained entity, they acted as supplements and provided extra room for the adjacent lodgings.

A number of factors helped to make this new type popular. The Hundred Years War came to an end in 1453, and for over a hundred years France had relative internal peace. In this period the kings both consolidated a France which approached its modern boundaries, and developed in it an alternative to feudalism, a structure of government and justice, emanating from Paris, and directed by the king; it was a development which had started before the Hundred Years War, but had been much delayed by it. By 1500 most of the great fiefs which had always been independent, or virtually so, or had been hived off by monarchs to their younger sons, had come directly under the king, by conquest, confiscation, marriage or otherwise: Guyenne in 1453, Burgundy and Picardy in 1477, Anjou, Maine and Provence in 1480, and Brittany, effectively, in 1491, the Orleannais in 1495; the Bourbonnais and the other lands of the Duc de Bourbon followed in 1527.

The greatly extended kingdom of France was administered by a network of local governors, bailiffs and sénéchals, and by a complex civil service at the centre, all paid by the king, and owing loyalty to him as his servants rather than as his vassals. The Parlement in Paris, and lesser parlements set up by the king in the provinces, acted as high courts, and gave endorsement to the king's pronouncements.

In this world of royal servants the arts of war remained of importance, but the arts of peace flourished alongside them. Its members were often highly educated, collectors of pictures and libraries, interested in the new classicism of the Renaissance; they displayed their interests and knowledge in the decoration of their houses. Many of them were new men, of bourgeois origin without military background or experience. Two of these acquired especial fame, along with great wealth, and expressed it in houses which developed the Louvre model. Jacques Coeur, son of a fur merchant of Bourges, made an enormous fortune as banker and merchant, trading in the Mediterranean and to the east, but combined his personal financial activities with various roles in the royal service under Charles VII; his house in Bourges, built between 1443 and 1453, was the most luxurious of the century in France.[5] In the next generation, Jean Bourré, coming from a rather similar background to Jacques Coeur, entered the service of Louis XI and became his chief financial minister. The château which he built at Le Plessis-Bourré between 1468 and 1473 had a scaled-down version of the courtyard plan of the Louvre, adapted to produce a suitable formula for a powerful seigneur: a corps de logis filling the main range of the courtyard; a range to one side containing a closed gallery above an open arcaded one, leading to a chapel; a range to the other side containing kitchen and offices; a gatehouse between miscellaneous accommodation giving entry to the courtyard. All through the sixteenth and into the seventeenth century this type of plan was to reappear, in adapted, contracted or expanded form. The entrance range could be reduced to the gatehouse, or omitted altogether, to produce an open courtyard plan that was to become exceedingly popular. By omitting the gallery, and sometimes putting kitchen and offices into a basement, the four-range plan could be reduced to an L-shaped one containing two ranges, or to a single long rectangle.

Le Plessis-Bourré anticipates Villeneuve-Lembron in its relative domesticity and lack of flamboyance. Indeed, Chiche-fache is to be found there too, among the twenty-four figures or groups of figures which decorate the ceiling of its salle haute. As at Villeneuve there are no knights, ladies or battles here: instead, strange beasts, odd scenes, a barber shaving a man, a woman riding a tortoise, a monkey riding on an elephant, a smith trying to shoe a goose, a man dropping stones into a well or carrying a sackful of rats. Each representation has a text describing the moral which it puts across: 'don't try and do the impossible', 'don't talk too much', 'look before you leap', and so on. A down-to-earth bourgeois attitude to life, perhaps, in origin, but if so it was to spread up the social scale. Rigault d'Oureille was noble by birth and a soldier by origin; and one finds the same kind of down-to-earth humour in the *Heptameron*, the collection of tales written by Marguerite de Navarre, the sister of François I, in which merchants, friars and servants feature, as well as kings and nobles, and a touching story of faithful love alternates with the story of a gentleman who served his mistress in faithful chastity for years, and then found her at the bottom of the garden lying on the grass, making love to her muleteer.

The château of Le Plessis-Bourré was built in about 1470 for Jean Bourré, chief financial minister to Louis XI. Its moat and towers echo the feudal tradition, but the château is infused with a new and gentler domesticity.

The range of inflections in the *Heptameron* reflects, in fact, the range to be found in the châteaux of the fifteenth and sixteenth – indeed, for that matter, the seventeenth – centuries. In the France of the Ancien Régime new forms and attitudes appeared, but the old ones never completely disappeared. Feudal nuances continued, both in the architecture of châteaux and in the lives and attitudes of the people who lived in them. This combination of the seigneurial, the classical and the down-to-earth is what gives sixteenth- and early-seventeenth-century châteaux their distinctive character.

To some extent towers and moats survived for straightforward practical reasons. France was a less peaceful place than England. Up till the mid seventeenth century

security was still important. The peaceful decades were never completely peaceful and they were interspersed with periods of civil war, of which the religious wars of the later sixteenth century and the Fronde (the revolt of the Paris Parlement and the great nobles against the king) are the best known but far from the only examples. For a new château to be surrounded by a moat crossed by a drawbridge, and to have loopholes for guns, was a sensible precaution. Châteaux could still be garrisoned. In 1569/1570 the occupant of the château of Montréal, near Périgord, contained twenty soldiers 'whom the seigneur has installed to guard this château'. We know this from the inventory made in that year, but there must have been many other examples. Le Plessis-Bourré had a capitaine and a garrison which defended it unsuccessfully against the Huguenot forces in 1594. It is likely that gatehouses were still being used, on occasions at least, to house troops; the gatehouses at Tanlay and Chantilly are grand classical pavilions, but the military devices carved on their façades suggest that this was their function. At Kerjean in Brittany and Cadillac in Gironde, to quote just two examples, the main buildings of the châteaux, with their big windows and handsome classical façades, are set in and behind a square of formidably fortified walls, of the same date as the houses; Cadillac, it is worth remembering, belonged to the Duc d'Épernon, the powerful governor of Provence and Guyenne, whose military dignity was supported by a permanent personal escort of twelve soldiers and three trumpeters.

But towers and moats were also valued as an expression of seigneurial and noble status. The servants of the king, if they were of any importance, were all seigneurs and noble, or soon became so, if they were not so by origin. This double aspect of Rigault d'Oureille is listed on an inscription which still hangs in the house: he is 'Messire Rigaud Doureille, knight, Comte of Meyrolle, Seigneur and Baron of Villeneuve, Le Cher and Villefranche', but also 'counsellor and chamberlain to the

The château of Cadillac (left and right) was built in the early seventeenth century by the Duc d'Épernon. Its formidable fortifications in the new Renaissance manner are evidence of the fact that in the disturbed politics of sixteenth- and seventeenth-century France security was still important, but are also used to express the ducal magnificence of its owner. The central tower of the main building of the château (right) contains the great staircase, following a common sixteenth-century arrangement.

king, who commanded a hundred men-at-arms in the expedition to Naples, governor and sénéchal of Agenais and Gascony'. The feudal structure continued alongside new structures of power. To be a seigneur, still more a baron or a comte, implied wealth deriving from seigneuries and power within them. Nobility and the lordship of seigneuries were technically distinct, but closely bound up one with the other. The king, anxious to ensure the loyalty of the old nobility, distributed the bulk of posts such as governor, sénéchal and bailiff among them. A provincial governor was a great man: almost invariably a grand seigneur in his own right, and in addition a power in his province because of his post, the troops of which it gave him control over, and the patronage he could exercise. When the king was weak, or the kingdom divided by faction, it was easy for him to set up as an independent magnate.[6]

Feudal levies – the result of seigneurs, as condition of their tenure of a fief, bringing when called a stated number of men to fight on behalf of their overlord – all but disappeared in the course of the sixteenth century. The king disposed of a standing regular army, supplemented by local militias raised by royal officers and paid for by the crown. But the officers were, for the most part, noble; they raised their own regiments from their own adherents, and the commanders at the top were usually grands seigneurs. Fighting was still considered the natural and most honourable occupation for a nobleman: noblemen of standing, even if in later life they moved on to other things, usually fought in the royal armies as young men. François I's campaigns in Italy, disastrous though their conclusion was to be, evoked enormous enthusiasm among them, and they dashed off to Italy to earn their spurs. Noblemen were still fighting in tourneys, organized as magnificent royal spectacles; however much some humanist scholars might disapprove, they were still reading romances, both the old medieval ones (*Perceval* was published in a prose version in 1530), and their modern successors brought up to date with classical allusions and elaborate new symbolism. The best-seller of the mid sixteenth century, in royal and noble circles at all levels, was the romance of *Amadis de Gaulle*, first written in Spanish, but translated into French by a noble author, Nicolas d'Herberay des Essarts, embellished with new material, and published in twelve volumes between 1540 and 1546. François I solaced his captivity in Italy after the disastrous Battle of Pavia in 1525 by reading it; on 6th February 1554, Gille Picot, the Sire de Gouberville, read it with his household to keep up their spirits, after a day of pouring rain, in the salle of his modest Normandy manor.[7] According to François de la Noue, a Protestant humanist writing disapprovingly about the new Spanish romances in Basle in the 1580s, 'their vogue was at its height in the reign of Henri II; and believe me one would have spat in the face of anyone who criticized/derogated them, so widely were they used for instruction, entertainment, and as subjects of conversation'.[8]

Sometime between 1560 and 1580 Michel d'Anjony celebrated his grand marriage into the Foix family by decorating the first-floor room in his donjon at Anjony with portraits of himself and his wife, and depictions of the Nine Worthies, the heroes of chivalry. Perhaps more typically, in the mid and late sixteenth century,

The château of Le Lude was largely rebuilt on earlier foundations in the mid sixteenth century. The great corner towers express the seigneurial dignity of its owner, but large windows and classical decoration pay tribute to the new culture of the Renaissance and make clear that security was now less important, although by no means to be ignored.

wider knowledge of the Greek and Latin classics provided a whole new repertoire with which to celebrate military glory. It was with scenes from the *Aeneid*, and all the drama of the Trojan War, that Claude Gouffier, Master of the Horse to Henri II, decorated his gallery at the château of Oiron in about 1548–50.[9] The classics were not only, or even mainly, used as vehicles for the display of learning.

This aspect of noble life had inevitable reflection in the architecture of châteaux. Brand-new nobles with no military background though they were, both Jacques Coeur and Jean Bourré felt the need to express their seigneurial status. The courtyard of Jacques Coeur's home in Bourges is luxuriously and triumphantly civilian, but if one goes round to the back, one finds it embellished with a slender tower, vertical seigneurial lodgings which inside and out are in the tradition of Septmonts and Oudon; and the tower at one external angle of Le Plessis-Bourré is unmistakably a donjon.

How an important seigneur of older lineage could express his status in the first half of the sixteenth century is amply demonstrated at the château of Le Lude, remodelled and largely rebuilt in this period by Jacques de Daillon and his son Jean.[10] Jacques de Daillon had served in the Italian wars under both Louis XII and François I; his son was a military commander, and later governor of Poitou, La Rochelle, Pays d'Aunis and Guyenne. The château was remodelled on the

foundations of the medieval one, and the result nicely combined modern and traditional elements. Its towers, moat, drawbridge and formidable machicolations all suitably enhanced a house which was the centre of a major seigneurie, with some twenty-five minor fiefs dependent upon it. But although moat and drawbridge gave it a measure of security, its machicolations were purely ornamental, with solid floors unpierced by openings above the corbelling, and its external walls were liberally pierced with large windows.

There are obvious parallels at this period between France and England. In English country houses one also finds a mixture of classical and traditional elements. But the nature of the mixture is different. In England, apart from in a very small, if interesting, group of self-conscious 'sham castles', moats almost completely disappear, and towers are less obviously harking back to castle prototypes. Above all, the main and most important traditional element in English houses, the great hall, has no parallel in France.

As a formula the English great hall was, for better or worse, an invention of such genius that it has lasted at least 600 years, and is still going strong – not in a country-house context, perhaps, but in university colleges and legal inns of court. Its achievement was to give vivid architectural form to an idea. The idea was that of an ordered hierarchy meeting with dignity and a degree of ceremony. The form came from its lofty height and arched timber roof, its high table on a dais at one end, its high chair under a canopy in the middle of the high table, its screen like a triumphal arch at the other end of the room, through which food processed to the high table while trumpets sounded from the gallery above the screen.

The hierarchy radiated down from the head of the household through his own immediate family to his servants (who, in those days, were included in the general term 'family'), in their three levels of gentlemen, yeomen officers and grooms. It stretched further than this to include his tenants. These were not present on a daily basis, but at certain times of the year, or on certain occasions, they were entertained en masse, and they came on individual business throughout the year.

This core was extended, at all levels, by friends and relatives of the family, visiting neighbours, substantial citizens from neighbouring towns and people of all kinds, who came on business or to solicit support or favours. All of these were fitted into the appropriate level of the hierarchy, were entertained, and shared in the ceremonial life.

The importance of the great hall undoubtedly declined when the family abandoned the dais and moved off to eat elsewhere, informally in a ground-floor parlour or formally in a first-floor great chamber. But much of its hierarchic dignity remained. A crowded hall where servants and visitors were visibly on show and generously fed remained an accepted and important element of the image of any family of standing. The hall still had its dais, where the steward and senior officials represented the lord; it still had its degree of ceremony, which elevated the ceremony of the great chamber upstairs. The lord still came down to eat in it on special occasions. In terms of ceremony, hall and great chamber worked together.

Food for the great chamber was carried with ceremony through the hall, where the occupants stood up in its honour. Visitors who were to be entertained in the great chamber, or who came more generally to visit the family, invariably entered by way of the hall, and in passing through it could experience the dignity of the family and the size of its household and following. When Lord Burghley, after visiting Christopher Hatton's great house at Holdenby, congratulated him on 'your stately ascent from your hall to your great chamber', he was underlining the relationship of the two rooms, and the fact that visitors experienced both.

There was no equivalent to the English great hall in France. A grande salle two storeys in height, with an arched timber roof and a dais, in something approaching the English manner – or tribunal as it was called in France – was a feature confined to the kings or royal ducs when they feasted or presided, raised above their nobility; it never became a standard feature of French châteaux, and such a room was never used to entertain people below noble rank. Although there was no shortage of substantial farmers in French seigneuries, they came to the château to pay their rent in money or in kind, and sometimes, depending on their tenure, to swear fealty to the seigneur; but although on such occasions they may have been fed at the third or fourth table, there was no tradition of their being incorporated into the ceremonial life of the château. As a separate class, highly conscious of its difference from, and superiority to, those who were not noble, the noblesse were just not interested in the kind of hierarchy suggested by the English great hall, and the procession through it to the great chamber. A French hall had status because the seigneur ate in it, and lost it once he ceased to do so. Socially, a château was the place in which the noble owner entertained his fellow nobles, and a staircase brought them together with speed and dignity without the interposition of another room.

As a result it was the staircase, rather than the hall, which was the linchpin of the sixteenth- and seventeenth-century château. An English house was entered by way of a hall, a French house normally by way of a staircase. Although there was sometimes a separate door leading directly from the courtyard into a salle on the ground floor, this was there just to give access to the hall; for other parts of the château use was made of the door opening directly into the staircase – or sometimes, particularly in the seventeenth century, into a modest vestibule at the foot of a staircase.

In fact, a French château was often not only entered by a staircase, but by several staircases. Earlier in the Middle Ages both châteaux and their English equivalents had usually consisted of a number of distinct, free-standing elements – towers, salle or hall, kitchen and so on – which of necessity had to have different entrances. Both countries followed a similar development, and the separate elements came together into a single building. For a time these cohering elements tended, even so, to keep their separate entrances in both countries. But the importance of the great hall in England meant that the entry into it took precedence over all the others, and, as corridors and careful planning made other entries unnecessary, these tended to disappear, except for a back door for provisions.[11] In France they survived and multiple entries are still to be found in some châteaux up to the late eighteenth century. On coming into the courtyard the visitor was likely to be faced by a series of entries, into two or even three staircases, and sometimes directly into a salle basse as well, if it was on a courtyard level. He chose the entry which gave him access to wherever he wanted to go. There was no 'front door'; there is still no French translation for the expression.

Impressive staircases took over some of the function of medieval donjons. Although these were often retained when sixteenth- or even seventeenth-century châteaux were rebuilt, perhaps the last unmistakable donjon to be erected in France was by François I at Chambord in the 1530s. It was called a donjon by contemporaries, and in spite of its classical embellishments there was no mistaking the symbolism of that massive square mass with its circular corner turrets, rising out of the courtyard of the château. A symbol indeed it was, for like a number of medieval donjons it did not serve as the royal or seigneurial residence; the king installed his lodgings in one corner of the surrounding ranges, and looked across the courtyard at it.

A characteristic of donjons, appreciated since at least the twelfth century, was that, as the tallest towers in châteaux were often anyway on a high point, a panoramic view could be enjoyed from their summits. The seigneurie, or group of seigneuries of which they were the centre, could literally be surveyed from them. In the

medieval romances, visiting knights climb up the tower to enjoy the view; in actual life the entourage of the Emperor Charles V, on a visit to Vincennes in 1377, went up to the roof of the donjon for the same purpose.[12]

The feature of the donjon at Chambord which has always made the biggest impression on visitors is its famous and ingenious double staircase which threads up through its centre and finally, by way of a smaller staircase, gives access to the roof, and to views of Chambord's amazing roofscape and the parks and woods all round.

The staircase takes its place in a series of staircases serving to give access to a high point, as well as to the main floors of the donjon or corps de logis to which they are attached. There are remarkable examples built at the châteaux of Nantes and Dijon in the later fifteenth century, for the ducs of Brittany and Burgundy, respectively. In both these châteaux an alternative formula to a donjon was evolved to express ducal dignity. A range of seigneurial lodgings, lofty but scarcely compact or high enough to be seen as a donjon, was attached to, and served by, a slender but very much higher staircase tower, which rose several storeys above it, and served both to provide a viewing point and to act as a beacon or symbol of the seat of the duc.[13] At Dijon the tower of Philip le Bon was built in about 1455–60, and rose through eight storeys, each containing one small room, and served by a staircase which climbed up a storey higher to give access to the roof; not surprisingly, the room on the top floor was used as an observatory in the eighteenth century. The date of the tower at Nantes is uncertain, but it was perhaps built a decade or two after the tower at Dijon. It is similar in plan, not quite so high, but much more richly decorated with late Gothic embellishments, and its two top floors have the attractive feature, not to be found at Dijon, of open loggias from which to survey the view or enjoy the evening breeze in hot weather.

The actual staircases at both châteaux are closed in the conventional manner. At Châteaudun the staircase built by the Duc de Longueville in about 1510–18 seems to relate to that at Nantes in function and lavishness of decoration, but each landing is open to the external world all the way up. This type of open staircase had been modestly pioneered at the château of Saumur around 1370, and at Châteaudun itself in the lovely staircase tower built by Jean de Dunois sometime between 1460 and 1468. But the later tower at Châteaudun is bigger, loftier, more elaborate, and much more clearly built as a belvedere tower as well as to serve the ducal lodgings. It is a glorious affirmation of ducal status from which one can look across at a very different status symbol, the massive unrelieved circular shaft of the donjon built by the Comte de Blois in the twelfth century.[14]

At the château of Meillant the great staircase attached to the ducal lodgings in about 1500 is as richly decorated as the one at Châteaudun, and although not open its large windows ensure a generous outlook. It goes up to the third floor, from which a smaller staircase leads higher still, to two octagonal rooms above the main staircase, the upper one with a balcony running round it, from which to enjoy the view. The end result is externally the most prominent feature of the château.

The château of Meillant was enlarged and remodelled by the Cardinal and Duc d'Amboise in about 1500, and the staircase towers date from this period. Each has its own entrance: that on the left served the salle basse and salle haute in the central block of the château, but the larger and more sumptuous one led directly to the apartments of the duke and duchess in the wing on the right.

Staircases all over France from the late fifteenth century onwards are wonderful in their richness and variety. A new type appeared around 1520, probably inspired by Italian example; instead of a circular staircase twisting round a central newel and applied to the front of the corps de logis, a 'dog-leg' staircase of two parallel flights, often under a richly decorated vault, was set in the corps de logis and running from back to front, so that at every landing views were to be obtained in opposite directions. The next refinement came in the early seventeenth century when staircases began to be built around the four sides of an open square or rectangular cage of stone, forming a well.

These staircases, often lavishly decorated with appropriate iconography, or the family coat of arms, became the new status symbol for noble residences; to some extent the donjon was replaced by the staircase, but one could also say that the donjon became the staircase, for the staircase, often in a prominent tower

The staircase at the château of Serrant dates from the 1540s, and is a fine example of the vaulted classical staircases which were to be such a distinctive feature of châteaux for the next hundred years.

and topped by a belvedere room rising above the roof, seems deliberately evocative of earlier donjons.

This is perhaps most obviously the case in the 'maisons seigneuriales', or manors as they tend to be called today (and were sometimes called at the time), built by the lesser noblesse in increasing numbers in the late fifteenth and sixteenth centuries. Their seigneuries were not important enough to entitle them to the full complement of moats, towers, crenellations and drawbridge. But they needed something to distinguish their residences from those of the richer farmers. There were two ways of doing this, both of which were commonly adopted: one was to build a free-standing dovecot – to which seigneurs were entitled, and which were forbidden to those who were not seigneurs; the other was to attach a staircase tower to their homes, and give it extra prominence by putting a room above it. Such a tower could be attached to one side – usually the centre – of a rectangular block; but a popular and agreeable variation was to build the main block on an L-shaped plan, and place the tower on the inside angle of the L.

These maisons seigneuriales, with their single staircase towers, were built by the dozen, and perhaps by the hundred, all over France, and are amongst the pleasantest and most friendly of French noble residences. The room above the staircase almost invariably has a good fireplace and its view and its seclusion make it desirable; it was clearly more than a room for a servant, but there is little or no evidence as to its actual use; perhaps it served as a study for the owner, or as a room for archives.

The staircase towers are often very modest in scale, midget donjons if donjons at all, but sometimes they are large and prominent enough to look like a donjon in the old sense.[15] It is possible that they were actually called 'donjons' at the time, at least colloquially. This would explain how by the later seventeenth century 'donjon' entered into the dictionaries as a term for the room above the staircase, or any room at the top of a house above the general roof level: in 1680 Richelet's dictionary gives one meaning of donjon as 'a place elevated at the top of a house, like a kind of little cabinet'.

Bigger châteaux inevitably had more complex arrangements. Staircases, prominent though they often were, shared the skyline with round towers in the old manner or square pavilions in the new fashion, all under steep-pitched roofs; the complex skyline that resulted was a perhaps deliberately up-to-date version of the skyline of a medieval château. In some châteaux, especially in the early sixteenth century, there could be two principal staircases; at Meillant and Châteaudun one of these was bigger than the other; at Villeneuve-Lembron and Goulaine they were identical, and placed at either end of the corps de logis to produce a symmetrical composition.

A common, but certainly not invariable, arrangement first appeared in the mid sixteenth century: just one principal, and often very grand, dog-leg or, later, open-well staircase, placed in the centre of the corps de logis and running right through it, giving access to the main lodgings on one side, and to one or more salles on the

other, usually with further lodgings beyond them, and often, though not inevitably, finished off, as in the smaller houses, with a room above the staircase, so that from the outside it appears as a central pavilion or tower. The arrangement is found at Serrant in the 1540s, and in a large number of châteaux thereafter. Cheverny is a perfect example: a central staircase, end pavilions and linking wings, all with prominent and separate roofs. The staircase, though the smallest element of the five, is the linchpin of the château, because of its central position, the richness of its decoration inside and out, and its function as the way by which the château is reached. In some châteaux, especially when there are no pavilions, the staircase emerges as the dominant visual element as well, and does indeed become the equivalent of a donjon – and the great staircase tower in the 1620s' new building at Brissac was certainly called the donjon in the eighteenth century, and perhaps always.

The English great hall, with its architecturally contrived link to the kitchen in one direction and the great chamber up a staircase to the other, encouraged ceremony, whereas a French house, with entry by way of a staircase or several staircases,

The château of Goulaine (above), largely built in the late fifteenth century, has two principal entrances directly into two twin staircase towers. That on the right leads to the salle basse and salle haute at one end of the main building, that on the left to the appartements of the seigneur. The dormer windows in the lofty roof light the attics or 'galetas', a common feature of châteaux often used for the storage of surplus furnishings and valuables, sometimes for the storage of grain.

did not. Certainly, there was less ceremony in French châteaux. It may also have been the case that French owners, confident in their unique noble status, could afford to relax, whereas in England, where all but a handful were equal before the law, social distinctions needed to be underlined by ceremony. At any rate, in the château the emphasis was on hospitality. 'Always open to friends' is the inscription in Latin over the door into the mid-sixteenth-century château of Saint-Amand-en-Puisaye. Around 1600 the chimney-piece in the salle basse at the château of Gatellier was decorated with the following exhortations:

A truce from ceremony
Take some wine
and
    If you come to drink with me
    By my faith, most welcome you will be.

These are just two locations, and there is a need for further examples. But there is powerful negative evidence to suggest that a similar atmosphere was found in other châteaux. Knowledge of English ceremony in households both royal and noble mainly comes from a remarkable series of household regulations issued for

The château of Cheverny (below), built in about 1600, is a perfect example of what became a classic later sixteenth- and early seventeenth-century arrangement: the main staircase was in the central tower or pavilion, with access to the salle basse and salle haute and the main guest apartments on the left, and to family apartments on the right.

individual households from the fourteenth to the early eighteenth century. Such regulations are almost entirely lacking in France. There are a handful of regulations for royal households, only three of them concerned with ceremony, and nothing at all for households other than royal.

Two of the royal documents are, in fact, descriptions of the household and its way of life rather than regulations: Olivier Le Marche's long description of the household of his master Duc Charles of Burgundy, known as 'Le Hardi' or 'Le Téméraire', written at his master's request in 1474; and Alienor de Poitiers's account of the household of his wife Isabelle de Bourbon, written sometime between 1484 and 1491. The orders for the household of Henri III of France, on the other hand, are straightforward regulations, promulgated by the king's directions in 1578 and (in much more detail) 1585.[16]

These three documents present a picture of life at least as formal and ceremonial as anything in England or elsewhere in Europe at the same time. The *Honneurs de la Cour*, in particular, is full of fascinating information. One learns how the different grades in the noble hierarchy can have dressers with five to one shelves, according to rank; that a chambre with two beds is superior to a chambre with one, and limited to great ladies, but the second bed is for show only, and so on. But it is doubtful if any of these are relevant to life in a noble French household. Duc Charles was in competition with his cousin, the king of France, and at least as rich and powerful; his aim was to unite the two main parts of his realm, Burgundy and

The swaggering architecture of the mid-seventeenth-century château of Beaumesnil makes one forget its comparatively modest size, for like many French châteaux it is only one-room thick. The entrance door leads directly into the main staircase in the central tower.

Flanders, into one kingdom, and rule them as king; he even had visions of becoming emperor. He kept a court as magnificent as any in Europe, based mainly on Brussels and Bruges rather than Dijon. Henri III, encouraged by his mother Catherine de Medici, was equally remarkable for his love of ceremony, but his reign lasted only fifteen years, and the formality of his court was in strong contrast to those of his predecessors and successors. Henri IV, in particular, was noted for his informality and Louis XIII's tastes, expressed as a boy by his fondness for going into the kitchens and cooking his own food,[17] led to his being criticized in later life for having 'all the skills of a servant and none of those of a master'.

In 1547 a French nobleman on a visit to England was shocked to see English Knights of the Garter kneeling bareheaded to serve food to their king. In 1644 the German Brackenhoff was admitted to watch Louis XIII's niece, the Duchesse de Montpensier (commonly known as 'the Grande Mademoiselle'), having her dinner, and commented that 'it was served without much ceremony. Affairs are managed with more magnificence by German princes.'[18]

Two other regulations are for less important families of royal blood: for the household of Margaret of Austria, based on Brussels and the château of Pont d'Ain in France, in the early sixteenth century, and for the Duc de Longueville (of illegitimate royal blood, but legitimized), based on the château of Châteaudun, in 1523.[19] The Pont d'Ain regulations are mainly concerned with good order in the household, and above all in the correct distribution of food to the many tables in the house. The Longueville regulations are also concerned with good behaviour (with fines or imprisonment laid down for bad language), and with ensuring that part-time members of the household do not try to evade the full duties of their periods of service. Neither shows any interest in ceremony.

Accounts in novels are not hard evidence, but they at least reveal an attitude. Agrippa d'Aubigné, in his *Avantures du Baron de Faeneste* (1630), relates how one Sunday the baron arrived unexpectedly with his three valets at the château of Sieur d'Enay. He is invited to join Enay at dinner in the salle, asks if his valets can join in the meal, and they are made welcome. At dinner the baron describes how his friend Engivaut plays games with his valets every Sunday. Enay says he does the same. Later that evening Enay, baron and valets all play Michou – a physical game, not a card game – in the salle together.[20]

A story in Ouville's *Contes* gives an agreeable picture of relaxed and mildly ribald life in a château of the 1630s. Its seigneur employs a lawyer from the local town to come once a year to hold his seigneurial court as his sénéchal, and invites his neighbours to dinner on the same day. One year this happens to be a Friday. The sénéchal arrives, finds no one in the courtyard, and being a friend of the family goes into the kitchen. This is equally empty, except for a vat of water full of live carp, waiting to be cooked. The procureur cannot resist taking one, and slips it into the front of his breeches. He then finds a lackey, who takes him into the salle, where a large company of ladies are warming themselves in front of the fire, waiting for dinner to be served. They invite the sénéchal to sit down in front of the fire, and so to conceal the carp he pulls his lawyer's gown over his breeches. The carp, overheated by the fire, starts to thrash around and push out the gown. One of the ladies notices the upheaval, misinterprets it and starts laughing, and then there is much laughter from the rest of the company.[21]

One is back in the same kind of world shown in some of Marguerite de Navarre's stories in the *Heptameron*. And it may be that this kind of easy-going jocularity shown towards inferiors, as well as to fellow nobles, was not untypical of life among the French noblesse at this period.

As Ouville's story shows, a salle in the early seventeenth century was still a room in which guests were received before food was served in the same room, much as is described in romances of the thirteenth century. Indeed, in many ways the accommodation of a sixteenth- or early-seventeenth-century château was little different from that in a late medieval one, even if now arranged in a single building, horizontally rather than vertically in a series of separate towers: salles basse and haute, sets of logis consisting of chambre, cabinet (the successor of the estude) and garderobe, kitchen and offices, chapel. Even the galleries, which became increasingly common in the sixteenth century, were a feature which first appears in the fourteenth.

Salles were still general-purpose rooms, put to numerous other uses besides reception and the serving and eating of meals. And these uses had not changed all that much: meals were often followed by dancing, masques and plays could be put on in them, and games played in them, including energetic physical games, if Agrippa d'Aubigny is to be relied on.

There are many representations and descriptions of such activities in royal salles, but all too few to document them in salles other than royal. One is given by the German traveller Thomas Platter, on the occasion of his visit to Marseille in 1597. He attended a ball in the grande salle on the first floor of the house of the Duc de Guise. The duc was sitting next to his mistress, who was dressed in cloth of gold; the duc himself 'to tell the truth was not good-looking, with his beaky nose, but he was resplendent in gold and silk'. Platter describes the vigour and variety of the dances, and notes that 'towards evening, when dancing stopped, cakes and sweetmeats were served, and Malvoisie wine to whoever wanted it'.[22]

Remarkable, if over-restored, frescoes in one room of the château of Grosbois show dancing, feasting and the performance of a masque or play; it is clear that actual events are being depicted. The frescoes are generally taken to represent scenes, probably in the main salle at Grosbois, at the marriage of Charles d'Angoulême to Françoise Nargaine in 1644, but another possibility is that they record the 'festin' offered to Louis XII at Grosbois on 18 September 1618.

Such entertainments were frequent and popular at the court, and it is likely they were also an acceptable feature of a royal visit. When the six-year-old Dauphin, the future Louis XIII, was sent for several months to the Gondis' château at Noisy to take refuge from an outbreak of the plague at Fontainebleau in 1607, a 'ballet des lanternes' was put on for him in the grande salle by the soldiers of his bodyguard, who had been taught to dance in the previous year; it was followed by general dancing. When his ten-year-old niece, the Grande Mademoiselle, travelled down to visit her father Gaston d'Orléans at Blois in 1637, a ballet was presented at her first stop, the house of her treasurer, Marchand, just outside Paris.

She remarks in her autobiography that for a ten-year-old girl the marriage of the gardener at her next stop, the château of Montglat, was more amusing. The wedding couple and their guests may well have been brought into the salle to dance for her entertainment, as was done for the Dauphin both in the salle at Noisy when the falconer of Monsieur de Paris was married, and several times in the grande salle at Fontainebleau. At Noisy the little Dauphin also amused himself by having a sparrow let loose in the salle haute, and flying a sparrow-hawk after it.[23]

One section of the household regulations of the Duc de Longueville, issued in 1523, is concerned with the profits of card games played in the duc's chambre and his salles:[24] the reference to 'salles' in the plural is probably to the 'grande salle' on the ground floor of the east wing, next to the great staircase, and his 'petite salle' or 'sallette' beyond it. With one exception, profits in the salles were to be the perquisite

of the furrier, whose job it was to provide tables, carpets serving as table-covers and cards; profits in the chambre were to be the perquisite of the valet de chambre. The exception was when the duc chose to play in his salles himself, when the profits of his table were to go to the valet de chambre. The impression given is of ducal and visiting gentilhommes' servants playing cards in the salle or sallette, and the duc on occasions coming from his chambre to join them.

In 1597 Platter went on from the Duc de Guise's ball to one in another house, belonging to a consul – one of the ruling body of Marseille (and noble by office) – and was intrigued to find dancing and card-playing going on in the same room.

> I was amazed to see the mistress of the house seated at a card table, with more than five hundred crowns in front of her, while her husband came and went with other people in the salle, without her taking any notice of him. She is a passionate gambler, and I am told she sometimes loses a thousand crowns in an evening. Fortunately, her fortune can stand it.[25]

Salles also played their part in funerals. As in all European countries in and around the sixteenth century, the funeral of a nobleman or noblewoman was a serious business. The surviving list of funeral expenses of Anne de Laval, widow of Vicomte de La Trémoille, who died at the château of Craon in 1553, and the inventory taken after her death, gives some idea of what was involved, including the provision of a funeral effigy depicting her.[26] The practice of having effigies at funerals was an English one, which the French kings had adopted in the fifteenth century, and which is then found in the sixteenth century at some grand but not royal funerals.

Initially, Anne de Laval's body lay in state in the Church of Saint-Nicholas in the town for five days, while bells were pealed and masses said daily. Meanwhile an effigy of her was made and set up in a smaller salle next to the grande salle, on a canopied bed, all hung with black; it was probably her actual death-bed, for the inventory lists no bed in the 'chambre where my late mistress died'. The effigy lay there for twelve or thirteen days and nights; seven priests stood or knelt round it, candles burnt all around it, and a cross covered with black taffeta stood at the foot of the bed. The summary of her funeral expenses lists the cost of the black mourning robes supplied for her thirteen demoiselles and femmes, the 3210 skins of the mouse-sized minivers, whose fur was used to trim them, and the black robes and caparisons supplied to her falconer, her two grooms and their horses.

It is possible that her body lay in state for a time on the bed before it was removed to the church. Such, at least, was the procedure after the death of the Duc de Longueville in 1574. He died at Blois; his body was embalmed, his entrails removed, put in a lead container, and taken to the family burial chapel at Cléry. The body was then conveyed in a coffin to Châteaudun, where the family's main château now was. It was met at the gates of the town by all his household and the clergy of the town, escorted to the château, and carried up, in this case not to the petite salle, but to the grande salle adjoining, where it was placed on a 'lit d'honneur' hung with black velvet and cloth-of-gold. Four candlesticks 1.8 metres high, ornamented with his coat of arms, stood at the corners of the bed, and a gold cross between two more candlesticks was set up facing it. The duc's almoner was installed in a chair covered with silk behind the bed, equipped with holy water and a sprinkler, to enable the seigneurs who came to pay their respects to sprinkle water on the corpse/coffin. The coffin was later removed to the chapel for the funeral service, and replaced by a splendidly clothed and robed wax effigy. Benches were set up round it, at which the duc's eight valets de chambre, the maître d'hôtel and gentlemen in waiting, and a selection of priests sat in constant attendance.[27]

Similar ceremonies are illustrated in Claude de la Ruelle's superb *La Pompe Funèbre de Duc Charles III de Lorraine*, published in 1608, to record the duc's funeral at Nancy. The duc died in his great château or palace in Nancy, and his body lay in state in his chambre there for fifteen hours, surrounded by hooded and cloaked members of his household, before being put in a coffin, displayed for a further period and then carried down to be displayed still further in the great Galerie des Cerfs. Meanwhile his effigy was dressed and laid out in the grande salle of the château. It lay there for fourteen days, and a full meal was served up every day on the table before the effigy, as though the duc were still alive.

But a salle was still above all a place in which to eat. Who ate where was graded by social rank. The basic division dated back to the Middle Ages and involved four tables: one for the family, one for the 'écuyers' (gentleman servants), one for the officers – that is to say, the senior non-gentle servants – and one (which could be still further subdivided) for the rest.

An engraving of the funeral banquet of the Duc de Lorraine, held in his château at Nancy in 1608. The body of the duc is laid out under the canopy, but a full-scale meal is being served to his empty table, as though he were still alive.

Another table, occasionally to be found, is a spin-off from the first table: it is the 'table des filles', the table at which the serving gentlewomen of the seigneur's wife sat. Châteaux could be described as one-, two-, three-, four-, five- and even six-table houses, and the importance of the house gauged by the number of tables.

In 1468 the château of l'Hermitage in Brittany was a four-table house, and all four tables were in one salle. We know this from depositions made at the time, consequent on a neighbouring nobleman, cousin to the owner, breaking into the château and removing all the contents of any value, while the owner and his wife were out.[28] In the salle meals were commonly served on silver plate to the first table, and a mixture of silver and pewter plate to the second. The miscreants went off with all the silver plate belonging to the salle, along with a set of tapestries, of violet embroidered with yellow inscriptions and coronets, which hung all round it. As a result the first table and guests of quality were reduced to eating or drinking from wooden vessels, like everyone else. To have the whole household eating in one salle in a château of this importance was peculiar to Brittany. Elsewhere the various tables were served in more than one room, and more than one salle was the result. In England there was a similar dispersal of tables, but 'hall' carried such a weight of symbolism and sentiment that there was a prejudice against applying the term to more than one room. There was one hall, and it was *the* hall. In France, where there was no such feeling, salles easily and confusingly proliferated.

The medieval arrangement of a salle haute above a salle basse was still a common one, indeed, far more widespread, and to be found in châteaux of all sizes, and not just the grander ones. The two rooms were now incorporated into the corps de logis, rather than being in a detached building. In what is met with often enough to be described as the classical arrangement, there is a stack of four large rooms, one above the other: a vaulted cellar, a salle basse, a salle haute and a huge 'galetas' or attic, lit by dormer windows, up under the open timbers of the roof.

In many châteaux, particularly the larger ones, the salle basse was still, as in the Bishop's Palace at Angers, the salle for the lower echelons – 'ceteri ad imos'. The second, third, fourth and, possibly, fifth tables were there. But the gentilhommes servants, including the maître d'hôtel and the various écuyers, being noble and extremely conscious of the fact, clearly disliked eating in the same salle as the servi-teurs. The seigneur wanted them there, to keep order in the salle. This is specifically spelled out in the household regulations for Marguerite d'Autriche at Pontdaims; the growing preference of the maître d'hôtel and his fellows for eating in another room is deplored, and they are instructed to eat in the salle.[29] Nonetheless, in the course of the sixteenth and very early seventeenth century, they clearly often succeeded in having the second table set up elsewhere, either in the salle haute with the seigneur, or in its own separate salle.

A salle basse where the seigneur did not eat, even if it were as large as the salle haute above it, was not grandly furnished. At the château of Thouars in 1542, the seigneur ate in one of two tapestry-hung salles, large and small, on the first floor, and the 'grande salle basse' contained four tables of different sizes, two dressers, an

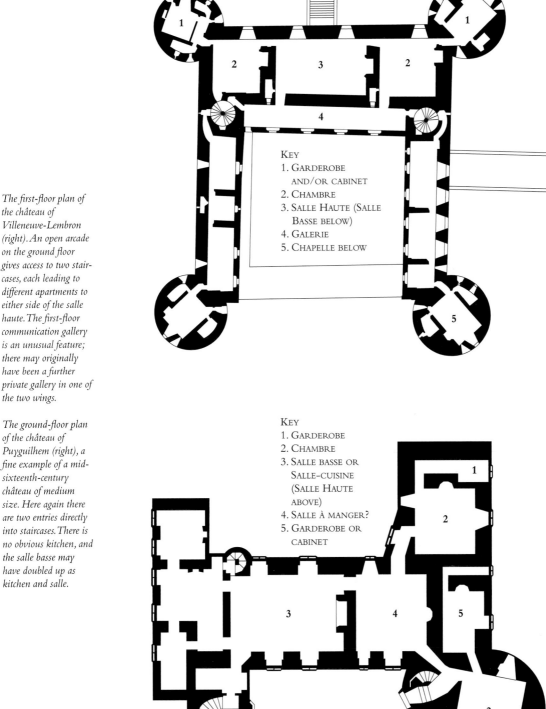

The first-floor plan of the château of Villeneuve-Lembron (right). An open arcade on the ground floor gives access to two staircases, each leading to different apartments to either side of the salle haute. The first-floor communication gallery is an unusual feature; there may originally have been a further private gallery in one of the two wings.

KEY
1. GARDEROBE
AND/OR CABINET
2. CHAMBRE
3. SALLE HAUTE (SALLE
BASSE BELOW)
4. GALERIE
5. CHAPELLE BELOW

The ground-floor plan of the château of Puyguilhem (right), a fine example of a mid-sixteenth-century château of medium size. Here again there are two entries directly into staircases. There is no obvious kitchen, and the salle basse may have doubled up as kitchen and salle.

KEY
1. GARDEROBE
2. CHAMBRE
3. SALLE BASSE OR
SALLE-CUISINE
(SALLE HAUTE
ABOVE)
4. SALLE À MANGER?
5. GARDEROBE OR
CABINET

old coffer, locked and containing unspecified papers, a big fireplace with logs supported on cast-iron andirons 'of little value', and 'a wooden perch, 3.6 metres long, composed of two pieces of wood, to put birds on'.[30] A good idea of the lack of prestige, but also the liveliness, of a French salle when the first table had been removed elsewhere is given in an entertaining romance, *La Description de l'Isle des Hermaphrodites*, published in about 1580:

> My guide asked me to dine with him at the table of the maître d'hôtel. The room to which he took me was far from clean, and the mingled smell of wine and food far from agreeable, but its habitués were so used to it that they ate there quite happily. It contained several tables, a lot like the refectory in a monastery; but a majestic silence was far from being observed, everyone talked at the same time and made so much noise all through dinner, cat-calling, shouting and laughing, that I suspect one would have heard more conversing next to the cataracts of the Nile.[31]

At the château of Gaillon, where Cardinal d'Amboise lived in some magnificence in the early sixteenth century, the first table was in the 'grande salle haute' on the first floor, above a lower and much less grande salle basse. At his death in 1550 it

At the château of Lanquais, largely rebuilt in the second half of the sixteenth century, the decoration of the salle basse (below) and the salle haute above it (right) expresses the way in which this arrangement of salles was often used: the household and less important guests ate in the less elaborate salle basse, the seigneur and his wife ate and received in the grander setting of the salle haute.

was hung with ten pieces of tapestry worked with his coat of arms, and furnished with a single table, a short bench for the cardinal, three more benches for his guests and a huge buffet on which to display his plate. That was all, and as the room measured 10 by 20 metres, the impression must have been one of somewhat chilly magnificence. The inventory does not itemize the contents of the salle basse.[32]

The salles at Gaillon and Thouars no longer exist, but one can get a good idea of the contrast between a salle basse for the household and a salle haute for the seigneur at the château of Lanquais in the Dordogne: two salles, originally of the same size, one above the other, the salle basse serviceable but simple, and the salle haute dominated by its superb fireplace, with doors to either side. The fireplace fills the end wall and the whole composition is carved with classical ornament of the greatest richness and magnificence.[33]

There were many houses, however, usually of more modest size, where there were two salles, haute and basse, but the seigneur was clearly eating in both of them, and the salle haute was the less important of the two. The two early-sixteenth-century salles at Plessis-Josso in Brittany provide a good example: in the salle basse the chimney-piece itself and the two wall recesses to either side, both elaborately finished and one framed by a richly carved archway, give an element of state to this end of the room, which is lacking in the salle above.

At the manoir of Mesarnou in Brittany, there was the usual combination of salle basse and haute, both handsome rooms, but it was when getting up from supper in the salle basse that the seigneur and three of his gentlemen were arrested in 1601 by a party of neighbours who had arrived on an apparently friendly visit, and been welcomed.[34] The fact that a number of these house inventories show that there was a bed in the salle haute suggests that it was the successor of the salle de parement, though no longer so called, and though the bed seems in some cases to have been in use.

The distinction between the two salles was now perhaps one between public and private, or between business and pleasure, or between male and female, with variations in different houses; the salle basse was, perhaps, a room for seigneurial business, where first and second tables were elided, and the seigneur and his gentlemen servants ate together and entertained male guests, while the lower servants ate at a different table, if they had not been removed to another salle altogether, or to the kitchen; the salle haute was where the first table was on occasion set up, when the seigneur and his wife entertained noble guests of both sexes, and where she and her ladies normally ate, or she entertained her women friends and relations on her own. A picture by or in the manner of Abraham Bosse seems to show an occasion of this sort – ten women eating together in what could well be a salle haute, a first-floor room in a château looking over the garden, with a bed to one side of the table.

A good example of joint seigneurial use of two salles is clearly shown in the inventory of the château of Montréal, near Périgord, in 1569.[35] Here, however, the

As in many smaller châteaux and manoirs the fifteenth-century salle basse at Plessis-Josso (above) is a more important room than the salle haute above it. The richly carved stone shelving inset into the wall was probably used for the display of plate at meal times.

serviteurs have been removed to a salle in the basement. It contained a 'buffet of little value', an iron pot, and nothing else worth listing, except two instruments of torture, which may have been used by the garrison of soldiers, who were probably accommodated in the gatehouse.

In the middle of the château was a stack of three large rooms, one above the other: the 'salle of the foresaid château', the 'salle haute' on the second floor above it, and a galetas up in the roof above the salle haute. The first was the most important of the three salles, hung with six pieces of 'almost new' tapestry, a long table and bench, a tapestry carpet, probably for the table, nine chairs of various kinds and a buffet with a tapestry carpet spread on it. In the salle haute there was another tapestry, a small table, an old carpet, a buffet, a 'couchette' and a large bed.

The galetas was crammed with valuable contents: coffers filled with clothes, ranging from 'a crimson satin dress decorated with silver plaques' to a pair of 'embroidered velvet shoes'; a big coffer with double locks filled with silver plate and other valuables; a coffer full of 'old and ancient deeds'; a coffer full of linen; harness,

A painting by or after Abraham Bosse (below) appears to show a salle haute being used as a women's room. This was one possible use for salles hautes, which not infrequently had a bed in them, sometimes used by the wife of the seigneur or an important guest, sometimes only on formal occasions, such as christenings, or for laying out corpses before funerals.

armour, furniture, altar hangings and seven pieces of new tapestry depicting the history of Judith and Holofernes. The list gives a vivid picture of what was at least one use of these great rooms up in the roof.

The basement salle at Montréal is described as the 'salle près de la cuisine', but in function it is what elsewhere came to be called a 'salle des serviteurs' or 'salle commune' or 'salle de commun'. The terms appear in about 1545 in the set of designs and plans for châteaux, attributed to Jacques Androuet du Cerceau, which was probably published in that year, or shortly before.[36] Later in the century such a room becomes increasingly common, and by early in the seventeenth century it was a standard feature. Such rooms were usually in the basement and smaller than the main salles. There was no kind of prestige attached to them. Their appearance over a hundred years before a similar development in English houses is an indication both of the strength of symbolism of the English great hall, and of the lower status of French servants.

One cannot assume when coming across a seigneurial residence with three or four large rooms, one above the other, that two or more of them were salles. A contemporary description of the château of Saffre, in Burgundy, in 1499, shows that this was not necessarily so: it is described as containing 'four storeys, cellar down below, salle above, a fine and large chambre above that, and then attics'. There were lesser rooms to either side.[37]

In his book of essays, *Les Contes et Discours d'Eutrapel*, published in 1585, Noel du Fail described the home of a gentleman at the time of François I. It contains only one salle, because to have more 'is for great people'.[38] Two or more salles was clearly a status symbol; the fact that a number of inventories show the salle haute to be empty suggests that it could be a status symbol with little if any practical function. Sensible noble families of modest or medium means confined themselves to one salle, perhaps with 'a fine and big' chambre above it, used either as a best chambre for guests, or their own chambre. But such a chambre could also be used for entertaining on occasions, and the difference between it and a salle haute with a bed in it was not so very great. At the manoir of Mesnil in the 1540s and 1550s there was only one salle, with a chambre above it, possibly Gouberville's own; his chambre was certainly on the first floor. The salle was an all-purpose room where, for instance, Gouberville found one of his servants straining honey in June 1549; in April 1550 he describes how he, two of his servants, Cantepye and Coubille, and a visitor from the neighbouring town of Valognes, who arrived with a serviteur, all had supper together there (though not necessarily at the same table). But at his other manoir, Gouberville, from which he took his name, and possibly also at Mesnil, he entertained guests of quality in his chambre.[39]

Noel du Fail gives an evocative description of the salle of this gentleman of François I's time:

> ... a stag's antlers, tipped with iron and fastened to the ceiling, from which
> hung bonnets, hats, collars, couplings and leads for dogs, and a big rosary for

The evocative and little-altered ground-floor grande salle at the fifteenth-century château of La Villeneuve-Jacquelot. There was no salle haute; a single salle was a feature of some smaller houses where to have two salles was regarded as pretentious.

communal prayers. On the two-stage dresser or buffet, a Holy Bible in the translation commissioned by Charles V more than two hundred years ago, and *Les Quatre Fils Aymon*, *Ogier le Danois*, *Mélusine*, *Le Calendrier des Bergers*, *La Legende Dorée*, or the *Roman de la Rose*. Behind the main door, many long and big poles hung with game, and at the back-end of the salle, on wooden supports fitted and fastened to the wall, half a dozen bows with their arrows and quivers, two fine big targes with two short broadswords, two halberds, two pikes 6.5 metres long, two or three coats or shirts of mail in the little chest, along with two powerful old-fashioned crossbows with their fittings. Further in, in the big window and over the chimney-piece, three acquebutes (it's a pity one now has to call them arquebuses); adjoining these, a perch for the sparrow-hawk, and lower down to one side, cages, traps, snares, nets, baskets and other equipment for hunting. And under the great bench of the salle, a metre wide, good fresh straw for the dogs to lie in so that they will be better and more vigorous for hearing and sensing their master near them. Finally, two good enough rooms for unexpected visitors and strangers, and in the fireplace good green wood mixed with a few dry faggots, to give a long-lasting fire.

This is an imaginary description, but the contents of the salle at the château of La Tour in Languedoc, as listed in an inventory of 1531, are not so very different. They include

nine javelins, held in a bracket made for the purpose, a good halberd, a crossbow with six strings, one of them broken, a case for a crossbow, two breastplates fitted with arm-pieces, one with a head-piece and gauntlets, the other with a helmet, all rusty; one arquebuse, a wooden bow, a shield with the figure of a man painted on it, an arquebuse of pine-wood ... two lockers, in which we found a book for recording the servants' wages, the *Canoniques of History* in French; another book about Merlin, in French ... a big chest full of linen and material.[40]

The armoury of the château is often recorded in inventories as 'hanging in the salle'. But 'salle des armes', the term so often found in châteaux today, with its suggestion of an outer hall for a bodyguard, is an expression of nineteenth-century romanticism, and is never used in contemporary sources, except in a few royal châteaux, where such a bodyguard was actually to be found. There was nothing like this in an ordinary château or manoir; an armoury, used both for fighting and hunting, was an appurtenance of everyday life, and hung in the salle which the seigneur used himself.

There was an intriguing simplest stage of all, below even the house with a single salle. In the houses of some modest noble families the whole household, including the seigneur, ate in the kitchen. Olivier de Serres, in his *Théâtre d'Agriculture*, written in 1600, records a saying of Anne de Montmorency, Constable of France, and one of the greatest figures of the mid sixteenth century, that

> a gentleman, once he has risen to an income of five hundred livres, no longer knows what it is to live well, because he wants to try to be important, and eat in the salle, at the mercy of his cook, whereas formerly he used to eat in the kitchen, and saw to it that he was fed as he wanted.[41]

In the house at Sommentrain where Elijonne de Goulangière lived with two successive husbands, Hubert de Maretz and François de Lespinasse, both members of minor noble families, an inventory of 1566 shows that there was no salle. The main room was the kitchen, and it was crowded with a remarkable miscellany of contents, including two beds, a big table, several benches, a buffet, and numerous cupboards and chests, filled with linen, pewter plates and bowls, and cooking implements of copper or iron. A chambre on the first floor containing the most valuable of the beds in the house, a buffet, two big chairs, two benches and a table was clearly also used for eating, perhaps to entertain prestigious guests; it is the only feature to distinguish the house from a substantial farmhouse.[42]

There is some evidence for houses where there was a salle, but it was used only for special occasions, and the seigneur normally ate in the kitchen. The wife of a seigneur, as related in the *Avantures du Baron de Faeneste*, orders some new tapestry for the grande salle of her château, but relates that her husband had first of all considered having it in the kitchen.[43] There are a number of other references to tapestried kitchens: Ouville, in one of his *Contes*, has a story of a soldier lodged in the attic of a strange house, who heard a noise below him, found a hole in the floor, lay flat on his stomach to look through it and saw 'a fine well-furnished room below his, hung with good tapestries, where there was a good big fire with plenty of game turning on two spits'.[44] As late as the 1660s Louis II de Condé (the 'Grand Condé'), returning from a journey to Dijon, where he was entertained by the magistrates of the local parlement, remarked to Louis XIV, 'your province of Burgundy is exceedingly prosperous; the kitchens there are hung with tapestry'.[45] Such rooms should perhaps be described as 'salles-cuisines', and some rooms which are today taken to be salles basses may in fact have been kitchens as well.

Cooking did not have the benefit of much equipment in the sixteenth century. A spit for roasting and one or two iron brackets and chains to suspend pots over the fire could be fitted to a big chimney-piece, such as was the standard in a salle basse, and could provide enough food for a moderate-sized household. An engraving of about 1580 shows what appears to be a handsomely fitted-up salle-cuisine of this type, with a cook seated before the fire, and a young gentleman making up to her.[46] It is to this kind of room that occasional references to kitchens hung with tapestry must refer.

Kitchens could get by with one big fireplace because baking was often carried out in a separate oven or ovens in another, free-standing building in the basse-cour, to avoid the danger of the ovens starting up a fire in the main house. The building was known as a fournil, and there was often a chambre over it, pleasantly warmed by the heat of the ovens below. In 1551 the Sire de Gouberville spent several days in his 'chambre dessus le fournil' at Mesnil, because a local curé had died in the chambre above his salle, and Gouberville did not like to sleep in the house, even though the body had been removed for the funeral. He spent at least three nights in the room, and entertained a friend to dinner there one evening.[47]

After telling his anecdote about Constable de Montmorency, Olivier de Serres gives his own suggestion for a seigneur of moderate means, of the early seventeenth century. His house should have an 'anti-cuisine' on the way to the kitchen, serving as a small salle or everyday eating room ('sallette du mangeoir ordinaire'); by this means he will have a room where he will be handsomely served and fed, can keep his people to their duty, but not have to mix with the 'dregs' of the household.[48] The implication is that there will be a salle for special occasions, but that he will normally eat in this smaller room.

'Mengerie' was the term used in about 1550 for a row of small rooms on the ground floor of the royal château of Saint-Germain-en-Laye, probably as rooms for the upper servants of courtiers to eat in.[49] 'Sallettes' or 'petites salles' are a feature of a number of sixteenth-century châteaux. Out of such rooms was to develop the 'salle à manger' of the seventeenth and eighteenth centuries, and indeed of today.

Sallettes could be rooms either for the seigneurial family or the gentilhommes servants, if they were eating away from the salle basse. As early as the 1480s it is stated in the *Honneurs de la Cour* that in the Burgundian court the gentilhommes servants are entitled to have canopies and 'dosserets' (backcloths, or decorated hangings behind the chair of a person of consequence) over and behind the tables where they eat in their 'salles ou sallettes'.[50] In 1570 the 'petite salle' next to the salle de commun in the gatehouse of the château of Saint-Fargeau was probably used by the gentilhommes servants.

But in a number of big sixteenth-century châteaux there was a 'petite salle' or 'sallette' next to the grande salle, for seigneurial use. In the mid sixteenth century at the château of Châteaudun, for instance, the Duc de Longueville (of an illegitimate branch of the royal family but legitimized) imitated royal usage, and both he and his wife had their own grandes salles, one above the other. These were huge rooms and cannot have been agreeable to eat in, except on big occasions. It is not surprising that both of them had a separate 'sallette' beyond their chambres on the other side of the staircase.[51] The Vicomte de La Trémoille had a similar arrangement of a small salle next to a large one, but on one level only, on the first floor of the château of Thouars in 1542. The inventory[52] gives the impression that the grande salle here was not in much use; it contained a large buffet of five stages, three large tables, two large benches, seven large pieces of tapestry and not much else. The room normally used by the family was what was clearly a smaller salle nearby, containing two tables, one large and one small, a dresser or buffet, four chairs, six stools, a copper bowl on the buffet, a copper 'fountain' to store water in for use as a wine

In the Middle Ages the more private meals were often served up in chambres, but this mid-seventeenth-century painting after Abraham Bosse dates from the appearance of sallettes or salles à manger, specialized rooms for meals and smaller than the grandes salles.

cooler, and five pieces of tapestry, depicting 'triumphs' and embroidered with the family coat of arms.

By 1621 the combination had moved down the social scale, and is found in the house at Reims belonging to Claude Thiret, a very rich tax farmer of a bourgeois family who had become maître d'hôtel to the Prince de Condé, and had been ennobled. His grande salle and sallette adjoined each other on the ground floor. Both rooms were furnished with the greatest richness. There were twenty-two chairs and eleven pieces of tapestry in the grande salle, and nine chairs and eight pieces of tapestry (of hunting scenes) in the sallette. But the salle was a grander and more formal room, hung with twelve pictures of 'emperors', as opposed to the pictures of Venus, and of Susannah and the Elders, in the sallette.[53]

The room was clearly being used as a salle à manger. The specific term, with its suggestion of specialization, of a room just used for eating, begins to appear in the early seventeenth century, in the form of 'salles à manger' or 'sallette à manger', sometimes clearly just for the family, sometimes probably for the upper servants.

There is a reference to one at Saint-Germain-en-Laye in 1606,[54] and in a number of Parisian houses in the 1630s. In the book of his designs for executed hôtels and châteaux, in Paris and the country, published by the architect Pierre le Muet in 1647, most of the houses have them. The term was still not a standard one, however; as late as 1683 the inventory of the château de la Lorie talks of 'la petite salle basse dans laquelle ordinairement on mange'.

One can get an idea of the people who were entertained in the salles or sallettes of a château or manoir from the journal which Gouberville kept in the 1540s and 1550s, and from the notes on the numbers of visitors entertained by the Chabannes family, given in a household account book of the château of Saint-Fargeau for 1570. These two sources throw light on two different levels of noble life: Gouberville a country squire living in a modest manoir, Chabannes a member of the upper nobility living in a large and important château.

In one year, from May 1549 to May 1550, five parties of noble guests came to eat and stay the night with Gouberville at Mesnil. Of these, the visit over which he took the most trouble was that, on Friday 31 May 1549, of Monsieur de Rouville. Louis de Rouville was Gouberville's boss: he was 'grand maître' of the royal demesne, the 'Eaux et Forêts', in Normandy and Picardy, and Gouberville, in addition to his active life as a gentleman-farmer, was in charge of the Eaux et Forêts in the Valognes area. Two days earlier he had bought four large turbots, two barbels and six large weavers; half a lamb, bought at the same time, and presents of game sent in by neighbours, were presumably for Saturday. Rouville came with two colleagues or gentleman servants, and a 'train' of unspecified size, had supper and stayed the night.

Three of the other visits were made by relatives of Gouberville. 'Ma cousine de Tocqueville' came to supper with her son and daughter, and stayed the night, although their own home, the manoir of Tocqueville, was only a few kilometres away. His uncle and sister, and his niece with her husband, the Baron de Crenoys, came for supper and the night on the way to or from their own châteaux. The Crenoys, who were Gouberville's richest relatives, were accompanied by two gentleman servants, and one gentlewoman, along with 'two other serviteurs'.

> On Sunday 29 September 1549, while I was at Vespers, Collin, the serviteur of Sieur de Cantapie, came to tell me that Monsieur Trexot had arrived at the house; I left immediately, and found him in company with the seigneur de Maisons, from Bayeux, Estienne Chiquart, Le Saulnes, sergeant at Bayeux, and several others.

They all stayed for supper and the night. Rolland Trexot was seigneur of Balleroy, and an important local official. He and his party were clearly what was called at the time 'survenants', unexpected visitors. Such visits were taken for granted, and any travelling nobleman seems to have expected hospitality and been given it without question.[55]

In addition to these noble guests there was a regular flow of other visitors, who came, usually on business, and were given supper and a bed: 'two friars', Richard Legros the barber and François le Buhotel the saddler, a man who came with medicine for the dogs, and 'maistre Richard' who came to bleed Gouberville. Others, noble or otherwise, came from time to time during the day, but did not stay the night.

Unlike Gouberville, the keeper of the Saint-Fargeau account book only thought noble visitors worth recording. Saint-Fargeau had more of these than Mesnil, as one might expect: in July 1570 alone, four parties each with up to six attendant gentlemen and suites, came and stayed overnight, as did one unattended 'capitaine', and one nobleman and suite came for dinner but did not stay. Only one group came for more than one or two nights: 'Mademoiselle Dufort' arrived on 7 July with her suite, two daughters and two gentlemen, and went off leaving daughters and attendant gentlemen behind for a fortnight's stay, after which she came back to collect them.[56]

This general pattern of short-stay visitors at both houses, coming in individual groups rather than large numbers of noble guests at any one time, would not have called for a great deal of accommodation; children and servants could sleep in a garderobe or in the chambre of their parents or employers, in a second bed. Richelieu's valet de chambre was sleeping in his master's bedroom in the 1630s; Richelieu, who was neurotic about security, perhaps with justification, used to search the room every night, and finding two bottles of wine under the valet's bed made him drink them straight off, as a precaution in case they contained poison.[57] The Grande Mademoiselle's chief lady was sleeping in her mistress's room at Saint-Fargeau as late as 1657.[58]

The 'two good enough rooms' which Noel du Fail allotted for 'survenants' and strangers in the house of his seigneur of the time of François I would have been quite adequate for the numbers of visitors at Mesnil, and it is unlikely to have had more than that. Saint-Fargeau would have needed a little more: the inventory of 1570 lists five chambres (two of them 'petite'), that seem to have been available for visitors rather than resident family or members of the household.[59]

In 1542 the château of Thouars, the main residence of one of the most powerful families in France, had only four such chambres. The most important of them, the 'grande chambre haute', was kept locked, because of the value of the tapestries in it, a set of several big pieces showing the history of Maccabeus. According to the inventory clerk,

> we were told by Paul Morier, tapissier, who opened the room for us and is in charge of these tapestries … that when it was known that the Queen of Navarre was coming to this town, they were brought here from l'Isle Bouchard, another château belonging to the family.[60]

A royal visit, even that of the queen of a pocket kingdom such as the kingdom of Navarre, must have imposed a strain on a château's resources; still more, a visit from

the king. For nineteen months, for instance, between 1564 and 1566 Catherine de Medici took her young son Charles IX and his brother the Duc d'Anjou round southern and western France, on a tour deliberately designed to establish the royal authority. They travelled with an enormous entourage and stayed at towns, villages, abbeys and numerous châteaux; they were at Oiron with Claude Gouffier for four nights, at Champigny with the Duc de Montpensier for four nights, at Brissac with the Cossé-Brissacs for three nights. All too little is known about how they were received by individual owners, but clearly very large numbers of people would have had to be fed and entertained.[61]

Big family events, such as weddings, could also bring large numbers to a château for a night or two. Another such event was the 'tutelle', or assembly for guardianship, which would take place when a seigneur died leaving a child heir. Guardianship had to be decided on by agreement, between all the relatives, who congregated at the château in large numbers for the purpose; 300 people, servants included, are said to have descended on the château of Cux in Burgundy for six days in 1613 for a tutelle.[62]

Up to the mid sixteenth century châteaux were geared to the kind of relatively modest visiting recorded at Mesnil and Saint-Fargeau, for the occasional big incursions produced by a royal visit, or for major family events. Everyone, apart from the royal or distinguished few who occupied the best chambres, was piled into the château in indiscriminate confusion.

The great château of Écouen built by Constable Anne de Montmorency in the 1540s and 1550s was deliberately designed to accommodate royal visits. It had two principal ranges, one to the north of its courtyard for royal visitors, the other to the south, for the Constable and his family.[63] A magnificent gallery in the west range joined the two together. Écouen was probably unique, and certainly out of the ordinary. Montmorency was for long the principal royal minister, and like Lord Burghley at Theobalds in England, was deliberately catering for frequent royal visits. But châteaux of all kinds in the later sixteenth and early seventeenth century were being built with more accommodation, perhaps as much as part of a general increase in luxury, much deplored by moralists at the time, as to cater for potential royal visits. When Louis XIII and his mother, Marie de Medici, came to Brissac in 1620, he for two nights and she for one, the recently completed (or all but completed) new building at Brissac could provide at least eight handsome sets of lodgings, independent of the family's own lodgings, in a separate pavilion. The king was given lodging on the ground floor, composed of a salle d'armes for his body-guard, an antechambre and chambre, both with splendidly gilded ceilings, and a clutch of cabinets and garderobes; the queen was on the floor above. No particular festin seems to have been laid on, and the total numbers involved are not recorded. The visit is briefly described in the journal of Louis XIII's doctor, and the rooms of the king's appartement kept their names into the mid eighteenth century.[64]

The visits to châteaux made by Louis XIII's niece, the Grande Mademoiselle, in 1637, on her way to and from her father's châteaux in Touraine, are described in her memoirs. It is not clear why this ten-year-old girl embarked on what amounted to a miniature royal progress, apart from the insatiable curiosity evinced all through her life. In addition to visits involving a meal only, she stayed at eight non-royal châteaux and six royal ones, three of them belonging to her father. At the former she records her appreciation of a good reception, when it occurred: Monsieur Marchand's masque and the gardener's wedding at Montglat have already been referred to; 'good cheer and an excellent reception' at Villemareuil; 'the fine, convenient and well-furnished appartements' at Selles, as beautiful as it was agreeable; the big dinner given to her at Fourchaud. Only of one château does she record her displeasure: La Motte in the Sologne was, according to her, in fact only a 'so-called' château, which turned out to be a 'little pavilion', quite inadequate for the entertainment of her and her train. Unfortunately she does not make clear how many people were accompanying her.[65]

The minimum accommodation to meet with the approval of an important visitor like the Grande Mademoiselle consisted, as it had done since at least the mid sixteenth century, of a fine large chambre, a garderobe and a cabinet. Stone-seated privies had been given up, except for servants; the gentry had a personal close-stool or 'chaise-percée', usually kept in their cabinet. The chambre de parement had long since disappeared, though perhaps one can see the salle haute as its lineal descendant.

In the fifteenth and early sixteenth centuries it had been common enough to find a chambre in the corner of the corps de logis, with the garderobe in an adjacent round turret; this was the arrangement at Villeneuve-Lembron, for instance.

In the sixteenth century chambre, cabinet and garderobe were frequently all fitted into a tower, producing the fat, low round towers which are a typical feature of châteaux of the time, and very much in contrast to the slenderer, taller towers of the later Middle Ages.

An alternative to such a round tower was the square tower with a high roof known as a 'pavillon', the geometry of which made it much easier to fit several rooms conveniently into it. Such pavillons first appear in the mid sixteenth century, and thereafter become increasingly common. What was known as the 'pavillon du roi' in the new range at the Louvre designed by Pierre Lescot in the 1540s perhaps set the fashion. In the designs printed in the so-called *Petites Habitations* of about 1545, Jacques Androuet du Cerceau, if he was indeed their author, alternates between the two types.[66]

A few older châteaux acquired what appears to have been deliberately designed as a new family pavillon, a virtually self-contained entity with a kitchen in the basement, a good staircase and appartements of identical plan piled up one above the other. Such a pavillon was added on to the château of Brissac, probably in the late sixteenth century; it was high, including two well-lit basements, originally rising straight out of the moat; the most richly decorated of the appartements was on the first floor, and belonged to Judith d'Acigné, who married Charles de Cossé, future first Duc de Brissac, in 1579, and who died in 1598.[67] One can appreciate how the existence of such a self-contained pavillon would have made it easier to deal with the visit of Louis XIII and his mother; the main body of the château could effectively be given over to them and their train.

There are other good examples of these self-contained pavillons with kitchens at the château of Lanquais in the Dordogne, dating, probably, from the 1570s, and the more modest pavillon of around 1630–40 added on to the late-fifteenth-century maison seigneuriale of Plessis-Josso in Brittany in about 1630.

But the ways in which the chambre and its appurtenances were increasingly personalized, the provision of ante-chambres and galleries, the enrichment and increased importance of the cabinet, everything that was to be finally signified in the early seventeenth century by the change of the neutral expression 'logis' into the new term 'appartement', with its insinuation of separation and privacy, deserves a separate chapter.

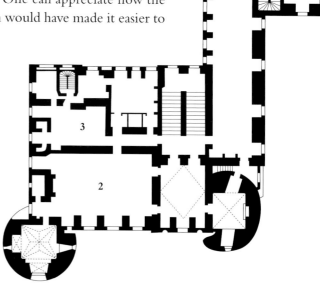

The soaring pavillon at the west corner of the château of Brissac (right) was added onto the earlier château, probably in the late sixteenth century. It provided compact accommodation for the family, and was detached at the end of a gallery, leaving the main body of the château free for grand events and important visitors.

In the plan of the first floor (above), 1 was the chambre of the Duchesse de Brissac, 2 and 3 the grande salle and chambre occupied by Marie de Medici when she stayed at the château in 1620.

4
PRIVATE PLACES

The cabinet at the château of Cormatin is the most magnificent surviving example of the many sumptuous little rooms installed in the early seventeenth century as the personal sanctums of their owners. A painting of St Cecilia, patron saint of music, over the chimney-piece bears witness to musical interests, and book-shelves are concealed behind the panelling.

WHEN GASTON-PHÉBUS walked with his knights up and down the gallery at Orthez in the 1380s, he was using a type of room which had only recently appeared, but which was to have a long history in France and Europe.[1] Galleries could, in fact, serve three main purposes, not necessarily exclusive: one could walk up and down in them, like Gaston-Phébus, or use them to go from one part of a building to another, or one could display fine things in them.

Galleries probably first developed as a means of communication. When a royal or seigneurial residence was made up of a number of separate elements, galleries were useful means of providing routes from one to another under cover. Such links may originally have been open, and made of wood, but the closed gallery of stone was a natural refinement or development, as was the discovery that these long closed spaces could be used for exercise in bad or cold weather, while open galleries turned out to be pleasant places for exercise or shelter from the heat.

The rambling collection of elements in the Palais de la Cité in Paris were connected by a series of galleries of varying sizes as early as the thirteenth and fourteenth centuries; the spacious gallery which Louis IX built in the mid thirteenth century as a link between the grande salle and the Sainte-Chapelle was ultimately, in the sixteenth and seventeenth centuries, to develop into the famous Galerie des Merciers, lined with booths and, as a combination of fashionable strolling place and shopping arcade, one of the main meeting-places in Paris.

The use of galleries for display was a later development, but grew out of their earlier functions. The business both of pacing up and down in a gallery, or moving along it to get from one place to another, could be made impressive, interesting or instructive by decorating it with images of one kind or another. So one finds frescoes of a scene from the *Aeneid* at Oiron in the 1540s, stained glass depicting the story of Cupid and Psyche at Écouen in the 1550s, or, much later, the paintings of landscapes installed in the 1620s in the gallery at Cormatin. By then

Small studies or 'estudes' for private work and the storage of books, manuscripts and valuables, begin to appear in the fourteenth century. A manuscript illustration (above) shows the authoress Christine de Pisan at work.

galleries were also being used for the display of portraits, usually of famous people rather than (though sometimes as well as) members of the family. The best surviving example is the gallery at Beauregard, into the walls of which 360 portraits are inset, like a stamp collection. The aim was to impress or instruct, rather than to display works of art of great value; the occupant of the gallery could learn, as he walked up and down.

A closed gallery on the first floor was frequently accompanied by an open gallery or arcade beneath it, as is to be found at Blois. The open gallery could be used for exercise in warm or wet weather, and they were also, at times, used for display, as with the paintings and horns of deer which are still to be found in the open gallery at Villeneuve-Lembron; the similar gallery at Oiron was originally frescoed with Claude Gouffier's favourite horses, all, sadly, long since disappeared.

Galleries could have varying degrees of privacy. A gallery of major communication, such as François I's gallery joining two wings of the château of Fontainebleau, or Constable Montmorency's gallery performing a similar function at Écouen, could be splendid features, but there was little privacy about them. The gallery which René d'Anjou caused to be constructed at his château at Angers in 1465 ran along one side of his own logis, and looked into his privy garden:[2] it would have been relatively private, with an agreeable outlook, but it gave access to the various rooms in the logis, and there would always have been people coming and going in it, as in the rather similarly arranged gallery in the Louis XII wing at Blois.

But the gallery at Oiron is literally out on a limb, filling the first floor of a separate wing; it led only to one room in a turret at the far end, probably Gouffier's estude, and the only access to it was through Gouffier's chambre. It was his own private gallery, accessible only to those whom he chose to take into it. It still has an extraordinary feeling of a secret world apart.

These private and personal galleries became a popular feature in the sixteenth century. Sometimes they led nowhere, sometimes to an estude or cabinet, or a private oratory, or a tribune looking down into the chapel, a combination which suggested one of their uses, as rooms of meditation for their owner, pacing up and down in them. An early example, perhaps the first surviving private gallery in France, is at Plessis-Bourré. It leads to the chapel, and is on the first floor above an open gallery; the two together fill a wing to one side of the courtyard, which joins the chapel to the principal logis. There is a similar arrangement, on a charmingly intimate scale, at the château of Bussy-Rabutin. It dates from the early sixteenth

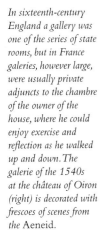

In sixteenth-century England a gallery was one of the series of state rooms, but in France galeries, however large, were usually private adjuncts to the chambre of the owner of the house, where he could enjoy exercise and reflection as he walked up and down. The galerie of the 1540s at the château of Oiron (right) is decorated with frescoes of scenes from the Aeneid.

century; but the gallery was to be redecorated by Roger de Bussy-Rabutin in the 1660s, and filled with portraits with long explanatory inscriptions, to provide, as he put it, 'a short history ancient and modern with all I should want my children to know of the subject'.

The gallery used in this particular way became a valuable tool towards the personalization of the logis – its development, not just as the private territory of its occupant, but as a territory in which he or she could express and develop their personality and their interests. Another means towards this was the provision of a 'cabinet'. Not everyone could afford a gallery, and in France they never became such essential status symbols as the 'long galleries' of England. But from the mid sixteenth century any logis of any pretensions had to have a cabinet.

Like a galerie, a cabinet was not in fact a new feature in the sixteenth century, although it had a new name: it fulfilled very much the same functions as the study or estude, such as had been provided for Charles V in his tower at Vincennes in the 1360s. By the 1440s, when Antoine d'Asti described the Duc d'Orléans's little estude or secret place in the thickness of the wall at Coucy,[3] he wrote as though he was describing a somewhat special and out-of-the-ordinary feature, for such rooms were still a rarity and a luxury, confined to royal or papal residences, or the houses of a handful of bishops or grands seigneurs.

In the sixteenth century they became a necessary element of all seigneurial residences of any pretensions. A chambre was only a semi-private room, to which access was taken for granted, not only by its occupant's family and friends, but by his servants; it was the domain of his valet de chambre, who frequently slept in it,

At the mid-sixteenth-century château of Bussy-Rabutin, the gallery filled the first floor of one wing (above), and led from the seigneur's chambre to his private chapel in the tower. In a combination typical of the period there is an open cloister or gallery on the ground floor beneath it.

on a truckle bed next to or at the foot of his master's. The occupant of a chambre could, and on occasion did, move into an adjacent garderobe when he wanted to be private; but garderobes had the disadvantage that they were also used by servants, who came in to look after the clothes stored in them, and sometimes slept in them. They were not as private as all that, and servants could use them to spy on their employers. In the anonymous *Amours, intrigues et caballes des domestiques* (1633), the valet de chambre tells how he ran up the backstairs to the garderobe 'where clothes are brushed', to which he had the key, and peeped into the adjacent chambre, in which his master was making up to one of his mistress's ladies.[4]

An estude was a deeply private room, probably kept locked, to which the owner had the key, and to which no one else had access except his secretary – his confidential servant. In his *Blasons Domestiques* Corrozet compares its relationship to the house with the relationship of the soul to the body.[5] He wrote, in fact, at the time when the estude was about to change its name, and be known as the cabinet, after the piece of furniture in which precious objects or private papers were kept; the name of the piece of furniture was transferred to the room in which it was most frequently found.

From the contents of someone's cabinet one could discover his or her interests and ruling passion, if there was one. Monsieur de la Vargue's cabinet at the château de Combes in 1569 contained his crossbows, a selection of swords, a table, a buffet, and a great many letters and legal documents in a locked cupboard.[6] In 1557 the cabinet of a doting grandmother at the château d'Esteban was filled with toys: a complete set of miniature silver plates, bowls, goblets, salt-cellars and all; dolls of all kinds, some mounted on horses; a miniature bed, complete with canopy, and a lady lying under it; a miniature litter of crimson velvet, with gold trimmings, with two dolls in it, and two toy mules with boy pages riding on them to carry it; little figures for a Christmas crib; bunches of flowers made of silk; a tiny horse of mother-of-pearl, with a gold man riding it; toy peacocks, cock, swans and other birds; a racket; a nutcracker; and so on.[7]

In contrast, at Chenonceau, the ruling passion of Henri III's widow, Louise de Vaudemont, was watering the memory of her husband with tears both real and allegorical. She retreated into her cabinet to mourn her husband, between his death in 1589 and hers in 1602. The results were described with some fascination by the Grande Mademoiselle, who visited in 1637:

In a series of designs published by Jacques Androuet du Cerceau in about 1545 (below), the corner towers normally contain a chambre, a cabinet for privacy and study and a garderobe for the storage of clothes or for a bed for a child or a servant.

There one could still see her chambre and her cabinet, which she had had painted in black, scattered with tears, skulls, tombs and a quantity of mournful emblems. The furniture was in keeping; the only ornament in the entire cabinet was a small portrait of Henri III over the fireplace of the cabinet.[8]

A cabinet similarly decorated for the widowed Duchesse de Longueville survives in the château of Châteaudun.

But it is the learned cabinets which are the most distinctive. Many of them survive, and as a group they are as powerful and evocative as anything to be found in France. Their golden age runs for about a hundred years, from the mid sixteenth to the mid seventeenth century. They are little rooms, often vaulted, often at the end of a gallery, decorated with the greatest richness of carved panelling and painting. The paintings are usually of mythological subjects, or subjects taken from the classics, as in the cabinet at Pibrac.[9] At Beauregard, towards the beginning of the series, Jean de Thier, Henri II's secretary, chose subjects which suggest the activities of a collector: classical busts, pieces of plate, books, musical instruments. At Oiron, several generations after Claude Gouffier's gallery, life-size figures of the Nine Muses, presided over by the goddess Diana, play their instruments between gilded columns and beneath a gold-encrusted ceiling. Often, concealed in the panelling of these cabinets, little doors open to reveal cupboards or nests of drawers, for books, paper or precious objects: the cabinet of Jacques du Blé was decorated in about 1620 at the château de Cormatin, as sumptuous a little room as one could hope to find, all blue and gold with St Cecilia, patron saint of music, over the chimney-piece, and other paintings or painted panels on other walls – landscapes, an Amazon, urns

The galerie at the château of Beauregard (above) was decorated in the early seventeenth century with a series of over 300 portraits of eminent historical figures, so that the room became a kind of visual encyclopaedia for the delectation and instruction of its owner.

Cabinets and galeries were often decorated with classical scenes as evidence of the cultivated tastes and studies of their occupants. The little vaulted cabinet of the late sixteenth century at the château of Pibrac (above right) was frescoed with scenes from Ovid for its owner, the poet Guy du Faur.

The sumptuous gilded cabinet of about 1640 at the château of Oiron (right) is encircled by figures of the Nine Muses.

overflowing with flowers – many of them brought down from Paris to be inset into the decoration.

In the first half of the seventeenth century cabinets reached their greatest heights of richness and fantasy. Their function as places for the cultivation of the personality developed still further. In his or her (more often her) cabinet individuals could not only study or write, they could enjoy intimate conversations with a few people – or just one person – or alternatively they could indulge in the pleasures of creative fantasy.

The French word 'rêver' undergoes a significant development at this period. In the sixteenth century, and well into the seventeenth, it was a pejorative term. It meant, indeed, 'to rave', or as Colgrave expanded it in his Anglo-French dictionary of 1632, 'to rave, dote, speak idly, talk like an ass'; he defines the noun 'resverie' as 'a raving, idle talking dotage, trifling, follie, vaine fancie, fond

imagination'. For Paul Monet, in his French dictionary published two years earlier, it went with delirium: 'people in a high fever' did it.

But by the time these dictionaries were published, the nuances of the word were already changing in certain select and influential circles. 'Rêvant' meant letting the mind and imagination run free – 'day-dream' is probably the best translation; it was an enriching occupation, and, in terms of the château, the best place to do it was in one's cabinet, or alternatively on a new architectural feature – a balcony, letting (by what came to be known in England as 'French windows') off a room in an individual's appartement, from which one could commune with nature.

Cabinets and day-dreaming occur frequently in the romances of Madeline de Scudéry. She talks of the need for solitude for day-dreaming:

> For when one has a lot of things to think about which are more worthwhile than the conversation one is listening to, one must go to one's cabinet and be by oneself, because it is certainly rude not to listen to anything of what people round you are saying, and to write off the company you are in. Myself, I am convinced that the only conversation one can civilly listen to while day-dreaming is the murmur of a brook or the sound of a fountain.[10]

She describes one retired cabinet as the perfect place for 'being by oneself – there was never a place so ideally suited for agreeable day-dreaming or better arranged for confiding a secret'.[11] Cleonie, in *Le Grand Cyrus*, 'much preferred to day-dream in her cabinet, or to occupy herself with a book there, than to be swamped by her mother's friends' (but she also had a balcony 'on which she used to day-dream when the weather was fine enough').[12] In *Clélie* the palace of Artaxandre and Amalthée had two cabinets at either end of a gallery, one 'so retired that one can't be in it without day-dreaming', the other looking on to a busy harbour 'so that one always has a choice, the outside world or solitude'.[13]

Cabinets keep occurring in her romances: places to retreat into when upset by a love-affair; to conduct private interviews in; to keep a picture which has an emotional association; to write poetry in. But they are also places for conversation among groups of like-minded friends. In fact, she describes two kinds of cabinets: smaller, more secret ones, and bigger, more social ones. It is in one of the latter that Scudéry describes Princess Clarinte entertaining twelve friends, 'a grand cabinet with a coffered dome, completely surrounded with objects. The princess was on a little day-bed, all the ladies on cushions, and the men standing, or half-kneeling by the ladies, on a large carpet.'[14]

She gives many loving descriptions of these sumptuous little rooms. A day-bed ('lit de repos') for the cabinet's owner was a frequent feature. The cabinet in the house of Cloramiste, in *Clélie*, 'had windows on three sides, with a beautiful view. It was full of pictures, books and musical instruments, surrounded by cushions embroidered with flowers, and the floor was covered with rush matting.' Another cabinet in *Clélie*

is painted and gilded throughout; there are mirrors on three sides, which reflect from above the beautiful landscape and one of the most beautiful gardens in the world, so that for those sitting on the sumptuous cushions which surround the room, or on the little day-bed opposite the door, there is something agreeable to look at in every direction – for the mirrors not only multiply beautiful countryside, parterre, and ponds outside and the company inside, but they multiply each other, and by their varied reflections agreeably deceive the eyes, and gently entertain the imagination.[15]

One is reminded of the mirror-lined cabinet which still exists in the château de Maisons. For Madeleine de Scudéry was not indulging in her own fantasies. She was writing about a world that she was familiar with, and attitudes and places that she knew; the cabinets and palaces which she describes are often based on real cabinets and actual châteaux or Parisian houses. She belonged (even if she was not always entirely accepted by its members) to the world of the Prétieuses (or

Précieuses), the select group of highly educated ladies from both the old and the new noblesse who moved round each other's newly built houses in the new and fashionable quarter known as the Marais in Paris, and whose influence radiated out from there to their own châteaux and the châteaux of other people all over France.

The members of the group could at times be pedantic, affected and irritating, but they were developing new forms of social relationship, and new types of individual sensibility. They wanted more than great dinners for many people in the salle, at which everyone got cheerfully drunk, with enthusiastic dancing afterwards, or the singing of rounds and the telling of stories – social life, in fact, as it had been lived for centuries. They developed their own imaginations and intellects. They also developed the art of conversation as the interaction of lively minds, not the disquisition of one person to a respectful audience; they developed the concept of the hostess, who could create such a social life in her own home, and the idea of personal relationships which were more than just sexual, though sex could play a part.

The cabinet was one place for the development of this way of life, but the chambre could also have a role, especially that section of the chambre known as the 'ruelle', and the child or near relative of the ruelle, the alcove.

When a bed was placed, as it usually was, with its head to the wall, the ruelle was the space, often sizeable, between the bed and the wall parallel to it. It formed, in fact, an inner space within the chambre. The sense of intimacy and enclosure which bed and wall gave to this space, and the feeling of privilege as a result of being close to the bed, gave it a special status from the fifteenth century onwards; distinctive and superior furniture for the ruelle is sometimes listed in inventories. Henri IV used to have a table set up in his and play poker dice with special cronies, as related by the eminent soldier Bassompierre, who was one of them; and Bassompierre also describes how the great Constable de Montmorency invited him and a 'good company of his familiar friends' into his ruelle in order to announce that he was going to give his daughter in marriage to Bassompierre.[16]

An alcove was a portion of a chambre divided off by an arch, or a beam, so as to become a room within a room. In a much-quoted passage, Tallement des Réaux, doyen of seventeenth-century gossips and a friend and admirer of Madame de Rambouillet, the queen of the Précieuses, describes how she had a disease, or skin complaint, which made it impossible for her to be close to a fire or in the sun without 'the blood boiling in her veins', and so in winter had to live in a room without a fire, and to get a little warmth was under the necessity of 'borrowing from the Spaniards the device of alcoves, which today are so much in fashion in Paris'.[17]

The Marquis de Rambouillet was on an embassy to Spain from 1626 to 1628, and perhaps his wife picked up the idea then; 'alcoba' or 'alcova' is a Spanish word of Arabic origin, and such subdivided rooms had been found in Spain since the beginning of the sixteenth century. In fact, similar features are also shown at much the same time in plans drawn in France by Sebastiano Serlio, and were actually installed in some of the lesser rooms of the château de Madrid for François I in 1527–47.[18] But the fashion did not catch on, and Tallement may be right in saying

that it was Madame de Rambouillet who brought about their increasing vogue from about 1630 onwards.

She installed her alcove in a little chambre off her antechambre, not her main chambre, the famous 'Chambre Bleu'. There was a fire in the antechambre in winter, and her circle could warm up at this before going in to see her in her chilly little room. There is no surviving plan of the alcove, but the inventories suggest that it was set between two closets, each in a corner of the room; there could have been little space in it for anything but the bed.[19] An alcove of similar size, with a charming group of three at the foot of the bed – the owner of the alcove, her admirer and her attendant – is shown in the frontispiece of Abbé Michel de Pure's *La Prétieuse ou le mystère des ruelles* (1656–8). But often there were no enclosing closets; the alcove went the full width of the room, and was entered either through a single opening or a screen of three; there was room in it for plenty of visitors.

In the mid seventeenth century the space around or next to the bed known as the 'ruelle', often divided off from the rest of the room by an arch to form an alcove, became a place for intimate meetings and conversations, as shown in the frontispiece of Michel de Pure's La Prétieuse ou le mystère des ruelles, *published in 1656–8.*

'Ruelle' and 'alcove' seemed now to have been used interchangeably. Their owners could receive visitors either lying in their bed or seated next to it, and their visitors could vary from a sizeable group to a single admirer – often a poet, come to read them a poem in their praise. They were said to 'tenir alcove', and their admirers were called 'alcovistes'. The practice grew up of individual ladies keeping or holding their ruelle on a particular day of the week. Somaize wrote about them in his *Grand Dictionnaire des Précieuses*, using pseudonyms for places and people; Mademoiselle de Scudéry, for instance, was 'Sophie', and of her he wrote that

> as for her alcovistes, they are identical in number with her acquaintances, for her wit and sweetness attract the largest and most distinguished section of the writing world to visit her … she lives in the district of Leolie [the Marais], and reading her works is the occupation and divertissement of all the ruelles of Greece [Paris].[20]

As Michel de Pure wrote about the Prétieuses, 'these terrestrial stars appear in two kinds of firmament, which modern science calls "Alcove" or "Ruelle". Both make up one sphere, and move in another similar/identical one called "conversation".'[21]

Conversation was what it was all about: lively, teasing, flirtatious conversations between a woman and her admirer, or witty, wide-ranging general conversations in larger, but never too large, groups. The use of the word in this sense was a relatively new one, as though people had suddenly become aware of a form of social activity which had in fact been developing for a hundred years or so. One can find the germ of it in Corrozet, celebrating 'the table' in 1539:

> Table where one talks about business
> Then about peace, then about war,
> Then about France, then about England,
> Then about virtue, then about folly.[22]

It has developed further in the description of supper with the Duchesse de Retz in 1591:

> All the evening was spent in an infinity of good and interesting talk, concerning the calamities of our time, and the hope or despair which each of us felt, depending on our different opinions. And as it is the privilege of a dinner-party to jump from one thing to another, without any connection, and without knowing why or how, we did exactly this without thinking, and sometimes talked about our own establishments, sometimes about law business, sometimes about the right time for ploughing – I've never heard conversation more disconnected or of better quality. A good writer could have made a book out of it to equal the *Saturnales* of Athénée or Macrobius. Finally, since conversation about love is the sauce of wit, we couldn't fail to talk about it.[23]

There can be no doubt that influence was coming from Italy, where one can move from the telling of stories in Boccaccio's *Decameron* to the general discussions in Castiglione's *Il Cortegiano* (1528): these Italian conversations were, in their turn, clearly influenced by the *Dialogues* of Plato and other classical authors. But French conversation was developing a little further than this, becoming lighter, gayer, agreeably spiced with gossip, not so much of a debate; even so, this element remained important, and these meetings in the Marais were still to some extent what had grown in the sixteenth century to be called 'academies', at which poets or writers read their new compositions, or rather formal debates were held on fixed topics.

In *Le Grand Cyrus* Madeline de Scudéry gives one account of how a conversation could develop. Stenobée, her daughter and two friends – one woman and one man – are in her chambre, having a long conversation about the nature of the ideal male friend, and other topics. Then more friends start coming in until there are about eighteen people in the room, and the conversation changes: 'There was general conversation, which lasted some time, a bit of talk about the news, then about a horse-race, which had just taken place, then about dress, and similar subjects.'

Personal relationships add a little spice: there were a number of admirers of the glamorous Artelinde in the room, and

> in her usual way, to keep them happy she started to pay attention to each one individually, and while she was talking to one it was fun for us to observe how fidgety the others were. I've never known a more agreeable after-dinner occasion.[24]

In *Clélie* Amilcar and Anacreon contrast the boring nature of big parties with the pleasures of small ones:

> big 'do's like weddings, that's to say a gathering of people who for the most part don't know each other, who don't know what to talk about, where there are more fools than sensible people, where none the less everyone talks non-stop without saying anything at all, where conversation is a confused noise rather than proper social interaction.

And in contrast,

> what I find really enjoyable is when five or six friends come together, not to do business or to annoy each other, but just to have a pleasant time, in which they feel free and happy and find all the enjoyment they want. The conversation is free, playful, and at times not to say funny; one says whatever one likes and whatever one thinks; one gives as much pleasure as one gets; the conversation is wittier than usual, because no one is trying to show off; one talks about absent friends and one's love-affairs; one anticipates further pleasure, by planning another gathering; the party is punctuated by agreeable songs, by music, a bit of a walk and a bit of conversation. One could say that both body and mind are content, and all one wants is to have a repeat of the same type of pleasure.[25]

What was also developing was the idea of a hostess, as the enabler and inspirer of gatherings of this type. The actual expression 'hostess' was not yet coming into use, but what did appear was the concept of the 'jour', the particular day on which a Parisian lady was at home to her friends. Michel de Pure explained it in 1656, in *La Prétieuse*:

> this kind of rendezvous is now being developed, to the general benefit. One lady selects one day, another another; so that anyone who wants to have a conversation or a meeting with a particular lady has no need of a confidante or go-between to arrange a meeting and relieve his pain. He just has to know the rota of ruelles, and the list of those who have them, and without any need of thinking up an excuse can meet up with the lady he fancies as

he wishes. This device was the invention of a contemporary nymph, and her success has made it so popular that it has become an obligation and a necessity. The obligation can be severe as the holder of 'a day' cannot give it up because her parents, or even less her husband and children are ill, but only because of the loss, absence, or affliction of a bosom-friend. She is also obliged to keep to her chambre even on a public holiday when the state-entry of a famous man, a joust, a fireworks display, a ballet or an outstanding comedy would normally have enticed her out.[26]

The holder of a jour needed a setting as well as a clientele, and in the choice of both she expressed and developed her personality. There was nothing new about particular sets of rooms belonging to particular people, but that they should express the taste and propagate the image of their owner by their decoration and furnishing was a new development in France, and it is perhaps significant that it is at this period that the term 'appartement' came into use as the name for such a collection of rooms. The most famous appartement in Paris in the mid seventeenth century was that of Madame de Rambouillet; it was made up of antechambre, little chambre with alcove, 'Chambre Bleu', and cabinet built over her garden, letting off the Chambre Bleu. The Chambre Bleu was one of the founding land-marks in interior decoration; it was painted a distinctive blue, a novel treatment which it made fashionable, and which was copied endlessly.[27] All these rooms let off a big salle, but this featured with little prominence in accounts of the Hôtel Rambouillet, for a salle was too large a room for the kind of gatherings over which Madame de Rambouillet liked to preside: small gatherings in her 'chambre à l'alcove', bigger ones in her Chambre Bleu or cabinet, and meals for a few chosen people in her antechambre.

The antechambre was a new arrival in private houses, although it had been found in royal residences in France since the 1560s. In effect, it fulfilled very much the same function as the sallette, and the chambre de parement before that. The function was a double one. People wishing to see the occupant of the chambre waited in the antechambre, or their servants waited there until they re-emerged; but the occupant of the antechambre also used it for the kind of small-scale meals that had previously been held in the chambre. By the mid seventeenth century it was becoming a common feature for the newly termed appartements, which now consisted of antechambre, chambre, cabinet and garderobe.

The successful evolution of fashionable society in Paris worked in two directions. On the one hand, social life there proved such an attraction that it pulled some owners away from their châteaux to spend most of the year in Paris. On the other hand, it spread fashions from Paris to the country, as châteaux were rebuilt or redecorated by families who owned a house in Paris, or knew what was going on there. The Chambre Bleu in the Hôtel de Rambouillet has long since been demolished, but the shade of blue which it made fashionable can still be savoured in Jacques du Blé's cabinet at Cormatin, 380 kilometres from Paris.

In about 1630 a chambre in one of the medieval towers of the château of Châteauneuf-en-Auxois was re-arranged according to the latest fashion, with a bed for the owner and his wife in an alcove, and their portraits above the doors leading to little cabinets to either side.

The Rambouillets are said to have left their own huge old château at Rambouillet all but unvisited for twenty-eight years.[28] It is hard to believe this of a château within such easy reach of Paris. But, true or not, on their few recorded visits they took the society which centred round them in Paris down to the country with them, for several days of jokes, amateur dramatics and amusement. They were pioneering the house-party.

Châteaux had been supplied with cabinets since the mid sixteenth century, but from the 1620s antechambres and chambres with alcoves begin to appear as well. There is a charmingly simple early alcove, probably of the 1630s, in the château of Châteauneuf-en-Auxois. It is on the first floor of the donjon, and was installed in the chambre of Marguerite de Vienne and her husband Charles, who bought the

château in 1627. Above the entry to the little cabinets on either side of the alcove are inset portraits of Charles and Marguerite. Between 1641 and 1660 the château of Sury-le-Comtal was lavishly redecorated for Pierre d'Escoubleau de Sourdu, Marquis de Sury, and at least four of the chambres were equipped with alcoves, far more lavishly decorated than the one at Châteauneuf.[29] One can plot the spread of the fashion all over France, starting in houses where the families had Parisian connections, but appearing, for instance, in the Brittany manoir of Le Plessis-Josso in about 1650, when the chambre at the end of the salle basse was redecorated and fitted out with an alcove.

François Mansart provided one antechambre and no chambres à l'alcove for one of his first commissions, the remodelling of the château of Berny, in 1623. By the 1640s his great château at Maisons, built for a powerful financier, was equipped with four complete

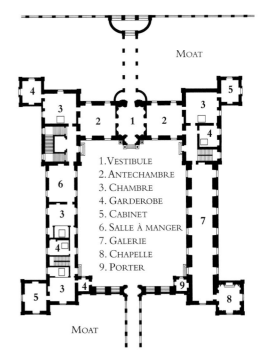

1. Vestibule
2. Antechambre
3. Chambre
4. Garderobe
5. Cabinet
6. Salle à manger
7. Galerie
8. Chapelle
9. Porter

The ground floor plan (above) of the demolished château of Pont, designed by Pierre Le Muet and built in about 1640, shows two early examples of chambres with alcoves, and twin sets of appartements containing ante-chambre, chambre and cabinet or garderobe, as was to become the fashionable arrange-ment. There was probably a grande salle on the first floor of the central range, but a smaller salle à manger on the ground floor was also provided.

An engraving of about 1680 by J.D. de Saint-Jean (left) shows a lady stretched out on her bed being visited by a young admirer.

appartements, the grandest of which included a chambre à l'alcove. This was in the superb appartement clearly intended for possible use by the king, and the alcove has become a magnificent rather than an intimate architectural feature.

Over much the same period the architect Pierre Le Muet, who specialized in work for robe and financial families, was installing alcoves and antechambres both in their Parisian 'hôtels' and in the châteaux which he designed for them in the country.[30]

In 1652 the Grande Mademoiselle, having made herself heroic or ridiculous, according to the point of view, by directing the military operations of the Fronde like an Amazon warrior or a seventeenth-century Joan of Arc, found it politic to leave Paris and lie low for some years in her château of Saint-Fargeau. She immediately set about bringing the huge old château up to date. Her very first improvement was to move the doors and chimney-piece around in her chambre to make an alcove. She went on to make herself a complete new appartement in another part of the château. She describes it with enthusiasm in her memoirs:

Alcoves, which started as small and intimate spaces, could become increasingly magnificent, as in this example (above) in the Chambre du Roi at the château of Vaux-le-Vicomte. A balustrade was the perquisite of royal or ducal occupants, and in the king's chambre only the grander members of the noblesse had the privilege of going inside it.

> It had an antechambre, where I always took my meals, and a gallery giving access to my chambre; in the gallery I hung the portraits of my closest friends, and put a billiard-table, because I enjoy games involving physical exercise. My chambre was rather charming, and led to a cabinet at one end, a garderobe, and another little cabinet, where there was room for me and nobody else. After eight months camping out in the attics, it was like finding myself in an enchanted palace. I fitted out the cabinet with a great many pictures and mirrors. In short, I was delighted, and thought I had made the prettiest place in the world.[31]

Twenty-five years or so later, the Grande Mademoiselle bought the château de Choisy, just outside Paris, and enjoyed herself as much as always rebuilding it and fitting up another lavish and fashionable appartement for herself. But the plan of Choisy included a room which was only just arriving in France, and which was to play an even more prominent role than the cabinet and the alcove: the salon.

5

THE CURIOUS HISTORY OF THE SALON

The salon doré at the château of Bussy-Rabutin is a provincial example of the sumptuous salons à l'Italienne that became fashionable in the grandest new châteaux of the mid seventeenth century. It was installed in the 1660s by Roger de Bussy-Rabutin, nostalgic for Paris and the court from which he had been exiled because of his scabrous Histoire Amoureuse des Gaules.

VAUX-LE-VICOMTE never ceases to amaze. As created by Nicolas Fouquet, Louis Le Vau and their team, and re-created in the twentieth century by the wealth and taste of the Sommiers and their successors, it is the most impressive château in France. It is triumphantly all of a piece. On one side one great basse-cour echoes another; on the other the great formal garden vanishes into the distance; and framed by the basse-cours, looking on to the vistas of the gardens, the main block is elevated on its moated island like an abode of enchanted beings.

The plan of this main building, and the way the plan is expressed in the architecture, is as simple, satisfying and splendid as the concept of the whole. A magnificent vestibule leads into an even more magnificent salon; to either side of the salon one great appartement matches the other, as one basse-cour matches the other; the architecture of the exterior exactly mirrors the plan and the arrangement of the rooms; the dome of the salon

rises over all. The ornament and decoration with which all this is clothed are dazzling in their combination of fresco and sculpture, allegory and fantasy, deep colour, flashing white and rich gold, mixed together with unfailing inventiveness and sensuous delight.

The rise and fall of Fouquet and of Vaux-le-Vicomte with him, is one of the best-known incidents in French history, although the rights and wrongs of it will always be debated: his modest origins as a respected and successful official under Mazarin, his appointment as Surintendant of Finances, the fortune this brought him, his lavish and perceptive patronage of all the best artistic talent of the time, the creation of Vaux-le-Vicomte, its year or two of glory and splendour, the apparent triumph of Louis XIV's reception there on 17 August 1661, Molière's masque by the waterside and the fireworks flaming out from the dome, Fouquet's almost immediate arrest, his two-year trial for peculation and subversion, his fifteen-year solitary confinement and lonely death in the prison of Pignerol.

Given the kind of person that Louis XIV was, and the aims that he set himself, it was impossible for him to accept Vaux-le-Vicomte. On and off over the previous centuries France had suffered from over-powerful grands seigneurs who set themselves up in virtual independence of the king. France had been torn by wars and factions as a result. Richelieu had set out to break the power of over-mighty nobles and partially

succeeded; but they had had their last fling in the civil war known as the Fronde. Thanks to the efforts of Mazarin and the young Louis XIV they lost. Louis XIV was determined to be his own Richelieu, his own Mazarin, to run the country himself and to ensure that all power emanated from him.

What was wrong with Vaux-le-Vicomte was not so much that it was too large, or even that it cost too much for the house of a subject. There were other châteaux as big or bigger, and perhaps just as expensive. But the brilliance with which every element was made to work together at Vaux turned it into a palace more splendid, and more luxurious, even if smaller, than any of the king's own residences. Its closest analogy was with Richelieu's great country palace at Richelieu, which had the same spread-out magnificence of basse-cours and gardens, but none of the architectural brilliance of Vaux-le-Vicomte. A better, even if not bigger, Richelieu was politically unacceptable, quite apart from the fact that it must have been personally galling to Louis XIV to see a subject, by birth not even a grand seigneur or anything near it, housed with much more style than he was himself.

In terms of the history and architecture of the French château, Vaux-le-Vicomte was a cul-de-sac. It was not just that the history of France and the French noblesse was to take a direction which made it an anachronism. The attitude to design which it expressed failed to catch the French imagination. In spite, or perhaps because, of the breathtaking simplicity of its conception, there was a remorselessness and even a lack of subtlety about it which was alien to the French genius. The satisfaction of a building in which the exterior mirrors and expresses the interior has seldom appealed to the French; they have preferred insides and outsides which play different games, so that the exquisite exterior does not reveal how the exquisite interior is fitted into it.

But there is one enormous debt which the French château, and the French house in general, owes to Vaux-le-Vicomte. It was the base from which that linchpin of French life, the salon, was launched on French waters. It is true that the salon as it

The salon at Vaux-le-Vicomte (above), designed by Louis Le Vau in the 1650s, was the most celebrated and influential example of a salon à l'Italienne. It had the essential attributes of such rooms: oval shape, domed ceiling, two-storey height, grand classical architecture, central position and windows giving on the garden.

The exterior of Vaux-le-Vicomte (left) exactly expresses the nature and function of the plan (right), with the domed two-storey salon placed between matching appartements. Like all seventeenth-century examples, the salon was designed for grand events, not as the main living room.

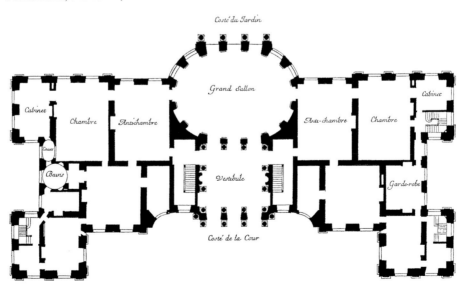

finally emerged was something very different from the salon at Vaux-le-Vicomte; but a continuous chain of development joins one to the other, and makes a curious story.

The word 'salon' was the French translation of the Italian 'salone', and both the word, and rooms so-called, appeared in France about fifteen years before Vaux-le-Vicomte. At first 'salon' was more an architectural than a functional description. A salon was a room which had at least some of a number of distinctive features: a square, oval, circular or octagonal plan; unusual height, rising up through two storeys, or at least into a cove, and often lit by two tiers of windows; magnificent architectural decoration, usually involving two or more tiers of classical orders, or one giant order; a dome or a cupola overall; a central position, on the main axis of the house; a ground floor situation, opening on to the garden.

Perhaps the first room in France to be described as a salon was at the château de Vizille, near Grenoble, belonging to the Duc de Lesdiguières. When an inventory was made here in 1642, there was already a room of that name at the end of a gallery in a separate building next to the main château.[1] It was a square room, panelled in walnut, and was hung with twenty-one pictures in gilt frames, dominated by a portrait of Henri IV on horseback, over the chimney-piece, and visible, by way of the entrance doors, all along the length of the gallery.

This salon no longer exists, but there is a similarly placed one at the château de Maisons, dating from a year or two later.[2] It is on the first floor, at the end, not of a gallery, but of a grande salle, into which it opens through a screen of three lofty arches. A portrait of Louis IV, in a magnificent surround over the chimney-piece, plays a similar role to the portrait of Henri IV at Vizille, and looks through the central archway down the length of the salle.

The salon formed part of what was called the appartement à l'Italienne, consisting of salle haute, chambre, cabinet and petit cabinet. It was described as 'à l'Italienne' because of the height of all the rooms except the petit cabinet, obtained by finishing them with lofty coved ceilings. The appartement was quite clearly designed for the reception and entertainment of royalty, and came into its own when Louis XIII and his wife spent a day at Maisons in the spring of 1651. Dinner must have been served to them sitting alone in the salon, divided off from the grande salle by a balustrade in the central arch, but visible to the rest of the company dining in the grande salle. It was a successful visit, and was followed almost immediately by its owner's appointment as Surintendant of Finances (the position that was later to be held by Fouquet).

But it was the architect Louis Le Vau who really caught the attention of his contemporaries with the far more distinctive way in which he introduced the salon to three châteaux built for rich financiers: Le Raincy in 1643, Turny in 1645 and finally (when peace came after the disturbed years of the Fronde) Vaux-le-Vicomte in 1656. All three salons were the dominant central feature of their respective châteaux. All were placed to project on the central axis from the garden façade, all were oval in plan, rising through two storeys to a dome, and were as prominent

Its height and rich decoration caused the room at the end of the grande salle on the first floor of the château of Maisons to be one of the first spaces in France to be called a salon. It was divided from the grande salle by a screen and a balustrade, so that the king, when visiting, could eat in solitary splendour but visible to the others in the salle.

Ander Prosp. des Schlosses de Rincij gegen dem Garten

outside as in. They turned inside out the kind of grand architectural treatment which in France had been reserved for the exterior of châteaux, and applied it to the interior, so that the salon became the secular equivalent of a magnificent church or chapel.[3]

The exteriors of Le Raincy and Turny are known from engravings, but there are no known illustrations of their interiors. The salon at Vaux-le-Vicomte survives, and is the best known and the most splendid of the few remaining French salons à l'Italienne.[4] Unlike the salons at Le Raincy and Turny it does not run through the house from front to back, but is preceded by a square vestibule, richly decorated but only a single storey in height. This acts as a prelude to the noble scale and architecture of the salon. It is divided into two levels, corresponding to the two storeys of the rest of the house: an order of Corinthian pilasters below, and sculpted herms holding baskets of flowers on their heads above. The surfaces are carved ashlar, marble or glass; all is sonorously splendid and only the dome is plain; Fouquet had been arrested and disgraced before Charles Le Brun had been able to fill it with a fresco which would have carried the eye through a teeming circuit of gods, goddesses and cherubs to Apollo throned high above in majesty in his Palace of the Sun.

Apart from its architectural splendour, the salon at Vaux-le-Vicomte caught the imagination of contemporaries because of its central position and relationship to the garden. It finally dethroned the staircase from its traditional sixteenth-century position on the axis of the house. This had been acceptable, and even desirable, when there was no very close relationship between garden and house, as had been the situation in the sixteenth century by and large, elaborate though the gardens often were. But once the axis of house and garden was combined, it seemed wasteful to give the grand axial view through the garden to a staircase rather than a habitable room.

As early as the 1580s, at the prestigious little château of Wideville, the staircase was pushed to one side and the centre filled by a salle haute above a vaulted salle basse, and there was a similar arrangement on a grander scale at Grosbois in the early seventeenth century. At the châteaux of Plessis-Belleville and Balleroy, François

The long-demolished château of Le Raincy was a precursor of Vaux-le-Vicomte, and also designed by Le Vau. It had a similar arrangement of two-storey salon à l'Italienne under a central dome, but this was up on the first floor opening on to a balcony, not directly on to the garden.

Mansart doubled the thickness of his central pavillon, so as to be able to interpose a first-floor grande salle behind the staircase and vestibule on the garden front.[5] At Maisons the grand staircase is pushed to one side of a central vestibule, and the vista of the garden could be enjoyed from windows and a balcony at one end of the grande salle.

But Le Vau went much further. In a revolutionary move for France, he took the main rooms down to ground level, and opened his salon to the gardens. At Vaux-le-Vicomte (and probably at Le Raincy), the salon is emphatically a summer room. There was no fireplace, and originally no glazing in the openings of either the salon or the vestibule that led to it. The great height of the salon, its marble floor, the air flowing freely right through it, and the vestibule, kept it deliciously cool in summer. Above all, by opening without impediment into the garden it was visually linked with it, so that from inside it was possible to look freely out on to it and along its central vista, or walk straight out into the garden from the salon, by way of a terrace, a bridge over the moat and two great flights of steps. As the whole main floor of the house was raised above the low 'sous-sol' (basement) containing the kitchen and offices, the salon was just sufficiently above the level of the garden for it to be possible to appreciate from it the intricate pattern of the parterres, interspersed with fountains, that stretched away into the distance in front of it.

The result was so effective and impressive that other salons à l'Italienne inevitably followed at the grand new châteaux for the great people of the time of Louis XIV: at Sceaux for Colbert in 1673, at Clagny for Madame de Montespan in 1676, at Marly for Louis XIV himself in 1679, at Choisy for the Grande Mademoiselle in 1680. They were rectangular, oval, or octagonal; all were centrally placed, two storeys in height and architecturally splendid.

At the same time the term 'salon' began to appear in French glossaries and dictionaries. In 1673 Blondel called it 'a state room or chambre de parade for the reception of guests of sufficient importance. Especially grand meals are served in it, concerts are given in it, or card and games tables are set up in it, as the most important room in the appartement.' In 1684 it was defined in the *Dictionnaire de l'Académie Française* as follows: 'Room in an appartement which is much higher than the other rooms, and which is usually domed and enriched with architectural ornaments and painting.' In 1690 Daviler expanded on this:

A big room in the middle of a corps de logis, or at the head of a gallery, or in a grand appartement, which must be symmetrical on all its sides, and as it is two storeys high and has two rows of windows, the shape of its ceiling should be domed, as in Italian palaces. The fashion for salons came to us from Italy. There are square salons, as at Clagny, octagonal ones, as at Marly, and ones of other shapes.[6]

Clagny, Marly and their fellows have all disappeared. Perhaps the only survivor from this period, apart from Vaux-le-Vicomte itself, is a delightful oddity, the 'salon dorée' at the château de Bussy-Rabutin. In 1666 the quarrelsome, amorous, extravagant, on-and-off scandalous soldier and courtier Roger de Bussy-Rabutin, whose privately circulated satire on the love-affairs of the court ladies of the time, *Histoire Amoureuse des Gaules*, had caused a furore and who had fallen foul of Louis XIV, was released from the Bastille, where he had spent eighteen months, on the grounds of ill-health, and was sent in disgrace to live in his family château, debarred from Paris and the court. After 1672 he was occasionally allowed to make short visits to Paris, but basically he remained in exile for sixteen years. Like others similarly exiled, in France and elsewhere, Bussy-Rabutin consoled himself and kept himself occupied with the pleasures of architecture and decoration.[7] In fact he was financially in no position to rebuild the old-fashioned, in Parisian terms, château which had been originally erected in the early sixteenth century, and partly rebuilt by his father, but he fashioned himself a newly decorated appartement and gallery, and filled the rooms with paintings and painted decoration of devices, mythical scenes, cryptic visual satires on his mistress, portraits of historical characters and famous soldiers, and views of the royal houses and monuments in and around Paris, which he was no longer allowed to see, and the court beauties, whom he was no longer able to meet. And as best he could, with limited funds and provincial decorators, he kept himself in fashion and created a salon à l'Italienne that in fact antedates by a few years the examples quoted in the previous paragraph.

He started work on this immediately. In February 1667 he wrote to his friend Mademoiselle d'Armentières and described how 'I have made a salon, in which I plan to put the portraits of my good lady-friends', or – as he described it four years later – 'the appartement is terminated by a grand salon, where hang the court beauties who have given me their portraits'.[8]

Bussy-Rabutin created an appropriately circular and two-storeyed salon by joining together the first- and second-floor rooms in one of the sixteenth-century round towers of the château, at the south-west corner of the corps de logis. It was the right shape, if in the wrong place, and on the wrong floor, for a salon (where one would expect a cabinet, and indeed Bussy occasionally refers to it as a cabinet and not as a salon), but he did the best he could. The decoration is in three bands: the lowest contains mythological scenes, framed by Ionic pilasters; then come the court beauties, each with a long inscription beneath; and then an upper row, punctuated by carved and gilded consoles. The long windows let out on to balconies, and at least one gave access to a view of the gardens across the moat. There is much lavish gilding, hence the name 'salon dorée' that was later applied to this festive and idiosyncratic room.

Occasional salons à l'Italienne continued to be built in French châteaux or town houses all through the eighteenth century. Blondel illustrated a sumptuous design for one in his *Maisons de Plaisance* of 1737, and gave a similar definition of its use to that given by his namesake in 1673: 'one can eat there, if the entertainment is of sufficient consequence, or give balls and concerts there, or come there for refreshment on the return from a hunt'.[9]

The early-eighteenth-century La Chipaudière, on the edge of St Malo, is one of the houses known as Malouinières, because they were built as country residences by the rich merchants of St Malo. It is a scaled-down version of the Vaux-le-Vicomte formula, but the modest central salon is on the ground floor only, and served originally as a salon à manger for everyday meals.

But in fact two-storey salons were few and far between. In the changed circumstances of the eighteenth century châteaux had little need of such splendid rooms: they had become holiday houses or family houses rather than centres of power or magnificence. Blondel found it necessary to describe as a 'salon à l'Italienne' what in the previous century would have been immediately recognizable just as a 'salon', because the term was now being applied to other kinds of room as well – single-storey rooms considerably less imposing and expensive than the great two-storey salons, but still called salons because they were of distinctive geometric form, or given a rich architectural treatment, or placed in the centre of one of the main façades.

The last remained the commonest and most distinctive use of the term. Vaux-le-Vicomte and its two predecessors had shown how attractive such a room was when in the centre of the garden façade, with windows opening and giving views into the garden; it was without doubt the best position in the house, and it remained so even if the room was more modest in scale and decoration. The visual influence of Vaux-le-Vicomte remained; in the early eighteenth century the central projection and distinctive roof of a handsome château like that remodelled by Paul Poisson de Bourvallais at Champs-sur-Marne, or modest 'maisons de plaisance' like those built by Saint-Malo merchants at La Chipaudière and Le Bos, obviously derive from it, but in the last two houses, as in châteaux elsewhere literally by the hundred, the salon only filled the lower half of the projection.

The question remained, what should such a room be used for? Should it be for eating (as at La Chipaudière), or reception (as at Le Bos), or both?

The kind of social life that had been pioneered by the Précieuses in the mid seventeenth century, and was further developed by Parisian hostesses on into the eighteenth century, really called for a specialized type of room. The alcove or the ruelle was well-adapted for more intimate gatherings, but limited in the number of

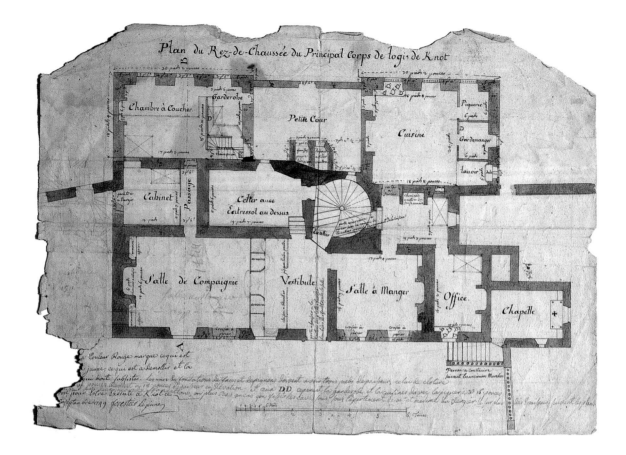

Plan du Rez-de-Chaussée du Principal Corps de logis de Knot

people it could accommodate. A traditional sixteenth- or early-seventeenth-century salle was too big, even the bigger cabinets rather too small for this kind of socializing. In fact, most of the entertaining at the Hôtel de Rambouillet seems to have taken place in the grande Chambre Bleu, rather than in the salle, the cabinet or the chambre à l'alcove. The Chambre Bleu had been Madame de Rambouillet's original bedroom, but by the time of the inventory of 1652 the bed had been removed from it. It was becoming what would later have been called a salon.[10]

This use of the word was still in the future, however, and to begin with awareness of the need for a specialist room for social gatherings produced either a smaller salle or a bigger cabinet. These were usually called a 'salle de compagnie' or 'cabinet de compagnie', though the terms 'cabinet de conversation' and 'salle d'assemblée' were also used. Salle d'assemblée seems to have been used for a room rather more richly furnished and prestigious than a salle de compagnie, but the distinction between them is not a clear one.

These rooms were likely to have been furnished with plenty of sofas and chairs, at least one mirror over the chimney-piece, tables for cards and games, often musical instruments, and whatever extras in the way of marble-topped wall tables, clocks, pictures, porcelain and tapestry suited the tastes and purse of the owners. The richly upholstered chairs and sofas required for a desirable salle or cabinet de compagnie were liable to be stained or damaged in a room used for eating and drinking, and a specialized room for meals became inevitable. At first, though, there

A plan of 1749 for alterations to the ground floor of the early-sixteenth-century château of Kernault (above) is a typical example of an eighteenth-century conversion. The grande salle, formerly serving both for receptions and eating, has been cut up into a vestibule and a salle de compagnie for receptions, and the former kitchen has become a salle à manger. Original house is shown in purple.

were two alternative possibilities for this: the antechambre of an appartement could be used for eating, or there could be a separate salle à manger outside the appartement system. Gradually, however, the salle à manger became the norm, antechambres were only used as washing rooms, and houses in the country, or smaller houses in Paris, often did without them.

How things were going is nicely shown in the plans drawn up in 1749 by the Parisian architect Forestier Le Jeune for modernizing the sixteenth-century manoir of Kernault in Brittany.[11] The former salle basse was subdivided into a small entrance vestibule leading to a salle de compagnie; the adjacent kitchen was converted into a salle à manger, and a new kitchen built on at the back; the salle haute, on the first floor above the salle basse, was divided into two chambres and a cabinet. The old double function of a salle, for reception and eating, had in fact been divided in two.

The contemporary plans of the ground and first floors of the château of Champs-sur-Marne (right) show the arrangement of a grand château of the early eighteenth century. The salon à l'Italienne was going out of fashion, and instead there were two salons, one above the other, the upper one probably for grand events and the lower one a salon de compagnie, opening on to the garden.

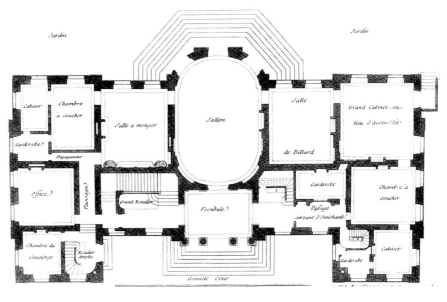

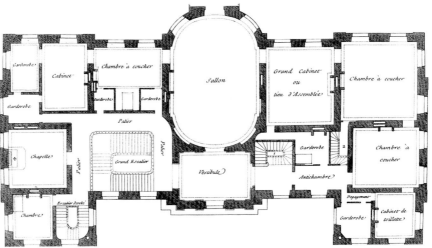

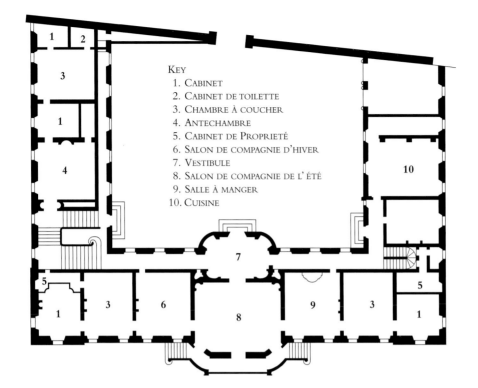

KEY
1. CABINET
2. CABINET DE TOILETTE
3. CHAMBRE À COUCHER
4. ANTECHAMBRE
5. CABINET DE PROPRIETÉ
6. SALON DE COMPAGNIE D'HIVER
7. VESTIBULE
8. SALON DE COMPAGNIE DE L'ÉTÉ
9. SALLE À MANGER
10. CUISINE

On the plan (left) of the ground floor of the château of Merville, the rooms are named as in an inventory of 1771. The rooms in the wing to the left formed a separate apartment for the owner.

Well into the middle of the eighteenth century the desirable centre position on the garden front was more often occupied by a room for eating, and was accordingly called a 'salon à manger'. But in 1743 Briseux, in his *Maisons de Campagne*, suggested that what he called the 'cabinet d'assemblée' should be put there,

> especially in houses in the country, where one puts the cabinet d'assemblée in the best position and the one best calculated to have agreeable views …
> As it is the main room, and the one most used, it needs to be bigger than the other rooms, and one must take care to place it well. A salon in the middle of the building is the perfect answer: from there the whole beauty of the garden is on display; and if the building is only one room thick, one gets the combination of a view of the entrance court and delicate views on all sides into the garden.[12]

The numerous cases in which his advice was followed or anticipated include the château of Merville near Toulouse, built by the Marquis de Chalvet-Rochmonteix in about 1750, and, at the other end of France, at Bagatelle, a 'maison de plaisance' on the edge of Abbeville, built in 1751–4 by Abraham von Robais, whose grandfather had been brought to Abbeville from Holland by Colbert in 1665 to establish a textile industry. In both cases the uses and names of the rooms are known from inventories. At Merville the central room is a summer 'salon de compagnie d'été', with a smaller 'salon de compagnie d'hiver' adjoining it, on one side, and a salle à manger on the other. The room above the main salon became a very agreeable library.[13]

At Bagatelle the centre contains a circular salon d'été between a rectangular salon d'hiver and a salle à manger. The miniature central salon, all rococo curves and delicious views to adjoining rooms and the garden, is a long remove from the magnificent rotunda at Vaux-le-Vicomte, but one led to the other, and the contrast between the two epitomizes the way the salon had changed and developed in a hundred years.[14]

In the second half of the eighteenth century this use of the central position became the commonest one, until gradually the term 'salon de compagnie' and finally just 'salon' began to be used for such a room, whether it was in

The salon de compagnie de l'été at Merville (below) is a relatively modest and charming principal living room opening on to the garden. The central room (above) on the first floor has always been a library.

a central position or not. The situation remained a fluid one for several decades; it was not until the nineteenth century that a room used for eating was always called a salle à manger, and a company room always called a salon.

The fact that, in effect, the company room pushed out the eating room, and took over both the best position and the most prestigious name underlined the fact that it had become the most important room in the château, and the focus of the life that was lived in it. It was, as Briseux had put it, 'the main room and the one most used'. This was the major development of the eighteenth century in France. For

The exterior of Bagatelle (left) shows how the Vaux-le-Vicomte formula was scaled down in the early eighteenth century for a modest but delightful château or maison de plaisance with a single-storey summer salon de compagnie opening on to the garden in the centre (below), and a smaller winter salon to one side.

The salle à manger of the château of Villette (right) possesses what became the standard fittings of an early- or mid-eighteenth-century salle à manger, at the time still sometimes called a salon à manger: a marble basin for washing hands and glasses, and a marble buffet for the display of plate.

centuries the most prestigious activity in both town and country houses in France, as in the rest of Europe, had been the serving of a sumptuous meal in magnificent surroundings. Now this was no longer the case. It had been overtaken by social life in a salon, the life of conversation, games and music, centring round pretty women in a room of great elegance, filled with, by the standards of what had gone before, comfortable and richly appointed chairs and sofas, the walls lined with pictures and mirrors, the glazed doors opening on to the garden. Far more time was spent in the salle de compagnie than in the salle à manger by both sexes; the English habit of the men staying on in the dining-room to drink and get drunk together never obtained in France, and was regarded as the height of barbarism or incivility. The whole company went together from the salon to eat in the salle à manger, and without

lingering for any great time over the meal, the whole company went back to the salon together afterwards. A salle à manger had to be spacious and handsome; it frequently had the feature of a marble buffet with shelves for the display of plate on special occasions, and a bowl for the washing of hands and dishes; in the second half of the eighteenth century it was often warmed by a porcelain stove, inspired by German examples, and these could be a handsome feature; but its contents, as is made clear by inventory after inventory, were always far less valuable than the contents of the salon.

For most people 'salon' means a social event as well as a room, a meeting together for often brilliant conversation of a circle of people presided over by a hostess. In this sense the salons of eighteenth-century Paris are famous, and innumerable books and articles have been written about them. It is worth remarking that in the eighteenth century this type of gathering was not referred to as a salon, and until the end of the century often did not take place in a room called a salon. Nobody at the time said 'I am going to Madame Du Deffand's salon this evening', or 'Madame Du Deffand is holding her salon today'. There was, apart from anything else, no room called a salon in her appartement in the Couvent de Saint-Joseph, large though this was, as is known from the inventory made of its contents in 1780.[15] The meetings which became so famous took place over meals in her salle à manger, and gatherings after or before the meal in her chambre.

In the eighteenth century what came to be called a salon was called, if anything, a 'société'. The custom of a particular woman being at home to the circle of her friends on a certain day had been started, as we have seen, by Mademoiselle de Scu-déry and others in the mid seventeenth century, and in their time the particular set which came to a 'jour' was sometimes called a 'cabale'. The practice continued, and became much commoner, into the eighteenth century, when every Parisian lady of any pretensions had her jour, and her own particular 'société', or circle of friends who came to it. Such sociétés could have a wide variety of characteristics: they could be gay, grand, fast, artistic, intellectual, political, or a mixture of all these qualities. It was these sociétés, and the jours which they attended, which had a particularly strong element of intellect or wit that came to be looked back on and written about as 'salons' in the nineteenth century, when such gatherings still went on, and were actually called salons. At the time Voltaire referred to them as 'those sociétés invariably presided over by some woman who offsets the decline of her beauty with the shining dawn of her intellect'. According to Madame de Genlis, writing in 1818, they were sometimes uncharitably referred to as 'bureaux de l'esprit' (intellect agencies).[16]

A hostess who had a jour usually offered a meal at it, either a large dinner or a smaller supper, where the company was often gayer and more intimate, and after the meal the guests reassembled in whatever the company room was called. From about 1770 onwards it was, in fact, increasingly called a salon; and the prestige and enjoyable nature of these post-prandial gatherings, and the frequently brilliant and expensive decoration of the room in which they were held, helped consolidate the supremacy of the salon in the country as well as the town.

From the mid eighteenth century it became increasingly common to warm the salle à manger with a stove rather than an open fireplace. The magnificent stove in the château of La Grange in eastern France is clearly influenced by German examples.

6
IN AND AROUND THE BOUDOIR

The late-eighteenth-
century boudoir at the
château of Moncley
epitomizes the intimate
elegance of these stylish
little rooms. A sofa in
an alcove, often lined
with looking-glass, was
a common feature.

IN 1820 THE IRISH NOVELIST Maria Edgeworth was on
holiday in France, and spent a few nights at the château de
La Celle, which had belonged to Madame de Pompadour.
She was intrigued to be put up in Madame de Pompadour's own
appartement, and wrote to her mother to describe it. She liked
the actual bedroom: 'high, comfortable, but not large … about
twenty feet square … with three very large mirrors', and its view

through two big windows, opening within a foot of the
ground into a large and beautiful old-fashioned shrubbery
garden with low rose acacias and rhododendrons in profuse
flower – the garden surrounded by lime trees thick and high –
but at the bottom arches are cut through the foliage and the
stems left so as to form rows of pillars through which you see
on one side fine views of lawn and distant country and on the
other the lime-grove is continued in arcades eight or nine trees
deep – well gravelled underneath – a miniature champs élysées.

But what really caught her fancy were the little rooms clustered around the main bedchamber. She described them at some length.

> The folding doors opposite to the folding doors of entrance into this bedchamber open into a pretty little dressing room and that into a pretty little cabinet about the size of that in which Lucy now sleeps – low sofas in tent stitch – painted wainscotting – in flowers and fruits and odd devices – large window and glass door opening to garden – to each room boudoir dressing room and bedchamber especially there are exquisitely contrived private exits and little dens of closets and antechambres which must have seen many strange exits and entrances in their day – and in their nights. In one of these small rooms our Adolphe now sleeps. Another which is our washing closet about ten foot by six – was I am sure Madame de Pompadours favourite retreat. The white wainscoat now very yellow is painted with grey imitation of Indian ink pictures of monkeys in mens and womens clothes in groups in compartments – the most grotesque figures you can imagine. I have traced for Lucy's diversion two of the best. Many of them are not only grotesque but dirty – for instance monkeys in old men and old womens clothes administering and receiving clysters … I have some notion of having somewhere read of this cabinet of monkeys and of having heard that the principle monkey who figures in it was some real person.[1]

Maria Edgeworth clearly got a frisson from imagining what she would have considered French goings-on in little rooms of this type, at La Celle and elsewhere. But so, for that matter, did the French. As L.-S. Mercier put it, in his *Tableaux de Paris* (1781–9),

> Our ancestors, who only knew how to build long rectangular salles, would have been amazed. Our suites of little rooms are shaped and put together like round polished snail-shells, and what used to be neglected dark awkward spaces now provide charming, well-lit accommodation. Two hundred years ago no one could have visualized the hidden secret stairs, the little unsuspected cabinets, the false doors which conceal the true exits, the floors which can be made to rise and fall, and the labyrinths in which one can hide and put off inquisitive servants while indulging one's tastes – a way out (opening into the garderobe of the next-door house) hidden from

The nature of the nests of smaller rooms attached to a bigger chambre which are one of the most attractive features of eighteenth-century châteaux is vividly suggested in these two paintings in one of the cabinets at the château of Chantilly.

everyone, except those in the know, but designed to foster the mysteries of love, and sometimes those of politics.[2]

Madame de Genlis commented,

Our forebears themselves had only three or four rooms in all besides their fine salons, antechambers and dining-rooms … today there is an infinite multiplication of rooms, cabinets, above all back exits and secret stairs. Appartements are planned so that all ways of access can be sealed off at will, independence secured as a result, and the surprising discovery of secrets made impossible. One might have thought that the architects were in the know about every family disagreement and every intrigue – or at least, if they were not, they could anticipate them.[3]

There is nothing quite like these carefully contrived clusters of little rooms in English eighteenth-century houses – or, in the rare cases where they occur, they are copied from France. In France they were only perfected in the middle of the century, as a combined result of refinements in planning and a change in attitude: the development of the entresol and the backstairs, on the one hand, and the change of attitude epitomized by the transformation of the cabinet into the 'cabinet de toilette' or the 'cabinet avec niche', colloquially known as the 'boudoir'.

For a chambre to be supported by a smaller cabinet and garderobe had been a common arrangement since at least the mid sixteenth century. In the sixteenth and seventeenth centuries all three rooms were normally of the same height. But if, where the floor-to-ceiling height was around 4.5 metres, an additional floor was inserted, then in the smaller spaces four low rooms could be obtained instead of two high ones. A little staircase was clearly needed to give access to the upper level, or entresol, as it became known, and this arrangement could be expanded into a system, with entresols on every floor at one end, or along one side, and backstairs running all the way up the house. Such back or secret stairs – what the French called 'escaliers dérobés' – had existed and been so named since the later Middle Ages, and feature frequently in romances as useful routes for intrigues, especially if they opened at the bottom into a garden; but they had not been arranged in a systematic way.

The entresol system had been anticipated in the hunting-lodge built by François I at La Muette in about 1540. This had three storeys of high rooms in the centre, corresponding to six storeys of low rooms in the four corner towers.[4] For a long time such a systematic provision remained unique, but occasional entresol rooms were to be found in châteaux of the later sixteenth and early seventeenth centuries, even if they were not specifically described as such. In 1623 François Mansart, for instance, provided a couple over the garderobe and another little room letting off the main chambre of the château of Berny.[5] The actual term 'entresol' appears in the 1661 inventory of Vaux-le-Vicomte, to describe two sets of little rooms in the north-west and north-east corners of the château; one of them contained seven beds for footmen.[6]

But it was not until the eighteenth century that the entresol system became a widespread feature. However useful backstairs and back entrances may have been for intrigues, this was certainly not the main raison d'être of the system, nor, as is sometimes stated, were entresol rooms mainly used as bedrooms for servants, although this was certainly one of their uses. The main advantage and attraction of the arrangement was that it was flexible, and could be put to all kinds of uses. Entresols and the rooms under them could provide studies, oratories, small libraries, storage rooms for clothes or documents, bedrooms for servants, 'garderobes de propriété' for chamberpots and close-stools, or be made into snug, self-contained 'petits appartements' which could accommodate children, tutors, governesses, and the less important guests, or be moved into by the owner or his wife in cold weather.

Entresols were practical, but also had aesthetic charms; the sequence of little spaces which they produced was in keeping with the taste of the mid eighteenth century for the ingenious and intimate. In 1754 the architect Pierre Patte attacked his contemporaries for their inability to think big; instead of grand suites of rooms in palaces, he complained that they were reduced 'to gracefully arranging petits appartements, and devising carved decorations for a salle de compagnie or a cabinet'.[7] This was true enough, but in terms of creative achievement the result was far from despicable. Above all, it was exceedingly enjoyable.

A typical arrangement was for a bedroom to open into a low-level cabinet or cabinet de toilette and garderobe de propriété, with a servant's room and a garderobe for clothes on the entresol above it. A cabinet de toilette was the result of moving the 'toilette' (the dressing-table) from the bedroom to the cabinet, and changing its nature in the process, from a room concerned with study, for intense and secret imaginings, to a room in which to make oneself desirable. 'Cabinets de toilette' were, in fact, often unpretentious little rooms, containing little except a chair and dressing-table. But sometimes they were expanded, prettily decorated, and made into attractive small rooms, occasionally including a little bed in an alcove. It must have been in a cabinet de toilette of this type that Laclos made Madame de Merteuil receive an admirer in *Les Liaisons Dangereuses* (1782), but made sure her maid was in the adjacent chambre in case he gave trouble.[8] Some of Boucher's paintings, or

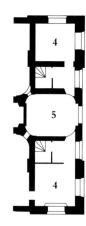

Entresol arrangements (above) as found at one end of a château of the 1770s.

KEY
1. CHAMBRE
2. CABINET DE TOILETTE
3. CHAPELLE
4. ENTRESOL
5. UPPER HALF OF CHAPELLE

At the château of Parentignat two low-ceilinged rooms, linked by a small staircase, are attached to a chambre of the same height as the two together, in the usual mid-eighteenth-century manner. In 1793 the chambre belonged to the owner of the château, the Marquis de Lastic, the lower of the two rooms (below, right) served as his study and the room above was the chambre of his young son.

the innumerable frivolous and mildly erotic engravings of Moreau le Jeune and others, suggest the setting of a cabinet de toilette rather than a chambre.

In 1764 Mademoiselle de Malboissière, staying at the château de Bourdonné, wrote with enthusiasm to a friend that

> my cabinet de toilette is delicious. It has two small windows, one of which faces north and looks on to the widest stretch of the moat and a charming landscape. It is upholstered with blue and white calico and has a fireplace and a little mirror; Mademoiselle Jaillié sleeps in it.[9]

White calico sprinkled with red flowers upholstered the chair and two armed chairs in the principal cabinet de toilette at the château of Le Marais in 1783, and in addition to a prettily fitted-up mahogany dressing-table the room contained a secrétaire, a writing-table and two cupboards built into the panelling. In the adjacent small garderobe (clearly what was sometimes called a garderobe de propriété) was a bidet covered in red leather, and a wash-basin and chamberpot.[10]

An alternative, or sometimes an accompaniment to a cabinet de toilette was a 'cabinet avec niche', or boudoir, a little personal sitting-room, with no dressing-table, but usually with a writing-table, a few chairs, and a sofa in a niche. The cabinet was still considered a place for day-dreaming, for letting the imagination run free, and the decoration of a cabinet of this type could express this; as the architect Jacques François Blondel put it in 1735,

Boucher's picture of a lady attaching her garter is redolent of the gentle sensuality associated with boudoirs and cabinets de toilette of the period.

nothing should be neglected to ensure that its decoration is gay and playful. It is here that imagination can take flight and abandon itself to the liveliest fancies, while in formal appartements the strictest rules of decorum and good taste should be rigidly adhered to.[11]

But the nature of the imaginings was changing: they were less intense, more frivolous, not to say straightforwardly erotic. Crébillon fils, in his novel *Le Sopha* (1742), which describes the history of a soul forced to transmigrate into sofas in various situations, had fun with the double nature of a cabinet, in which his sofa was installed. Its owner professes that it is for religious reading and serious reflection, but the way in which the sofa is upholstered (pink, with silver trimmings) and the voluptuous way in which its mistress tries it out, makes the sofa realize that 'she did not intend just to use me as a show piece'. He soon discovers that she has two lots of books, religious books on the open shelves, and love stories in a secret cupboard. The episode ends when her husband discovers her making love to a priest on the sofa.[12]

A cabinet with a sofa, or a similar piece of furniture, as its focal feature, usually placed in a recess and that recess often lined with looking-glass, came to be known as a 'boudoir' – a room to sulk in. The term suggests its potential use as an instrument of sexual warfare or politics, and from the start, the boudoir had erotic connotations. One of its earliest recorded appearances is in 1727, when Mercier de Compiègne published *Manuel des boudoirs, ou Essais érotiques sur les demoiselles d'Athènes* in four volumes.[13] Thereafter, the same note was sounded in literature, in real life, and also in themes of decoration.

Boudoirs were not necessarily for women. In the mid eighteenth century Madame de Pompadour's brother the Marquis de Marigny specified that his boudoir should be 'very small, very warm', and decorated only with paintings of nudes.[14] In the late 1770s the boudoir of Louis XVI's brother the Comte d'Artois at his exquisite little château de Bagatelle was described by the writer Louis Petit de Bachaumont as 'displaying every variety of voluptuous painting by our modern masters, Greuze, Fragonard, Lagrenée etc.... A rose-coloured bed, and mirrors all round, to reduplicate the attitudes of the lovers.'[15]

Jean-François Bastide's novel *La Petite Maison*, published in 1752, is concerned with the seduction of the courtesan Mélite by the Marquis de Trémicourt at his voluptuous 'little house' on the banks of the Seine. This is described in such detail as to suggest that it is based on an actual house, or possibly an amalgamation of several houses, for its erotic equipment: no fewer than two boudoirs, an elaborately decorated cabinet de toilette, painted by Boucher with scenes of lovers, and a bathroom equipped with bed as well as bath – this seems almost too lavish for a real life 'little house', however luxurious.[16] The first boudoir had walls covered with looking-glass, with the joins between the sections hidden by artificial trees covered with flowers, with candles on their branches; in the alcove was a green and gold 'ottoman', and the paint throughout had been devised by its painter, Dandrillon, to exude the scent of jasmine, violet and roses (Dandrillon was a real-life decorator and sculptor who had perfected such a process). The final seduction took place in the second boudoir, which was hung with dark green silk, filled with sofas, day-beds and chaises-longues, and had just enough light to see the erotic engravings by the best masters which hung on the walls.

The Parisian courtesans, or actresses supported by rich nobles or financiers, were renowned for their boudoirs. J.-H. Bonardi du Mesnil describes how, as a boy of sixteen or seventeen from a modest Normandy château, he was bowled over by the boudoir of 'a girl of good background, very well educated and kept in splendour by a friend of my father, one of the richest financiers and wittiest men in Paris'. In the boudoir,

> walls, ceiling, alcove were all made of nothing but mirrors, except for some garlands of flowers which held them together and were themselves supported by cupids. It was a real fairy-land. I felt I was seeing the goddess of love in her sanctuary. I was at first stupefied, and then intoxicated.[17]

Poems backed up the reputation of the boudoir. It was contrasted, in its favour, with the salon de compagnie:

> All your salons de compagnie
> Honestly can't hold a candle
> To our informal boudoirs
> Where we enjoy our sweet diversions.[18]

The change of behaviour from one to the other was underlined:

> Women's expressions
> Are completely under control
> With a decency in the social circle
> Which they abandon in their boudoirs.[19]

And Sylvain Maréchal, in his 'Scheme for the house of a friendly philosopher', planned to have

> A little cellar for my wine
> Below the boudoir.
> In a well-arranged house it is necessary
> For Venus to be close to Bacchus.[20]

These attitudes were summed up by N. Le Camus de Mezières, in his *The Spirit of Architecture, and its analogy with our sensations* (1780): 'The boudoir is seen as the shrine of sensual pleasure ... Such a delectable retreat should only arouse gentle emotions, and bring peace to the spirit and pleasure to all the senses.'[21]

Madame de Genlis, looking back in 1818, when 'boudoir' had become a standard expression, commented that 'what grumpy and carping old survivors of the Ancien Régime find especially shocking is to hear women calling their cabinets "boudoirs"; for this bizarre word was formerly only used for the cabinets of courtesans'.[22]

But one can wonder whether Madame de Genlis's old gentlemen were as shocked as she claimed to be herself; she was always trying to live down her youth as the mistress of the Duc d'Orléans, and had become excessively straight-laced as a result. In fact, 'boudoir' occurs regularly throughout the eighteenth century in respectable contexts, as well as erotic ones. The Prince de Croy had two at his town house at Condé in 1745, and the inventory suggests that they were little more than studies.[23] In 1768 Dumont showed one in the master suite of what appears to be a family house at Versailles; it adjoined the two-bedded room of 'the young ladies'.[24] In about 1778 Victor Louis included one in an unexecuted design for the château of Argent-sur-Sauldre, where the client was Nicolas de Dupré de Saint-Maur, Intendant of the Généralité of Bourges.[25] In the 1780s one finds the 'boudoir de Madame' in the château de Caillé in Brittany,[26] and an oval boudoir next to the 'chambre de Madame' in Chaussard's plans for the château de l'Hermitage, made in 1784.[27] In the survey plans of the château of Chantilly, drawn up in 1785, there are three tiny boudoirs shown, two for the Duc and Duchesse de Bourbon, adjacent to each other in their joint suite in the Petit Château, and one for 'Mademoiselle', the daughter of Louis XVI, in the main building;[28] those in the Petit Château date from a remodelling of its interiors in about 1730, though they may not have been called boudoirs from the start. In an inventory of 1791 two boudoirs are listed in the Marquis de Lastic's château de Parentignat, one belonging to the Marquise, which has disappeared, and one attached to the best appartement, which is still there, though largely redecorated.[29]

Antoine Caillot, when describing the sumptuous Parisian boudoir of the actress Annette d'Hervieux in 1788 (where she entertained 'a seigneur of the highest rank', and the two lovers could watch 'their voluptuous embraces reflected in all their variations' in the mirrors which lined it), commented that 'Mademoiselle Dervieux and nymphs at other theatres set the boudoir-style for young women of quality or in the upper ranks of the bourgeoisie'.[30] Courtesans in France, unlike those in England, had a recognized position, and set fashions which modish young-marrieds were happy to copy, the term 'boudoir' and all.

However, for those with reservations the alternative name of 'cabinet avec niche' or just 'cabinet' could be, and often was, used for a room of identical type and decoration, such as the prettily-decorated cabinet avec niche in the dauphine's appartement at Versailles, which the Duc de Luynes saw and described in 1747.[31] Twenty or so years later the cabinet avec niche decorated in 1781 for Marie-Antoinette at Versailles was, and still is, as mirror-lined and voluptuous as any courtesan could have wished for.

But whatever they were called, and however they were decorated, these prettily decorated, playful and intimate private sitting-rooms were obviously desirable, and there is no need to explain their popularity. Many vanished examples are listed in inventories, and an idea of their quality can be gained from the description of their contents; one can but regret the disappearance of the Marquis de Lastic's boudoir at Parentignat, as described in 1791: crimson silk embroideries framed in grey on the wall, sofa, chairs and stools all in matching crimson and grey, marble-topped tables of mahogany and ormolu, and porcelain-and-ormolu vases and candlesticks reflected in the mirror over the chimney-piece.[32] A good many others survive, or survived until recently, none more delicious than the little boudoir at the château de Millement, dismantled only a few years ago: everyone's dream of a Louis Quinze boudoir, all swirls and curls and pink and white and gold, and festoons and swags, and endlessly reflecting mirrors. The boudoir of the 1780s in the château de Moncley is, in contrast, coolly neoclassical, but just as desirable in its own way, with its painted arabesques, looped curtains, and spindly chairs and tables as elegant as the ladies who once sat on them.

But it would be a mistake to see boudoirs in isolation. They were always part of an appartement, which was decorated throughout with consistent prettiness or elegance: the main bedroom, in which the bed was often framed in an alcove between closets, and there might be a pair of turtle-doves carved above the archway, to celebrate the love-making of a royal mistress as at Madame de Pompadour's Champs, or of a newly married couple, as at the château of Lantilly; the boudoir or cabinet avec niche itself; the cabinet de toilette, which if there was a boudoir was usually a small and relatively simple room, but if there was none, could be larger and more

The boudoir of c. 1750 in the château of Millement (right) was perhaps the most evocative of Louis Quinze boudoirs until it was unfortunately dismantled in recent years.

Two turtle-doves often feature in the decoration over the bed alcove in eighteenth-century chambres. This example (left) at the château of Champs-sur-Marne is in the room once occupied by Madame de Pompadour.

At the château of
Haroué the corner towers
were made use of to pro-
vide cabinets attached to
chambres. The one in the
south-west tower (left),
decorated with arabesques
in the Chinese style,
is one of the most perfect
of smaller French
eighteenth-century
interiors.

At the château of
Parentignat a bed alcove
of c. 1750, with
entrance lobby and
cabinet to either side
(below), repeats with
Louis Quinze gaiety
the formula evolved
in the seventeenth
century.

richly furnished; sometimes a salle or 'cabinet de bain', though this, supposing there was one, was more usually in the basement or in a separate building in the garden; and in addition, whatever there was in the entresol, if one there was, perhaps including what the Parentignat inventory calls a 'garderobe chambre à coucher', a spare bedroom suitable for a friend or a child, with a small bed in a niche (though a room of this nature was sometimes on the same level as the main bedroom).

Unlike eighteenth-century country houses in England, where the bedrooms of the owners were almost invariably on the first floor, the favoured position for them in France was on the ground floor with french windows opening into the garden, sometimes their own little private garden. At the château of Ansouis an appartement opening on to its garden and the bonus of a superb view were combined in an unusual way. Ansouis was the ancient seat of the Sabran family: a proud château on a lofty hilltop remodelled as a Baroque palazzo in the early seventeenth century. In 1698 the château was sold to Jean-Baptiste de Villeneuve, whose son had married the daughter and heiress of the last Sabran of the senior line. The Villeneuves were a new robe family. In about 1750 the Villeneuve of the day, Louis-Elzéar, a counsellor in the Paris Parlement, remodelled the top floor of the château to make

At the château of Ansouis an octagonal chambre opening on to a garden with bed alcove, a boudoir (above), and nests of smaller rooms, were installed on the second floor for the wife of the owner in about 1760, as shown on the plan (far right). Stucco panels in the chambre (right) depict her with her children.

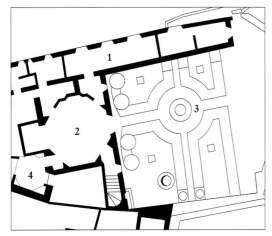

The terrace garden at Ansouis (right) is linked to the chambre through its french windows and has a superb view over the surrounding country-side.

KEY
1. BOUDOIR
2. CHAMBRE
3. JARDIN
4. CABINET DE
    TOILETTE

an up-to-date appartement for himself and his wife (or perhaps just for his wife). He formed a little roof-garden, prettily laid out with box hedges and statues of children, and with a panoramic bird's-eye view over many miles of rolling Provençal countryside; a well in one corner dropped three storeys through the château to a huge rain-water cistern in the basement. Round the garden were grouped an octagonal chambre opening on to the garden, with an alcove for a bed, looking straight out into a long boudoir or cabinet, proportioned more like a small gallery, with a niche for a sofa at one end, a smaller octagonal cabinet de toilette and a selection of closets. There was no entresol. All the rooms were decorated with delicate rococo plasterwork framing low-relief panels depicting a variety of subjects: scenes of the four seasons in the boudoir, of children being washed in the cabinet de toilette, and of daily incidents in the life of Madame de Villeneuve in the bedroom. All are charming, but perhaps the most delightful is the one captioned 'Solicitation maternelle', which shows her seated at a table teaching her child in a miniature version of her own chambre, complete with a bed in the alcove, a window, and a shelf of books. All in all, this hidden paradise up in the skies is one of the most delectable of the many delectable appartements in eighteenth-century châteaux.[33]

LA GARCONIÈRE
A
MESSIRE
HENRY AUGUSTE
DE CHALVET ROCHEMONTEIX,
GRAND SENECHAL
GOUVERNEUR DE LA VILLE DE TOULOUSE
ET PAYS D'ALBIGEOIS,
MARQUIS DE MERVILLE,
SEIGNEUR DE GAUJOUZE,
&c.

7

WERE THEY EVER THERE?

MADAME DE GENLIS'S NOVEL *Les Veillées du Château*, published in 1784, starts with the departure of the Clémire family from their house in Paris to their château in the depths of Burgundy. They have not visited it for many years, but Monsieur de Clémire has just been given command of a regiment and the expense involved in this has driven his family to Burgundy, in his absence, to economize. So Madame de Clémire, her three young children, her mother Baronne Delby, and her son's tutor, the Abbé Fremont, prepare to set out for the country, along with part of their household, including Madame de Clémire's maid, Mademoiselle Victoire, and the children's nanny, Mademoiselle Julienne. Madame de Clémire bravely accepts the necessity of this drastic step because of her love for her husband. Not so her servants. 'The house,' writes Madame de Genlis, 'was all filled with noise, bustle and dismay … the servants who were going and those who were staying behind were equally dissatisfied.'

Mademoiselle Victoire, one of Madame de Clémire's maids, unburdens herself to Monsieur Dorel, the maître d'hôtel, as she gloomily does the packing:

> It's crazy to go and shut oneself up in an old château which has never been lived in, and to leave in the middle of winter instead of remaining in Paris, where at least Madame can enjoy herself! how can three children, the eldest of whom is nine and a half, fail to be exhausted by the journey ... To go hundreds of kilometres in January!... Is it really necessary to turn oneself into a hermit, and run off to the end of the earth, just because a husband is leaving to join the army!

Monsieur Dorel was equally upset to be staying in Paris and separated from Mademoiselle Victoire. Caroline and Pulchérie, the two daughters of Madame de Clémire, had to listen to similar complaints from their nanny, Mademoiselle Julienne, who could not conceal her bad humour; she had never left Paris, and had an invincible horror of the provinces. After several days' journey, the unhappy party arrive at

> an old dilapidated château surrounded by water and made even more grim and rustic than usual by frost, snow and all the rigours of the time of year. The children were especially struck by the crude simplicity of the furniture.

The gaiety of al fresco life in a château in the hot French summers of the mid eighteenth century is suggested in this picture by an unknown artist. The château in the background has not been identified, and it is possible that the picture illustrates a theme rather than an actual gathering.

'Why are there only black leather chairs and armchairs in the salon,' asked Caroline … 'What big chimney-pieces… What little window panes.'

All the doors and windows are badly fitting, and the abbé starts a cold on the first day.

The novel reinforces a picture widely believed by the English, and indeed by the French: that in the seventeenth and eighteenth centuries the French noblesse deserted their châteaux and, unlike their country-loving English counterparts, spent all their time lounging around Versailles, or living it up in Paris. Was this true?

This kind of viewpoint is almost impossible to quantify, without a great deal more detailed research than has so far been carried out. It is not difficult to find examples of châteaux deserted, or largely deserted, by their owners, and other examples of châteaux inhabited by them; the impossible question to answer is one of proportion.

Without statistical backing one is left with one's own necessarily subjective impressions and contemporary comments which can contradict each other, as is the case, for instance, with Arthur Young in his *Travels in France* (1792), and Madame de Genlis writing at almost exactly the same time in *Les Veillées du Château*.

In September 1787 Arthur Young commented that

the present fashion in France, of passing some time in the country, is new… Everybody that have country seats are at them; and those who have none visit others who have. This remarkable revolution in the French manner is certainly one of the best customs they have taken from England; and its introduction was effected the easier, being assisted by the magic of Rousseau's writings.[1]

But in *Les Veillées du Château*, Madame de Genlis, at almost exactly the same time, says almost exactly the opposite. She presents château life as something that flourished forty or fifty years earlier, and had since fallen into disuse. She makes the children's grandmother, the baronne, say to her dismissive little Parisian grandchildren:

My children, when I was young, we happily spent eight months of the year in châteaux like this one. There was much more real fun to be had in them than in those little houses which you have visited in the surroundings of Paris: dazzling dwellings, which provide neither pleasure nor freedom, and where health and fortune are equally at risk.[2]

One can say with some confidence that the popular view is grossly over-simplified, as regards both France and England. There was no shortage, all through both centuries, of English families who quite happily abandoned their country houses, sometimes for years at a time, and of French families who regularly resided in their châteaux for substantial periods. There is straightforward architectural evidence for

this in the number of châteaux that were new-built, rebuilt or substantially remodelled in the period; families were not going to embark on the expense involved for
buildings which they had no intention of using. But here again there has been no
analysis of the thousands of French châteaux in order to get an overall picture of
which decades were especially prolific, or lacking, in new work.

It is, of course, a ridiculous over-simplification to talk of 'the French noblesse'.
There were different patterns for different groups within it. The robe families, in
both Paris and the provinces, usually owned châteaux, on the whole of moderate
size, within convenient distance of the parlement or other nobility-conferring court
to which they belonged. When the courts were in session they lived in their hôtels
in the relevant town, but in the summer, Easter and Christmas recesses they went
off to their châteaux.

The grand court families inevitably spent much time at Versailles, they usually
owned an hôtel in Paris as well, and a string of châteaux, some more important than
others, which could be several hundred kilometres away from the capital. It was
always tempting for them to acquire, in addition, a château or 'maison de plaisance'
within reasonable distance of Paris (if they did not own one already) and to go there,
especially in the hot summer months, rather than make a long and tedious migration, with all their households, to their hereditary châteaux.

But everywhere there was also a provincial noblesse, older than the robe families,
distinct from them, though more and more intermarrying with them, often very comfortably off, but with their town house in a local provincial capital, social, administrative,
or both, rather than in Paris. One can cite, for instance, Valognes, in the Cherbourg
peninsula, where the local noblesse of the Cotentin spent a winter season and had
town houses of such elegance that the town became known as 'la petite Versailles' or
'la petite Paris', even though it had no parlement or court of any importance.[3]

A major difference between France and England in the later seventeenth and
eighteenth centuries was that English country houses still had a role as centres of
political power, whereas French châteaux had lost it. In the sixteenth century in
both countries landowners had been able to produce substantial military power –
from their tenantry, their households or their feudal vassals, or by virtue of their
position as local governors in control of locally raised troops. They could exert pres-
sure on the king and exact concessions from him on the strength of it. After the mid
seventeenth century in both countries, for different reasons but to the same effect,
they lost power of this kind. But the English aristocracy and gentry developed a
new kind of power, at both a local and a national level. Locally they were automatically created Justices of the Peace by the Lord-Lieutenant of their county, and, apart
from administering justice in person in their own little 'Sessions' (a task which they
did not always take too seriously, and sometimes left to the local clergymen, who
were also usually JPs), met together four times a year in the county town for quarter-sessions, which dealt with more serious crimes and law-suits, and also acted as
local-government bodies, concerning themselves with such matters as prisons,
workhouses, road-construction and bridge-building.

At a national level, the head of an untitled landed family of any ambition aimed to become a Member of Parliament, preferably for the county; the heads of the grander families, who were usually titled and therefore members of the House of Lords, and not eligible for the House of Commons, usually in effect controlled the election of one or more Members of Parliament, because of their local standing.

Control of Members of Parliament was an essential element in the power-stakes: the more Members a landowner was able to field, the greater his political weight, and the likelihood of the appointment to important executive jobs, or well-paid sinecures, of himself, his family and his following. But to acquire such control usually involved much hospitality and help to the members of the electorate, which included local farmers, minor gentry, local professional families and tradesmen. This local political support was known as a landowner's 'interest'; cultivating one's interest was a major concern of the English landowning classes, and was impossible to do adequately without spending some time in the relevant country house, and living in some style there.

There was no inducement of this nature for an eighteenth-century French nobleman to live in his château. Important posts were either purchased, or made directly by the king at the centre, and the route to them came from sedulous attendance in Paris or at court, not by cultivating an interest in the provinces. It was his court connections not his local power-house which made a nobleman sought after; on the other hand, the expense of life as a courtier or military commander could get him into serious debt: in 1764, for instance, an Englishman visiting his cousins at the château of Bonnemare, in Picardy, described to a correspondent his dinner at a neighbouring château, 'moated round with tourelles, drawbridge &c.', where the owner,

> a gentleman of the first rank in the kingdom … has just sold his last estate … His grandfather's father himself had made shift to dissipate about £9000 a year in the service but he has the honour of being a Lieut. General, of having a cross of St Lewis – it is a great loss to our family not only as a good neighbour but also as he was their particular friend, has a good heart and had great interest at Versailles – which he would have used for their family in case of need.[4]

There was no local gathering of landowners at the equivalent of quarter-sessions; seigneuries had their own seigneurial courts, but justice (or, too often, injustice) in these was never dispensed by the seigneur himself but by his representative, usually a local lawyer who had bought the post from him. Seigneurial justice was anyway increasingly being replaced by royal justice, administered by the royal judges of the 'bailliages' and 'sénéchaussées' in local towns, just as local administration was largely controlled by 'intendants', powerful officials appointed directly by the king, usually belonging to lesser non-local noblesse, rather than by the governors. The importance of these substantially decreased, and although it by no means immediately disappeared and their prestige (like that of Lord-Lieutenants in England in this century) remained considerable, by the late seventeenth century Madame de Sévigné could write that 'all that is left of their former power is useless honours, the sound of trumpets and violins, and an air of royalty'.[5] Later on in the eighteenth century the post could become so nominal that many governors lived in Paris and only occasionally visited their province.

One exception to the general centralization of power in the crown was the survival, in about one third of the country, of the provincial États. There were ten of these, the most important being the États of Brittany, Languedoc, the Dauphiné, Provence and Burgundy, based on Rennes, Toulouse, Grenoble, Montpellier and Dijon. Unlike the États-Généraux, which did not meet at all between 1614 and 1789, they met yearly to vote the contribution which the province would make to the central exchequer. (In the rest of France the annual taxes were decided on at the centre.) Like the États-Généraux they were made up of members representing the three estates, sitting separately from each other. The chairman of the whole assembly was always a bishop, an archbishop or a grand seigneur. These annual meetings were of some importance, and could be attended by members of major noble families with properties in the province, who were likely to spend some time in châteaux near the relevant town before or after the meeting.[6]

But on the whole what took a nobleman to his château, or kept him from leaving it, was not the pursuit of power or the cultivation of an interest, but sentiment, pleasure or good stewardship: because it was his ancestral seat and a symbol of his position; because it was pleasant to be in the country in the hot summer or golden autumnal months, building, gardening, entertaining friends and neighbours and being entertained by them, and, perhaps above all, hunting or shooting; and because it was sensible to spend time at his château to make sure that the estates, which were the main source of his income, were being properly administered, that his steward was not cheating him, and, in some cases (which perhaps grew commoner in the second half of the century, partly under English influence), to engage actively in farming himself.[7]

As examples of families who, at one time or another, deserted their châteaux, one can look at the Rochefoucaulds, the La Trémoilles, the Saulx-Tavanes, the Polignacs and the Rosanbos. According to Saint-Simon, the Duc de la Rochefoucauld (whose family are said to have adopted a purple livery in mourning for the Crucifixion) was so heroically or slavishly devoted to Louis XIV that for ten years he never slept a night in a different place from the king; meanwhile the great château of La Rochefoucauld, with the echoing Renaissance arcades and mighty donjon, slept on unvisited. 'Not even a valet,' commented Saint-Simon, 'could have danced attendance more humbly or assiduously.'[8] Louis XIV rewarded him with the appointment of Grand Master of the Garderobe. The great La Trémoille château of Thouars, looming above the little town, had been rebuilt in the grand manner in the 1630s. At the time of the inventory taken in 1702, it was still being maintained and inhabited in style, but the inventory of 1741 shows a different picture. The family then had, in addition to Thouars and half a dozen or so lesser châteaux, a house in Paris, another in the Parisian suburbs, a house in the town at Versailles, an appartement in the palace there, and the 'Maison de Gennevillières', in the Île-de-France. Thouars was 327 kilometres from Paris. Gennevillières was just outside it, and the latter had clearly taken over from the former as their residence in the country. The inventory shows Thouars in decay, and it is symptomatic of the shifting centre of gravity that all the more readable books formerly in the library at Thouars have been removed to Gennevillières. This was a large house, which would have been called a château today (it has been demolished), but it had none of the family and feudal connotations of Thouars.[9]

The Polignacs had been for centuries far and away the grandest and most powerful family in the Velay, the mountainous and volcanic district in the Massif Central around Le Puy. They had been vicomtes de Polignac since the early Middle Ages. They had huge estates in the Velay and elsewhere in the Massif; they served continuously from 1632 to 1792 as governors of Le Puy; for centuries before this they had been conducting a vigorous feud with its bishop, whose cathedral topped one of the volcanic pinnacles at Le Puy and looked over from the town to the huge fortified château of the Polignacs on another. The Polignacs also had a large house in the town, and the château of Lavoûte-Polignac, topping a precipice above the

In the 1770s the château of Lavoûte-Polignac was abandoned by the Polignacs when they gave up their centuries-old rôle as the leading family of the area and moved into the inner circles of Louis XVI and Marie-Antoinette at Versailles.

valley of the Loire a few kilometres down-river from Le Puy; they had modernized this early in the seventeenth century, and preferred it to the windy heights of Polignac. From the sixteenth century the family moved on the national stage as well as the local one, as soldiers, courtiers and churchmen, culminating with Cardinal Melchior de Polignac, prince of the church, diplomat and patron of literature and the arts.

Up till the early eighteenth century the family maintained a presence both in the Velay and at the centre, but then the expense of living on a grand scale in Paris, and at court, of life as a military commander or an ambassador, of the purchase of regiments for younger sons, took the family into increasing debt, and led to the gradual sale of seigneuries and seigneurial rights, until little was left except the châteaux of Lavoûte-Polignac, rented out to an Yssingeaux merchant, the ruins of the château of Polignac, and the rump of their hereditary estates.[10]

In one sense the extravagance and the sales paid off. Yolande de Polignac, wife of Jules-François-Arnaud XXII de Polignac, became the intimate friend of Marie-Antoinette, and the governess of her children; money, sinecures and royal favours were lavished on the whole Polignac clan, Jules-François-Arnaud was created Duc de Polignac in 1783, and by the time of the Revolution the Polignacs had become gilded court aristocracy, with a château near Paris and only the distant memory of their feudal grandeur in the Velay.

The story of the Le Peletiers de Rosanbo is a different one. Louis Le Peletier, son of a rich Parisian merchant and financier, and himself prominent in the Parlement of Paris, and its Premier Président in 1707, married the heiress of an ancient line of Brittany nobles seated at the château of Rosanbo. On the strength of this marriage and inheritance Rosanbo was erected into a marquisate in 1698. This gave a satisfying feudal gloss to a relatively new robe family, but its members continued their connection with the Paris Parlement, and although Rosanbo was modestly modernized by a Parisian architect, their interests remained based on Paris and on a clutch of châteaux in and around it. Between 1776 and 1806 Louis Le Peletier, Marquis de Rosanbo, Premier Président of the Paris Parlement like his grandfather (and the last individual to fill that position), paid only one visit to Rosanbo. The bonus resulting from this for the social historian is that the 561 letters which Pierre de Guermarquer, 'régisseur' at Rosanbo, sent to his master in Paris form a fascinating thirty-year record of life in a Brittany seigneurie in all its details.[11]

In contrast to these families is the great variety of those still very much involved with their châteaux. One can start with three grands seigneurs of the late seventeenth and early eighteenth centuries – the Comte de Grignan at Grignan, the Duc de Saint-Simon at La Ferté-Vidame and the Duc de Sully at Sully-sur-Loire.

The Comte de Grignan was Louis XIV's Lieutenant-General, that is to say military representative, in Provence, and kept what amounted to a little court at the great Renaissance château which his forebear had built on the hilltop above the town of Grignan. Owing to the good fortune that he married the daughter of

Madame de Sévigné, one can chart in his mother-in-law's correspondence with her daughter the amount of time which he and his wife spent at Grignan in the 1670s, 80s and 90s, the splendour in which they lived there, and the richness with which they enlarged, furnished and embellished it – a splendour of which too little remains today, since it was largely gutted and dismantled in 1794, and insensitively 'restored' in the early twentieth century.[12]

The Duc de Saint-Simon was in a different category, perpetually disgruntled because Louis XIV did not employ him. On the strength of his memoirs he is thought of as the archetypal haunter of Versailles, and retailer of its gossip; but his memoirs also show how attached he was to his own château of La Ferté-Vidame, and how constantly he went off to spend time there.[13] Although he rebuilt the service court on a grand scale, he left untouched the enormous and amazing sixteenth-century, moated main body of the château; perhaps its feudal fantasy appealed to him, because essentially he disliked and disapproved of Louis XIV for what he saw as his destruction of tradition, the feudal system and the power of the noblesse. The towers of La Ferté stood for tradition, in contrast to the endless aggressive horizontality of Versailles.

The Duc de Sully was another grand seigneur who owned a great medieval château at Sully-sur-Loire, where he redecorated some suites of rooms, but otherwise left it untouched. We have a picture of life there in 1716 from Voltaire, who had been ordered out of Paris as a punishment for writing some satirical verses, and had gone into retreat at Sully. There he found a large house-party assembled, mainly for sport, but pursuing a vigorous social life at the same time.

'Enjoy the pleasures of Paris, dear Sir,' he wrote to a correspondent,

but meanwhile, by royal command, I am at the most agreeable château and in the best company in the world. Some people may imagine that I am in exile, but the truth is that the Regent has commanded me to pass several months in a delectable company assembled for the autumn – plenty of intelligent and what is even better, sociable and friendly people, great sportsmen for the most part, who are taking advantage of the fine weather here to slaughter partridges … As for myself, I shoot very little, but rhyme a lot, and turn everything that chance offers to my imagination into verse.

Voltaire describes one delightful al fresco party which went on through the night, in a 'great open-air salle enclosed by lime-trees, and lit by a myriad of lights', in which 'magnificent refreshments were served to the accompaniment of music, followed by a dance for more than a hundred masked dancers, wearing superb "guerillons".'

He celebrated his stay in verse:

I'm writing to you from the riverside
Where I've stayed for more than two years,
The nicest people
Who have been seen for a long time in France
The Chapelles, the Maniscamps,
Voluptuaries and sages
Who as they rhymed, shot, and argued
On the happy banks of the Loire
Spent the autumn and the spring
Less in philosophizing than in drinking.[14]

At Sully one can see how great, at châteaux all over France in the last summer months of the eighteenth century, was the attraction of the gardens, arranged as they were in a mixture of enclosed and open spaces which provided delicious outdoor rooms of various sizes, for both parties or more intimate gatherings. Such gardens, and the surrounding countryside, feature prominently in a curious and charming manuscript, *The Description of Embleinvilliers, by five authors*, 'ninth edition, revised, augmented and corrected in 1729'.[15]

The *Description* is concerned with the autumn spent in 1728 by 'Amilcar' (Monsieur de Charmoy) and six or seven friends at his 'pretty country house' at Embleinvilliers, near Verrières on the banks of the Bièvre, 16 kilometres from the centre of Paris. The house is described at some length, but the gardens, and the views from it, in even greater detail: the terrace above the river, the groves of lime-trees and horse-chestnuts (the latter 'where birds love to come by the thousands to sing of their loves' mixed with rose-trees, honeysuckle and lilac), the open-air 'cabinet' surrounded by ancient elms, the menagerie or aviary of ornamental birds, the dairy, the kitchen-garden, and the huge view from the terrace, embracing neighbouring châteaux, meadows studded with wild flowers and covered with grazing flocks, the winding river with groves of willows along it, in the shade of which 'country shepherds like to come together, for nowhere could be better suited for a bal champêtre, so that they are continuously filled with the soft music of fifes, straw pipes and bagpipes'. Indeed, 'here everything recalls the age of Seladon and Astrée, and a moving beauty instils a taste for pastoral life'. In short,

> autumn had never been so peaceful, one could compare its days to those of the Golden Age, and we filled these happy days with the liveliest enjoyments which the country could provide. I would need a volume to list for you all our hunting and fishing expeditions, our picnics on the lawn, the firework displays and illuminations of Amilcar's gardens.

Outings were made to neighbouring châteaux, walks taken in the surrounding countryside, there was fun to be had at the fair in Longjumeau, hunting in the forest of Verrières, and dances full of pretty girls all the autumn in Verrières itself. Back at Embleinvilliers 'we often relaxed on the grassy beds in the groves, and watched young Télémaque and Amilcar running races and showing their skill in all kinds of games, and the winner being crowned with flowers by one of the ladies'.

The fanciful classical names under which the friends are described – Amilcar, Aglatide, Aristide, Aglatidas, Télémaques, Aminta, Hellissemonde – conceal, in fact, a rather grand house-party – Monsieur de Charmoy himself, the Comte and Comtesse d'Hautefort and their young son, the Comte de Verteillas and his daughter, the Comte d'Essoine, the Abbé de Saint-Orce de Montferrand – sword rather than robe families, and rich and fashionable ones, spending a holiday of Arcadian artificiality, which could have been painted by Watteau or Fragonard, in one of the most fashionable areas on the outskirts of Paris, crowded with elegant châteaux and maisons de plaisance where similar holidays were being enjoyed by similarly fashionable people.

It is a contrast to move down to Brittany and look at the Barbiers de Lescoët, Comtes and Marquis de Lescoët, at their châteaux of Kerno and Lesquiffiou. These were not far distant from Rosanbo, but the Barbiers came from a different class of noblesse from the Le Peletiers: not a Paris Parlement family but solid well-established Brittany people, a junior branch of the Barbiers who had built the great sixteenth-century château of Kerjean, served as soldiers and priests, but when not away in the army lived almost continuously at their châteaux. A wealth of letters and other documents survives to illustrate their life there:[16] farming, gardening, breeding horses, hunting, organizing the local militia, improving their châteaux, buying books, picking up the latest news from Paris, entertaining their relatives and neighbours and being entertained by them. At Lesquiffiou in 1741

One breathes nothing here but joy and pleasure. Our daughters are dancing with the other girls; they are making an amazing row, but we're only young once. My son plays the violin for his sisters to dance to … Nothing but fun and games, dances, races, competitions, and hunts here, one after the other. The menfolk are leaving at this moment to hunt. They'll eat at Cosquer, and find all the neighbours there … yesterday there were twenty people to dinner, and more than thirty in the servants' hall.[17]

All this took place in September, at the same time of year as the holiday at Embleinvilliers, for September was the liveliest month at châteaux all over France. But there is no Watteauesque flavour to the vigorous fun in Brittany, and moreover the Barbiers lived all the year round at their châteaux, and do not even seem to have had a town house in one of the local towns. It is interesting to move from them to one of the grandest of grand seigneurs, who was by no means all the year at his châteaux, but who remained deeply involved in, and frequently visited, his properties, remote though they were from Paris.

The Duc de Croy was a young professional soldier who owned enormous estates in the north of France, stretching over into what is now Belgium, and centring round the town of Condé and its château. At the end of the War of the Austrian Succession he found himself with time on his hands, and after what seems a not especially serious attempt to get a position at court, settled down to a pleasurable existence divided between court and Parisian society, hunting and improvements on his estates, and looking after the regiments which he still commanded. He made improvements to the château at Condé, and built a new church in the town, but the bulk of his energies went into building and planting at the nearby forest-surrounded château de l'Hermitage, where he could indulge to the full his passion for hunting, and for field sports of all kinds. Everything is recorded in his journals.[18]

At the beginning of 1751 he planned out his life as follows:

Arrangements for 1751, and for the future.
15 April. Leave Paris for l'Hermitage. Walks, gardening, building and builders, outdoor life.
15 May. Go to Sobre. Stay there till 15 June. Hunt with my two packs, walk, a bit of building.
15 June to 15 July. Go to Plombières and Bery, tour around in order to visit the garrisons, and because there is not much sport available.
15 July. Go to Compiègne, the Paris neighbourhood, and Versailles, till 20 August. Attend court, go to the pleasantest country areas and shoot a lot.
20 August to 1 September. Go to Courière, Le Petit Quesnoy and the Lille and Carrin neighbourhood. Shoot a lot.
1 September to 15 November. To l'Hermitage and nearby places, such as Beloeil and Enghien. All kinds of sport, especially stag and boar hunting

with my two packs. Building works and builders.

15 November. To Condé for the presentation of my accounts, business, arranging my papers. End up at Lille, shooting in its neighbourhood, till 15 December.

15 December. To Paris and court, see my mother and my children, attend court. Building works, and see friends, until 15 April, when start again as before.

In all, 4 months in Paris, three and a half months at l'Hermitage, 1 month at Sobre, 1 month touring, a month and a half at court or near Paris, and a month at Condé.[19]

It was scarcely to be expected that Croy would keep to this programme to the day, but over the next few years he kept to it well enough. There were variations: his mother bought a château at Ivry near Paris and he spent some time there every year; his son and daughter-in-law became enthusiasts for the theatre, and from 1768 Croy put on an annual theatrical season at l'Hermitage for them, as well as hunting there. But, however spent, his long autumn visit to l'Hermitage and Condé remained a constant feature.

While he was there, or on the way up or back, he did a good deal of visiting at other châteaux, especially to the Prince de Ligne at Beloeil and Beaudour, and the Duc d'Arenberg at Enghien, and often found huge parties assembled, for balls or hunting, or both. He was at Beloeil, for instance, for a fortnight in November 1750, for the visit of Duc Charles de Lorraine, and found between twenty-eight and thirty-five people staying there, in addition to himself, and a succession of hunts and balls, the latter attended, amongst others, by the local canonesses, young ladies of good family who, all over France, in the eighteenth century, were installed comfortably in religious houses, and enlivened the social life of their neighbourhood.[20]

His own biggest entertainment was given on 4 July 1752, for the visit of the Prince and Princesse de Soubise to Condé and l'Hermitage. He put up twenty guests at Condé, in addition to the thirty-five servants that they brought with them, his own household staff of eighteen, and twelve extra servants brought in for the occasion. He allowed anyone in the town who wanted to come into the salle à manger, and around 130 people at a time crammed into the room, which was not large, to watch dinner being served to all these grand people. Next day there was a dinner at l'Hermitage, a tour of the house and park, and music and illuminations in the evening.[21]

Croy gave another dinner for eighteen people at l'Hermitage to celebrate the completion of building work there. But much of the time he was alone with two or three friends, relaxing and enjoying himself. On 24 June 1750, 'I got up at four in the morning to enjoy the beauty of the dew and the dawn of the feast of St John, on which I enter on my 33rd year.'[22] Two years later he celebrated his birthday in a more spectacular fashion, even though he had only two friends staying with him.

On St John's Eve he arranged

a superb soirée, we three had supper for the first time in symmetry at the
rond point of my avenues. Huge torches reflected in mirrors made a blaze of
light, which gave my people the idea of rushing off to Mons and lighting
bonfires on the road at the end of my two avenues. This combined with the
sunset on one side and the moon on the other to produce a delightful
effect.[23]

Croy was a grand seigneur, and although he invited the less grand families of the
neighbourhood to his big entertainments, he himself only visited at the grandest
châteaux. A more detailed picture of the entire society of a neighbourhood can be
obtained from the autobiography of Dufort de Cheverny.

Dufort belonged to a rich Parisian robe family, had a château near Paris and as a
young man purchased the socially prestigious post of 'Introducteur des
Ambassadeurs'; as such he was responsible for all the considerable protocol when a
new ambassador came to France and had to pay his separate respects to the king and
numerous other members of the royal family. He lived, however, too extravagantly
in Paris, got into debt and determined to economize by moving to the country. He
sold on his post, and in 1764 bought the great early-seventeenth-century château
of Cheverny near Blois; Cheverny had already been erected into a 'comité', and
Dufort got the title of Comte de Cheverny confirmed to him on the strength of
his purchase.

Dufort built an orangery in the garden at Cheverny, and contrived a sizeable theatre in the château itself. Many of the local families were musical, 'and as a result
every year we could make up a very gay and pleasant society without any need of
importations from Paris. By the end of six months I found myself as well-established
in the neighbourhood as if I had been there for ten years'. There was a vigorous and
agreeable society in Blois and the châteaux around it, and he described its make-
up in some detail in his autobiography.

The great man of the neighbourhood was the Duc de Choiseul, the former chief
minister of Louis XV. He had bought the château of Chanteloup in 1761, and in
1770 fell out with the king's new mistress, Madame du Barry, and was exiled there
in disgrace. For four years he lived there all the year round in great style, had what
amounted to a court and made it one of the rare eighteenth-century examples of
a château with a political role, for it became, in effect, the centre of the opposition.
On the death of Louis XV in 1774 he was allowed to return to Paris, but he still
spent a considerable time each year at Chanteloup, up to his own death in 1785.

The château and seigneurie of Guelaguette had been bought by Paul Boesnier-
Delorme, son of a rich wine merchant and formerly with a post in the Eaux et
Forêts, the department which ran the royal domains in France. Guelaguette was an
old 'château en pavillon' in great need of improvement; he lived with his sister, spent
eight months there, and the rest of the year in a house in Blois.

A lively drawing of about 1770 shows the Berckheim family at dinner in the château of Schoppenwihr. The hostess, Madame de Berckheim, is seated at the centre of the far side of the table, and the company includes family, friends, the tutor, and the music-teacher who taught the harp to one of the daughters.

Closer to Cheverny a naval officer, Claude-Michel Bégon, 'écuyer, sieur de La Sestière', lived at the château of that name, and 10 kilometres away, at the château de Comeré, the Baron de Comeré was 'ruined and discredited. He and his wife lived off the remains of their fortune, and were happy enough to marry their daughter to a rich citizen of Blois'. At the château of Beauregard (famous today for its gallery), halfway between Chambord and Blois, lived the Comte and Comtesse de Gaucourt; 'he was a real country gentleman'.

Madame de Pompadour's brother, the Marquis de Marigny, lived at the château of Ménars. He owed his marquisate and much of his wealth to his sister, and carried little weight after her death in 1764; but he was a genial man (if a little vulgar), with good taste in architecture, on the strength of which he had become 'Intendant des Bâtiments', in charge of royal buildings. Ménars had been rebuilt rather grandly, to the designs of Soufflot. Dufort describes him as 'a millionaire, thanks to his wife's fortune … spent his income in magnificent embellishments to his property and lavish hospitality to friends en route from Paris or Versailles, and to some hangers-on whom he had picked up in Blois'.

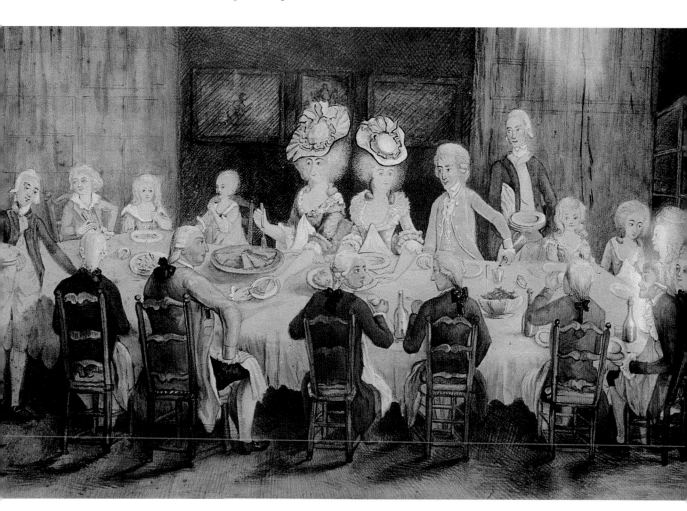

The old Marquis de Saumery, governor of Chambord, 'had been in the Order of Malta, and lived in patriarchal splendour at Saumery'. At Diziers, nearby, the Marquis de Diziers

> was an intelligent man, who had had to retire from the navy because of bad health … his brother Guyon, Marquis de Guerecheville, a retired captain of dragoons, had his own property next to Ménars. Next door was Comte Hurault de Saint-Denis, belonging to a younger branch of the Hurault family.

The Comte de Maillé inhabited a property called Roujoux or Rougeou as a suzerain of Cheverny, and Dufort had rights of 'haute justice' over it as a result.

> His family was a very old one, related to the Prince de Condé, and lived in style. There were three brothers, all childless, and one sister. The eldest lived at Rougeou; the next brother, the Marquis de Maillé, was a retired naval officer, and lived near Saumery; the youngest, the Chevalier de Maillé, was Chamberlain of something-or-other, and lived, modestly but respectably in Blois.

Monsieur Le Ray, 'Grand Maître des Eaux et Forêts', came from Nantes, had bought the great Renaissance château of Chaumont, and 'was mixed up in every possible kind of speculation. He and his associate Monsieur Rousseau had a business partnership with an able group in Blois.' In 1770 he was appointed Intendant of the Invalides, and acquired a magnificent property at Auteuil, where at one time he let a subsidiary house to Benjamin Franklin.

Monsieur de Termont, the Bishop of Blois,

> lived mainly in Paris, devoted himself to pleasure, but was respectable and in every way an excellent Bishop when he was in residence. He was a great benefactor to his family, and was always surrounded by them when he was at Blois. He spent part of the summer at his property at Madon.

C.-F. de Vezeaux, Marquis de Rancoigne, was 'a former Musketeer, and seigneur of the property of Herbault-en-Beauce. I [Dufort] soon saw a lot of him; he was talented and intelligent, and became one of the faithfuls of our local society', as did B.-B. Herry de Maupas, who was still serving as a captain of dragoons, and was 'an outstanding man in every respect'. New arrivals included Monsieur Phelipeau, the Archbishop of Bourges, who 'owned a property at Herbault, 10 kilometres from Cheverny, and came there for the first time after I had established myself in the neighbourhood', and the Marquis de Polignac, who set up a royal stud farm at Chambord, and spent six months of the year there.[24]

The mixture of people in the Blois area – grand families, local gentry families, decayed families, *nouveau-riche* families, military or naval families, clergymen (worldly or otherwise), sporting or musical families, families coming down from Paris for the summer months, families living all the year in their châteaux or with a town house in Blois – is redolent of a way of life to be found, with variations, all over Europe from the eighteenth to the twentieth century. In England it would be called county society. Anyone who has ever known it – or still knows it, for it can still be found – will immediately recognize it. Similar societies were in existence all over France in Dufort de Cheverny's time. Admittedly, the further the area was from Paris, the more likely there were to be houses belonging to grand families, to which their owners seldom, if ever, came. But there were still châteaux or more modest gentry houses by the thousand, revolving round their local centres and very far from abandoned.

In his memoirs de Frenilly describes the roads out of Poitiers in the 1770s and 1780s:

Those little roads led to a mass of good big and sometimes beautiful châteaux, which turned those melancholy landscapes into the most sociable and lively areas in France. I visited there a lot. At that time the grander and richer local families did not feel in exile in their little capitals, and were not yet drawn by ambition or a search for superior society to leave the places where they were the social kings, and go to Paris in search of their equals and betters. Estates, tenants, rank, posts, duties, pleasures, friends, relatives and fortune all gave them roots in one district. They lived there and died there. Out of this grew local character, and out of local character grew a national character in which everyone had a local flavour: one wasn't French without distinction and in a mass, but French because one was from Poitou, Brittany, Burgundy or Picardy … What I have said about Poitiers is even more true of the Parlement towns, and truer again of provinces with their own assemblies – the Pays d'État.[25]

Whether it was for eight or six or four months, or just for a few weeks, all over France the ponderous biannual move from town to country and country to town was going on, by horse, by coach, by wagon or by boat. In his memoirs General d'Andigné recalls with nostalgia the family migrations to and from Angers in the 1770s:

I spent my childhood, according to the custom of those days, half in the town, where we spent the winter, and half at our family property at La Blanchaye, which we shared with the younger brother of my grandfather. The voyages – and 'voyages' is the right word for them – from country to town were sometimes made by horseback and in litters, but more often in a boat, by way of the River Oudon, on which one embarked just above Segré. A day was needed to travel 38 kilometres! But the journey was charming, and I remember with pleasure our spring-time return to the country in our man-drawn boat, and the pretty banks of the Mayenne and the Oudon.[26]

Château life was not always sophisticated, and not always crowded with people. 'I had company at carnival time,' wrote Madame de Cadillac in 1746 from her château at Tournecouppe to her mother Madame de Riquet at her château at Bonrepos,

> Madame de Gontaut, whom I hadn't seen since her marriage, and several other people … they danced, they acted comedies, all this entertained me very little … I prefer the solitude in which I presently am, alone by my fireside with my books and my writing-table, going from one to the other … This is wonderful weather, just right for life in a beautiful country like yours – take full advantage of the rest and fresh air and build up a stock of health for the winter. As for me, I stock up with sleep, I go to bed at ten, a few people come to dinner, but they are the sort who leave at five, so I am very much on my own and happy to be so. I go for walks, I read and I sleep, and it all keeps me from getting bored.[27]

The Riquets were a Toulouse family, and the letters of other Toulouse or Bordeaux families show how important a part getting in the vintage or otherwise looking after their property played when they were at their châteaux. 'My first act this morning was to go out on the terrace,' wrote the Abbé de Bertier, in 1756, staying at the family château of Pinsaguel near Toulouse, 'where I found Monsieur de Bertier walking with his pipe in his mouth, clad in his riding coat, and teaching Monsieur Dechaux the art of cultivating the soil and making the farm capital produce.'[28] The great writer and thinker Montesquieu, who came from a Bordeaux Parlement family, sank himself in country life when he was staying at his château of La Brède, and dressed so roughly that he was mistaken for a peasant, as he walked round his farms.[29]

But, not surprisingly, it was the big events, the house-parties, dances, theatrical performances or hunting on the grand scale, which stuck in the memories and reappeared in the memoirs of people who stayed in châteaux in the half-century before the Revolution. Hunting was one of the great attractions of château life, and grands seigneurs pursued it in the grand manner. Hunting with the Prince de Condé at the château de Chantilly, with its baroque stabling as grand as a palace for 250 horses and its 108 hunt servants in livery, was something quite extraordinary; the Condés were of royal blood, and lived like royalty, on the basis of immense wealth. But others hunted grandly enough.[30] At Chanteloup Arthur Young climbed to the top of the pagoda which had been built by the Duc de Choiseul, looked for the hunt over the acres of forest and long rides radiating through it, and commented sourly enough on 'the mischievous animation of a vast hunt, supported so liberally as to ruin the master of it … Great lords love too much an environ of forests, boars and huntsmen, instead of marking their residence by the accompaniment of neat and well-cultivated farms, clean cottages and happy peasants.'[31] At the château of

A modest family group assembled in the château of Davayat in about 1760. Genre pictures of this type are common enough in England but exceedingly rare in France.

Brienne, in the 1770s and 1780s, the Comte of Brienne (army minister in Louis XVI's penultimate government and brother of Cardinal Lomenie de Brienne, who was chief minister at the same time) came for the summer months for a season of hunting, balls and theatre, in the manner of the Duc de Croy.

Brienne had a hundred horses in his stables, half of them carriage horses, half for riding, and a hundred hounds, two thirds stag hounds and one third boar hounds. His hunts had two uniforms, worn not just by hunt-servants, but by everyone who hunted: scarlet coat, gold and silver braid, sky-blue velvet collars and facings for the stag hunters; green coats, silver braid, and collars and facings of crimson velvet for the huntsmen. One way and another, the field could consist of 250 riders.[32]

J. de Norvins used to stay there in the 1770s, and was amused by the balls which took place during the hunting season:

At the château the ball was held on two levels; while we were dancing on the ground floor, the big salle d'office in the basement was converted into a ballroom for the ladies' maids' ball, attended by the upper menservants and the local farmers and petite bourgeoisie. It was always bigger than our ball, and there was abundance of every kind of refreshment.[33]

Châteaux of all kinds in these decades before the Revolution are brought to life in memoirs and letters. Provincial life in Poitou in 1789, at the château of Monts, 48 kilometres from Poitiers, and the nearby château of Madame de La Brousse, is described by de Frenilly. Monts was 'a vast Gothic château, approached through three great courts, bristling with towers and turrets, and suspended above a terrace on the edge of a ravine'. It belonged to a Beauty-and-the-Beast couple, the Vicomte de La Chastre and his pretty young wife. The Vicomte's face had been hideously mutilated as a result of a childhood accident, but he was still a viscount, aged twenty-five, extremely rich, and 'basically one of the best fellows in the world'. In spite of his disfigurement, he had found 'a charming wife, from one of the best families in the province, but endowed with nothing except two sisters, canonesses and as poor and charming as she was – the three sisters Turpin, in the flower of their youth and beauty', aged between eighteen and twenty-one.[34]

De Frenilly, who writes very much from the standpoint of a sophisticated Parisian venturing into the provinces, was introduced at Monts by his friend, the Chevalier de Tryon, and found himself in

an immense salon with a beamed ceiling, hung with tapestries of the loves of Gombault and of Macé, and lit by two candlesticks by the light of which circulated a crowd of local squires (for the drones of Poitou descended there in swarms, clumsy, badly turned out and still smelling of the kennel)… It was a society which I found charming once the viscount was out shooting, the Chevalier de Tryon had gone off to annoy his mother, and the local flitterbugs had flown off to other perches. I looked out for occasions such as these, took advantage of them, and as a result spent happy days and moonlit nights with the three charming sisters, around their piano – for they were excellent musicians – on the beautiful terrace, or in the woods.

Not far away,

Madame de La Brousse used to cram all the young and lively company she could get hold of hugger-mugger into her château. That year she must have had fifty guests, and I, Count Charles de Vittré and two others hatched a plan to go and add ourselves to the crowd, masked and dressed up like courtiers from the great days of Louis XIV. We spent eight days arranging our clothes, wigs and transport. We unearthed an ancient berlin of the right period, gilded, carved and lined in red, and four horses, one black, one white, one bay, and one piebald. Our coachmen and three footmen wore livery in keeping. In this splendid outfit we drove across 50 kilometres of countryside, to the astonishment of the inhabitants, and finally tumbled into the middle of a ball in the salon of Madame de La Brousse. Among the many beauties there were the three goddesses of Monts …[35]

Provincial life in another part of France, a good deal closer to Paris, is described in the memoirs of J.-H.-A. de Bonardi du Mesnil. His father had bought the small château of Le Mesnil, near Rouen, in about 1769, and lived there for much of the year. For most of the time society was limited. It consisted of an inner circle made up of the neighbouring seigneur, 'Monsieur de S–, a proper village squire and a former infantry captain … decent, loyal, brusque, gay and outspoken', Monsieur de Blosseville, who was the Procureur-Général of the Chambre de Compte at Rouen, and Monsieur Delorme, who ran the nearby glassworks (for some reason the glass industry was open to nobles without their being deprived of their noble status as a result). The outer circle was made up of

> several gentlemen glass manufacturers, working under Monsieur Delorme, whom my father had picked out of the crowd to admit to his acquaintance; some lawyers, whom my father, who was not averse to law-suits, treated with a respect which on the whole they deserved; and a specialist in seigneurial business whom he had brought in to live in the house, and who stayed on there when he was away.[36]

'That was our world,' comments Bonardi. But it was enlivened by the summer arrivals. Monsieur de Merval spent six weeks a year in 'a superb château a few kilometres from us, kept house in great splendour, and was frequented by the best society of Rouen'. He was a financier, exceedingly rich, related to all the robe families and the provincial noblesse, and anyway distinguished in his own right, 'because of his superior character'. As an impressionable teenager Bonardi was bowled over by a summer visitor (the same lady whose boudoir he had visited in Paris) when she came to stay on her way to Dieppe, along with her lover and his hangers-on,

> an exceedingly pleasant architect and a musician. They enchanted us with their professional skill, and amused us with their wit. There were continual entertainments in honour of the woman of my dreams. The architect devised the scenery, and the lighting, the lover wrote the verses, the musician sang them, and I, overcome by love, desire, fear, hope and admiration, offered my divinity the homage of a pure heart in silence, and seemed to please her more than all the others. That was how I spent the evenings; in the mornings she taught me Italian, and we passed whole hours closeted together tête-à-tête, virtuously occupied in this agreeable study.[37]

A quite different form of entertainment was the outdoor dances which Madame de Bonardi gave every Sunday in the summer for 'all the young people of the village, from farmers' sons to local seigneurs. We had a supremely good time.'

In contrast again, for young Bonardi, the height of sophistication was reached when he went to spend a week with his father's friends the Nicolays, at their 'superb' château at Auny, near Pontoise, about 40 kilometres from Paris. The Nicolays were one of the richest and most distinguished of the Paris robe families, and to Bonardi life at Auny seemed

the epitome of the house of a grand seigneur in the country. Luxury at once in the grand manner and exceedingly enjoyable, exquisitely good manners and liberty that never went too far … I've never spent eight days in a house-party as agreeably as there … The house-party was made up of plenty of lawyers, most of whom had plenty of wit – and of plenty of well-born women, who were no longer young but still had all the charms of breeding and good manners; they had left their grand airs in Paris and brought nothing with them but their good humour. Every day after dinner six open carriages each pulled by six horses were waiting in the courtyard for those who wanted to go on expeditions, ready to convey them to the most attractive places in that splendid countryside. Madame de Melian (widow of the Intendant of that name) and I were always in the same carriage. She went hunting for wild-flowers, and gave me lessons in botany. In the morning, by her invitation, I went to see her in her room. There she gave me lessons in good breeding and good temper. Above all she gave me a good example … When I tried to make love to her, she skilfully and kindly made fun of me.[38]

A drawing by Césarine de Barante (above right) shows Madame de La Briche and her family and friends in the petit salon of her château of Le Marais in 1819. Madame de La Briche, seated in the chair on the left, divides a skein of wool held for her by her grand-daughter, her friend Frédéric d'Houdetot is sketching to the far left, and his sister is playing the clavecin on the right, watched by his wife.

The château of Le Marais (below right), designed by the archi-tect Barre in the 1770s, was one of the most perfect of the many châteaux built by rich financiers in the vicinity of Paris. Madame de La Briche inherited it from her uncle in 1783.

Among châteaux in the Paris region frequented in the holiday season by clever Parisians, one of the most glittering was the château of Le Marais, where Madame de La Briche started to entertain the cream of the Enlightenment in the 1770s, and continued to give scintillating house-parties, balls, soirées and theatrical perfor-mances into the early years of the Revolution.[39] The one criticism of life in this exquisite neoclassical mansion was that it was too like life in Paris; this had more particularly been the case in the time of the builder, the financier Le Maistre (whose heir Madame de La Briche was), who, according to de Frenilly, kept it 'so to speak under glass, putting on slippers to walk on the parquet, and gloves to handle the candlesticks', or, as another writer expressed it, 'it was not the château of a grand seigneur recovering from court life in the country, but the huge and magnificent mansion of a rich Parisian capitalist, who wanted to feel that he was still in Paris'.[40]

House-parties at Le Marais could run up to thirty people, and even more were crammed in on the night when a theatrical performance was put on in the little theatre. There were the usual diversions of a château house-party: carriage expedi-tions through the countryside, or to neighbouring châteaux, walks, a village wedding; Le Marais was not just a maison de plaisance with little land attached to it, but the centre of a sizeable property, and Madame de La Briche enjoyed visiting the tenants at her nine farms and three mills, and in 1786 gave an open-air dinner,

followed by dancing, for her peasants under one of the avenues of the park. On this occasion she also opened the entire château to the public:

> there were a thousand precious objects which could easily have been damaged, but I was certain that my act of trust would act as a good safeguard. I did not deceive myself; more than a thousand peasants went through the rooms without causing the slightest damage. The Comte de Brienne, who was staying with me, gave me the idea of permitting this, although everyone expostulated against it; one couldn't do better than follow his advice, for he was the epitome of the good landlord.[41]

What one can see coming to fruition in these châteaux is the idea of the house-party, and the holding of house-parties as one of their main functions. Houses had previously been geared for the supreme moment when one or more great, and possibly even royal, people arrived and were put up in style, in one appartement or a couple of them, each of several rooms, and their numerous servants fitted in as best could be, sleeping by the bed of their employer, or put up in the basse-cour. Bigger incursions there might be, often for a single night, after a ball, a wedding or a hunt, but then people could be crammed in happily, several to a room; they did not expect too much. One source describes how in hospitable houses in Brittany, admittedly modest ones, guests slept in, in effect, dormitories, two to a bed, women on one side of the room and men on the other, and young people on mattresses on the floor or, if needs be, on hay in a barn,[42] but this would not do for house-party life. This was based on the concept of sizeable numbers of people coming together for a week or more, to enjoy themselves and be entertained with outings on horse or on foot, picnics, sport of all kinds, visits to neighbouring châteaux, perhaps a ball or two, and lively conversation, card or other games, and billiards in the salon and the rooms around it. All this was another aspect of that feeling for comfort and elegance which had produced the clusters of little rooms round the main chambres, and the intimacy of the boudoir. All but the most important guests at an agreeable house-party could not hope for as much as this, but they could expect an elegantly furnished chambre to themselves, preferably with a cabinet de toilette adjoining, or a little garderobe with a bed for a child or a servant, or, even better, both.

What, in short, was needed was a large number of well-appointed bedrooms, and increasingly, in the eighteenth century, new houses were provided with this, and old houses adapted to obtain it. At Embleinvilliers in 1728 the house-party consisted of only eight people, but the description of the house shows it could cope with more, though it was clearly not a very large house: there were five appartements on the first floor, some of them double ones, and nine on the second floor, and these last were not servants' rooms but 'were furnished with exquisite taste; there were Indian fabrics and each appartement had a dressing-table supplied with bottles of scent, and everything down to the smallest detail that a nice feeling for comfort could provide'.[43]

A corner of the grand salon of Le Marais as photographed in the 1920s when it was the home of the notorious Boni de Castellane and his millionaire American wife. In the eighteenth century its grandeur was considered more suited for a Paris hôtel than a country house.

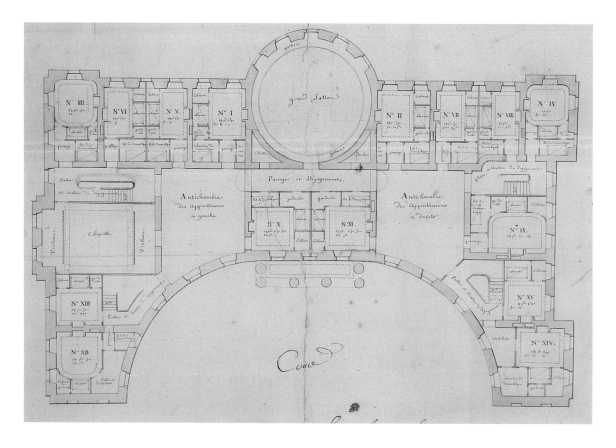

As a result of alterations at Condé in 1748 the Duc de Croy was delighted to have increased the number of appartements to eighteen by raising the roof.[44] The much more modest alterations to the Brittany manoir of Kernault in 1749 were mainly designed, in addition to forming an up-to-date salle de compagnie and salle à manger, to get more bedrooms by dividing up the big old rooms on the first floor.[45]

But perhaps the most symbolically significant alteration was the similar conversion of the, of course, much larger and grander first floor of Vaux-le-Vicomte to the designs of Jean-Baptiste Berthier in 1767. The nature of this is clearly shown by his surviving plan, drawn in two colours to show new and old work, and it transformed the archetypal house built for grand entertaining of a few people, including the king, in the mid seventeenth century to a house designed to accommodate up-to-date house-parties in the mid eighteenth century.[46]

Eleven years later, at the château of Moncley, the architect Bertrand produced (for the Président of the Besançon Parlement) what was clearly meant to be a neo-classical reinterpretation of Vaux-le-Vicomte, adapted for changed ideas about style, and changing forms of social life. The house was grouped around a giant two-storey circular grand salon with a gallery, obviously inspired by the one at Vaux; but the provision of bedrooms has nothing to do with Le Vau. The family appartements were all on the ground floor, and the first floor was given over to guests, in the form of, as the inscription on the plan puts it, 'fifteen master appartements, along with

The many bedrooms shown in the plan for the first floor of the château of Moncley (above), as drawn by its architect C.-J.-A. Bertrand in 1779, vividly suggest the function of late-eighteenth-century châteaux as venues for large house-parties in the summer months. The appartements of the family were on the ground floor, as was often the case in France.

garderobes, servants' rooms and cabinets'. The rooms vary in size, but the beds in all of them are neatly tucked into alcoves, as had become standard, especially for guest rooms, with a tiny (for the most part) cabinet and garderobe to either side of the alcove; the servants' rooms are mainly fitted in between the bedrooms and the corridor, and very few of them have windows. The floor heights were not sufficient to allow for entresols. Moncley is especially interesting because many of the bedrooms retain their original furnishings, curtains and pretty neoclassical wallpapers.[47]

The rooms are numbered with Roman numerals on the plan, and here and elsewhere there were corresponding number-plates on the doors, an anticipation of hotel usage which became quite common in these multi-bedroom houses. There were, for instance, twenty-nine numbered rooms at the château of Ormesson in 1775 and twenty-one at the château of Le Marais in 1783, as shown in their inventories;[48] and the numbering survives in place on the upper floor of Montgeoffroy.

The guest rooms on the first floor at Moncley all have only one bed. There are two big several-roomed appartements on the ground floor, each with two bedrooms, annotated as 'for husband and wife', and the Président and his wife also had separate bedrooms. It was less usual, in eighteenth-century France, for husband and wife regularly to share a bed, as they often did in England. But plans or inventories frequently show rooms with two and even three beds in them, and although in some cases these were clearly rooms of less importance designed to fit in extra accommodation, in some cases they were actually the best chambres, and were clearly designed for a husband and wife sharing the same room. A grand late-eighteenth-

Newly-married couples in French châteaux shared a bed, but in later life rooms with two single beds were a common feature, as in this splendid example at the château of Longpra (right), furnished in neoclassical taste under Louis XVI.

century example survives at the château de Longpra, with its two splendid neo-classical beds. It is not clear why this arrangement is found in some châteaux and not in others.

Young visiting bachelors could not expect a room to themselves. One of the most charming products of château life in eighteenth-century France is the poem 'La Garçonnière', and the accompanying picture, emanating from the château de Merville, near Toulouse. Four young men used regularly to come and stay there, and were always given the same room, which became known as the 'Garçonnière' – the bachelor-pad. In 1762 they wrote a poem about life in the Garçonnière, and at Merville generally, had it printed, and presented it to their host along with a pic-ture showing their occupation of the room with its four beds – one of them is writing, one painting on an easel, another brandishing a cello and the fourth play-ing the flute.[49]

The second-floor rooms at Embleinvilliers were strung out along a corridor, and at Condé the Duc de Croy was delighted with the convenience of the corridor (or 'collider' as he called it) which he had had inserted there.[50] No plans survive, but it sounds as though these may have been examples of what became the favoured plan for the first and second floors of eighteenth-century châteaux, a corridor running from end to end along the length of the building, with rooms to either side; light came from windows at both ends, usually supplemented by indirect light from the staircase coming up in the middle of the corridor. Sometimes the rooms were of the same depth on both sides, but often the corridor was over to one side, so that one set of rooms was smaller; these could be servants' or children's rooms. There was often a 'lingerie' (linen room) on this floor, and sometimes a room for dirty linen as well – a useful feature, for owing to the long intervals between washes the dirty linen must have piled up alarmingly.

In France, unlike England, the rooms of the master and mistress were usually on the ground floor, with access by french windows directly into the garden. The room of the mistress of the house was as much a sitting-room or reception room as a bed-room, though more intimate or private meetings could take place in her cabinet de toilette or boudoir, if she had one. There were, for instance, eleven chairs of various kinds in the chambre of Madame de Saint-Paul at the château de Beauregard in 1772, and thirteen in that of the châtelaine of the château de Flines in 1793. Guests in any well-appointed chambre would also expect at least a few chairs (and a writ-ing-table, either in the chambre or an adjoining cabinet), so that they could receive a few friends there if they felt like it.[51]

But the 'salon', 'salle', 'pièce' or 'cabinet de compagnie', or whatever it was called, ultimately to surface just as the salon, had become the pivot of château life, both when the house was crowded for house-parties and when there were only a few people there. In the bigger houses there were usually two salons, one larger than the other; they might be distinguished as 'salon d'hiver' and 'salon d'été', with the salon d'hiver as the smaller one, because it was easier to warm and because summer was the time for large numbers of visitors; but when a house was crowded then both

A distinctive feature of many eighteenth-century châteaux was the long central corridor giving access to the many bedrooms on the first floor, as at the château of Montgeoffroy. The rooms were often numbered, in anticipation of the system later to be found in hotels.

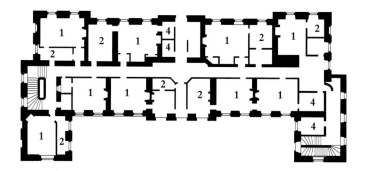

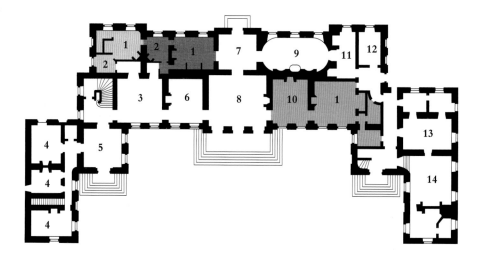

salons would be called into use, and when just the family were in residence, one
would expect them to use the smaller one, in summer or winter.

Salon life in grand or rich houses is described by de Frenilly and Dufort, at Le
Marais and Chanteloup respectively. At Le Marais,

> a huge salon, really too grand, filled the middle of the house. On each side
> was a smaller salon lit by two windows. Small gatherings took place in the
> first of these, between the salle à manger and the appartement of Madame
> de La Briche. Concerts were given in the second, next to the billiard-room.
> The big salon was for the mob.

Elsewhere there are descriptions of readings aloud, of playing the game of 'proverbs',
of Madame de La Briche 'playing her pieces on the piano', or Florian singing her
'delicious romance' to her accompaniment.[52]

At Chanteloup the regular evening routine after dinner ran as follows:

> The company reassembled in the salon at eight o'clock. The Duchesse de
> Choiseul loved backgammon, and fleeced me and the Comte de Boufflers;

KEY
1. CHAMBRE
2. CABINET OR
   GARDEROBE
3. BILLARD
4. CHAMBRES DES
   DOMESTIQUES
5. VESTIBULE
6. SECOND ANTE-
   CHAMBRE
7. PETIT SALON
8. GRAND SALON
9. SALLE À MANGER
10. CABINET
    BIBLIOTHÈQUE
11. BUFFET
12. LINGERIE
13. OFFICE
14. CUISINE

The grand salon of Montgeoffroy (above) opens on to the forecourt and is axially aligned on the avenue of approach. The axis continues through the petit salon behind it into the garden.

meanwhile the Duc played chess with the Abbé Billardi. The rest of the company occupied themselves with conversation, or looking at engravings of superb quality. Supper was good and substantial, but unpretentious; one sat down to table at nine and left it at ten. Then one started on backgammon again, or some other game, up till midnight. At midnight or one, those who wanted to went to bed; but the Duc and Duchesse, Madame de Gramont, the Abbé Barthélemy, the Abbé Billardi, Monsieur de Gramont, etc., stayed up. Never in my life have I heard more interesting conversation; it went on till three in the morning. Eight days have never passed so quickly in my life – apart from the etiquette, which was a bore. One wore what one liked all day; but when one came down to the salon at eight, one had to be dressed as though at court. All the women had their high hair-dos and were splendidly dressed and coiffeured.[53]

Madame de l'Épinay's château of La Chevrette was described by Diderot in the 1750s:

By the window which opened on to the garden Grimm was sitting for his

portrait and Madame de l'Épinay was leaning over the back of the chair of the artist. A draughtsman, sitting at a lower level on a stool, was drawing her profile in pencil. In a corner Monsieur de Saint-Lambert was reading the latest pamphlet which I sent you. I was playing chess with Madame d'Houdelot. Good old Madame d'Esclavelles, the mother of Madame de l'Épinay, had all her children round her, and was talking to them and their tutor and governess. Two sisters of the man who was painting my friend were embroidering, one by hand, the other on a frame. The third was practising Scarlatti on the clavichord.[54]

A not dissimilar group is portrayed in a water-colour by Baron de Tott, showing Madame de Tessé reading aloud to her friends in the salon of the château of Chaville in the 1780s; the baron has depicted himself drawing the group in one corner; the Comte de Tessé has gone to sleep.[55]

These were all clever or famous people, the cream of French intellectual and social life; but the scenes are not all that different from the provincial group charmingly and naïvely depicted in the château of Davayat, at much the same time. Similar scenes were being enacted in the salons of châteaux of all types all over France, then and for at least a hundred years to come.

The architectural decoration of the salon at Chaville, as drawn by Baron de Tott, is rather grand, but the furniture is remarkably sparse. Families kept their grandest furniture and best pictures in Paris, or at their town houses in provincial towns. In the country there was not much gilt, and relatively simple upholstery. In 1771, for instance, it was in the salon of his town house in Toulouse that Monsieur de Chalvet kept his most richly upholstered set of seat-furniture, hung his crystal chandelier and displayed his collection of oriental porcelain; the salon in his château of Merville was much less elaborately fitted out.[56] The furnishing of the salon in the château of Le Marais was considered inappropriate for a château, and too much in Parisian style. Châteaux had become essentially holiday and family homes, just as they remain today.

INTERLUDE 1
PUTTING ON A SHOW

The gaily-decorated theatre of about 1840 at the château of Digoine, is one of the best nineteenth-century examples of the many private theatres of all sizes and degrees of elaboration installed in French châteaux from the eighteenth to the twentieth centuries.

THE FRENCH HAVE ALWAYS had an instinct for spectacle and presentation. Already by the seventeenth century the style and showmanship with which both women and men dressed and carried themselves spark out from the engravings of Leclerc and Abraham Bosse. When one looks down one of the many avenues, leading to a château, such as began to be planted in the sixteenth century, and proliferated thereafter, and sees the symmetrical façade and piled-up skyline at the end of it, one can have the feeling of looking at a stage set. It is more the other way round, however. Perhaps the enthusiasm with which the French took to the proscenium theatre was because it appealed to a sense of showmanship which already existed.

A taste for the theatre that started in Paris in the sixteenth century spread to châteaux in the seventeenth, and in the eighteenth and nineteenth centuries became almost an obsession. By then, whenever a house-party assembled at a château, one of the first things the guests got involved in was amateur dramatics – or at least the acting of 'Proverbs', the eighteenth-century French equivalent of charades. In most châteaux this led, at best, to a temporary stage set up in a salon, a gallery or an orangery, or out of doors in the garden, but in a sizeable minority it meant the creation of a permanent theatre. One can watch a similar process in England; and amateur dramatics in a country house, and the problems which it led to, were immortalized by Jane Austen in *Mansfield Park*. But the French enthusiasm for country-house dramatics started earlier, and was carried much further than in England. Four actual country-house theatres are known to have been built in England and Wales in the eighteenth century, as compared to at least twenty in France; in the nineteenth and twentieth centuries the comparable figures are four in England and Wales, and fourteen in France.[1] This is exclusive of royal theatres, where the contrast is even greater. Monarchs and emperors in France created theatres at their numerous residences from the seventeenth to the later nineteenth century, and in doing so must have encouraged the noblesse to follow their example; but in the same period not one royal theatre was installed in England. Even Victoria, an enthusiast for the theatre, never got further than having a temporary stage set up in one of the state drawing-rooms or the Waterloo Chamber at Windsor.

The moving spirit behind entertainments of all kinds at the French court in the later sixteenth century was Henri III's mother, Catherine de Medici. For some decades Florence and Paris were running in tandem in the development of the proscenium stage; it is not absolutely certain where it came first. The numerous entertainments were sometimes put on out of doors, sometimes in temporary buildings, sometimes in a converted grande salle, or its Italian equivalent. A grande salle with an existing raised dais at one end was obviously adaptable. The prototype of a proscenium stage was perhaps in the Salone del Cinquecento of the Palazzo Signoria in Florence, as converted for d'Ambra's play *La Cofanana* in 1565.[2] One end of the 'salone' was raised (if it was not raised already) and a single proscenium opening formed, supported on Corinthian columns, with a coat of arms above the entablature. A similar but more elaborate arrangement on a very grand scale was shown on the plans for the Tuileries, published by du Cerceau in his *Plus Excellents Bastiments* in 1579, but possibly drawn up earlier.

The Tuileries plans were never carried out, but meanwhile the enormous late-medieval grande salle of the hôtel known as the Petit-Bourbon, next door to the Louvre, was used for court entertainments in 1572 and 1581, and frequently thereafter. Engravings were made of the ballet put on in 1581. The salle ended in three arches, one large and two small; the theme of the ballet was the story of Circe, and she was seen enthroned on the dais under the big arch, with her château behind her; the action and scenery of the ballet spilled out into the main body of the salle, where the king and queen sat at one end to watch; most of the spectators were accommodated in narrow galleries, cantilevered out from the side walls.[3]

Henri IV's chief minister, the Duc de Sully, in his capacity as 'grand maître de l'artillerie', built a grande salle at the Arsenal in Paris, and it became a second venue for royal events.[4] A third great room was added to these two by Cardinal Richelieu

The medieval grande salle of the Hôtel de Petit-Bourbon in Paris, as arranged for a performance of the Ballet Comique de la Reyne in 1581, was a pioneer of the auditorium and proscenium stage in France.

when he built a grande salle on to the Palais Cardinal in 1641 – to become the Palais-Royal, and a favourite royal residence of Louis XIII on Richelieu's death in 1642. His grande salle, sometimes called the Salle de Spectacle, was a more sophisticated descendant of the grande salle at the Petit-Bourbon, with galleries down the side, and the stage behind a single great proscenium arch at one end. It was remodelled or rebuilt over the centuries, and its site is now occupied by the theatre of the Comédie-Française.[5]

All these rooms were used in a very fluid way, for weddings, dinners and balls, as well as for ballets and plays. The stage or dais at one end was to elevate whatever or whoever was appropriate at any particular moment. Circe was enthroned on it in the Petit-Bourbon in 1581; so were Louis XIII and his ministers when the États-Généraux met there in 1618 – their last meeting before 1789. At the opening performance in Richelieu's Salle de Spectacle, Anne of Austria watched the performance of Desmarets's *Mirame* seated by Richelieu in the body of the Salle (the play was considered a great failure); then the curtain fell, and rose again to reveal a magnificent grey-and-silver throne, in a superb salle; Anne of Austria processed up on to the stage to sit on the throne, from which she presided over the ball which followed.[6] At the ball held to celebrate the marriage of the King and Queen of Poland in the same Salle in 1645, Louis XIII escorted the Queen of Poland on to the stage, and they danced the branle together, watched by the court; then the general ball commenced, and the king took his seat on a throne on the stage, and watched the courtiers dancing down below.[7]

Ballets and plays proliferated in the seventeenth century; masques did not necessarily need a stage, and king, queen and courtiers frequently danced in them; plays were put on by professional actors. Both began to take place in private houses and in the country as well as in palaces and Paris. The ballet of the *Lanterniers*, danced before Louis XIII at Noisy in 1607, and the masque shown in the frescoes at Grosbois, have already been referred to.[8] At the end of 1630 the entertainment which Nicolas Goulas put on for Gaston d'Orléans in his hôtel in Paris started off with a comedy in the salle basse, followed by a 'collation' in the salle haute, and then descent to a ball in the salle basse.[9]

An alcove and a stage were the two fashionable improvements with which the Grande Mademoiselle solaced her exile at the château of Saint-Fargeau in 1653. Her installation of an alcove has already been dealt with, but the stage came first, as she describes:

> On my arrival, I thought of nothing except of fitting up a stage as quickly as possible. There was a grande salle at Saint-Fargeau, which was very suitable for this, and I listened to comedies there with more pleasure than I have ever experienced. The stage was well lit and well decorated; the company which acted was not large, but it included some well-turned-out women.[10]

At much the same time Madeleine de Scudéry relates a similar conversion in *Clélie*, as put on for the wedding of Lysonice and Cloramiste, and describes the scenery; as is often the case with her, she may be describing an actual event under pseudonyms.

> I called our Masquerade 'The varied effects of love'. As the château where we were staying had a grande salle, I had a big stage erected across one end of it. On one side of this one saw a representation of a magnificent palace, on the other a pleasant landscape; on the right hand Love at Court was

shown under a painted and gilded arch; on the other side Love in the Country, under an arch and quiver decorated with flowers.[11]

In the seventeenth century representations of plays and masques spread from Paris and the court to châteaux. A masque put on at the château of Grosbois, perhaps in 1641, is represented in one of a series of frescoes which line one room there.

It was inevitable that Fouquet should put on plays during his short but splendid reign at Vaux-le-Vicomte. Molière's presentation of *Les Fâcheux*, specially written by him in fourteen days for the occasion, took place by the water in the gardens, and was one of the episodes in the famous and fateful last fête given by Fouquet to Louis XIV at Vaux on 17 August 1661. A few weeks earlier, on 12 July, the English Queen Mother, Henrietta Maria, had been entertained at Vaux, and for her Molière put on *L'École des Maris* inside the château, probably using the alcove in the Chambre des Muses, still only partly furnished and without a bed, on a proscenium stage.[12]

These were all professional performances; what was to prove the special characteristic of the château in ensuing centuries was the scope it gave for the amateur's
delight in dressing-up, in and out of doors. It was a delight which had already been
expressed in the court ballets in Paris, and Madame de Rambouillet had exploited
it at the château de Rambouillet to satisfy her inexhaustible taste for giving people
surprises. In the 1630s, or thereabouts, the Bishop of Lisieux visited her at
Rambouillet.

> At the foot of the château there was a large meadow. In the middle of this,
> by some freak of nature, was a circle of huge rocks, growing among which
> large trees gave a very agreeable shade. The Marquise proposed a walk in the
> meadow to the Bishop. When they were near enough to the rocks to see
> through the foliage of the trees, he saw something gleaming here and there,
> and as they got closer he seemed to distinguish female forms in the
> dress of nymphs. The Marquise, at first, gave no signs of noticing what
> he saw. But when they actually reached the rocks they found
> Mademoiselle de Rambouillet and all the young ladies of the château,
> convincingly disguised as nymphs, and making the prettiest sight in the
> world, sitting on the rocks.[13]

*At the château of
Malle plays were being
put on by an amateur
cast by 1722, if not
before. Cut-out figures
from the Commedia
dell'Arte preserved in
the château (below and
right) were probably
used as stage props.*

But it was not until the eighteenth century that the inhibition which made
it seem demeaning for a lady or gentleman to act was broken, and the great
age of amateur country-house dramatics began. It can be introduced by a
letter from Alexandre de Lur-Saluces to a friend, written from his château
of Malle near Bordeaux on 28 August 1722:

> Doubling up the parts was a good idea of yours. I've already assigned
> the part of Pierrot to Monsieur de Montarlier, and that of Harlequin to
> Sieur Chaumette – I'm confident that he'll do it very well. Monsieur
> Cadet will be a wonderful Gaufichon – it's not a negligible part.
> Monsieur La Moth will be the Doctor. The performance is fixed for 22
> October. Lur-Saluces is keeping the part of Mezzelin for himself. To
> complete his appearance he's ordered a costume and a little jet-black
> wig, as short as that of a priest.[14]

Several pages of scribbled notes for plays survive in the château archives. The
play about which Lur-Saluces was writing was *Useless Precaution or Mistrust
Revenged*, and the action took place 'before the house of Gaufichon'.
Hanging in the salon at Maille today are life-sized cardboard figures of characters in the Commedia dell'Arte which must have served as elements in
the scenery of this or other plays; and the fact that a pretty rusticated arcade
at the end of a terrace at the top of the garden is carved with similar figures
suggests that this was the outdoor setting for other performances, and the

arcade may have served as the 'house of Gaufichon'. It is possible, however, that indoor showings were also put on in the orangery. Orangeries, which were usually sizeable spaces and stood empty during the warm months, when the orange trees were carried out into the gardens, were sometimes converted into temporary theatres; but it was in a separate extension to the orangery at Chantilly that the opera *Oronthée* was put on before the Grand Dauphin in 1688, and a *Ballet des Vingt-Quatre Heures* before Louis Quinze in 1722.[15]

A grande salle, in a château which had one, was another obvious venue for theatrical performances. It was in the grande salle at the château of Sully-sur-Loire that Voltaire put on his *Artémire* to entertain the house-party during his sojourn there in 1719, and it was probably in the grande salle in the château de Maisons, making use of the three arches at its end, that a comedy was going to be put on in 1722, as part of three days of entertainment devised by its owner, Président Desmaisons, in which

An arcade in the garden (below right), which is also decorated with carvings of figures from the Commedia dell'Arte, was probably used for outdoor representations.

every kind of intellectual delight would have taken place in varied succession. More than thirty seigneurs had been asked, and as many ladies. A comedy was going to be acted, and Mademoiselle Le Couvreur, the celebrated actress, had already arrived. Cardinal Fleury had been invited, and had accepted. Voltaire was going to read his tragedy *Mariane*. On the day of his arrival he was taken ill, and by nine in the evening was in a fever. The doctor … diagnosed it as smallpox. Consternation in the château,

and the whole event was cancelled.[16]

Voltaire was an indefatigable visitor to châteaux, perhaps the first professional country-house guest. He was always in demand, because a house-party of which he formed part could be guaranteed to go with a swing. He was also an indefatigable devotee of the theatre, his own and other people's, acted himself, got neighbours or the rest of the house-party to join in, created theatres of his own at the château of Cirey in the 1730s, and at the châteaux of Les Délices in Switzerland and Ferney in France in the 1750s, and was as responsible as any one man for the great eighteenth-century vogue for amateur dramatics.

Voltaire retreated to Cirey in 1734. The château had two attractions for him: its position and Madame du Châtelet, the wife of the owner. It was close to the border between France and Lorraine, which was still an independent country; he was, as usual, in trouble with the authorities because of his writings, and wanted a retreat where he could lie low and make a quick get-away, if necessary. He was already, before the move, conducting an affair with Madame du Châtelet, and she lived at Cirey with him; her husband was an army officer, and away most of the time, on duty.

The château is still remote today, in lonely wooded country of great beauty: a perfect hideout, for love, work and safety. Voltaire added on a new wing for himself, at his own expense, and created a little theatre at the top of the main building. It is still there, a delightful evocation of the pleasures and intimacies of country-house acting. It is very simple, just a big attic under the roof, a few benches down on the floor, a little box up in one wall, and a small stage and proscenium fitted in at one end, cleverly lit from a concealed window up at the back. The proscenium arch itself, and the charming simple stage-set of a kitchen, which is still in position, may possibly date from after Voltaire, but the box is certainly of his and the Châtelets' time, and so is the pleasing (if much effaced) conceit of a matching box, with people in it, painted on the opposite wall.

Both Voltaire and the Châtelets acted in plays put on here, and so did their guests, friends, and neighbours from nearby châteaux, especially Monsieur and Madame de Champbouin and the Comtesse de Neaulle. Cirey is a remote place, however. They sometimes had difficulty in getting together both a cast and an audience, and were forced to put on performances by marionettes as an alternative. So, at least, wrote Voltaire's niece, Madame Denis, who came there on her honeymoon in 1737;

The little theatre (right, above) originally installed by Voltaire in an attic under the roof at the château of Cirey, where he took refuge with his lover Madame du Châtelet in 1734, survives, along with a stage-set, to give a vivid impression of the modest charm of many château theatres. In an adjacent attic (right, below) is a selection of stage props of various dates.

but in 1738 the garrulous Madame de Grafigny, who came to stay there with her lover Leopold Desmarets, wrote of four plays underway, constant rehearsals and excitements, the pleasure of finding that everyone was talking of how wonderful an actor Desmarets was turning out to be, but also the strain of keeping up with Voltaire's restless vitality. She wrote to Pampan, the secretary of King Stanislaus of Lorraine:

> Pampan, my dear Pampan, we've just finished the third act which we've rehearsed today… It's midnight, we're going to have supper … I'm knocked out. This life we're leading is the devil. After supper Madame du Châtelet is going to sing an entire opera … One never draws breath here. Today we rehearsed *L'Enfant Prodigue* and another piece, in three acts with constant repeats. We went on redoing *Zaïre* until three in the morning … That comical Voltaire doesn't learn a word of his role until just before he goes on the stage, and then he's the only one who acts without a mistake.[17]

For the rest of the century private theatres were coming into existence all over France. They varied enormously. Some were even simpler than the theatre at Cirey, some little jewels of theatre architecture. At the simplest end one can find a stage being knocked up at one end of a salle or salon, or in an orangery, and a curtain being hung across it. At the château de Merville, one is described in 'La Garçonnière' in 1762:

> To amuse the company
> They propose a comedy.
> A stage is immediately arranged.
> All is ready, the play begins.[18]

In March 1770 the son of the Duc de Croy got the house-party of fifteen or more people acting proverbs 'on a portable stage which could be erected in a moment in the salon'.[19] At the château of Parentignat, the old salle haute on the first floor had become the 'Salle de Comédie' by the time an inventory was taken in 1791, but the conversion seems to have consisted of little except arranging a stage, setting pictures of Venus on overmantels above the two doors behind it, and running 'a large curtain of India cotton, ornamented with red flowers on a white ground' across it.[20]

In contrast (leaving aside the royal theatres at Versailles and elsewhere) were the complete little theatres with galleries and boxes constructed at the Palais Bourbon in Paris, and at Chantilly, in the 1770s, by the Condé family as their own town and country theatres; both have been long since demolished, but the exquisite designs for the theatre at Chantilly survive.[21] Others, perhaps equally elaborate, are known only from descriptions, often no more than a passing reference: the theatre at the château of Étioles which Monsieur Le Normant d'Étioles constructed in the early

1740s to amuse his pretty young wife, not yet reincarnated as Madame de Pompadour;[22] the theatre at Passy at which the opulent financier La Poplinière invited all the stars of Paris to sing and dance in the operas of his friend Rameau, who also played the organ in his chapel;[23] the theatre at the château of La Chevrette, which Louis-Denis La Lire de Bellegarde d'Épinay constructed in about 1749 to set off his brilliant daughter Madame d'Épinay, as Dufort de Cheverny recollected with nostalgia:

> La Lire acted brilliantly there; Madame d'Épinay, Monsieur Dupin de Francueil, Receiver-General of Finances, and Monsieur Dupleix de Baquencourt, Maître des Requêtes, were completely absorbed in it. A superb theatre, constructed in the orangery, attracted the best society of the neighbourhood. I came as a spectator, they suggested that I become an actor; I agreed, and found myself introduced into delightful society, filled with talent. The intervals between acting were filled with music and intrigues.[24]

It is hard when visiting the empty and echoing interiors of the château of Chambord today, where almost nothing seems later than the time of François I, to realize that it once had fitted into it what Arthur Young, who saw it in 1787, described as 'a neat, well-contrived theatre'. It was installed in the 1740s by the Maréchal de Saxe, who was occupying Chambord as tenant of the king; it was regularly used by his successors the Polignacs. Dufort de Cheverny used to watch comedies there in the 1770s, when he had moved to Touraine. He himself added to the amenities of the neighbourhood by building his own theatre to one side of the main building at Cheverny; it has gone, but it is shown inside and out in a set of naïf but charming little views of all his improvements in and around the château, which remains at Cheverny. It was clearly quite an elaborate affair, the unsightly protrusion of which was one reason for its demolition.[25] Another theatre, formed in the 1750s under the central dome of the château of Fontaine Française, was almost certainly simpler, closer to the roof-top theatre at Cirey, for there is no trace of it under the dome today, and all that remains is the memory that Voltaire visited and acted there, and some pretty fans, painted to serve as programmes.

The most perfect surviving private theatre of the eighteenth century in France is at the château of Vezenobre, to the north of Nîmes. It was built in 1754,[26] as a separate pavilion next door to the château; there are stables underneath, but owing to the slope of the ground access to the theatre and its vestibule is at ground level on the side facing the château. The exterior is elegantly simple; inside all is white-and-gold rococo plasterwork, with exquisite little boxes, surmounted by the family coat of arms, to either side of the stage.

There were some houses where the annual season of theatrical performances was the great social event of the summer or autumn in that particular neighbourhood. This was clearly the case at l'Hermitage, where the Prince de Croy encouraged his son's enthusiasm for the theatre, and the theatrical season grew more and more elaborate. It started in 1766, when the house was in the course of being rebuilt, so a small temporary theatre was contrived in the basse-cour. The scenery depicted l'Hermitage at dawn, and Croy's son, daughter-in-law, daughter and their friend the Duc d'Harvé acted, on the first night

before an audience of 200 made up of 'workmen, household servants, and officials of the garrison'. There were sixty-two people (fourteen gentry and forty-eight others) staying in the house and forty horses in the stables, 'not bad for a house where building works were going on'.[27]

It all grew much more ambitious when the remodelled house, incorporating a salle de comédie, was finally completed in 1771. The theatrical season opened on 3 October, and there were performances every few days all through the month: 'The theatre excelled for large-scale performances, and the scenery for these was better than anything to be found in any other private theatre.' The stage

A set of crude but lively little drawings showing improvements made at the château of Cheverny by Dufort de Cheverny, who bought it in 1764, include a view of the interior of the theatre (above) which he attached to one corner of the château (left).

was opened up at the back so that the surrounding forest acted as

At the château of Vezenobre a theatre was built in a separate pavilion in 1754, as shown in an engraving of about 1820 (below). It survives complete, though in need of restoration, as the most perfect private theatre of the eighteenth century in France.

an enormous backcloth, against which the movements performed by the well-trained soldiers from Condé, who provided the extras, made an amazing sight, which would have seemed like magic to anyone who had unexpectedly come across it in the middle of a wood. On big days there were at least 800 people in the auditorium and although the splendid entrance court was illuminated, there was chaos when the carriages were leaving. The final performance on 30 October was a remarkable one, and ended magnificently. A big crowd came, from the three regiments at Valenciennes, the one regiment at Condé, from Raime and from all over the place. We kept forty or so on to supper, after which they were brought back to the salle, which an hour earlier they had left as a richly decorated theatre,

and which they now found opening through a sumptuous screen of columns into the grand salon, and the two together forming a superb and brilliantly lit ballroom. The experts were much taken by it, and indeed it succeeded beyond our dreams, and became something unique when I had the end of the room opened up and one saw the forest all illuminated and making a unified extension and promenade on the same level and alignment as the rest – there was a burst of clapping, expressing the admiration which the effect deserved.

The whole of October was filled with an active and noisy social life running into the small hours, from young people staying at the château and a stream of guests,

> not bad, for a Hermitage which I had intended should live up to its name, and which had completely changed its function – thirty-one gentry staying, including our four charming grandchildren, and in all a hundred and one people sleeping in the house.[28]

L'Hermitage was rebuilt, without a theatre, in the 1780s, after the Duc de Croy's death. But the device of providing a backcloth by opening the back of the stage to the landscape beyond can still be seen in the little theatre at the château of Verderonne, where it was perhaps inspired by the arrangement at l'Hermitage, but may even have preceded it. The simple but charming theatre was installed by the Andlau family in one end of a barn in the basse-cour, it is said in 1760. At the back of the stage an arch opened on to a view into a water-garden, today agreeably in the style-Anglais, but perhaps originally a formal design. At some later stage the archway was filled in, but it has been reopened in recent years.

The château of Brienne was another place which a combination of balls, plays and hunting, all on the grand scale, made the social hub of its neighbourhood during the months that the Comte de Brienne was in occupation, often with his brother the Cardinal, who had an appartement in one wing. There was an exquisite little theatre in the basement under this, and a private staircase going down from it to his box in the theatre, which was screened (so that the Cardinal could watch theatrical performances on Sundays without causing offence).[29]

Ten or more years later, the château of Le Marais was another place which acquired a theatrical season. It started in a small way, with two comedies by the novelist and dramatist Florian put on in 1787, with young Norvins, later to be Napoleon's biographer, helping out. According to Madame de La Briche,

> Florian was both actor and impresario, Norvins filled the part of prompter and compère. The kindness people have for me extended to these plays: it was agreed that I was a good and natural actor; that a hay barn made an excellent theatre; that a decor of lavishly daubed paper was charming, etc. etc.[30]

The Le Marais season survived the Revolution, and became an increasingly big event from 1807 till about 1826, owing to Madame de La Briche's daughter the Comtesse de Molé becoming an enthusiast for the theatre. The season in 1807 ran for three weeks, from the last Sunday in August until the second Sunday in September.

> There were two performances in each of these three weeks, one on Saturday, called the dress rehearsal, for the hoi polloi from Dourdan, Arpajon and neighbouring villages, the other on the next day, for the aristocracy from nearby châteaux who came on for conversation and ices in the salons after the show, and who filled the drive with a mass of carriages worthy of the grand turnouts leaving the Paris Opéra.[31]

The theatre at Le Marais seems to have remained a simple affair of painted cardboard in a barn, and no trace of it survives today, but while it was enjoying its post-Revolution season a far more highly finished little theatre was being created by Talleyrand at Valençay, the huge Renaissance château which he had purchased in the 1790s. In 1808 Napoleon forced Ferdinand VII of Spain to abdicate, ultimately in favour of Napoleon's brother Joseph, and sent Ferdinand and the Spanish royal family into exile and what amounted to gilded imprisonment at Valençay, where they remained until 1813. He instructed Talleyrand to see that they were treated well, and to 'do everything possible to amuse them. If you have a theatre at Valençay, and could arrange for actors of comedy to go there, it wouldn't be a bad idea.'

There was no theatre at Valençay, but Talleyrand immediately created one, and it was inaugurated with an opera on 10 March 1810. The fact that it was, in effect, a royal theatre encouraged the creation of an exquisitely finished interior: a white-and-gold auditorium under a shallow dome supported on arches, all decorated with delicate neoclassical stencilling, and with Grecian maidens holding up lights to either side, or in the daytime silhouetted against the windows, for the room was clearly intended for use in daylight as well as at night. On at least one occasion the royal family became performers rather than spectators, and went up on the stage to provide a concert, Ferdinand on the flageolet, his brother Carlos on the flute and their uncle Antonio on the trumpet. After their return to Spain in 1813 Talleyrand continued to use the theatre almost up to his death in 1838, and seventeen stage-sets survive.[32]

The château theatres of the nineteenth and early twentieth centuries have the same kind of variety as those of the eighteenth, ranging from a curtain-rail fixed across the ceiling at one end of the salon, as still exists at the château of Commarin, to miniature theatres complete with boxes and galleries, like the little jewel of about 1850 at the château of Digoine; but for the family coats of arms which liberally sprinkle its decoration, this could have been imported complete from the Parisian boulevards, and it was indeed installed by the Parisian architect and decorator, Pierre Luc Charles Ciceri.[33]

Most of these theatres, simple or elaborate, are fitted into an existing building in the 'communs' (service court) or basse-cour, like the theatre at Digoine. But at Brissac a sizeable theatre was installed in the main building of the château in 1890: there was in fact a space waiting for it, for the salle haute on the second floor of the towering early-seventeenth-century corps de logis had ceased to have a function, and was already empty at the time of the inventory of 1732; by joining it up with the attic above it was possible to obtain both a theatre rather larger than the usual in châteaux, and give it a handsome approach up the great seventeenth-century staircase. The particular reason for its installation at Brissac was that its ebullient châtelaine (formerly Duchesse de Brissac, but now Vicomtesse de Trédern as a result of a second marriage) had a passion for singing in opera herself, and money to spend, as one of the two heiresses of the Say sugar fortune.[34]

Even larger supplies of new money produced the theatre at the château of La Verrerie, at Le Creusot.[35] Le Creusot was the industrial kingdom of the Schneider steel family. They made no attempt to conceal the origins of their great wealth –

The theatre at the château of Valençay (above) was installed by Talleyrand in 1810, when the Spanish royal family was put in his custody after Napoleon's conquest of Spain.

rather the opposite; they turned the buildings of the original eighteenth-century glassworks into a château, immediately next door to their huge and ever-expanding steel mills, and transformed the conical glass furnaces in the courtyard into a chapel and a little circular theatre – an ingenious twentieth-century variation on the theatres and chapels formed in circular towers in the seventeenth and eighteenth centuries. The architect for the château and its adjuncts was Ernest Sanson, the most successful designer of châteaux and Parisian hôtels of his generation, and one of the architects responsible for a revival of the Louis-Seize style. The theatre interior is, as a result, coolly classical, in contrast to the ebullient richness of theatre interiors like that at Digoine.

Events in these nineteenth- and early-twentieth-century theatres included both plays and operas, and were sometimes put on by professionals brought in for the occasion, sometimes by amateurs, sometimes by a mixture of the two. At Cirey and Valençay, and probably others of the earlier theatres, the servants were invited in to boost the audience, but later events seem to have been more exclusive. They were usually made the occasion for big house-parties, and invitations were sent out to

In 1890 the Vicomtesse de Trédern, formerly Duchesse de Brissac, created a theatre on the top floor of the château of Brissac, and took the leading roles in operas put on there herself. Here (below) she poses in costume with members of the chorus before the main entrance of the château.

neighbouring châteaux, and sometimes to the officers of a nearby garrison town, if there was one. The staging of de Corvin's play *Danicheff* by the Duchesse de Rohan and a cast of her family and friends at the château of Josselin in the early 1900s was given a whole page in the Parisian newspaper *Le Gaulois*, with detailed descriptions of the costumes, and critiques of each actor: the numerous members of the Rohan-Chabot family, and a string of counts and barons. There was an audience of more than a hundred, of whom forty were put up in the château.[36] Operas staged at Brissac produced enthusiastic comments in the 'Livre d'Or', the French equivalent of a visitors' book, but one to which guests were, and still are, expected to contribute comments and, still better, verse and pictures, designed to give pleasure to the hostess: 'Enchantress and genius of Brissac, the château of delights … Your wonderful voice opened its golden wings … its music in its flaming flight, brought with it everything that makes the spirit vibrate and sing.'[37]

At the château of Boisset-les-Prévanches, the owners, Monsieur and Madame Thiry, installed a theatre or 'salle des fêtes' in the basse-cour in 1912. In the winter the room was used to store the orange and palm trees which were carried out on

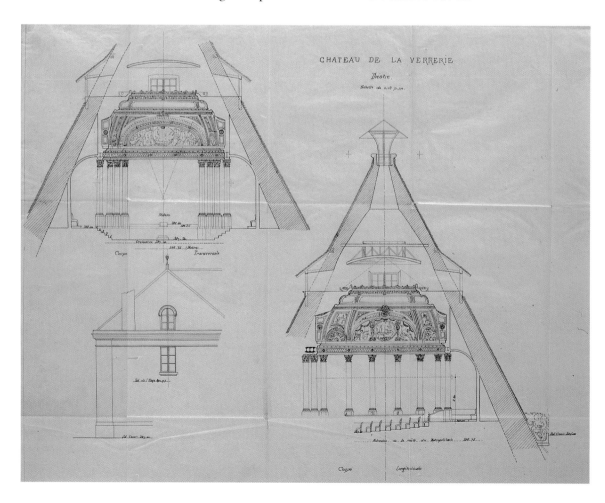

The château of La Verrerie at Le Creusot is unique among French châteaux in having been created out of an earlier glassworks by the Schneider family, whose steel mills were next door. A circular theatre, designed by Ernest Sanson, was installed in 1906 in one of the original pyramidal glass furnaces (left and above).

to the terraces in the summer, when the room took on its alternative function as a theatre. The modesty of the fittings – a stage, a very simple proscenium arch and a curtain – was probably similar to those in many eighteenth-century château theatres, and suggest why these so often vanished without trace. At Boisset the costumes are still stored in the cupboards which line the billiard-room, the pink toile de Jouy curtains survive, and photographs show the audience and the cast – on stage, assembled outside the château and at the dinner given after the performance. The shows put on were mostly operettas, the cast was always an amateur one, and the audience, of about fifty people, was made up of relatives, neighbours and officers from the nearby barracks in Évreux.[38]

Apart from plays and operas or operettas, whether put on in a purpose-built theatre or an improvised one, the denizens of châteaux were, and are, always ready to dress up, for fancy-dress balls (of which the most remarkable took place in Paris), or on impromptu occasions. But the inter-war years were not financially propitious ones for châteaux owners, and no new theatres were installed during this period.

In the 1950s the theatre in the château enjoyed perhaps its final flowering, when Charles de Beistegui created one in the château which he had bought a few years before at Groussay. This Franco-Mexican millionaire had already marked the end of post-war austerity by the fancy-dress ball he had given in the Palazzo Labia in Venice, and his theatre shows the same flair for going over the top with style. A semicircle of eighteen boxes, abundantly draped in crimson velvet and damask, surveyed a stage; one of the stage-sets represented a mirror-image of the auditorium. The theatre, which was designed by the architect Emilio Toiry, was in one of the wings which Monsieur de Beistegui added to the château, and was inaugurated on 18 March 1957, with a performance of Marivaux's *La Fausse Suivante*, presented by actors of the Comédie-Française, with decor and scenery designed by Beistegui, before an audience which included the President of France, Jean Cocteau and the cream of European society.[39]

The exquisite private theatre at the château of Groussay (below right) was created by Charles de Beistegui in 1955.

At the château of Boisset-les-Prévanches a theatre was created in the orangery in 1912, and a photograph of about the same date (left) shows a performance in progress. The cast was an amateur one: the audience, photographed at the same time (below left) include the owner and his wife in the front row, and a selection of friends, neighbours, and officers from the barracks at Évreux.

Numerous photographs in the albums of French châteaux testify to the French upper classes' passion for dressing up. Here (right) a group of descendants of the Napoleonic Prince de Wagram pose in early nineteenth-century uniforms in the château of Grosbois, which had belonged to him.

INTERLUDE 2

PLUMBING —OR THE LACK OF IT

In the late nineteenth century a bedroom at the château of Serrant was converted into a bathroom, and a bath inserted into the eighteenth-century bed alcove. At a time when bathrooms were few and far between in French châteaux, Serrant was in the remarkable position of being equipped with ten of them.

IN THE MIDDLE AGES washing and relieving oneself were catered for in France in much the same way as they were in England, or, indeed, all across Western Europe. At least from the fourteenth century all houses of any pretension were plentifully provided with latrines, privies or whatever one likes to call them; in France the commonest term in the fifteenth and sixteenth centuries was 'retrait' – retreat. A retrait was a little separate room, and contained a stone seat with one or more circular holes in it, either letting on to a shaft dropping down to ground level, or corbelled out from the surface of the main wall – usually a wall on the perimeter of the château, so that excrement dropped down to the surrounding ditch or moat. The number of seats in each individual latrine was a matter of status; single seats adjacent to the chambre of the owner, family or important guests, two or more seats in a row elsewhere. In a residential tower with a retrait on every floor, each seat could drop into a common shaft, which got larger and larger at each storey of descent; or alternatively, as in the donjon at Largoet, there could be a stack of individual shafts descending from floor to floor, on the same principle as flues in a chimney-stack. In a few châteaux, such as Pierrefonds, there were towers containing latrines and nothing else; at the mid-sixteenth-century château of Assier a semi-circular tower, linked to the main château by a narrow corridor, rose out of the moat and contained a six-seater retrait.[1]

The standard method of washing was in a tub, brought into the chambre and filled with hot water heated over the fire, as is shown in numerous contemporary illustrations. The tub, to judge from illustrations in manuscripts and occasional surviving descriptions in inventories, was often set up under some kind of curtained baldachin or canopy, either for warmth and to retain rising steam, or to mark the importance of the occasion.

The height of medieval luxury was to have a separate appartement for bathing, consisting of two rooms, a small vaulted room known as the 'étuve', warmed either by a hypocaust under a suspended floor, or by flues in a narrow partition wall, and an adjacent room containing one or more 'baignoires', or tubs, for water. The latter room also had a fireplace, which both warmed it and piped heat to the adjacent étuve. This was a room to sweat in, prior to the dip; sometimes it may also have been fitted to provide a steam bath. The adjacent 'chambre des étuves', as described in the inventory of the château d'Angers in 1471–2, contained just 'a lockable cupboard with two doors, two small wooden forms, and two large bath-tubs, one complete and the other in pieces'.[2]

An intimate bath-tub meal is depicted in a manuscript illustration of about 1500. Depictions of this period often show the bath-tub protected by a canopy.

In the Middle Ages this kind of accommodation was only for the very great or very rich, and, to judge from the known surviving examples, was extremely rare. The system derived ultimately from Roman examples, but probably came to France by way of Byzantium, the Near East and the Crusades. The Pope had it at Avignon, the ducs of Brittany had it at Suscinio, Jacques Coeur had it at Bourges; there are considerable traces left of the last two, and a handful of other examples have been identified.[3]

The medieval system of privies continued through the sixteenth and indeed well into the seventeenth century. Corrozet gave the retrait a write-up in his *Blasons Domestiques* in 1539:

Highly convenient retreat
Whether in the country or the city
Retreat which no one enters
Except to purge his stomach

Where the arse is enthroned in majesty
Retreat which one hesitates to enter
Or lift the cover of the seat
For fear (to tell the honest truth)
That the stink will escape.
Retreat where one relaxes.
But it's better for me to shut up
Rather than describe your odours
To my audience or readers.[4]

Corrozet both suggests the disadvantages of retreats, and reveals that the seat now could have a cover; this seems to be a refinement of the sixteenth century. However, new techniques or sophistications also began to appear. The most important was the gradual replacement of the medieval type of latrine by the close-stool, or 'chaise-percée'. This was just a box with a receptacle in it, but with the advantage that it could easily be emptied, and kept clean and odorous. Close-stools usually belonged to individual people, and were a status symbol; lower mortals had to use the old techniques. At Saint-Germain-en-Laye in the mid sixteenth century the king and queen had close-stools; the more important appartements had their own retrait; minor courtiers and officials had to use one of two communal retraits, but acquired an undesirable habit of relieving themselves on the staircases, a practice which was still to be found at Versailles in the eighteenth century.[5]

But already, at the château d'Esteban in 1557, a noble family was well supplied with both close-stools and another new arrival, the chamber-pot: six close-stools, covered in cloth or velvet, depending on the importance of the user; thirteen chamber-pots similarly graded, six of copper and seven of tin.[6]

The close-stools were often kept in an individual's cabinet, along with all his or her other valued belongings. Brantôme describes how two gentlewomen, servants of a lady at court, one very splendidly dressed in cloth-of-gold, retired into their mistress's cabinet, while she was at church, to make love to each other, which they did with such energy on her chaise-percée that it collapsed under them, and the cloth-of-gold lady literally fell into the shit.[7] It was not until very much later that a specialized little room, usually known as the 'cabinet de propriété', developed; its descendant was the modern 'cabinet de toilette', but this, as has been discussed, had a quite different meaning in the seventeenth and eighteenth centuries.

Occasionally étuves and adjacent baignoires continue to be found in a royal or grand context. The system remained the same, but could be combined with lavish decoration in the new Renaissance manner. François I installed a bath appartement

DAMPIERRE

THERMÆ

Eſtuues

An engraving in J.A. du Cerceau's Plus Excellents Bastiments de France *shows the 'étuve' or sweat bath installed in the base of a tower at the château of Dampierre.*

under his gallery at Fontainebleau in 1529, and another in Paris for his mistress, the Duchesse d'Étampes.[8] The étuve built by the Cardinal de Lorraine at the château de Dampierre in the mid century was considered sufficiently unusual and remarkable to be illustrated by du Cerceau in his *Plus Excellents Bastiments*. It must, indeed, have been a beautiful room, stone-lined and stone-vaulted, as was the usual arrangement for étuves, but articulated with a Doric order, and equipped with shell-headed alcoves to sit in.[9] It was at the base of the tower in the northern angle of the château, adjacent to a 'chambre des baignoires'. Du Cerceau gives no information as to how it was heated, or how water was brought to the baths. He also mentions, but does not illustrate, the 'poêle étuves baignoires' at Maulnes, the remarkable pentagonal château built by the Duc d'Uzès in the mid sixteenth century.

Bath appartements continue to be a rarity in the seventeenth century, and an intriguing passage in Savot's *L'Architecture Française*, published in 1624, suggests one reason why there were so few of them.

> Étuves and baths are not needed in France in the way they are in outlying regions where they are customary, though less so today in some regions than they used to be … we can do without them more easily than the ancients, because of our use of linen, which nowadays keeps the body clean more conveniently than was possible by means of their étuves and baths.

None the less, Savot gave instructions for any seigneur who was still out of date enough to want to wash. Appartements de bains should be situated on the lowest floor

> to make it easier both to bring water to them, and to vault them, and consist of four rooms, including a room for the furnace, a vaulted chambre de l'étuve containing a stove and hot water cisterns, and the cabinet de bain, containing one or two baths and also vaulted, but higher than the étuve and more richly decorated.[10]

Louis XIII installed baths of some richness at the Louvre and at Versailles: the latter were superbly redecorated and perhaps enlarged by Louis XIV, when the appartement contained three rooms, and an octagonal marble bath three metres wide and one deep. In a non-royal context, at the château of Pibrac, near Toulouse, the Le Faur de Pibrac family built a 'pavillon des bains' sometime between 1638 and 1676. It was in a wood at some distance from the château, and surrounded by a garden; it contained an elaborate grotto, described in an inventory of 1676, but it has long since been demolished, although its plan has been recovered by excavation.[11]

There was a circular cabinet de bain with a small single bath, apparently in an alcove to one side, as part of the royal appartement at Vaux-le-Vicomte.[12]

It does not amount to very much; and though no doubt there were other examples, and more may come to light, one can reasonably assume that the great advances

made in the science of hydraulics in France and elsewhere were, as far as châteaux were concerned, mainly used for the provision of garden waterworks, and that, as far as domestic hygiene was concerned, all but a handful of sixteenth- and seventeenth-century châteaux relied on the old system: close-stools for the gentry, latrines (now increasingly called 'lieux' – 'places' – rather than retraits) for the servants, and bathing in a tub carried into the chambre or cabinet – if bathing there was at all.

Little in the way of plumbing or sanitary fittings of any kind is shown on the many plans in Le Muet's book of his own designs, and one must conclude that the houses relied largely on close-stools. The same was true of the internal arrangements of the château of Richelieu, but for the servants there was a provision of 'latrines' which was far from impressive at the magnificent château of the most powerful man in France: the corps de logis of the château was set a little way back from the perimeter of a moated rectangular island, with four extruded corners shaped like fortifications; the latrines (so-called on the contemporary plan) took the form of little pavilions at the four points of these, and presumably dropped their contents directly into the moat.[13] A similar arrangement is to be found at the château of Missery in Burgundy, but here there was just one latrine turret, which survives, complete with its stone seat – and appears to date from as late as the eighteenth century.

In the course of the eighteenth century Savot's complacency was abandoned, and the provision of service rooms reached a new pinnacle of ingenuity and inventiveness. That same feeling for gaiety, intimacy and sensual pleasure which developed the cabinet and produced the nests of little rooms around the chambre

At the château of Richelieu (above), built for Cardinal Richelieu in the 1630s, four 'lieux' or privies were installed at the four corners of the château above the moat. A similar if more modest arrangement survives at the château of Missery, where a single eighteenth-century privy turret is corbelled out over the water (right).

was exploited to turn the acts of washing and relieving oneself into a decorative and enjoyable business.

Lovely rococo designs for salles and appartements de bains, and that (for France) new product of hygiene technology, the 'cabinet' or 'lieu à soupape', are to be found in the treatises of Blondel, Briseux and Mariette. A soupape or 'valve' was the French abbreviation for a water-closet, an invention which came to France from England, so that in France in the eighteenth century it was sometimes called a 'soupape à l'Anglaise'. But no English design attained the rococo splendour with which it was ensconced in the Hôtel de Soubise in Paris, as published in Mariette's *L'Architecture Française* in 1737–8: virtually a royal throne in a lofty alcove set in a spacious and elegantly panelled room.[14]

In his *Maisons de Plaisance* (1737), Blondel wrote enthusiastically about the invention, and gave his own delicately frivolous design, carved with monkeys, those favourite accompaniments to the French toilet in the eighteenth century. He wrote:

> The lieux à soupape are very suitable to be placed adjacent to the main appartement, because they never smell … They can be very prettily decorated, and it is usual to enclose them in a panelled or marquetry box and place this in a niche formed like an alcove, to either side of which are little doors, one of which gives access to the garderobe, which is behind the cabinet, and the other serves as a cupboard for storing scented waters.[15]

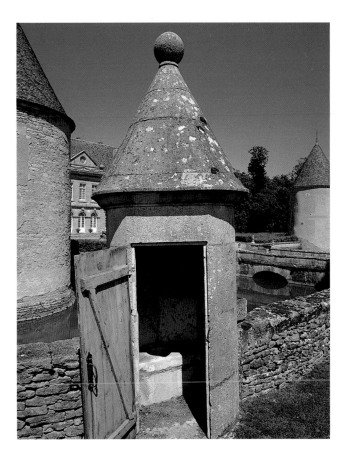

Briseux, in his *Maisons de Campagne*, listed lieux à l'Anglaise as an optional accompaniment to his ideal appartement de bains, which otherwise consisted of antechambre, salle de bains, étuve, chaussoir (boiler room), and chambre de bains; the last was to be fitted out with bed, chairs and fireplaces, as a place to recover in and receive company after the bath.[16] Two similar appartements were illustrated by Blondel in his *Maisons de Plaisance*, one of them supposedly designed for a 'Seigneur in Florence'. Both were delicately and elaborately decorated with rococo ornament. One of the salles de bains was 'large enough to contain two baths', which was more usual than rooms with a single bath, 'whether it be that two people can keep company and amuse themselves with each other, or because the arrangement is more symmetrical, or because it is intended to have one bath for hot water and the other for tepid water, according to the season'. The baths took the form of tubs in alcoves, which became the common French arrangement, in contrast to England, which in the eighteenth century favoured the plunge bath.[17]

A year or two before these descriptions were published Voltaire had arranged a little appartement de bains during his time at the Marquis du Châtelet's château of Cirey. Whatever Voltaire did was given top publicity, and one may wonder whether it was the sight of the plans for this (the architect is not known) which set off Blondel's and Briseux's designs.

Madame de Grafigny stayed at Cirey in 1738, and described the appartement de bains in ecstatic language which epitomizes (as do her descriptions of Madame du Châtelet's own rooms) all her generation's taste for pretty, small-scale things:

Oh, what an enchanting place! the antechambre is no bigger than your bed, the chambre de bains is entirely lined with tiles, except the floor, which is of

An engraving (left) in Blondel's Maisons de Plaisance *(1737) shows a bathroom fitted with two tubs, a common feature at the time. Blondel also gives the plan of the room (right above) and an enlarged detail shows the connection of the tub to a boiler and cold-water tank.*

The water-closet or 'soupape à l'Anglaise' installed in the Hôtel de Soubise in Paris, as engraved in 1737 (below right).

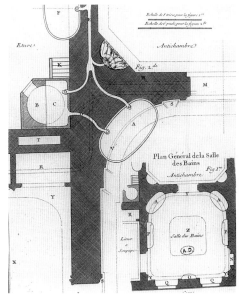

marble; there is a cabinet de toilette, of the same size, the panelling of which is varnished a clear celadon green – divinely gay, and exquisitely carved and gilded – furnishings in proportion, a little sopha, charming little armchairs en suite, all carved and gilded, corner cupboards, porcelain, engravings, pictures, a dressing-table, a painted ceiling. The chambre is richly decorated and similar in every way to the cabinet, furnished with mirrors and amusing books on lacquered stands. Everything seems made for Lilliputians – indeed, I've never seen anything so pretty … I keep longing for you to have something similar, knowing your good taste for little nests … the chimney-piece is no bigger than a chair, but it's a jewel that one longs to put in one's pocket.[18]

Voltaire's appartement de bains has gone without trace, as part of what seems a deliberate policy of the nineteenth-century owners of the château of Cirey to efface all traces of his adulterous and free-thinking memory. In inventories, in plans, in letters, in contemporary publications, one comes across descriptions of or passing references to other appartements or single salles de bains, some never executed, too many others demolished or altered out of all recognition. For the most part they are situated as Savot and Briseux recommended, either in the basement (or on the ground floor, if there was no basement), or in a separate wing or a free-standing pavilion. Robert de Cotte made a series of variant designs

in 1728 for a very splendid pavillon de bains at the château of Saverne, the huge country residence of the archbishops of Strasbourg. Most consist of a vestibule leading into a central 'salon', containing a sofa between two matching baths in alcoves, with bedrooms and garderobes to either side; most are of two storeys. But none of the projects seems to have been carried out.[19]

One would like to have seen the salle de bains described as existing in 1741 in the house rented by the Duc de La Trémoille in the Parisian suburbs: a sofa and six armed-chairs of gilded wood upholstered and fringed in white mohair, a fireplace, a copper bath in a painted case, four big taps of gilded ormolu, and overall 'a canopy and curtains of Dutch bazin serving to enclose the bath' – an eighteenth-century descendant of the common medieval arrangement.[20] Or to know more about the 'corps de logis de bains' in the garden of the château de Bourdonné, in which Geneviève de Malboissière described her father as sleeping in 1764, when she was lodged in the main body of the château.[21] Or to have seen the appartement de bains – 'rechauffoir', antechambre, salle de bains, chambre à coucher – in the basement of the château of Le Marais, before it was dismantled in the nineteenth century.[22] Or to have illustrations of the baths in the Palais-Bourbon in Paris, or the many other luxurious Parisian baths in hôtels particuliers or the appartements of courtesans, described in contemporary sources but long since demolished. Or, indeed, to have more details of the portable and re-erectable salles de bains (complete with bed, chairs, two baths, and exterior decoration with trellis-work) which were advertised in Parisian newspapers in the 1770s as suitable for the garden.[23]

Few enough survive – some royal bathrooms, a couple or so others in Paris, but only a handful of rooms in actual châteaux, none of them complete, although more may remain to be discovered. In about 1730 the Comte de Toulouse, Madame de Montespan's son by Louis XIV, created a bathroom in the basement of the château de Rambouillet. The tiles are still in position, but all traces of a bath have disappeared. The little 'salle de bains' designed by Clérisseau in 1767 for the rich Marseille merchant Louis-Joseph Borély, at the so-called château Borély or (in Marseille nomenclature) Bastide Bonneveine just outside Marseille, contained a covered marble bath in a semi-circular niche off a small octagonal room with a pretty ceiling, and an even smaller 'boudoir' adjoining. The rooms are still there, but the bath has been removed in recent years.[24]

At the château of Gatellier a simply decorated but very charming salle de bains of about 1760 is complete except for the sad loss of its two bath-tubs (in use as tanks in the garden within living memory). The room is in the basement and measures about 5.5 by 6.5 metres. There are adjoining recesses for two oval baths in one of the short sides, and an alcove for a bed in the centre of the long side, between two glazed doors: one is for access and the other leads into a little room which was probably a lieu or 'garderobe de propriété'. There is a fireplace opposite the bed alcove; fireplace and openings are all nicely adorned with simple but elegant curves and mouldings of the period.

To the best of my knowledge no eighteenth-century soupape à l'Anglaise survives in position in a French château. Mention should be made, however, of the delightful little oval lieu which adjoins the circular cabinet in the south tower of the château de Haroué. The château was designed by Boffrand for the Prince de Craon in 1720–31, and the lieu is clearly shown on Boffrand's plan.[25] It now contains a water-closet, the machinery of which is nineteenth-century or later, although the simple joinery of the box may be earlier; what the original technology was (if any) is uncertain. But the decoration of this little room – inlaid marble floor, ceiling painted with flowers and trellis-work, and the seat tucked into one end of the oval – has something of the gaiety to be found in Blondel's and Mariette's more elaborate designs for these necessary but seldom more than utilitarian rooms.

A problem working against adequate provision of bathrooms or plumbing in most eighteenth-century châteaux, however, was the lack of an adequate piped-water supply.

A few examples of elaborate systems of supply are known. Madame de Pompadour's brother, the Marquis de Marigny, who had a taste for luxury, installed a 'machine hydraulique destinée à monter l'eau au château', at his château of Ménars in 1763, to the designs of Simon Auercoust, a protégé of the architect Gabriel.[26] Substantial remains of this survive, but exactly how it worked has still to be established. It had no architectural pretensions, unlike the exceedingly grand neoclassical 'château d'eau' or pump-house which adjoins the château of Le Bouilh, near Bordeaux. This, like the château itself, was designed by Victor Louis for the Marquis de La Tour du Pin in 1787, and unlike the château, of which only a third was built, it was completed. It survives as one of the most impressive remaining examples of water architecture in France. The water supply was powered by a ram,[27] fed with water flowing through a deep channel under the cupola which lights the main chamber; the water is still flowing, but nothing is left of the pumping machinery.

The early-eighteenth-century bathroom installed for Louis XIV's natural son by Madame de Montespan in the château of Rambouillet is still lined with the original tiles, but no trace of the bath remains.

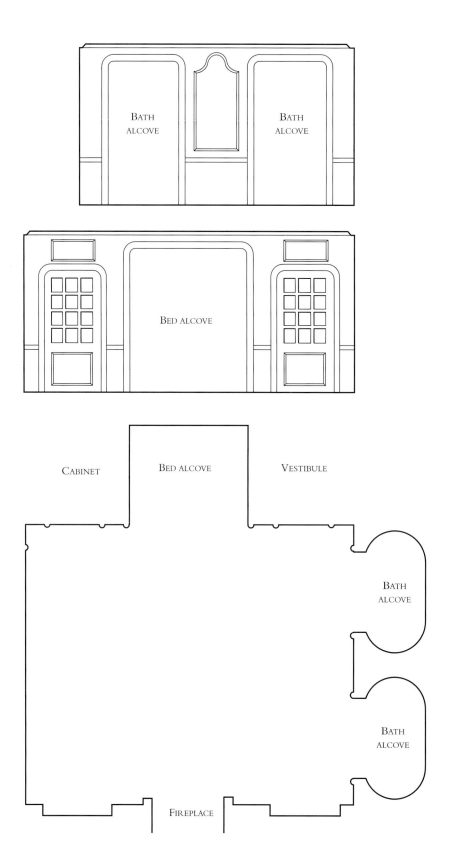

BATH
ALCOVE

BATH
ALCOVE

BED ALCOVE

CABINET

BED ALCOVE

VESTIBULE

BATH
ALCOVE

BATH
ALCOVE

FIREPLACE

*The new main building
of the 1760s at the
château of Gatellier
contained a bathroom
in the basement (left)
fitted with two tubs in
alcoves, a fireplace and
an alcove for a bed. The
tubs have disappeared
but otherwise the bath-
room survives complete.*

*A glimpse of the inlaid
marble floor of the
eighteenth-century
'lieu' in the château of
Haroué (right).*

However, in the vast majority of châteaux, although the desire to have elegant bathing and sanitary accommodation may perhaps have existed, the technology was lacking, and they had to do what they could with a servant pumping away down the well (as shown in a surviving drawing at the château de Barbentane[28]) or, at best, a horse-pump fixed to the well, and worked by a horse repeating an interminable circle, as shown in a 1781 design for the installation in the basse-cour of the château of Le Buissant.[29] At the château of Montgeoffroy there was originally a hand-pump fixed to the outside wall of the kitchen; the pump has gone, but the decorative brass tap from which the water emerged in the scullery survives. This was the only pump-

fed water point in the château in the eighteenth century.[30] The handsome marble cistern for washing glasses and possibly cooling bottles, outside the salle à manger, was fed from a cistern which had to be filled by hand. A tin bath in an elegant rococo frame, now up in the attic, was clearly also designed to be filled by hand. It does not feature in the 1775 inventory, and it is not certain when it came to Montgeoffroy.

At the château of Gatellier there is now a nineteenth-century hand-pump on the wall outside the room containing the cistern which fed the bath. It must have replaced an eighteenth-century pump similar to the one (made in Lyon and dated 1784) which survives in the entrance court of the château of Sury-le-Comtal nearby.

The eighteenth-century arrangement known to have existed at the château de Flines is probably typical. All water derived from a hand-pump fitted to a well in a room in the basement of this agreeable late-eighteenth-century château; this may possibly have pumped water up into the cabinet of the salle à manger, immediately overhead, or into the kitchen or one of the adjacent rooms, also in the basement. But there was certainly nothing resembling a soupape à l'Anglaise, or indeed any sanitary accommodation in the house. Instead there was a four-seater lieu for the family in a separate little building adjoining the orangery in the garden – four seats in a row, two large and two small, the seats with elegant carved backs in the same style as the joinery in the house. Nearby was another little building for the servants, also with four seats, but these all of the same size and with no

The magnificent neo-classical château d'eau (left) designed by Victor Louis in 1787 to supply water to the château of Le Bouilh.

A design (above right) for a horse-worked pump to raise water in a series of buckets from a well in the basse-cour at the château of Le Buissant. The system was known in France as a 'noria', and fragmentary remains of one survive in the temple at Montgeoffroy, illustrated on p.236.

A design (below right) for a hand-worked pump to be inset in a well at the château of Barbentane.

carving. The arrangement survived within living memory, but only the ruins of the two buildings remain.[31]

In the provision of plumbing France and England in the eighteenth century were not dissimilar from each other; if anything, France was in the lead. If most houses still relied on close-stools and tubs placed in front of the bedroom fire and manually filled with water, a sizeable minority had proper bathrooms, often of considerable elegance. England went in for the plunge bath, France for the tub-bath, preferably two of them; but both countries had an ideal of the bath as an aesthetic and sensual pleasure, as well as a practical and hygienic convenience, and expressed this in the elegant and at times frivolous design of their bathrooms.

The French tradition of exotic bathrooms went on into the Napoleonic period. Napoleon's sister, Pauline Borghese, installed luxurious bathrooms at all her many residences; they have all been broken up, although one of her marble baths, with gilt taps in the form of swans, has been moved to the château of Le Grange. The Empress Josephine's elegant neoclassical bathroom survives at the château de Malmaison.

But from perhaps the 1830s onwards, in England as well as in France, the idea that a bathroom, still less a lavatory, could be aesthetically and physically enjoyable, disappeared. Before the twentieth century most new-built English country houses had only one bathroom, or at most two – one for the gentry and one for the

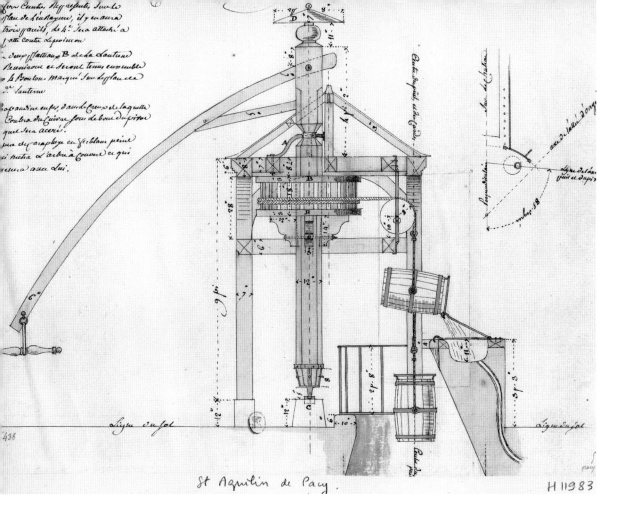

St Aquilin de Pacy.

H 11983

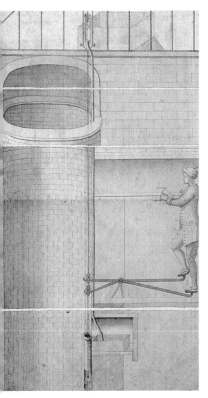

servants – and a tin bath in front of the bedroom fire remained the commonest way of washing into the twentieth century. Water-closets, on the other hand, became necessary fittings for country houses both new and old. The simple device of the S-trap – an S-shaped bend in the waste pipe from the pan – had got rid of the smell which had been their main disadvantage, and from the 1830s more and more houses were able to have them in abundance, as water, pumped up to a tank in a water-tower, made running water available on every floor.

The triumph of the water-closet did not extend to France, or at least to French châteaux, and bathrooms were even less in evidence. The Duc de Doudeauville, who hunted from his château of La Gaudinière, new-built in 1863–70, with a feudal lavishness reminiscent of the château of Chantilly in its great days in the eighteenth century, when asked if he was installing bathrooms in the château, replied, 'I am not building an hôtel.' It is instructive to look at the plans of the Angers architect, Édouard Dainville, who was much employed in building or enlarging châteaux on a considerable scale all over Anjou in the mid nineteenth century.[32] The thirteen châteaux where he worked between 1856 and 1881, and the plans of which survive in the Archives Départementales in Angers, score between

In the eighteenth
century at the château
of Montgeoffroy, a tap
in the kitchen (above
left) was fed with water
by a hand-pump fixed
to an external wall, and
was the only water-
point inside the
château. The marble
basin outside the salle à
manger (left) was filled
from a hand-filled tank
in the cupboard above
it. A tin bath (above
right) was also hand-
filled.

them two bathrooms and one water-closet; and the water-closet is to be found in the last of the series, the château de la Tremblai, plans for which were made in 1881. Up till then his châteaux had to make do, like their predecessors, with a not over-abundant supply of 'lieux'.

Plumbing was first installed in the château of Flines in the 1860s. A horse-worked pump delivered water up from the well to a water-tower on the terrace over the entrance gatehouse to the courtyard. Two outdoor water-closets were installed on the terrace, which communicated with the house at first-floor level, and an outside bathroom was inserted into the ground floor of the gatehouse, where its tiled floor is all that survives of what was considered in the neighbourhood at the time to represent the height of progress.[33]

Horror stories about the plumbing, or more often the lack of it, in French châteaux used to be a favourite stock-in-trade of English visitors who had stayed in them. The retreat from the aesthetic bathroom, common to both countries, in France was perhaps in part a reaction against eighteenth-century frivolity and worldliness: Voltaire's bath appartement at Cirey was ruthlessly blotted out and nothing took its place. But in France the retreat from worldliness was not replaced by that passion for hygiene which spawned so many English country-house water-closets. One reason was, no doubt, the lack of a running-water supply; but this lack was perhaps itself a symptom of the fact that running water and up-to-date plumbing were not considered a first priority, since the technique to provide them certainly existed.

At the château of Montgeoffroy, running water came into the house in the 1830s.[34] A machine of the type known in France as a 'noria' – an endless chain of buckets lowered and raised down the shaft of a well, usually operated by a horse moving round the well – was installed in a well protected by a little pump-house, disguised as a Doric temple, at the end of the main vista rising up from the axis of the salon. This raised water sufficiently high to gravity-feed it into the ground floor of the château, and operate a fountain in a pond before its garden façade.

Steam-driven pumps appeared in a few châteaux at the end of the nineteenth century. At the château of Thoiry the ruins of the late-nineteenth-century pump-house survive in the purlieus of the château,[35] and there is an evocative drawing of the vanished pump-house at Madame Heine's château of Roquencourt, later to be inherited by her daughter, Princesse Murat.[36] At the château of Avignon, built by the Noilly-Prat family in the 1890s on the proceeds of the drink of that name, the

A hand-worked pump of the 1780s (below) in the courtyard of the château of Sury-le-Comtal.

technology of water-supply reached heroic proportions. About a hundred metres from the château a great classical engine-house (now sadly denuded of its steam-driven engines) proudly bears the inscription 'Eaux du château d'Avignon 1896', and looks across two shallow reservoirs, formally arrayed like a water-garden in front of an orangery, to a lofty water-tower. Water was pumped from the Rhône, which runs immediately below the engine-house, up into the water-tower and then fed by gravity to the château and its surrounding gardens. All this is in the grand manner after which the bathroom in the château, one of the beneficiaries of the system, comes as rather an anti-climax – a good solid bourgeois bathroom, with a tub-bath in one corner and no hint of extravagance about it.

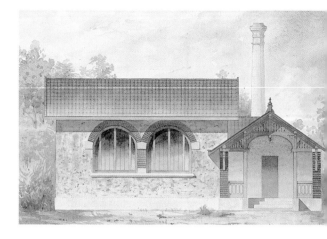

But the history of water-supply at French châteaux is in need of research. There is no doubt that the château of Boisset-les-Prévanches, where running water did not arrive until the early 1900s,[37] was far from untypical, and that there were many

The temple (below) built in the 1840s at the end of the garden vista from the château of Montgeoffroy contained a 'noria' or horse-worked pump.

By the late nineteenth century the luxurious château of Rocquencourt was a rare example of a château supplied with water from a steam pump and the designs for the pump-house survive (left).

châteaux in which it did not come until substantially later – or at best only came to the kitchen and a single bathroom. In the 1960s when the Vicomte de Baritault's English wife came to the château of Roquetaillade, magnificently restored by Viollet-le-Duc, she found one bathroom, no water-closets and sixty chamber-pots.[38]

But at the end of the nineteenth century baths and water-closets began to appear in some quantity at a handful of châteaux. A number of water-closets were installed in the château of Montfort at the end of the 1880s, and in September 1889 evoked a letter from Comtesse Antoine de Nicolay, wife of the owner, to her mother-in-law:

> The WCs are fine. There is one detail in the seat which could have been made differently, but it's minimal. Antoine's one comment was to express a fear that those endowed with a modest development might completely disappear through the hole (Queen of Spain model) and only be stopped by the valve. Perhaps a rod and a loop, like those supplied to hospital beds, would be a sensible provision to rescue those unfortunate enough to get into trouble.[39]

At the château of Avignon steam pumps in a pump-house (below), prominently inscribed 'Eaux du château d'Avignon 1896', pumped water directly from the Rhône up into a water-tower, from which it was fed to the château and gardens.

A generous supply of bathrooms and WCs was often a sign of new money, whether coming through the husband or the wife. When the fashionable Parisian architect Ernest Sanson largely rebuilt the château of Mennetou-Salan for Prince and Princesse d'Arenberg in the late 1880s, he provided it with two water-closets and no bathroom. His lavish conversion of the historic château of Chaumont in the 1880s for the Prince and Princesse de Broglie was financed by her fortune as heiress of the Say sugar fortune, and was much more lavishly equipped with water-closets – twelve in all, spread over four floors. But it still had only one bathroom.[40]

When the sixteenth-century château of Serrant was restored and modernized around 1890, under the architect Lucien Magne, it was fitted out with ten bathrooms. These were skilfully fitted into little closets in the thickness of the tower walls, inserted into former bed alcoves, or, in one case, disguised as a bedroom wardrobe. The influence at work here was probably not that of the client, the Duc de La Trémoille, head of a historic French family, but of his wife Marguerite (d. 1868), whose father Comte Tanneguy Duchâtel owed his title to his having been Louis-Philippe's chief minister, and who came from a different background.

Probably the most technologically up-to-date (though far from the most beautiful) château to be built in France in the decades before the 1914–18 War is the enormous Trevarez in Brittany, built by a millionaire Brest merchant

and entrepreneur, James de Kerjégu, between 1894 and 1906. His architect was Walter-André Destailleur, son of the better-known Gabriel-Hippolyte-Alexandre Destailleur: father and son between them specialized in providing sumptuous neo-Renaissance châteaux paid for by new money, sometimes allied to old blood. Their masterpiece is in fact outside France: Waddesdon Manor, a brand-new exotic transplanted, as it seems, from the valley of the Loire to a Buckinghamshire hilltop for Baron Ferdinand de Rothschild, in one of the handsome baths of which the Baron actually expired in 1898.

In terms of design Trevarez is a bit of a brute, but in terms of technology its lavishness is in striking contrast to the standard French château of the time; greater, indeed, than anything which could then have been found in England. It had electricity, lifts, central-heating, refrigerators, and plumbing in abundance, all supplied from Paris: twelve water-closets, two showers and eight bathrooms, one of them with two baths in it. Five of the bathrooms contained tub-baths, the remainder, including the double bathroom, had plunge baths, set flush into the tiled floor; all the bathrooms had heated towel cupboards.

Trevarez was badly damaged and stripped of most of its contents and fittings during the Second World War. Tracing the remains of its bathrooms has become a matter of industrial archaeology, at its strangest and most evocative in the former double bathroom, where only the shattered and ghostly outlines of the fittings remain around the holes in the floor which once contained the two plunge baths, side by side.

Judging by the exterior of Trevarez, and surviving photographs of the grand rooms of the interior, the bathrooms, fitted with the massive commercial plumbing of the day, would have been its most satisfactory internal feature. But a few bathrooms with a hint of eighteenth-century aesthetic ebullience are to be found elsewhere, such as the magnificent marble tub-bath installed around 1900, underneath the chapel in the nineteenth-century tower built out into the moat at Sully-en-Bourgogne; but above all in the fittings installed by the Marquis de Castellane at the château of Le Marais also around 1900, including at least one wash-basin with exquisitely chased ormolu fittings made to Louis-Seize designs. This expressed the taste of the celebrated Boni de Castellane, who restored the chateau and who used to beg his guests 'to wear tea-gowns which would not clash with the delicate tones' of his salons.

A massive and shapely bath, installed in about 1900 in the basement under the chapel and overlooking the moat at the château of Sully-en-Bourgogne.

The extension to the Rothschilds' château d'Armainvilliers, built in the 1880s, was as lavishly equipped with bathrooms as Trevarez: seven on the main bedroom floor alone, almost an average of one to each bedroom, and opening directly into them. In 1925–30 a rather staid bathroom with an encased tub, installed in their château de Ferrières when it was first built in the 1860s, was transformed with Art Deco furniture and decoration by Clément More for Baronne Édouard de Rothschild.[41] Peacocks fly through Art Deco clouds in the alcove above the bath and the commode is rich with characteristic inlay.

New châteaux, or châteaux newly modernized, in the 1920s often have the solidly functional fittings of the period; and since the Second World War the blessings of modern plumbing have spread to more and more châteaux – but still by no means to all of them.

INTERLUDE 3

THE HOUSEHOLD

A noblewoman is addressed by her maid, from a set of illustrations to a late-fifteenth-century romance called Les Amours de Jean de Montfort, *in the Musée Condé at Chantilly.*

ONE OF THE BEST-KNOWN illustrations in the *Très Riches Heures du Duc de Berry* shows the duc at dinner. He sits at table alone with an abbot or bishop, in front of the fireplace, as was the usual arrangement, though protected from too great a heat by a fire-screen; a canopy projects over his head from above the fireplace. A crowd of richly dressed noblemen and others are watching him, and warming their hands at the fire, but are not grand enough to sit at the same table with him, although one of them is leaning over the back of the duc's chair to hear or join in the conversation.

As prominent as the duc in his wonderful blue-and-gold robe, which sweeps to the ground and flows under the table, are the three servants standing in the foreground. They are superbly elegant figures dressed in the height of fashion in patterned robes of different colours, two with different coloured stockings on either leg; they wear spurs and carry swords or daggers. A similarly dressed servant is partly concealed at the end of the

table. A fourth servant stands behind the duc, inviting the bystanders to 'approach, approach', and warm their hands at the fire. He too wears a splendid robe, of red and gold with gold tassels, and carries a long rod of office over his shoulder. Although he is older and less glamorous than the young men in the foreground, he is clearly a person of authority.

Servants waiting on the Duc de Berry in about 1415. A detail from one of the illustrations to the Très Riches Heures du Duc de Berry.

To the left and right of the picture are two more soberly dressed servants, without arms and spurs and wearing plain grey cloaks and black scarves and necklets. The contrast between these two and the other five epitomizes the basic division in all big medieval households: between 'gentilhommes' and 'serviteurs', noble and non-noble. The elegant three in the foreground are the 'écuyer panetier', the 'écuyer échanson' and the 'écuyer tranchant'; the older man in the background is the 'maître d'hôtel'. These were the four noble servants who attended the meals of their master. They would all have been of good seigneurial families, and, as noblemen, entitled to carry swords; Gaston de Foix's three waiting écuyers, as has appeared, were his three bastard sons.

In the *Très Riches Heures* picture, the figure on the left is the écuyer échanson. He holds the duc's covered golden goblet in his right hand; with his left hand he has lifted the cover off the duc's golden tasse, his tasting-cup, so that his non-noble assistant, the 'sommelier de l'échansonnerie', or wine-waiter, can pour in some wine, for it to be tasted prior to the duc's goblet being filled. The prime reason for tasting was to detect poison, not to ensure that the wine was of adequate quality.

The figure in green towards the right is the écuyer tranchant – the carver. He holds a knife above a plate of portions of meat, which he has just cut up. The figure on his left is the écuyer panetier, who was responsible for serving up the bread, and the food generally. The young man in red at the end of the table is not one of the duc's household, but the visitor's écuyer, who has come with his master, as was the practice, and is cutting up his meat, or tasting it. The figure in the background is the maître d'hôtel, in overall charge of serving the meal, and indeed of the whole household; he was always an older and soberer man than the gorgeous young écuyers. The little servant crouched down to the right, feeding the dog, is probably one of the 'valets servant', who did the heavy work of carrying food and plate from the kitchen and adjacent rooms: it was only in the ultimate stage of serving the lord and his guests that the écuyers were interposed.

The écuyers, besides serving at table and, as will appear, running the stables, acted as bodyguards and companions to their master. Olivier La Marche, in his description of the écuyers of Charles Le Hardi, Duc de Bourgogne, written in 1474, is dealing with a household of exceptional size, but what he has to say could be applied more generally to these dashing young men of good family but little fortune in all big households:

> The écuyers accompany the prince wherever he goes, on foot or horseback, act as bodyguards, and wardrobe masters, and sleep next to his room to keep watch over his person. When the duc retires to his chambre after having worked on his affairs all day, and given constant audience, the écuyers go with him to keep him company. They sing to him, read him romances and novels, talk about love and war, and fill up his time with entertaining novelties.[1]

The 'gentilhommes servants' were the sparkling, snow-covered peak of the household mountain; under them was the grey solid mass of the serviteurs, who did all the manual and most of the clerical work. They worked in four main areas: indoors in the kitchen, in the offices and chambres, and outside in and around the stables.

The kitchen, in a big household, was presided over by the 'écuyer de cuisine'; perhaps in very early days or very grand households he may have been noble, but, in spite of his title, he was not normally so; even so, he was a figure of importance, with a sizeable staff of 'cuisiniers' under him, and under them the lowest element of the household, the 'happelopins' who turned the spits and the 'enfants' or 'garçons de cuisine', the kitchen-boys, who were clothed and fed but paid no wages, because they were effectively apprentices, coming into the kitchen to learn their craft.

The adjacent offices could be a conglomeration of rooms, small and large: an 'échansonnerie' for the dispensing of drink, the equivalent of an English buttery, with access to the cellars; a 'paneterie' for bread, a 'fruiterie' for fruit and a 'sausserie'

The late-fifteenth-century kitchen in the château of Scorbé-Clairvaux. From the Middle Ages on into the eighteenth century, kitchens were often vaulted for security against fire.

for spices, each with one or more sommeliers in charge, and possibly with some unpaid 'garçons d'office' under them. Outside the kitchen, and communicating with it by a hatch, was the 'dépense', the servery, in which the valets servants waited to collect the food.

The chambre staff included a number of 'valets de chambre', the 'tapissier', in charge of tapestries and hangings and the 'fourrier', in charge of furs and other hangings. ('Valet' was the general status term for serviteurs; a valet was the equivalent of an English yeoman, and etymologically of the same root as 'varlet'.)

The 'écuries' were, inevitably, in the charge of the 'écuyer d'écuries'; the basic definition of an écuyer, as his name expressed, was a horse-riding gentleman. The stables had to contain horses or mules for the master and his family; for the maître d'hôtel and all the écuyers in the household; for one or more trumpeters, such as are seen sounding away to greet May morning in front of a proud cavalcade in one of the *Très Riches Heures* illustrations; and also to mount the pages, the young boys of noble birth who came into a household for education in the ways of a gentleman. Since one of the first duties of a gentleman was to learn to ride a horse, these boys were put under the charge of the écuyer d'écurie, though they also went in to the house and served at table.

At the valet level the stables contained the 'palefreniers' and 'muletiers', the grooms who looked after the riding horses and the mules; the 'valets de pied', from at least the fifteenth century also known as the 'lacquais', who ran alongside the horsemen to add to the impressiveness of the cavalcade; one or more 'braconniers' to look after the dogs; and probably a 'fauconnier' in charge of the falcons. A porter had his quarters by the outside gate, and supervised who went in and out.

Though gentlemen and serviteurs made up the two main sections of a big medieval household, there were three other elements: priests, professionals and women. The priests always included one or more 'aumôniers', in charge of distributing alms, and one or more chaplains, in charge of the chapel which was an inevitable feature of any large medieval château, although it could vary very much in size, and in the number of priests attached to it. The professionals could include a doctor, an organist, a secretary, and the receiver and clerks who took in incoming rents and kept the accounts: they were technically classed as 'serviteurs', but, in terms of status, they were somewhat uneasily poised between the gentle servants and the serviteurs.

French medieval households, like medieval households all over Europe, were predominantly male. Effectively, women looked after women or babies, and did the laundry. Just as the lord had his noble écuyers and his non-noble valets de chambre, so his wife had her noble 'demoiselles' and her non-noble 'femmes de chambre'. There were no women in the kitchen, and the bulk of the cleaning (such as it was) was done by men. The demoiselles usually consisted of an older woman of dignity and authority, known as the 'demoiselle de compagnie', and a greater or lesser number of young women (depending on the grandeur of the household and the number of daughters in the family), known as the 'filles'.

Lists of wages, legacies and funeral expenses made at the time of the death of Richard Picque, Archbishop of Reims, in 1389, give some idea of the size and nature of his household.[2] He was one of the greatest princes of the Church in France, in some ways the equivalent of the English Archbishop of Canterbury, for it was the Archbishop of Reims who crowned the French king. He had a château and palace in Reims, the château of Courville and at least two others in the country, and a house in Paris.

For someone of his importance, his household does not strike one as an especially large one. He had a basic establishment of about thirty-eight people, twenty-nine indoor and nine outdoor, including five noblemen and four clerics. There were no women. In addition, twenty-four named individuals served in the agricultural establishment, which forms one of the most interesting features of the wage-list, in charge of pigs, sheep, wagons, wagon-horses, barns, forges and wine-cellars, distributed through the various properties, but the largest proportion at Courville.

A final group consists of the three 'capitaines' of the three châteaux. There is no mention of payment to any kind of garrison, but the wages of the captains vary so much in size, and are so much larger than the average, that it is possible that they had to pay the individual garrisons out of them. The archbishop's armoury was kept in the château of Porte-Mars at Reims. It included complete sets of armour – coats of mail, iron gauntlets, bassinets, and iron helmets covered with cloth – for eight mounted men. This mounted and armed entourage would certainly have included the four écuyers, the maître d'hôtel, possibly the captains, and the archbishop himself, to whom must have been apportioned the gilded bassinet and the saddle trimmed with gilded copper, which feature in the inventory.

From the archbishop one can move on to the household of François de La Trémoille, Vicomte de Thouars, and his wife, as revealed in the household roll, 'La Maison du Vicomte et de la Vicomtesse de Thouars en 1534'.[3] The vicomte was a great nobleman, but though he was no greater in his field than the archbishop in his, his household was substantially larger, even allowing for the fact that he was married with children, which inevitably increased its size. There are ninety-one people on the roll, including nineteen women, four of them noble, headed by the Dame de Puybouillant, the vicomtesse's demoiselle de compagnie. The basic male household consisted of about fifty-six people, forty-one indoor and fifteen outdoor. The list includes ten or so noblemen, all seigneurs of one place or another, and forty-six serviteurs. There are in fact twenty noble seigneurs on the list, including four maîtres d'hôtel and two tutors for the vicomte's sons, but only half of these are likely to have been at the château at the same time, because they were serving for only half the year, three months on and three months off, in alternation. This was clearly not the case in the archbishop's household in the fourteenth century. Quarterly service seems to have been a later development, which enabled those who served in that way to look after their own property for the remainder of the year; there was a similar development in England, where the arrangement still survives with the members of today's royal household, who pass only a portion of the year 'in waiting'.

In addition to the gentle servants, and serviteurs, a third group on the roll consists of the vicomte's council. There were five members, including a lawyer, and with one exception the small size of their salaries (40 to 50 livres) makes clear that they were receiving retainers, and were not full-time staff. The exception is John of Saint-Avy, Abbot of Les Pierres and 'head of our council', who is paid 500 livres a year 'for the conduct, negotiation and despatch of our business'. He is the best-paid person on the list, and it seems likely that he was substantially in residence.

He is the only cleric on the roll, which clearly does not include the priests attached to the chapel built on to the end of the château in the fifteenth century, with a tribune or gallery on the upper level at its west end, from which the family could attend mass.

A person of great importance was the receiver-general, the chief financial officer of the vicomte. He was the second best-paid member of the household, receiving 310 livres a year, as compared to the 500 livres of the head of the council, and the 300 livres of the senior maître d'hôtel. But he was not noble; he comes at the head of the list of serviteurs, followed by the secretary, who was paid 100 livres a year (as was the apothecary).

Wages varied considerably, from the Abbé of Les Pierres's 500 livres to the 3 livres paid to the water-carrier. Gentlemen got paid substantially more than serviteurs, with the exception of the receiver, the secretary and the apothecary; most of the gentlemen were paid between 120 and 240 livres, whereas the chief cook only received 30 livres. Women, of all ranks, got a third to a half as much as men of equivalent position.

One can get some idea of the lives and lifestyle of the servants at Thouars from the detailed inventory of 1542.[4] It is more personal than many inventories: as he goes round, the inventory clerk meets the various members of the household, who unlock doors, chests or cupboards for him, and show him the departments in which they work, or the rooms in which they live and sleep.

The atmosphere and fittings of the échansonnerie and the rooms around it come across especially strongly. At Thouars there was not a separate paneterie and fruiterie, as, for instance, at Tarascon; the offices had been simplified, as was the tendency of the times, and everything was in the échansonnerie, and the adjacent 'dépense' and cellars, the whole presided over by four sommeliers, who were possibly only in service two at a time, under the same arrangement as the gentilhommes.

The échansonnerie was the ancestor of the French 'office' and English butler's pantry of later centuries. At Thouars it was a snuggish little room, with a fire blazing in the fireplace, cupboards full of plate on the walls, a bin full of bread, a tray on a trestle table for plates and napkins, another big table and a bench covered with old tapestry for sitting on. The sommeliers clearly slept in the room, for two bundles of their bedding were stored in one of the cupboards; one suspects that they ate in it too, when they could get away with it, rather than in the bleak vastness of the adjacent salle basse.

A hatch protected by bars (for the security of the plate kept in the room) enabled bread, wine and candles to be handed out to whoever was entitled to them. There were ten copper candlesticks on a ledge in the window (and one sommelier told the clerk that there were more out in the chambre), candles stored in a locked coffer and wax in another locked chest in the cellar. Down in the cellar, which was lit by seven iron candlesticks fixed to the wall, were barrels and jars of wine, and two big ropes to haul them up and down; the sommeliers told the clerk that having the empty jars was one of their perquisites.

Most of the serviteurs slept on bedding kept in the place where they worked. For one of the household to have a room to himself was a rarity. The two maîtres d'hôtel in residence each had one; the senior of these, Monsieur de Roncée, had three pieces of verdure tapestry hanging in his. The tutor to the La Trémoille eldest son slept with his pupil, side by side in two canopied beds, one big and one small. The other gentilhommes probably slept in groups together, although the inventory is not clear about this; certainly the women did, the two children's nurses in the 'chambre des nourrices', the vicomtesse's three demoiselles in a 'chambre des filles'; the senior demoiselle de compagnie, the Dame du Puybouillant, slept in the adjoining garderobe. Lockable coffers and cupboards assigned to the belongings of the various women were distributed in the chambre des filles, and another room under it.

Households varied, of course, very much in size. Gouberville, a typical Normandy 'hobereau' or squire, had a household of around twelve people at Mesnil-au-Val in the 1540s, eight men and four women, and some of these were farm workers, or combined household and farm work.[5] But even Gouberville had one noble servant, his invaluable assistant and constant companion Thomas Langlois, Sieur de Cantepye, who disappeared from Mesnil from time to time to look after his own little seigneurie, and had his own servant, Collin. At the château of Quermelin, in Normandy, in 1584, the Marquis and Marquise de Coatmeur had a total household, indoors and out, of around thirty people, including ten women; the marquis had a maître d'hôtel and three gentilhommes – as opposed to the ten or so at Thouars – the marquise and her daughter both had their own demoiselle.[6]

Going up, rather than down, from Thouars, the royal household, and the household of the Duc de Bourgogne, living at a royal level in Burgundy and Flanders, were running into several hundred by the fifteenth century. But the Thouars household, to judge from other examples, represents a fair average for the establishment of a grand seigneur, from the sixteenth to the mid seventeenth century – the households could be a lot larger or a bit smaller, depending on the size of the family, the number of women servants and the organization in the basse-cour, but the basic male indoor household remains fairly consistent: forty-seven for the Duc de Longueville at Châteaudun in about 1517, forty-one for the Vicomte de Thouars in 1534, forty-one for the Comte du Lude at Le Lude in 1617, fifty-five for Cardinal Richelieu in around 1630, fifty-four for the Duc d'Épernon in 1644, at the château of Cadillac and elsewhere.[7]

Richelieu, because of his position, had an enormous outside establishment, including what was in effect a school for young noblemen set up in the stables; but his basic household was little larger than would have been expected for any grand seigneur of the time. The Duc d'Épernon was Governor of Guyenne and noted for his ostentatious style of living; he had no fewer than sixteen gentilhommes (inclusive of maîtres d'hôtel), six pages and three trumpeters. In 1644, feeding humans and animals in the household was let out, for a stipulated sum, to an outside contractor. Touissant Bridon, 'argentier', agreed to feed the basic fifty-four – twelve guards, nineteen or so servants of servants, twenty-seven coachmen, postilions, wagoners, grooms, muleteers, blacksmiths and cellarmen – and the duc and his family (probably with an agreed number of guests) – in all 130 people – along with fifty-five horses and thirteen mules.

It is likely that during the first half of the seventeenth century the maître d'hôtel ceased, in some households, to be noble. A maître d'hôtel had always had an ambivalent double role, ceremonial and practical. At the head of the écuyers he was the orchestrator and main household figure in the serving of grand dinners; he was also the chief administrator. A nobleman was likely to be better at the first role than the second. It is possible that, in households where there were two maîtres d'hôtel, the two roles were divided between them; the position of their chambres at Thouars, one on the first floor, the other close to the kitchen, suggests this. Here, both maîtres

The household of the Duc de Lorraine watch round the body of their master in 1608, from the illustration by Claude de la Ruelle.

d'hôtel were noble, however. Richelieu, if his contemporary biographer Aubery is to be relied on, had two maîtres d'hôtel, one of whom ate in a separate room with the gentilhommes, while the other presided over the table of the 'officiers'.[8] The second of the two, Daicque, seems not to have been noble.

In the second half of the seventeenth century a major change, of which the evolving position of the maître d'hôtel may have been the precursor, took place. Noble gentilhommes and demoiselles largely disappeared from noble households, and these households in general grew smaller.

According to de Callière, in his *La Fortune des Gens de Qualité* (1661),

> a courtier of our days once remarked that a gentleman could consider himself sufficiently well set up if he was smart, scrubbed and seemly; and that in reality it wasn't always by spending a lot of money that he could show himself off … my advice would be that a strong hand of personal qualities is more important than a string of valets. A train of pages and footmen that never gets further than the courtyard of the Louvre, is not

going to make much impression in the cabinet, and is what one expects of seigneurs from the extremities of Brittany, who show their noses at court once or twice in their lives, along with a suite suitable to the Great Mogul. This sort of display will only impress the middle classes and provincials.[9]

Behind de Callière's remark lay the fact that the balance of power in French society had changed, and that a huge household, and the physical power which it expressed, was a way of antagonizing the king, not of extracting favours and offices from him. Success came from attending court, not from living in grandeur in the country. As the châteaux ceased to be power centres huge households were no longer appropriate for them, and in Paris were ruinously expensive and also, as de Callière pointed out, ineffective. Households shrunk at all levels, including that of the noble servants.

In 1692 Audiger, in his *La Maison Reglée*, suggested thirty-one to thirty-three people as suitable for the establishment of a grand seigneur, including ten outdoor servants in the stables; the variation depends on whether he has four or six lacquais. Whatever the size, it is less than half that of at least some grand seigneurs earlier in the century. The suggested household is given only one écuyer, who is the only apparent nobleman on the list. This does not include the establishment of the seigneur's wife, who is given her own écuyer and noble demoiselle servante, but no other noble filles.[10]

The households of the cadet branches of the Bourbons, the Duc de Condé and the Duc d'Orléans, remained enormous. The Duc de Condé, living mainly at the château of Chantilly and the Palais-Bourbon in Paris, had 239 servants in livery in 1775, ninety-eight indoor and 141 outdoor; the numbers of members of the household out of livery are not recorded, but including as it did maîtres d'hôtel, écuyers, tutors and secretaries along with all the female staff, noble and non-noble, the grand total must have been not far short of 300.[11] But

An early-eighteenth-century maidservant, from a cut-out figure in the château of Malle.

the Condés were a family of royal blood, however distantly related to the king, and also of enormous wealth; they maintained a household of this size not least because the king and queen were constantly coming to stay at Chantilly, and all visiting royalty were similarly entertained there. One is in a world apart, to which there was no equivalent in England. Outside this world, even Audiger's suggested total was not necessarily reached by grand noble families. In 1777 the Comte de Choiseul-Gouffier, one of the richer noblemen of his day, had a household of around twenty people inside and out, and this included two secretaries and a nanny.[12]

Noble servants survived into the eighteenth century in a small way: a grand seigneur could have his écuyer, acting as a kind of aide-de-camp, his wife had both an écuyer, who accompanied her when she went visiting and sat in the antechambre while the visit was taking place, and a demoiselle de compagnie. According to Madame de Genlis, retailing her memories of the Ancien Régime after the Revolution,

> ladies who lived on their estates had demoiselles de compagnie, literally for
> company in the loneliness of a château; they had them in Paris for
> respectability… but towards the end of the eighteenth century people no
> longer had them in Paris, and although they were still to be found in the
> country, there were far fewer of them.[13]

Écuyers largely disappeared too, and ladies went visiting just with a footman or valet de chambre in attendance.

At a substantial French château in the eighteenth century one would expect to find a household, inside and out, of between ten and twenty people, the variation depending on the size, wealth and tastes of the family. An 'intendant' or 'régisseur', who ran the whole property, might be living in a house in the basse-cour or a pavillon in the forecourt; an 'aumônier', the priest who officiated in the château chapel and distributed charity in the neighbourhood, might live in another pavillon. The main household would be run in partnership by the maître d'hôtel and the cuisinier. The officier, who was the descendant of the medieval sommelier and in charge of plate and glass, the valets de chambre and femmes de chambre, formed an upper stratum and usually ate with the maître d'hôtel in the office. Any secretaries, tutors and governesses were likely to eat with the family, though sometimes they might be relegated to the office. The four to six lacquais (footmen), the kitchen staff, the 'servante', who was a general maid of all work, the assistant in the office, the woman in charge of the laundry and the porter, ate in the salle de commun, presided over by the cuisinier. The coachman, postilion, groom and one or more gardeners usually ate outside the château, and were given subsistence money on top of their wages.[14]

The porter in a big household was usually called the 'Suisse'; in the later seventeenth century big Parisian households started using the Swiss as porters, and their distinctive uniform, with cocked hat and pike of office, became a familiar feature

Pareil a l.d. Envojé arser

of the entries to all hôtels particuliers and châteaux of any pretensions. By the end of the eighteenth century 'Suisse' had become the general term for any porter, whether Swiss by origin or not.

An eighteenth-century kitchen in a château was usually vaulted, as earlier kitchens had been, as a security against fire. It contained, in the traditional manner, one, or perhaps two, open fireplaces for roasting and boiling, fitted up with spits and chains on which to hang cauldrons, but from the late seventeenth century inevitably had the new feature of a 'potager' or stewing stove, a row of little circular openings above apertures for charcoal. Soup and sauces were heated up on this, and there was sometimes a smaller one in the office on which to make coffee. A pump, inside the kitchen or on the wall outside, delivered water into a stone sink, and there was a brick-lined bread-oven built into one corner, unless this was in another room.[15]

The salle de commun could be a sizeable room, with a big fireplace, but the furnishings, as listed in most inventories, were of the utmost simplicity: a wooden table, or tables, and benches, and that was all. The office was likely to be more inviting, with big fitted-cupboards for china and glass, a fireplace, and a table with cane- or rush-bottomed chairs grouped round it, and coffee brewing up on a potager. In 1783 the office of the château of Le Marais was hung with three pictures – a big

A 'Suisse' keeping watch (above), from a design of c. 1755, for a porter's lodge at the château of Uzès. The job of porter in grand French houses from the seventeenth century was usually filled by a uniformed man of Swiss origin, and the name was later retained for porters in general.

The eighteenth-century stove in the old kitchen in the château of Le Touvet (right) is a 'potager', the ancestor of the modern kitchen range, with separate burners heated from underneath by charcoal. Its free-standing position and magnificent hood are unusual features.

one of game and sporting gear, another of fighting birds, and more game over the chimney-piece.[16] Le Marais was a financier's château, found excessively opulent at the time, and such a grand office may have been considered part of the excess.

The femme and valet de chambre were probably sleeping close to their mistress or master in one of the entresol rooms. The other male servants were usually up on the top floor. At the château of Le Touvet in about 1750 the chambres of the aumônier and the intendant, the chambres des lacquais (four beds), the chambre des cuisiniers (two beds), the chambre des secrétaires (two beds), and a 'chambre de chirurgiene', for sick servants (three beds), were all up on the top floor. Only the chambre des secrétaires and the chambre de chirurgiene had a fireplace.[17]

At the Archbishop of Auch's country residence, the château of Mazères, in 1776, there was a servants' dormitory, called the 'salle des domestiques', probably the old salle basse under the huge grande salle of the fourteenth-century archbishops, long since subdivided. It contained seventeen double-beds, arranged in fourteen cubicles along the sides of the room. Each cubicle could be screened off by a cotton curtain, and contained a straw-seated chair as well as the bed; the three extra beds were perhaps in the centre of the room, and kept for visiting servants. The room, lit by a central lantern, contained no other furniture.[18]

The valet de chambre and the femme de chambre, being in constant attendance on their master or mistress, could establish a close and friendly relationship with them. Marie-Judith de Vienne, the widowed owner of the château of Commarin, relates in her 'livre de raison' how, when visiting in Franche-Comté in 1744, she arranged a marriage between her valet de chambre, Saint-Jean, and a rich peasant's daughter:

> It's quite a romance. I arrived here on the 7th of May. I had heard that the daughter of a worthy local peasant was widowed and well-endowed; he sent to see her and married her on Tuesday. She has six thousand francs, is young, pretty and brings a good trousseau. It's a real fortune for him. As he was mad to get married, I arranged this match for him.[19]

According to Norvins, writing in the context of the château of Brienne in the 1770s,

> the valets de chambre in grand houses were still more or less like those whom our dramatists depicted in their comedies. Neither Molière nor Dancourt nor Marivaux completely invented the type, which is why characters of this kind drew so much applause. These valets de chambre thought of themselves as almost members of the family and enjoyed a kind of reciprocal familiarity, which in my days could still develop at times into blows of the cane, if their masters thought that they had passed the limits of respect. Like the characters in the comedies, they were intelligent, loyal and

cheeky. They were chastised, and they were cherished. They all had to know how to cut hair, shave, read, write, and run fast. At the château of Brienne, where they were five of them, they also had to be outstanding at shooting, playing billiards and acting into the bargain. With these skills they provided a back-up to social life there which it was frequently necessary to make use of; for in those days it was not considered demeaning to get on such familiar terms.[20]

There were without doubt households with more than twenty servants, but there were also a great many lesser châteaux or 'maisons nobles' which had fewer than ten. The returns for the tax known as 'capitation' are a useful source of information, because in order to be assessed each owner of a house had to return the number and type of employment of its occupants. In 1790, for instance, before the Revolution had effectively altered noble society, the average number of servants in noble households in and around Toulouse was 3.08. Comte de MacCarthy's household, including family, amounted to twenty-nine; the senior Président of the Toulouse Parlement had a household of twenty-three; the titled noblesse had, in general, four to eight servants; the rest two to four.[21] In Brittany, which was well known for its large number of virtually penniless nobles, 16 per cent of the noblesse had no servants at all in 1710, and 43 per cent only one or two; only 1 per cent had between nine and twenty-three (one, or possibly two families).[22] The household of Chateaubriand's father at the château of Combourg in 1770 is a typical enough

Family and household assembled in the courtyard of the château of Montgeoffroy after Sunday mass in the chapel, from the picture painted in collaboration by the fifteen-year-old son of the house and his tutor in about 1830. The clock is a real one, inset into the picture.

Details from the picture of Montgeoffroy.

example of modest, but not indigent, noble establishments all over France: a woman cook, a femme de chambre, two footmen and a coachman.[23]

In smaller households all the servants ate in the salle de commun; at the lower levels there was no maître d'hôtel, one of perhaps two footmen doubled up as valet de chambre, and the coachman came in to help out and served at table for big dinners.

When one moves on into the nineteenth century, and even beyond, the servants' world remains in many ways much the same. Sizes of households do not change very much. Towards the lower end, at the château of Longpra, on 1 January 1836, Monsieur de Longpra gave a New Year present of thirty francs to his aumônier and six francs to each of his servants, six in all: the 'young male indoor domestic', his wife's femme de chambre, the female cook, the kitchen maid, the coachman and the gardener.[24] At the recently built château of Montfort in 1833, the owner, Comte de Nicolay, laid down that 'the coachman must serve at dinner when there is company',[25] and there must have been a similar arrangement at Longpra. Towards the upper end of the scale the Harcourts and the Broglies, two old and grand families, had households, including stable staff, of about sixteen for the Harcourts (in the 1870s), and fourteen for the Broglies (in 1910).[26] A photograph of about 1900 shows a staff of sixteen servants posed around the régisseur and his wife at the Duc de Rohan's château of Josselin.

The household staff of the Duc de Rohan (below), grouped around the régisseur and his wife outside the main entrance of the château of Josselin in about 1900.

The office gradually ceased to be used for eating in by the upper servants; even in big châteaux everyone ate in the salle de commun, now sometimes called the 'salle des gens'. Chef and maître d'hôtel presided over their respective domains, but new technology was coming into the kitchen, most notably towards the end of the nineteenth century in the huge cast-iron ranges, in France, unlike England, often sited free-standing in the middle of the kitchen floor.

A distinctive feature of châteaux as opposed to English country houses was the importance of the 'lingerie' where linen was stored and ironed. Linen was washed at much less frequent intervals in France; sometimes there was a great wash only twice a year, and this became a significant event in the château calendar. As a result, very large quantities of linen were needed, and whereas English country houses could make do with a linen-cupboard or linen-closet, a château often had a size-able room; a 'cabinet de linge' appears in the 1590s at the château of Pompadour,[27] and in the seventeenth and eighteenth centuries a separate lingerie becomes increasingly common, and its contents feature at length in inventories. At the château of Flines in 1793, for instance, its contents included 151 pairs of sheets and 638 towels; in 1843 the château of Longpra had 118 pairs of sheets for the gentry, ninety-one and a half pairs of coarser quality for the servants, 693 towels, 711 dish-cloths, 599 kitchen aprons, and much else, including four bath-robes.[28]

Comte Christian de Nicolay, writing in the 1960s, recalled with nostalgia the lingerie at the château of Le Lude, the 'damp, steamy, strangely scented smell of recently bleached and ironed linen', the skill with which the laundry-maids wielded their ponderous irons, and the sound of their 'light and hasty footsteps' along the corridors, as they distributed the linen to the bedrooms.[29]

Linen on display in the lingerie or linen-room of the château of Le Lude (left). The lingerie in a French château was usually a sizeable room, since very large quantities of linen were stored in it, owing to the practice of washing linen only at long intervals.

The family with the most opulent lifestyle in the late nineteenth and early twentieth centuries was probably that of Prince Joachim-Napoléon Murat and his wife, the heiress of the Furtado-Heine banking fortune. They were renowned both for the splendour of their entertainments at their Paris hôtel on the Rue Monceau, and their lavish hospitality at the château of Rocquencourt, and the château of Chambly, where they kept their stud and huge hunting establishment. In 1910 they had a household of twenty and a 'laveur des automobiles', who by 1910 had taken the place of coachmen and groom. The staff included three valets de chambre, two femmes de chambre, two junior filles de chambre, and three footmen; there had been five of these a few years before. For their big receptions in Paris they hired extra maîtres d'hôtel and footmen for the occasion.[30]

But what especially impressed contemporaries about the Murats was the enormous outdoor staff which they maintained at Chambly and Rocquencourt. They normally spent July and August at Rocquencourt, and in addition to a small permanent caretaking staff hired staff by the day or the month for their time there: there was a total outdoor staff of forty-three in 1913, including twenty-three in the park and garden, nine in the laundry, and a cowman to look after the 'vacherie de luxe'. At Chambly there was an outside staff of thirty-nine, including four grooms, nine gamekeepers, eight at the home farm, three in the infirmary and dispensary, and two mechanics to run the electric-light plant.

An impressive feature of Chambly is the standard of accommodation provided for servants and staff. The furnishings of the servants' bedrooms in 1901 were far removed from the bed and chair in curtained cubicles provided for the servants at Mazères in 1776. All the servants had individual bedrooms, however small. They were furnished with bed, night-table, well-appointed writing-table and washstand, two chairs and a mirror – but no carpet. The bedrooms were all up on the top floor, with their own bathroom. In the stables was a games-room or 'salle des jeux' – furnished with chairs and sofas, a games-table, chess and domino sets, a billiard-table, various other games equipment, ten pictures of racehorses, four cigarette-lighters and three blue-enamel spittoons.[31]

At much the same period there was also a 'salle des jeux des domestiques' at Trevarez.[32] It was at the end of the long corridor which ran through the basement past kitchens, servants' hall, lift, refrigerator room and telephone exchange. This was equipped with a railway along which wagons could be pushed – one for dishes and one for coal (there is a similar basement railway at Josselin). Adjacent to the salle de commun were ranges of lockers, each one assigned to a servant. There are twenty-four of these, evidence, in their number, of the size of the staff at

Disused lockers for servants in the château of Trevarez (below). It was the usual practice for each servant to be allotted his own lockable compartment, and the number of lockers at Trevarez reflects the size of the largest and most lavish of late-nineteenth-century châteaux.

A nurse and her charges photographed at the château of Kernault in about 1900 (above).

Trevarez, and, in their decay, of the disappearance of this way of life.

All over France similar rows of lockers survive, in varying numbers, in the basements of other châteaux. Of course the set-ups at Chambly and Trevarez were far from typical: château life was on the whole much more modest in scale, in terms of servants as well as the lives of their owners.

Enough remains of memoirs or contemporary letters to bring life to the skeleton provided by plans and inventories. Vignettes emerge. In the Broglies' household, in Paris and at their château of Saint-Amadour, as their daughter recollected,

the maître d'hôtel was ceremoniously referred to as 'Monsieur Lepage', and was the most important figure in the household. It was essential to be in his good graces. He had entered into service with my grandmother as a young man, stayed with the family for fifty years, and only left it to die. He knew everything that was going on, and was nicknamed 'the Prince'. My mother claimed that he copied the voice and gestures of the Prince de Sagan, who was often in our company at Dieppe.

All the servants were more or less related to each other. My mother's femme de chambre was the sister of the maître d'hôtel, my father's valet de chambre was the nephew of the coachman, and so on.[33]

Such interrelationships were typical; so was long service and corresponding devotion to the family. The Nicolays' coachman at the château of Montfort recommended his successor not long before he died, after many years' service; his young daughter married the new coachman, and became one of the femmes de chambre at Montfort. As a small child she had been petted and loved by the Nicolay parents and been a playmate to their children, riding round the park with them on a go-kart pulled by a goat imported from England. As a young girl they had had her up to the salon to sing and dance the pavane for them, accompanied by the countess on the piano. When she and the coachman married, Comte de Nicolay officiated at their wedding, invited them up to the château afterwards, and sent them back to their house in the village carrying bottles of champagne with which to celebrate.[34]

In and around 1910, when the Broglies' daughter, Comtesse Jean de Pange, went to stay with her parents-in-law in Lorraine, at the eighteenth-century château of Penge, one white-coated servant waited at dinner, and put a quiche Lorraine on the turning 'lazy Susan' in the salle à manger which was lined with Louis-Quinze boiseries or cupboards filled with porcelain given to the family by Louis's father-in-law King Stanislas. But her parents moved en masse from Paris to the country, footmen and all. They had decided to make Saint-Amadour their principal residence, rather than Dieppe or Paris, where from then on they spent only four or five months a year. But they couldn't conceive of living a simple life in the country. They transported their entire town establishment down there … the bad temper of the servants showed how ill-adapted they found the new setting to their habits and tastes.[35]

The Harcourt household made a similar migration to the family château at Sainte-Eusoge, but there the coachman and femme de chambre, inevitably married to each other, remembered what fun the Saturday evening dances in the salle de commun were. About thirty people came to them, a mixture of Paris servants, the staff which stayed permanently at Sainte-Eusoge, and people from the village. The big table was pushed to one side, the women decorated the walls with garlands of flowers, and music was provided by the chef's piano-accordion. 'The people of Sainte-Eusoge were simple and natural, and it was contagious. Everyone had a good time.'[36]

The maître d'hôtel of the Prince and Princesse de Murat photographed at the entry of the ballroom of their Paris hôtel (above).

One can move right up to the 1930s and find life going on without much change, at the château of Beaumanoir in Brittany, as related by Comte Henri de Saint-Pierre, as well as at others all over France. The château, like many others, was shared, in this case by his parents and grandmother; when the latter died, her bachelor son moved into her rooms. There was an indoor staff of nine, a maître d'hôtel, the femmes de chambre of the two ladies, the valet de chambre, the woman cook, the kitchen maid, a nanny, a governess, and 'Miss Agnes', brought from Ireland to teach the children English. The governesses ate with the family. In the servants' hall, the maître d'hôtel and the cuisinière sat opposite each other at the centre of either side of the long table, with the indoor servants to either side, and the outdoor servants at either end. Maître d'hôtel and cook stayed seated all through the meal, and were waited on by the others. The cook had come to Beaumanoir when she was nineteen, and stayed to her mid seventies.

The office was next to the dining-room. It was not used for eating in, except by the nanny and children, who had their meals there until the children were about eight, when they ate in the dining-room with the grown-ups, and at the same times. There were no longer horses in the stables; cars had replaced them, but there was a 'valet des chiens' to look after the fifteen shooting dogs, and do outside work. The chauffeur's wife had been the femme de chambre, but now worked part-time in the house, mainly on the ironing. Washing was done by a 'lavoir', who had a house nearby.

The 'garde' was an important man, part-gamekeeper, part-forester, and in charge of the outside staff, apart from the jardinier and the two under-gardeners. The château was to a considerable degree supported off its land. Fruit, flowers and vegetables came from the gardens, fuel for the fireplaces in the big rooms from the woods, and there were pigs, poultry, ducks and a cider-press in the basse-cour. There were twenty-five farms on the estate, paying their rent partly in money, partly in days of labour at the château, partly in supplies of butter and poultry, under the system known as the 'redevance', which went on in France until suppressed by law in 1945.

In many ways, looking back at the way of life in châteaux, the big break in continuity came neither with the 1914–18 War, nor even with the Revolution, but with the War of 1939–45.

The Duc and Duchesse de Lorge photographed with the indoor and outdoor staff of their château in Britanny at the time of their marriage in 1932 (below).

IN PRAISE OF THE BASSE-COUR

The late-nineteenth-century poultry-house in the basse-cour of the château of Beaumanoir. Fanciful farm buildings, placed within easy reach of the château and convenient for visits by the châtelaine and her friends, were a popular feature in the nineteenth century.

FASHIONS HAVE COME AND GONE in the château, towers have been replaced by pavillons, grande salles have been divided and cut up into smaller rooms, the salon de compagnie and the boudoir were new arrivals of the eighteenth century, moats became unnecessary and were filled in, or retained for reasons of sentimentality or tradition, the cabinet de toilette was hived off from the cabinet, and the salle de bains from the salle, but from the fourteenth to the twentieth century châteaux have had one constant element, which has preserved the same name and the same function: the basse-cour. Since the war, admittedly, its function has begun to change: its barns and byres have been tidied up and are let out for weddings, or alternatively it is the château which is let out for weddings and the family has made itself snug in the basse-cour. There is no adequate English translation of 'basse-cour'; 'farmyard' is the nearest, but even this misses some of the nuances and uses of the term. It is near enough, however, and underlines the contrast between France and

At the formidable early-fifteenth-century château of Tarascon (left), the low buildings of the basse-cour nestle up against the main castle. The kitchens were in the basse-cour, and food had to be carried outside and across the moat into the main building.

At the fifteenth-century château of Olhain the main building and the basse-cour were on separate moat-surrounded islands linked by a drawbridge. Another drawbridge led to the basse-cour, and entry to the main building was only by way of it (above right). Its buildings were much rebuilt in later centuries (below right), but still give a vivid idea of the relationship of these two basic elements of a château.

England, where to have a farmyard attached to a country house has been unthinkable since the eighteenth century, if not before.

The name dates back to at least the fourteenth century. The basse-cour was perhaps first called the 'low court' because it was built on a lower level than the main bulk of the château, formidably impregnable on a hilltop.[1] Down below, looking up, like the villagers in Kafka's *The Castle*, at the sanctum into which many of its denizens were never going to penetrate, was a lower world of barns, stables, cowhouses, dovecots, wash-houses, winepresses, bakeries, and sometimes kitchens, the function of which was to keep the people up above fed and serviced. Alternatively, the term may simply have been used because the buildings in the basse-cour were smaller in scale than those around what came to be called the 'cour du seigneur'. One can still get a vivid feeling of the contrast, on a large and small scale, at Tarascon and Olhain, both dating from the early fifteenth century: at Tarascon the basse-cour like a decreasing echo alongside the looming cliff of the main château; at Olhain both château and basse-cour more modest – suited to the seigneurie and residence of an officer in a ducal household, not to the ducal household itself – but the basse-cour, with low buildings around an irregular court, delightful as a foil and introduction to the château: the only approach to this was and is through the cows, pigs and ducks of the basse-cour. At both Tarascon and Olhain, as in numerous other examples, basse-cour and main building were on separate fortified islands, linked by drawbridges to each other and the outside world.

In 1322 the basse-cour at the château of Mareuil, belonging to the Bishop of Arras, contained (as far as can be made out from the inventory, which is not altogether clear) a kitchen, a bakehouse, stabling for two cows and seven horses, together with three beds for the people looking after them, accommodation for forty-one pigs, a barn, and the 'women's chamber', apparently for women labourers, for along with four beds and bedding, the room contained 'three forks for the barn'.[2]

The kitchen in the basse-cour is the only one mentioned in the inventory; there is no kitchen in the main château. There was a similar arrangement at the château of Tarascon, as shown in an inventory of 1457, and here one range of buildings survives, although much altered. In 1457 it contained a large and small kitchen, a 'garde-mangerium' or larder, a 'chansoneria' for wine, a 'fructeria' for fruit, a 'panetaria' for bread and a 'sausseria' for spices.[3] All these rooms had hatches, with stone ledges in front of them, from which the servants could collect food and drink, and carry them across the second drawbridge to the halls and chambres of the château. Effaced inscriptions over the hatches probably gave the uses of the rooms.

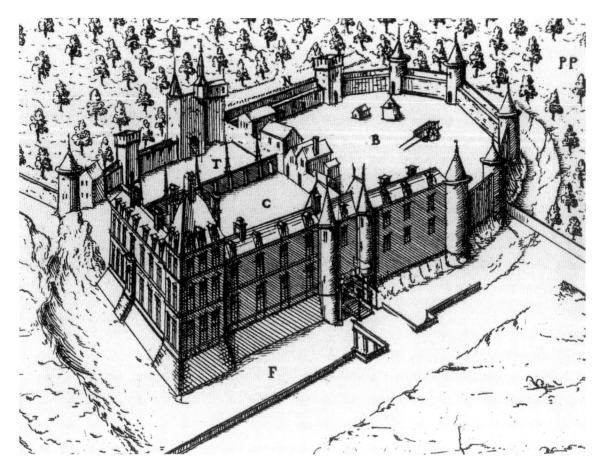

On a much smaller scale a similar arrangement is to be found at La Poissonière, the little maison noble built in the early sixteenth century by Loys Ronsard, the father of the poet, and here the inscriptions survive. At La Poissonière the basse-cour was in fact the only court, for the corps de logis was too small to have a court of its own. It ran along one side of the basse-cour: two salles, two chambres, a stair-case tower to give access to them, and a few more rooms. The kitchen and other ancillary service rooms, much as at Tarascon, were in a separate building, running along one side of the basse-cour and partly dug into the rock, in the steeply rising ground to this side. Latin or French inscriptions and carved symbols give their uses: 'La Fourière' (the straw-house) over the barn, with carvings of two bales of straw; 'La Buanderie Belle' (the good wash-house) over the wash-house; 'Cui Des Videto' (be careful to whom you hand it out), with a jug and tumblers over the échanson-nerie or buttery; 'Vulcano et Diligentiae', with carvings of four cauldrons, over another room. There were formerly rooms, probably accommodation for servants, on the first floor along this range. It is likely that stabling for animals was on the other side of the court, where the wall has been demolished.

With the sixteenth century one has emerged into the period when there is enough in the way of surviving buildings, illustrations and inventories to give a good

A bird's-eye view (left) of the château of Vallery in J.A. du Cerceau's Les Plus Excellents Bastiments (1576) *suggests the relationship of basse-cour to main château and the nature of the former, which contained barns, stables, cow-houses, dovecot and well-house.*

The huge barns in the basse-cour of the château of Fleury (below) date from the early seventeenth century. An archway in the range to the left links the basse-cour to the main forecourt of the château.

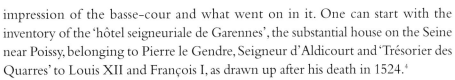

impression of the basse-cour and what went on in it. One can start with the inventory of the 'hôtel seigneuriale de Garennes', the substantial house on the Seine near Poissy, belonging to Pierre le Gendre, Seigneur d'Aldicourt and 'Trésorier des Quarres' to Louis XII and François I, as drawn up after his death in 1524.[4]

The house had two courts, the 'grand cour' and the basse-cour, to one side of it; the latter was close to the kitchen, but this and its supporting rooms seem to have been in the main building, not separate in the basse-cour. The 'grand cour' only contained stacks of wood and tiles, a couple of wagons and a well. In the basse-cour were more tiles, a barn filled with hay, and stabling for horses and cattle: two 'étables à chevaux', accommodating five mares, an assortment of saddlery, and beds and bedding for the grooms; and in the adjoining 'étable à vaches' eight cows, two calves, four heifers and a bull. A loft filled with barley ran over both 'étables'.

A good many basse-cours, some on a very large scale, are illustrated, and their plans given, in du Cerceau's *Les Plus Excellents Bastiments de France*. They contain, as du Cerceau himself puts it, 'stabling, barns, presses, and the other accommodation (lieux) needed in a basse-cour'.[5] Some of them also contain a dovecot. Du Cerceau often marks stalls, and sometimes shows what seem to be wagons and round wine- or cider presses in plan in the barns; occasionally he draws a wagon, standing uncoupled in the courtyard. On the whole the buildings are utilitarian, and arranged asymmetrically, though some of the barns are very large; at Verneuil there is a more ambitious, and more or less symmetrical arrangement of a tall and imposing circular dovecot between two barns, each with two large arched doorways set with rustication.

There was no call for the basse-cour to be anything but utilitarian at these 'plus excellent bastiments', because entry to them was always separate from entry to the main building's court or courts. Where, in less grand houses, the basse-cour was the way of approach to the main building, there could be more of a show. At Martainville, near Rouen, the early-sixteenth-century château is a remarkable exercise in symmetry, all in a late-Gothic idiom: the main building a compact block, on a symmetrical plan, with four corner towers and a further tower over the entrance; and facing this a basse-cour with parallel ranges to either side, and, at the end, a dovecot on the axis of the entrance to the house.

At the château of Fleury, the main building (itself mostly rebuilt in the eighteenth century) is approached by a very large courtyard of imposing grandeur, entered by a tall gatehouse, with long ranges of stabling to either side of it, and access through the stabling on one side to a series of huge and nobly architectural barns.

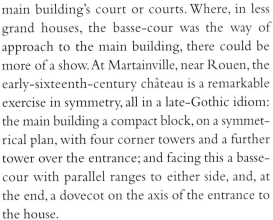

But very often, in the sixteenth and early seventeenth centuries, the approach to the main building was through an irregular basse-cour, presenting, usually, to the outside world high stone walls with few openings in them, broken by an archway or gatehouse into the court. Through the archway one might see the generous spaces of the court, the main building across it, perhaps with a small forecourt of its own, and around it an irregular range of buildings, or separate small buildings, one or two storeys high, housing horses, cattle, pigs, poultry, barns and lofts for hay and corn; a free-standing bakehouse (sometimes with a bedroom above it), a wash-house, a well protected by a pentice, often bedrooms for servants; sometimes also a round dovecot in the centre of the yard, although this inevitable adjunct to a seigneurial residence was often outside the building complex, in an orchard or a field.

Such complexes can be found all over France: at, for instance, Plessis-Josso in Brittany, Crosville-sur-Douve in the Cotentin, and Ango, near Dieppe, the last with one of the most splendid of sixteenth-century dovecots in its courtyard; or, with the main building separated from the basse-cour by its moat, as at Commarin in Burgundy, Clairvaux in Deux Sèvres, and Longpra in the Dauphiné.

Two vignettes help to give life to basse-cours of this date. In 1616 Louis XIII, as a boy of fifteen, was amusing himself at the basse-cour of his own château, Le Plessis-les-Tours, outside Tours, first by knocking a tennis ball around it, then by driving his 'little carriage, pulled by two of its team of six little horses' round the well in the centre. This, like many wells, was protected by a tiled timber roof supported on timber pillars. His friend and écuyer, the Sieur de Liancourt, was doing the same, in his own little carriage; the king got distracted, watching or competing with him, cannoned into one of the supporting columns of the well, brought the whole roof down on one of the horses, and only just escaped being killed himself.[6]

In 1652 the Grande Mademoiselle was in retreat from Paris, and in hiding from Louis XIII, to whom she had not endeared herself by her exploit in turning the cannon of the Bastille on his troops during the revolt of the Fronde. She took refuge, travelling semi-incognito, with Madame Le Bouthillier at Le Muet's great new château of Pont. While she was there Madame de Marsilly, a friend of her hostess, came to stay, with her servants, and was given a separate supper, in ignorance of the Grande Mademoiselle's presence in the house. Her servants were sent to sleep in the basse-cour, across the moat from the main building, 'and as the kitchen had windows giving on to the moat, her servants, taking a stroll, noticed that another supper was being prepared in the kitchens, and told their mistress about it in the morning'.[7]

But from the late sixteenth century one starts to find a new arrangement: an 'avant-cour' with courts to left and right of it, one serving as the basse-cour, the other containing the stables and sometimes the kennels, what might be called the superior element of the basse-cour, now separated out from it, with the étables for

*At the château of
Richelieu, basse-cour
and stables were placed
to either side of the
avant-cour leading to
the main building, a
grandly formal
arrangement which
became popular in the
larger châteaux.*

horses elevated to the more dignified level of 'écuries' (although the two courts were sometimes both called 'basse-cour'). Such a disposition seems to have been created in the late sixteenth century at the Gondis' demolished château of Noisy,[8] and certainly existed, on an enormous scale, at Richelieu, where there were two courts to either side of the central avant-cour. Main building, courts and all have gone, except for the pavillon originally serving as gatehouse leading to one of the courts. The grandest surviving example of this arrangement, as of so much else, is at Vaux-le-Vicomte, where the two courts survive all but complete. Both courts are described as 'basse-cours' in the inventory of 1661.[9] Their façades are rendered out of brick, with stone dressings, to maintain a hierarchy with the ashlar of the main block; they contained appartements for Fouquet's principal officers in pavillons at the corners, as well as stable and farm accommodation. In reduced versions of this plan there could be the basse-cour on one side, and a single range of stables on the other, as at Balleroy and the demolished Liancourt; or a single court only, with the stables in the range facing the forecourt.

The main object of such arrangements was to eliminate the need to get mixed up with farm animals and carts on the way to the main entrance. By the eighteenth century it had become unthinkable to design a new château or maison noble entered by way of a basse-cour, though this arrangement was still to be found in older châteaux. But the basse-cour was still firmly anchored to one side of the main buildings, with its activities visible from their windows, and the quacking of ducks, cackling of poultry and mooing of cows clearly audible to the denizens of the château.

NOUVELLE MAISON RUSTIQUE

The ideal arrangement of a basse-cour is described in detail in Liger's *Nouvelle Maison Rustique*, which was published in 1721, quickly became a best-seller, went into new editions throughout the century and was in the library of every château. Liger is concerned with the more modest seigneurial residences, and writes as follows:

> The basse-cour is the supply-base of a country house, and its make-up should reflect its revenues … It should consist of some low buildings for the farmer and the domestics, of stables, cow-byres and sheep-pens, of cellars, winepresses, barns, lofts, piggeries, poultry-houses, dovecots or pigeon-lofts. No great skill is called for if all these elements are scattered at random, as is often found in the provinces: each owner can thus consult his own fancy; but order and the benefits that it brings come from arranging all these parts in one mainly symmetrical building.
>
> I am of the opinion that a basse-cour should never serve as an introduction to the forecourt of the main house, but that from the windows of the latter the owner should be able to see all his establishment laid out in the basse-cour, the way into which should be to the right or left of his forecourt, so that animals and farm gear can hive off to their own departments without stopping in the forecourt.
>
> The barn should be on one side, the cow byre and sheep-pen on the other, the farmhouse opposite the house of the owner; by this arrangement everything will be under his control.[10]

Although Liger recommends against having basse-cours in front of, and as an approach to, the house, the frontispiece to his book shows them only approachable through the main court, which as a result is pullulating with farm activities, perhaps shown like this in order to get the maximum into one engraving, but giving a vivid idea of what life was still like in the more rustic of maisons rustiques.

In general basse-cours were now built to one side of the forecourt, and sometimes in a range of buildings completely separated from the main house, though never very far away from it. Houses which had been previously entered through the basse-cour could be adapted to make a new entry. There is a good example of this at the château of Gatellier. As built in the sixteenth century this was entered by way of a gatehouse into the basse-cour, and from the basse-cour by way of another gatehouse into the enclosed main courtyard of the château. In the mid eighteenth century the entrance route was shifted round ninety degrees. One range of the main courtyard was demolished, to open it up, and the range opposite the demolished one was rebuilt and given elegant Louis-Quinze façades; the house now had an axial approach through handsome gates and gateposts to the entrance in the new façade, and the basse-cour became a charmingly rural appendage to one side, as it still is today.

A sensible owner could keep an eye on what was going on in the basse-cour from the windows of his own appartement, if Liger's advice had been followed, and he and his wife often took an active interest in the cows and poultry which lived there.

The Duc de Choiseul, the able Chief Minister of Louis XV, lived in great splendour at his château of Chanteloup, and occupied himself in building, hunting, farming and entertaining his friends and neighbours, all on a princely scale. He installed a herd of Swiss cows and two bulls in his basse-cour, with a Swiss cowman to look after them. Arthur Young, who came there in 1787, two years after the duc had died, wrote with appreciation:

> As a farmer, there is one feature which shows the duc had some merit; he built a noble cow-house; a platform leads along the middle, between two rows of mangers, with stalls for seventy-two, and another appartement, not so large, for others, and for calves. He imported 120 very fine Swiss cows, and visited them with his company every day, as they were kept constantly tied up. To this I may add the best built sheep-house I have seen in France.[11]

A gouache by Blarenberghe shows the huge basse-cour at Chanteloup, with its tall dovecot backing on to the main house, and the long range of the cow-house, the flat roof of which formed a terrace accessible from the gardens; over the balustrade of this terrace the duc's guests are surveying the busy and agreeable mixture of cows, horses, poultry, wagons and people in the basse-cour below them. An enamel painting of much the same date, probably also by Blarenberghe, depicts a gentleman showing the aviary and poultry-yard to his children.[12]

The Duc de Choiseul was an enthusiastic farmer and installed a range of magnificent cow-houses in the basse-cour to one side of his château of Chanteloup. Its flat roof formed a terrace accessible to the garden, from which the duke's guests could survey the farm activities, as depicted in the picture of about 1780 by Blarenberghe (above).

The duc's pride in visiting and showing off his dairy herd is not all that far removed from English landowners' interest in farming and what in England at that time was called 'improvement' – from Coke of Norfolk's agricultural achievements at Holkham, for instance. Choiseul was probably to some extent inspired by English examples. But at Holkham Coke's farm-buildings, grand though they are, are on the other side of the great park from the house; to have the farm in his back yard would have offended his sense of propriety, and that of his fellow landowners, and the nearest they could come to it was to have a pretty dairy in the garden, well separated from the cows which supplied it.

At the château of Barbentane, near Avignon, an elegant little basse-cour was built next to the house in the 1760s, and, as at Chanteloup, though on a far more modest scale, was clearly designed with visits from the family and their guests in mind. The function of each part is inscribed in incised capitals over the relevant doorway – 'vaches', 'poules', 'pigeons', 'cochons', and so on – and a balustraded terrace walk, with a pretty view over the countryside, leads to little domed turrets, containing poultry and pigeons, at high level at the corner of the courtyard.

From the Barbentane basse-cour it is not all that great a step to the famous 'hameau' or 'ferme-ornée' of Marie-Antoinette at the Petit-Trianon, and its less well known precursor at Chantilly: both of these are essentially basse-cours transformed into toy villages to become the plaything of royal or noble ladies, but

Among the accommodation of the elegant basse-cour built in the 1760s immediately next to the château of Barbentane is a raised walk linking two dovecots (right).

containing the same mixture of animals and activities to be found in basse-cours all over France.

Most eighteenth-century basse-cours are more down to earth, whether accommodated, as Liger recommended, in one symmetrical building, or arranged in an agreeably haphazard way, in the traditional manner. One development, quite commonly met with, was to make a distinction between the basse-cour and the farm: the latter let out to a tenant and farmed commercially by him (usually on the shared-profit system known as métayage), the basse-cour run from the château, but now limited to providing accommodation for poultry, perhaps a cider press, a wash-house and a workshop for repair work: the bigger farm animals and farm machinery were all in the farm, probably with some arrangement for supplying the château with free milk and butter as part of the rent. Farm and basse-cour often adjoined each other. At the château of Canon in Normandy they are symmetrically arranged to either side of the château, round two courtyards of nobly simple architecture, on a scale considerably grander than that of the château itself.

But old arrangements could last on into the nineteenth century. The château of Longpra in the Dauphiné is a medium-sized château of the greatest charm, an eighteenth-century remodelling of an earlier building, on a moated site, handsomely furnished in the time of Louis XVI, with furniture by one of the best of provincial

At the château of Vauboisseau (right) an elaborate basse-cour at once ornamental and useful was built in 1870 on the far side of the stables from the château. The farmhouse is seen on the left and the roof of the château rises above the trees in the left centre.

Access to the château of Longpra is still through the basse-cour (below), across the moat from the main château, a corner of which is seen on the right. In 1844 its accommodation included cow-byre, hen-house, goat-house, workshops, stables, wood-store and dovecot.

cabinet-makers, and with a Holy Family bought in Italy in the little chapel. It was rather more, in short, than a country squire's house. But it was, and still is, approached through its spacious basse-cour. In 1844 this contained stables, a harness room, the coachman's room, a cow-byre, a coach-house, workshops, a bakehouse, a barn, a loft, a butchery, a hen-house, a goat-house, a storehouse for vegetables, a dovecot perched on the open-sided pentice known as 'les halles', and a building called the 'mayonnerie', which had been used for the cultivation of silkworms in the eighteenth century.

There were two elderly horses in the stables, two 'fine cows' in the cow-byre, two old carriages, a chaise and a cart in the coach-house, firewood piled up in the pentice; six pairs of pigeons in the dovecot, three old goats in the goat-house, eighteen hens and cocks and five chicks in the fowl-house, three big vats for washing clothes in in the bakehouse, shelves for apples in the vegetable store, and an assortment of choppers and butchers' gear in the butchery. The mayonnerie was no longer in use for silk culture, and had in effect become a conservatory; the stands for the silkworms were still there, along with a stove, five orange trees, five double-flowered laurel trees, thirty flower-pots and a lot of wood.[13]

The laverie, or wash-house, at the château of La Jaillière (below) adjoins the pool in which washing took place; the slatted room on the first floor was used for drying.

In general, in the nineteenth century, the basse-cour, if new built, was moved further away from the château; it became more like an English home-farm, though usually much closer to the main house than would have been the case in England. Sometimes it was straightforwardly called 'the farm'; occasionally it was called the 'servitude', or service-yard. But the old term 'basse-cour' is often found as well.

Nineteenth- and early-twentieth-century basse-cours were often arranged as a group of different buildings of contrasting character and very carefully designed to be pretty or fanciful. When Madame Armaillé, going to visit her mother-in-law for the first time at the château of Briottières, at the end of the nineteenth century, describes how 'I saw a pretty basse-cour where my mother-in-law amused herself by rearing poultry and pigs. The buildings were new, and in very good condition',[14] she is describing something to be found all over France – a new-built basse-cour of characterful design, and a châtelaine coming to visit it. The occasional distinction between basse-cour and ferme continued, but the farm was now more likely to be taken in hand by an owner, who saw himself as a 'gentleman-farmer' on the

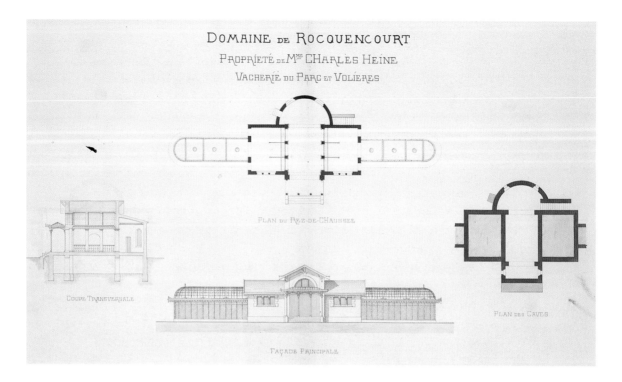

DOMAINE DE ROCQUENCOURT

PROPRIÉTÉ DE Mme CHARLES HEINE

VACHERIE DU PARC ET VOLIÈRES

PLAN DU REZ-DE-CHAUSSÉE

COUPE TRANSVERSALE

FAÇADE PRINCIPALE

PLAN DES CAVES

English model. At the château of Montfort, newly built in the 1830s, there was no basse-cour, but a model farm was built about a kilometre from the house. The specification laid down that it should include

> a cow-house for five cows and two or three calves. As Madame de Nicolay pays frequent visits to see the cows, the arrangement of the cow-house must make it possible for her to have access without getting dirty … The dairy to have a little reception-room for Madame de Nicolay above it.[15]

The laundry was always done at the château, and often in the basse-cour, but the technology – or the lack of it – varied from château to château. The old system, once found in villages and towns all over France as well as in châteaux, was to wash in a pond, or on the banks of a stream or river, on an inclined stone surface running down to the water, on which linen and laundry would be beaten with flat wooden paddles to get the dirt out, and afterwards hung out to dry.

In or adjacent to the basse-cour, there was often still a pond for washing. Sometimes it was surrounded by pillars and covered over, sometimes with a loft on top for drying in, and the whole could be made into a rather pretty composition.

An alternative to this system was a 'buanderie', or laundry, an enclosed room with a stove to heat water, big vats to wash in, and sometimes a tank of cold water: next door could be a room for ironing. At the château of Rocquencourt, just outside Paris, the buanderie adjoined a free-standing 'séchoir', a drying shed enclosed by

At the luxuriously-appointed château of Rocquencourt, a vacherie or cow-house for six cows (above), described in the inventory as a 'vacherie de luxe', was built separate from the basse-cour in the garden. There was a dairy at the back and aviaries to either side, and the whole was designed as an attractive feature for visits.

slatted wood and with a lantern at high level, all designed to stimulate a through draught, which could be increased by a steam-driven fan.[16]

Rocquencourt belonged to the Heine family, rich bankers whose ultimate heiress was to marry a Murat and finance the lavish Murat entertainments of the Belle Époque. The main buildings of the farm or basse-cour were across the public road from the château, in perhaps deliberate isolation, but a de luxe cow-house ('vacherie de luxe') with adjoining aviaries, was allowed in the pleasure grounds of the château, close to a winter garden, and hot-houses for camellias. The vacherie de luxe consisted of a central pavilion, containing an ornamental dairy, with stalls for six cows in the cow-shed behind it, and pretty cast-iron aviaries in wings to either side. More rooms were added later on, and in these and the dairy were displayed enormous quantities of faience and porcelain, including faience figures of a bull, cows, a 'fox playing the flute', and around seventy different birds.[17] It was all in the Petit-Trianon tradition, but it is the more down-to-earth basse-cours which draw and retain the affection.

Cows water in the pond at the edge of the basse-cour of the château of Allonville, as photographed in 1909. A close relationship of farm life to château was still frequently to be found in France, but would have been virtually unthinkable in England.

INTERLUDE 5

TO HORSE

Luxuriously appointed 'selleries' or harness-rooms were a feature of châteaux in the later nineteenth century. This example was fitted up in one of the original sixteenth-century towers at the château of Montgeoffroy.

THE HISTORY OF THE STABLES in French châteaux has never been written, and is in need of research. The horse was at least as important in the life of the French noblesse as of the English upper classes, and the architectural expression of it was at least as grand and in one or two examples considerably grander.

Horses have always had to be kept in considerable numbers in French châteaux, for fighting, transport, recreation and sport, and although the fighting element ultimately disappeared, if a good deal later than in England, the others continued, and were still as important in the nineteenth century as they had been in the eighteenth and seventeenth.

Horses, and an 'étable' or 'écurie' to contain them, are frequently listed in early inventories, usually in the basse-cour. Only perhaps in the seventeenth century was a clear distinction made: cattle and sometimes sheep in the étable, horses in the écurie. It is not certain when the system of fastening horses in

The late-sixteenth-century stable range to one side of the forecourt of the château of Fleury (left) is perhaps the earliest surviving stable block in a French château. The bridge on the left leads across the moat to the main building.

individual stalls first developed, but it was probably not before the sixteenth century. Only towards the end of that century did stables of any architectural importance appear, perhaps under the influence of Italy, and the cult of horsemanship and the horse there. An early example was at the château of Montargis. Louis XII's daughter, the Duchesse of Ferrara, came from Italy to live in this huge medieval château when she was widowed in 1560, and one of the improvements she made was to build a large stable block backing on to the curtain wall in the main courtyard. It is shown on the plan in du Cerceau's *Plus Excellents Bastiments*. It consisted of three parallel rows, each containing stalls for at least twenty horses, with a symmetrical façade on the courtyard flanked by staircase turrets. This façade is unfortunately not shown in du Cerceau's bird's eye view of the château, in which only the three pitched roofs of the three naves are recognizable as seen from the rear, rising above the curtain wall. The stable block was clearly two storeys high, presumably with hay-lofts and possibly sleeping-quarters for grooms on the upper floors.

What really brought stables into the realm of architecture was the development of great formal and symmetrical plans, such as first appeared in France in the late sixteenth century, in which the main block of the château was approached through a forecourt lined by subsidiary buildings, including the stables and the other buildings of the basse-cour. An early example was the Gondis' château at Noisy, built at the end of the 1570s; the forecourt at Fleury is perhaps the earliest summary example. One of the most extensive ever built was Richelieu's château of Richelieu, which dates from the 1620s and 1630s.[1] In this kind of layout, to be in keeping with the character of the whole the façades facing on to the forecourt had to have

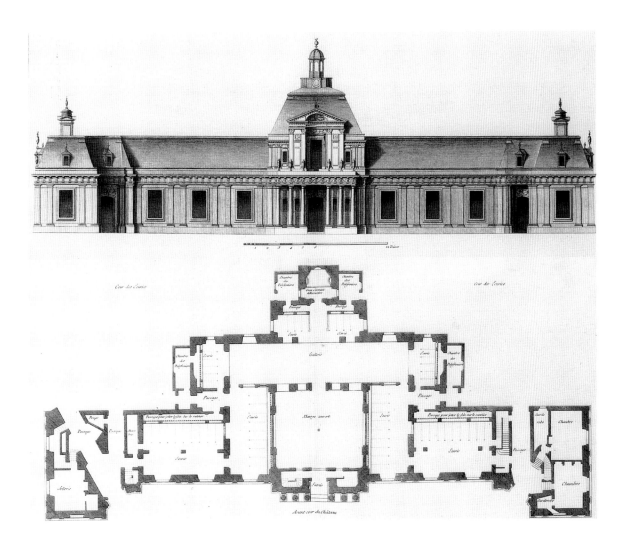

The magnificent stable block designed by François Mansart for the château of Maisons (above) is shown in the book of engravings known as the Grand Marot. *The big space in the centre was a riding-school. The stables were demolished in the nineteenth century, all but the fountain or watering-place for the horses, shown on the top of the plan.*

architectural coherence. On the other hand, the notion of architectural hierarchy which was implicit in a plan of this type meant that any subsidiary courts were given subsidiary façades, in comparison to those of the main building; they needed to be seemly and symmetrical, but not too grand.

Noisy and Richelieu have long since been demolished, but a good example that survives, on a more modest scale, is at the château of Balleroy, as built to the designs of François Mansart, probably in the 1630s. Here the stables form two ranges, framing the avant-cour; the basse-cour is concealed behind one of these ranges, and is irregular and without architectural pretensions, but the two stable blocks have agreeable matching façades, looking at each other across the court.[2]

Mansart went on to design much grander approaches for the château de Maisons in the 1640s; they were never completed, but the half which was built contained the stables, and these were so magnificent that they were probably the first French stables to be fully illustrated. The two façades appear prominently in the set of illustrations of Maisons engraved by the Perelles in the late seventeenth century.[3]

The central feature on the courtyard façade is more reminiscent of a church than a stable block. This was because it was intended to be the mirror image of the chapel of the château, in the centre of the unbuilt range across the avant-cour. It also needed

The former watering-place of the Maisons stables has been incorporated into a late-nineteenth-century house (left). The water-basin has been removed, but the decoration survives intact.

The superb stables (above right) built by the Duchesse d'Angoulême at the château of Chaumont (in Burgundy, not Chaumont-sur-Loire) are a near contemporary of the demolished stables at Maisons. The stabling is in the vaulted ground floor (right): the existing boxes are late-nineteenth- or early-twentieth-century insertions, but an original plan shows the space divided up into stalls for eighty-seven horses. The two grand flights of external steps suggest that the first floor may have been intended for large-scale entertainments.

to be two storeys high, however, for what was behind it was not the actual stabling, but a riding-school for the 'haute-école' or art of manège, which had been imported to France from Italy in about 1600 and adopted with enthusiasm there. One result of this was that horses became stars as well as their riders. They were now bought and sold for very high prices, and as stars, they needed star accommodation.

But the grand central entrance of the stables at Maisons was not designed for horses but for humans – for Président René du Longueil and his guests, perhaps above all in anticipation of a visit by the king, who did indeed come to Maisons in 1651; it gave access to a staircase, leading up to the viewing gallery from which to watch the displays of horsemanship in the riding-school down below. Entry and exit for horses were at either end of the façade, and stalls for sixty-two horses were arranged in groups around the riding-school.

The stables at Maisons were demolished when the ground around the château was laid out and developed for building in 1834. Only a tiny portion of them survives, but this is remarkable enough. At the back of the stables, on the central axis in line with the main entrance, was a covered drinking fountain decorated as a grotto. This is now incorporated into a private house on one of the new avenues which replaced the park and gardens. The actual drinking basin has been removed, but everything else is there. The decoration, complete with coupled sea-horses, is so lavish that the fountain cannot conceivably have been for use just by horses and grooms; the young noblemen who rode the horses for the manège must have ridden, after their display, straight from the riding-school to the fountain to refresh their mounts.

An almost exact contemporary of the stables at Maisons survives at the château of Chaumont in Burgundy. It was built between 1648 and 1652 for Henriette de La Guiche, Duchesse d'Angoulême, to the designs (it is said) of François Martel of Charolles. It contained stalls for eighty-seven horses, to either side of arcades of Tuscan columns, on a vaulted ground floor. Two magnificent external staircases on either side led to the floor above, and there was a further attic floor under the roof. The main entrance into the stabling is through a central door, surmounted by an equestrian statue of the duchesse's father, Philibert de La Guiche. He had been Master of the Artillery under Henri III and Henri IV, and cannon are incorporated into the decoration of the pediment over the door.[4]

These stables are a little mysterious. Why so magnificent? They had no architectural relationship to a basse-cour or to the château – at the time a huge courtyard building of mixed dates. Their most prominent external features, apart from the central doorway and its statue, were the staircases leading to the upper rooms, and the chimney-stacks which served them; but these rooms are purely utilitarian today, although they may have been intended to have decoration which was never carried out. Henriette de La Guiche's husband, the Duc d'Angoulême, was Governor of Provence, where he would have had a military establishment, but there seems no reason for this to have been transferred to his wife's château in a rather remote part of Burgundy. There was no riding-school at Chaumont, and the establishment was most probably a hunting one.

There is no other example of an equestrian portrait decorating the stables in a French château, but in the eighteenth, and possibly also the later seventeenth, century the carving of a horse, or horses, or at least a horse's head, became a common feature. If the horses' and stags' heads carved over doorways at the château of Dampierre date from the late seventeenth century, like the rest of the stables, they are an early example of what was to become one of the most attractive features of French stables, and one with which there is no parallel in England. The horse carvings can take the form of elaborate reliefs, but right through into the early twentieth century no stables in a château, however modest, were complete without at least the carving of a horse's head over the entrance door or archway.

A prancing horse was a popular motif; there is a nice example of about 1750 over the stable entrance in the château of Commarin, and identical horses are to be found in a number of other châteaux, on into the nineteenth century. At Montgeoffroy, in the 1760s, where the stables shield the basse-cour and look over the forecourt to the chapel range, a horse is rearing up on its hind legs, with wildly waving mane.

There is nothing in a château quite as elaborate as the enormous group of 'the Horses of the Sun' carved on the stables of the Hôtel de Soubise in Paris. For quality and invention, however, it would be hard to equal the lively rococo horses of around 1740, framing a clock over the archway in the stable range at the château of Bizy, and the inventive architecture and waterscape of which they form a part.

The château and marquisate of Bizy had been bought in the 1720s by Comte Fouquet de Belle-Île (later created Duc de Gisors), the grandson of Nicolas Fouquet of Vaux-le-Vicomte. It is interesting to compare the stables at Vaux and Bizy. The Vaux stables are in the tradition of the grand

formal layout, and occupy one of the twin basse-cours. They are large and hand-some; the ranges for the stalls, instead of many vaults supported on columns, as at Chaumont and in many other stables, are spanned by a single brick and stone bar-rel vault, which is extremely impressive. Even so, inside and out, the stables are utilitarian architecture, and very much subsidiary to the château.

At Bizy the architect's fancy and ingenuity were lavished on the stables, and the château was in fact never built; in the end, a temporary residence was formed in one range of the basse-cour, to be replaced in the mid nineteenth century by a Renaissance palazzo designed for the Franco-German banker Baron Schickler.

The stables, which formed the entrance range to the basse-cour, were brilliantly combined with the necessary water-supply. This was treated as a decorative adjunct as well as a practical one. The water came from a reservoir pond in a cascade down the hill, on the axis of the stable archway, passed through the large and decorative Fontaine du Dauphin, and then went underground beneath the archway, to re-emerge in a drinking trough and a pond for washing the horses, on the same axis in the centre of the basse-cour. Two ramps were taken down into the wash-place in matching rococo curves. The water then went on to supply a fountain by the site of the proposed château.[5]

An easily available water supply was vital for horses, more so than for humans, who drank wine, not water, servants included, in eighteenth-century châteaux. The tank for washing them and the basin for watering them could be made decorative features, as at Bizy. There is another highly decorative water-trough of much the same date in the stables of the château of Champlâtreux. Château and stables were built from 1751 to the designs of Jean-Michel Chevotet for Mathieu-François Molé, Premier Président of the Paris Parlement, who had married the daughter of one of the richest of the financiers. The three pediments on the garden front of the château are filled with classical deities preparing for hunting and fishing, presided over by Diana under the central pediment.[6] Champlâtreux, in fact, like so many châteaux,

was essentially built as a summer resort for sport, and the stables, as a key element in this, were decorated accordingly.

The most opulent stable fountain of all is in the central rotunda of the huge stables at Chantilly, built by Louis-Henri de Bourbon, Prince de Condé, between 1719 and 1735. The Chantilly stables are grander than many palaces, grander indeed than the château of Chantilly itself, as it was in the eighteenth century. They are royal, rather than noble, in scale, but their architecture, and the size and splendour of the hunt establishment which was based on them, must have encouraged the building of grand stable buildings all over France.

Eighteenth-century stable buildings naturally vary much in size and elaboration, but they are always agreeable and sometimes architecturally delightful. However modest, they invariably contained accommodation for carriages as well as horses, in one or more 'remises' or carriage-houses entered by big arches off the courtyard. Towards the end of the century, under neoclassical influence, they sometimes have a geometric plan: at Le Bouilh they are built on a semicircle, at Moncley they were to have been built round a circular court, only about two thirds of which was completed.

Hunting continued to be of the first importance all through the nineteenth century, as a reason for going to châteaux, and sometimes even for building them, and the grander nineteenth-century stables are as impressive as any of the eighteenth century, Chantilly and other royal stables excepted. At the château of La Gaudinière, built in the 1860s by the Duc de Doudeauville largely or entirely as a base from which to hunt in the Fôret de Fréteval, long ranges of stables lined the approach to the château in the formal seventeenth-century manner, and the departure of the

The stable block at the château of Bizy (above) was designed in about 1740 by Pierre Contant d'Ivry for a château that was never built. The pool and fountain in the fore-ground were for the watering and washing of horses, and is approached by two curving ramps. Through the archway is a glimpse of the fountain and cascade that carry the vista up the hill.

Photographs in a commemorative volume privately printed in about 1870 show the Duc de Doudeauville (in the foreground, below left) about to go hunting at his newly-erected château of La Gaudinière.

duc and his family and guests for hunting was accompanied with a pomp and sense of showmanship which seems to be a deliberate re-evocation of eighteenth-century hunting splendour, at Chantilly and elsewhere. At Le Luart, where stables and château both date from the 1860s, the stables are as grand as the château. At Chaumont, in about 1878, Ernest Sanson designed the stables round two courts, one for the horses of guests and the other for the horses of the family, with accommodation for grooms on the first floor in both courts, and a basse-cour for cows, pigs and poultry forming a third courtyard at a lower level.[7]

Water was now mainly piped to the individual stalls (where the space between manger and hayrack was sometimes lined with marble). Fountains accordingly ceased to be architectural features. Their place as the prestigious focal point of the stables was taken by two novelties, the covered court and the 'sellerie', or harness-room.

Harness-rooms had certainly existed before, but they were normally utilitarian and practical rooms, rather than places for display. In the later nineteenth century they were carefully fitted up as rooms entered by family and guests as well as grooms, with a splendid array of highly polished harness displayed on the walls, sometimes

The bronze figures and sofa in the harness-room of the 1880s at the château of Contenson (left) make it clear that the room was not just intended for use by grooms.

A number of the larger stables of the late nineteenth and early twentieth century at French châteaux were planned round a covered court, used for washing down or mounting the horses. This example (right) is at the château of Gâtines and dates from about 1900.

The arrival of the car was greeted with enthusiasm at French châteaux. Above, the Marquis de Broc and his family or friends strike typical attitudes around his pioneer steam-car at the château of Le Perrays in about 1880. The stoker or 'chauffeur' at the rear makes clear the origin of this term.

A late-nineteenth-century photograph (left) shows the owner seated at the wheel of his new open car at the château of Schoppenwihr.

Departures for an
outing from the château
of Josselin, as illustrated
(above) in an article of
about 1900, show the
overlapping of two
stages in the history of
transport.

with comfortable seats for visiting gentry and even, as at the château of Contenson, with a central bronze of hounds and a horseman. The especially elegant circular form of the sellerie at Montgeoffroy is due to its being created in the nineteenth century in the medieval tower at one end of the eighteenth-century stables.

The covered court was a feature made easy to create in the later nineteenth century by new techniques of glass and iron roofs, as found especially in covered markets and railway stations. The more ambitious nineteenth-century stable blocks were now often ranged to either side of such a court, sometimes with the harness-room at the centre. The covered space was used for the grooming and hosing-down of horses, perhaps also for the cleaning and polishing of carriages, and riding parties could assemble there and mount their horses as they were led out from the stalls to them. The arrangement became a common one, and in a few of the largest stables it could be extremely imposing. Nothing like it is to be found in England.[8]

Towards the end of the century the automobile became the new toy and status symbol of the French upper classes; the pride and pleasure which they took in their gorgeous de Dion-Boutons and Dietrich-Lorraines comes across vividly in photographs, and on occasions the passion for cars virtually drove out the previous passion for horses. The new cars fitted happily enough into the former carriage-houses, and could be driven out and cleaned in the covered courtyards, although

Ligny-le-Ribault (Loiret). — Château de la Frogerie — Les Communs

separate accommodation was sometimes provided; plans for Chaumont show a covered 'cour des automobiles' to one side of the model farm, next to the 'logement des mécaniciens' and close to the electric-light plant and the elephant-house.[9]

When the novelist Eugène Sue acquired a château in the 1850s, his enemies made fun of his 'terrestrial paradise in the heart of the Sologne' where 'the dogs strut up and down in a kennel which many labourers would be pleased to live in', and 'the horses are warmly and stylishly installed in their own desirable residence'.[10] The marble-lined and glass-and-iron-roofed stables of the nineteenth century, with their harness-rooms concealed at their heart like treasure chambers, are indeed equine palaces, and the dogs were often handsomely housed too, if not as magnificently as the horses, perhaps, but far more stylishly than they would have been in England, in kennels that are architectural rather than utilitarian. They often have a dog's head carved on them, to go with the horse's head on the stables, which they sometimes adjoin, but not always, especially if they were built for shooting-dogs rather than hounds. At the château of Beaumanoir the kennels are right next door to the château, and Comte Henri de Saint-Pierre vividly remembers the pleasure which it gave him as a child to look through the windows and see the kennel-man in his 'big boots, leather leggings, brown jacket, flat cap, with a whip in his right hand and a stick in his left hand', marshalling his fourteen dogs, coupled in pairs and perfectly trained – 'they always had to keep behind him'.

The ebullient building, with its covered court, shown in an old postcard of the château of La Frogerie (above), followed the model of contemporary stables but was always built and used as a garage.

Kennels at French châteaux were often more elaborate than their English equivalents. The example shown in an old postcard of the château of De Coulonges (above right) is joined with a pavilion for tea or refreshment. At the late-nineteenth-century kennels at the château of Beaumanoir (right), a dog suns himself on the specially provided platform and surveys the canine sculpture under the gable.

8
BACK TO THE LAND

The eighteenth-century feature of a chambre with two grand beds in it is translated into medieval language in one of two superb bedrooms at the château of Roquetaillade, restored and remodelled internally by Viollet-le-Duc and Duthoit.

ENORMOUS NUMBERS of châteaux were rebuilt, new built or restored – and restoration often amounted to virtual rebuilding – in France in the nineteenth century. The results are to be found all over France, though they are thicker on the ground in some regions, which, for various reasons, were especially in demand. A recent survey of châteaux in the Sologne, to the south of Orléans, for instance, showed that out of a total of about 560 châteaux two thirds had been rebuilt or reconstructed between 1800 and 1914 – impressive evidence both of nineteenth-century activity and of the huge number of châteaux in some parts of France.[1]

These châteaux form a forgotten or neglected chapter in the history of French châteaux. French taste – or at least French château taste – is more or less where English taste was forty or fifty years ago. Nineteenth-century châteaux are considered hideous, or at best of no interest, and if there is money available it is deployed in toning or scraping them down, and if possible replacing their highly charged flavour with what is considered a more tasteful one in the eighteenth-century manner – now considered the golden age, as far as the owners of most châteaux are concerned. Some appreciation of the nineteenth century is, it is true, beginning; a few châteaux of this period are being included on government lists of 'classified' or 'inscribed' buildings, a few articles and a handful of books take nineteenth-century châteaux seriously.[2] And seriously they deserve to be taken, at least as a social phenomenon, and sometimes as an architectural one as well.

Behind the efflorescence of château-building – not as the only cause, but as an important cause – lay a social and political ideal and programme. In 1920 the sixty-year-old Marquis de Lastic, owner of the château of Parentignat, looked back on the history of his family in the eighteenth century, and felt able to say:

> Our family survived that century of loose morality and scepticism without singeing its wings too badly, and after the shattering impact of the Revolution the nineteenth century found it back in its home country and on its estates, following its rightful traditions of honour, religion, and faithfulness to the past.[3]

In the 1840s the old nobility were far from a spent force. The bulk of them were 'legitimist' supporters of the senior Bourbon line, and as hostile to Louis-Philippe and the Bonapartes as they were to the Republic. They still had estates, wealth, prestige and hopes, far from ridiculous, that the true Bourbon line would be restored, and the noblesse reassume its rightful position under them. Most English people do not realize that if Charles X's grandson, the Comte de Chambord, had been able to accept the tricolour as easily as his ancestor Henri IV had accepted the mass, France would have become a monarchy again in 1873, and he would have left the château of Chambord to ascend the throne as Henri V.

The fact that there were now local elections both to the provincial Conseils Généraux and the central government gave a rich and popular landlord a political role which his family had not held before the Revolution. New châteaux were in part a reflection of this. The noblesse hoped to win the country districts for the monarchy by living on their estates, restoring or rebuilding their châteaux, fostering agriculture and local industry, giving local employment, attending the parish church and, if necessary, rebuilding it, in general acting as the patrons, leaders and benefactors of their neighbourhood, and in some cases standing for election themselves. The ideal was stated by the Abbé Methivier in 1861:

> Every rural parish which does not contain a large estate crowned by a worthily inhabited château lacks an element essential to its morals and well-being. The château serves the village like a public fountain on which all the inhabitants can draw. Workmen of all kind find employment there, the day-workman can fill his day there, it provides help for the needy, care for the

sick, good advice for those in difficulties, support for the oppressed, an intelligent interest and a powerful defence for all the needs and interests of the neighbourhood, and a good example and the authority which this confers, for the population as a whole.[4]

In his monumental two-volume history of Maine and Anjou, Baron de Wismes, writing in the 1860s as a local nobleman and landowner, emphasized the need to update and improve 'the modest residences of the local gentry', which were no longer adequate for present-day needs and interests:

One of the main essentials for our time is to fight against the disastrous attraction which is pulling men of fortune away from the country into the towns; but if there is nothing to set against all the seductions of luxury, comfort and elegance which residence in the towns can provide, few people will be prepared to shut themselves up in an antiquated and gloomy mansion for the sake of a principle. To remedy this situation country-house life needs to be reinvigorated on the English model and to enrich its natural attraction with all that art and good taste can supply, above all to be given a secure foundation by large-scale farming and the exercise of the patronage which falls naturally to the lot of a resident proprietor. This is the path which is open to us, and by which we can both renew ourselves and once more acquire a legitimate influence on the country.[5]

Farmers were prosperous in the mid nineteenth century, and the income to be derived from farms and forestry was increasing. Napoleon III promoted agricultural improvement both by running his own model estates, and by pumping capital into the agricultural infrastructure and building roads and railways which gave farmers easy access to the growing markets in the towns. He was eager for the support of the old families, and however unenthusiastic most of them were about the Bonaparte dynasty, they were not averse to benefiting from it. In addition, some of the old families had received substantial injections of capital in the late 1820s, in the form of compensation, inaugurated by the Bourbon monarchy, for losses under the Revolution. How this compensation was administered, and who benefited from it, had been the subject of much dispute and complaint; but those who did so had capital available both for investing in land-purchase and agricultural improvement, and for spending on building and landscaping. Other families, especially of the lesser noblesse, had kept out of trouble during the Revolution, and done well out of buying up confiscated land on the cheap, so that they ended up considerably richer after it than they had been before – something which their descendants tended to gloss over.

The owners of historic old châteaux which had been abandoned or fallen into disrepair went back to live in them. The château of Josselin, which had long been in ruins, was restored and its interiors lavishly redecorated by the ducs de Rohan;

the ducs de Polignac reoccupied the château of Lavoûte-Polignac. Restoration, in the case of a medieval château, could entail the replacement of later features by new detail and decoration in a medieval style, as was done to sensational effect by Viollet-le-Duc and his pupil Duthoit at the great fourteenth-century fortress of Roquetaillade. But where a château was not thought to be of great value owners felt free to remodel or replace it, perhaps with the token retention of what were considered the more interesting original features, often so 'restored' as to be virtually rebuilt.

The new or new-modelled châteaux which now started to rise in increasing numbers out of the French landscape were designed to speak out with a triple tongue, for traditional values, good stewardship, and modern comfort and elegance. Traditional values involved the building of a chapel and the embellishment of the château with a full historical apparatus of high roofs, towers, turrets and pavillons, evoking whatever golden age of the past appealed to the particular proprietor, up to the time of Louis XIII but seldom later. Coats of arms, ornamental wrought-iron wind-vanes and other symbols of noblesse, which had been effaced or stripped off at the time of the Revolution, now had a second spring, caparisoned every surface and sprouted on every skyline. Any illustrious forebear or historic incident connected with the family or the location was celebrated in frescoes or carving, and men in armour or ladies in wimples supported beams, framed doorways or gleamed in the stained-glass of the windows.

In the purlieus of the château new forests were planted, and herds of cows, bred from fashionable Durham bulls imported from England, issued from model farms

The château of Josselin had grown ruinous, but from the 1860s the Ducs de Rohan went back to live there and restored it as their principal residence. In the grande salle or salon (above, as shown in an old photograph), the chimney-piece is original, but the furnishing and decoration are typical of the ponderous and evocative richness of the mid and late nineteenth century.

The magnificent fourteenth-century château of Roquetail-lade had been much altered, but Viollet-le-Duc and Duthoit took it back to their version of the Middle Ages. The staircase (right) fills the lower floors of the original donjon and was lit by one of the most splendid paraffin lamps ever constructed.

The château of Villiers (left), built in about 1885, is typical of the hundreds of new-built châteaux of the later nineteenth century, detached on an eminence in English-style parks, with the basse-cour removed to a discreet distance, but resolutely French in their symmetry and high-roofed silhouettes.

Nineteenth-century châteaux have frequently been redecorated as fashion swung back to the eighteenth century, but the interior of this château of the 1870s near Angers (right and below left) is almost unaltered. The galerie leading from either side of a central staircase is a typical feature, and the château retains its light fittings, originally made for paraffin, and especially prominent in the inevitable billiard-room.

or from prettily embellished basse-cours to graze the meadows. But neither basse-cour, farm or stables were too close to the château. Modern notions of what was desirable kept them at a suitable distance, though often much closer than they would have been in England. The ideal was now a château free-standing on a hill-top, with gardens and a park around it; an existing house, if on a low-lying site, was often abandoned for a new and higher site nearby, especially if it was small or considered architecturally undistinguished; the old buildings were sometimes kept, or kept in part, as the nucleus of communs or basse-cour.

The château itself, however heavily weighed down with traditional symbols, had to have high ceilings, large windows and an up-to-date plan. This meant a handsome salon, often opening on to a terrace, a billiard-room, a salle à manger, and a study, also serving as a library. The larger châteaux had both study and library, and two salons, one large and one small. A popular feature was a spacious corridor or gallery, on to which the main door opened, giving access to the principal rooms. Up-to-date elements often included a hot-air heating system, and big sheets of Saint-Gobain plate glass in the windows; a popular device was a window in the place of the traditional mirror over the chimney-piece in the salon, made possible by diverting the flues to either side. Modernity seldom extended to the plumbing, and new techniques of lighting were slow to arrive. From about 1870 onwards, paraffin lamps began to replace candles (or in some cases colza-oil lamps) in the main downstairs rooms. Gas was virtually unknown, as was electricity before 1900.

Entresols, and the whole elaboration of little rooms around the chambre, largely disappeared; servants now normally slept together on the top floor, and social life in the salon became more important than private life in the appartement. Boudoirs were rarer than in the eighteenth century. The usual arrangement was just a chambre with a cabinet de toilette adjoining; the latter was essentially a dressing-room rather than a sitting-room or occasional secondary bedroom, and often contained little more than a dressing-table, a washstand, and a chamber-pot in the cupboard. Running water in the cabinet de toilette or even near it was a great rarity. The cabinet de toilette of the mistress of the house, or the one attached to the main guest bedroom, could be a sizeable and agreeable room; the Duchesse de La Trémoille's cabinet de toilette, at Serrant, fitted up in the 1890s, is a beautiful example (and here there was even a bathroom adjoining).

In England in the first half of the nineteenth century it was common enough for amateur water-colourists in a family to make a detailed record of the interior of their homes, room by room. There was no such tradition in France, and as a result records of the internal appearance of châteaux before the arrival of photography

In the cabinet de toilette of the Duchesse de La Trémoille at the château of Serrant furniture and fittings in the best taste of the Belle Époque meld harmoniously with a coffered sixteenth-century ceiling. A photograph of the 1920s (below) shows the room in its original state, but it survives today little altered (right), although the overmantel portrait of the duchesse is a successful insertion of recent decades.

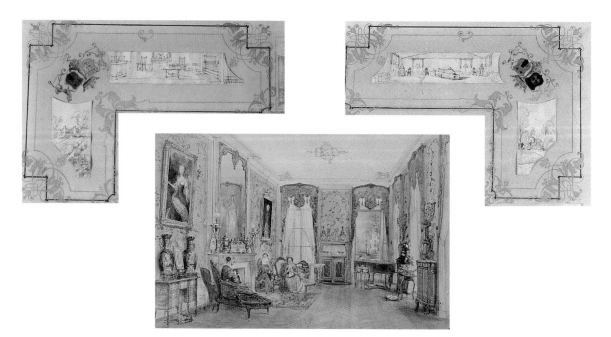

In 1839 the artist
Caron painted a view
of the château of
Courcelles and added
views of the interior of
the château around its
perimeter, to provide a
comprehensive and very
rare record of how a
château was furnished
and decorated under
Louis-Philippe.

The views are repro-
duced here in a slightly
different arrangement
from that in Caron's
picture. The view of the
salon (centre, top) is in
fact taken from a sepa-
rate painting, also by
Caron, of 1850. The
window is shown open
on the right to give a
glimpse of the recently-
built water-tower or
château d'eau, bringing
running water to the
château and still a rare
feature in the 1850s.

are much rarer and all the more valuable when they come to light. They show interiors still relatively empty and uncluttered, although the furniture tends to be growing heavier, and to be moving gradually from the walls into the centre. The lavish vegetation, heavy velvet drapes and fat velvet-upholstered sofas and chairs which combine with the increasing number of objects to produce the strong flavour that most people associate with the nineteenth century arrived only in the last decade of the century, along with the use of the camera to record it.

Baron de Wismes had talked of 'reinvigorating country-house life on the English model'. The English upper classes, securely placed in the political structure, as a whole far richer than their French counterparts, and enjoying as a result all the panoply of English country-house life – large houses, money, servants, broad estates, spacious parks, lodge-gates and lodges, and deferential cottagers and tenantry – were regarded with some envy by the French noblesse, as it fought to establish or at least retain its social, political and economic position. To some extent the new nineteenth-century châteaux were influenced by English models. The removal of farm-buildings, the dignified isolation of the house in its park, the avenue winding through this park, the model farms and the enthusiasm for agriculture and estate management which produced them, all owed much to England. Certain features inside the château were English-inspired or imported from England, particularly towards the end of the century, when 'le hall' made its curious appearance in a sprinkling of châteaux. English sporting or racing prints, or their French equivalents in the same style, began to line corridors and hang in the less important rooms, and English children's books, along with an English or Irish nanny, became a common feature.

A rare view of the salon of the château of Cany (below) shows a salon as furnished in about 1860, before the arrival of the potted palms and plush sofas made familiar in old photographs. A separate billiard room was later to become an almost invariable feature of French châteaux, but at Cany the billiard table was in the salon until the château was reordered to the designs of Ernest Sanson in the 1890s.

The 'hall' made its first French appearance at the Rothschild château of Ferrières, built to the designs of Paxton and Stokes in 1853–63.[6] The hall at Ferrières was top-lit, two storeys high, and filled the centre of the house in exactly the same manner as the hall at Paxton's slightly earlier Mentmore, designed for an English Rothschild in 1851. The Mentmore hall had been a pioneer in England of the use of a room of this name and type as a sitting-room, rather than an entrance vestibule, circulation space, or dining hall. The Ferrières hall (always so-called, in French and English) was used in the same way, as drawings and photographs show. Later French halls include ones at Contenson (1880s), Grosbois (c. 1890), Chambly and Le Luart, and the early-twentieth-century ones at the châteaux of Rochefort-en-Yvelines and Le Claireau.[7]

In both the eighteenth and nineteenth centuries, when the main rooms were usually on the ground floor, it was a problem to know what to do with a salle haute on the first or second floor, in the sixteenth- or seventeenth-century manner. At the château of Serrant this was converted in the 1890s as a joint library and billiard-room, as shown in a photograph of about 1920 (above).

At Grosbois the Prince de Wagram and his Rothschild wife created a hall by joining up the salle haute and the salle basse of the seventeenth-century château and running a gallery round the junction. At the new-built Contenson the room was divided in two by the great Gothic staircase, with its neo-medieval frescoes; according to the article in *Fermes et Châteaux* in 1905 one side was 'reserved for smoking and billiards, the other is the domain of the ladies'.[8]

According to the memoirs of Comtesse Jean de Pange, the widowed Madame de Rochetaillé and her brother and relatives normally sat in the sitting end of the hall, and life at Contenson was 'freer, more impromptu and much less regulated' than life in her own family château at Broglie.[9] A French hall seems, in fact, to have been intended as a less formal room than a salon, even though much the same kind of activities went on there. It was a big room, designed for large house-parties in houses where there was plenty of money, and a touch of Anglophilia. There was a billiard-table in the hall at the Murats' Chambly, as well as at Contenson;[10] the hall at Grosbois contained a grand piano, divans, at least one writing-table, and a table piled high with books, the ancestor of a modern coffee-table. Mary King Waddington, writing in the early twentieth century, saw such book-covered tables as examples of English comforts and 'a very rare thing in a French château'.[11]

In general, in spite of the occasional influences, there were substantial differences between nineteenth-century English country houses and French châteaux, partly due to basic differences of attitude between the two cultures, partly because most French owners had less money to spend.

The almost neurotic differentiation of the Victorian country house into various zones, often allotted to different wings – for gentlemen and ladies, for family, children and guests, for men servants, and women servants – is barely to be found in France. The English ideal in the nineteenth century was that servants should, if possible, be neither seen nor heard except when waiting at table or admitting guests at the front door, and that tradesmen delivering their wares or their services should be equally invisible. The Victorian answer to this was the service court – sometimes two service courts – with all the servants' and service rooms grouped round it, and stretching out to one side at the back of the gentry part of the house, shielded from view by plantations of bushes and trees, and approached by a back or side drive, which either discreetly broke off from the main drive well before the house was reached, or had its own separate entrance on to the public road.

The practice of putting kitchen, hall and other servants' rooms in the basement of the main house, which was common enough in both France and England from the sixteenth to the eighteenth century, was largely abandoned in new houses built in England in the nineteenth and twentieth centuries. One reason for this was that

What the French called 'le hall', in imitation of the living-halls which became fashionable in Victorian country houses in England, began to appear in some of the grander châteaux in the later nineteenth century. The pioneer was the hall at the château of Ferrières (below), designed by English architects for Baron James de Rothschild in 1853–63.

basements were said to be dark and damp, and that properly looked after servants deserved more salubrious quarters. But the other reason, often stated at the time, was perhaps more important: from the windows of the basement (unless it was sunk in an area, as it sometimes was) servants could survey the activities of the gentry, in entrance court and gardens, and impinge on their privacy, which was not the case if they were securely isolated and shielded in a service wing.

The French upper classes were less sensitive. The servants' living and working quarters normally continued to be provided in the basement; with the virtual disappearance of mezzanines their sleeping quarters were now in the attics. There was no service wing, and usually no service yard, or only a small one; deliveries came up the main drive and went in through a side door in the basement, but all in full view of the main part of the château.

The gentleman's wing or appartement, made up of billiard-room, smoking-room and sometimes study and gun-room, with bachelor bedrooms on the floor above – all carefully isolated from the women in the morning-room or drawing-room – was equally conspicuous by its absence in most French châteaux. The nearest equivalent was the 'salle de chasse', lined with sporting trophies and with its own external entrance, in which sportsmen congregated in the more ambitious new châteaux built mainly as centres for field sports. On the other hand, the billiard-room became as essential an element of a new French château as of an English country house, but it was seen as an extension of the salon, not as a retreat from it. Billiards was just another game, to be enjoyed in the evening or on a wet day, like cards and backgammon, and in the earlier decades of the nineteenth century the billiard-table was sometimes set up at one end of the salon, if it was a large one. When a 'salle de billard' was provided, the normal position was next to the salon, and the two rooms were often joined together by an archway, or double doors normally left open, so that the friendly click of billiard balls became a background to the conversation or the rattle of dice and smack of cards in the salon; billiards was more normally played by the men of the party, but was not confined to them. A 'fumoir' or smoking-room is sometimes to be found in a nineteenth-century château, sometimes tucked away in a tower, but it was not the invariable feature it became in the larger English country houses, and it was not necessarily adjacent to the billiard-room. Very often the owner's study also acted as a smoking-room.[12]

The lack of differentiation in French châteaux made planning them a simpler matter than was the case with the manic complexity of a Victorian country house in England. Instead of a main block sprouting out into an enormous service wing and a smaller gentleman's wing and family wing, the necessary accommodation could be fitted quite easily into a single compact block; and whereas the diffuse and rambling nature of a Victorian country house made some kind of irregular picturesque composition a natural way of fitting the various elements together, in France there was seldom a problem of giving the single block of the château symmetrical façades, if that was what was desired. And since the English taste for the picturesque never bit so deeply in France, and the French retained a taste for

A 'hall' of about 1880 at the château of Contenson, as illustrated in the magazine Fermes et Chateaux *in 1905. It consisted of three parts: a sitting end, a billiards end, and a central staircase. Frescoes around the top of the staircase show the owner's family and friends in the guise of a medieval hawking party.*

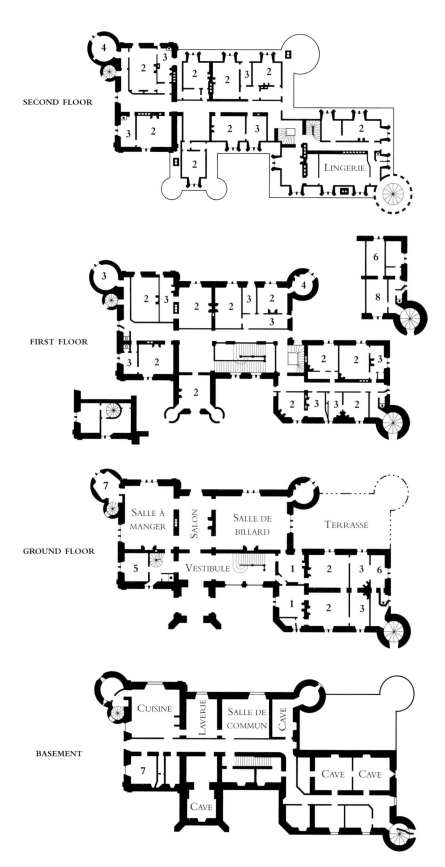

SECOND FLOOR

FIRST FLOOR

GROUND FLOOR

SALLE À MANGER   SALON   SALLE DE BILLARD   TERRASSE

VESTIBULE

LINGERIE

BASEMENT

CUISINE   LAVERIE   SALLE DE COMMUN   CAVE

CAVE   CAVE

CAVE

KEY
1. SALLE D'ATTENTE
   CABINET
2. CHAMBRE
3. CABINET DE
   TOILETTE
4. BOUDOIR
5. VESTIBULE DE
   CHASSE
6. SALLE DE BAIN
7. OFFICE
8. FEMME DE
   CHAMBRE

Plan of the basement, ground, first and second floors (left) of the château of Vouzeron (right), designed by G.-H.-A. Destailleur for the banker Baron Eugène Roger and built in 1887–93. Destailleur, unlike many nineteenth-century architects, pre-ferred a degree of asymmetry, but the château is still far more compact than an equivalent large house of the same period in England, partly due to putting all the service rooms in the basement. The small size of the salon compared to that of the billiard-room is a curious and untypical feature. The 'vestiaire de chasse' on the ground floor is a reminder that one of the main functions of the château was as a centre for field sports.

symmetry, many French châteaux continued to be largely or wholly symmetrical all through the nineteenth century. A rival group, to which Viollet-le-Duc belonged, supported the idea of more irregular compositions; perhaps it was influenced by the ideas and arguments of the English architect Pugin and his successors. A number of châteaux involving a degree of calculated asymmetry were built, mostly towards the end of the nineteenth century, but the symmetrical design remained the commonest solution for a new-built château.[13]

It was easier to fit the servants into the basement of a compact block, which was not overpoweringly large, because there were fewer of them than in England. For an English duke to confine himself to a household of sixteen servants, as did the Duc de Rohan at the château of Josselin, would have been unthinkable. The reason may have been in part a taste in France for a simpler lifestyle, but this taste was encouraged by the straightforward fact that the French upper classes were poorer than the English ones. In 1878 John Bateman published his invaluable *The Great Landowners of Great Britain and Ireland*.[14] This was a survey of income derived from land, based on the exhaustive county by county returns of income made by order of Parliament in 1872–3. Bateman's 1878 edition was confined to landowners owning at least 1200 hectares (3000 acres), living on an income of at least £3000 a year. A new edition in 1879 was enlarged to include possessions of at least 800 hectares

(2000 acres) and at least £2000 a year; the supplementary class were placed humbly beneath a line at the bottom of the relevant page. The supplement increased the number of qualifying landowners from about 2500 to about 3800. The income of many landowners soared far above the minimum £3000 or £2000, even though (a major lack) income derived from property in London was not included. The richest landowner, in terms of landed income, in the 1883 edition, was the Duke of Buccleuch, with an income of £231,855 derived from 184,000 hectares (about 460,108 acres), in fourteen counties.

Historians of nineteenth-century France have no equivalent of Bateman or Parliamentary Returns to simplify their work and illuminate the landed incomes of France, but there is no doubt that a combination of the French Revolution and the Code Napoléon resulted in an, on the average, far smaller size of landed

The château of Challain-la-Potherie (below), built for the Rochefoucauld-Bayers family to the design of René Hodé in 1846–54, was one of the most impressive expressions of the return of the noblesse to their country estates in the 1830s and 1840s.

estate in France, and made impossible the huge accumulation of property in many counties, of which the Duke of Buccleuch provided (and indeed, still provides) so extraordinary an illustration. The bulk of French owners of châteaux would have failed to make even the below-the-line classification in Bateman. The imposing mass of the Rochefoucauld-Bayers château of Challain-la-Potherie, for instance, was supported by an estate of 596 hectares (1470 acres), and other châteaux rebuilt or remodelled at the same time in Anjou had estates of the same kind of size, ranging from 440 to 717 hectares.[15] In the Sologne, where estates were rather larger, the château of La Ferté-Imbault was based on an estate of 10,000 hectares (24,000 acres) in 1814, but this was quite exceptional; in 1848, however, half a dozen or so Sologne châteaux were based on property ranging from 1700 to 4915 hectares.[16] But even Sologne should be compared with, for instance, the sixty-seven, sixty-eight and seventy landowners recorded by Bateman as having estates of 12,000 hectares (30,000 acres) or more in Devon, Lincolnshire and Norfolk respectively.

Of course there were historic families with châteaux and estates dotted over several départements, the combined acreage and income of which could add up to a considerable total. But even these tended to get divided up among different children, thanks to the effect of the Code Napoléon. One is left with the impression that many new-built châteaux were larger than the income available to support them from the lands attached to them, especially as the Code exercised its effect on succeeding generations. It may be that the owners who enthusiastically went back to the land in the mid-century were over-optimistic about the increasing income that agricultural improvements would bring them. A model farm, or farms, could turn out to be as good a way of losing money as of making it. At the château de Saint-Amadour, for instance, the agricultural improvements and model farm inaugurated by Comtesse Pauline d'Armaillé and continued by her heir, the Prince de Broglie, failed to survive the latter's death in 1906. His widow confided her affairs to her brother-in-law, Pierre de Luppé, who immediately persuaded her to close down Saint-Amadour, and, as her daughter recalled, set about

> liquidating as soon as possible the model farm and the Durham herd, which he said cost a fortune and made no profit. All the dream of being 'gentleman-farmers' which had captivated my parents for fifteen years cut no ice with Pierre, who was above all a good business man and hostile on principle to Anglomania.[17]

Saint-Amadour was only a satellite of the family's main property at Broglie, and it could survive expensive hobbies of this kind. But the châteaux which had the best hope of survival were those which were supported on more than income from land.

All through the centuries French châteaux, like the country houses in other countries, had been heavily indebted to new money, and to the new rich who bought land and built themselves, and whose daughters married into old families and enabled them to restore and rebuild. The nineteenth century was no exception, though the source of the money was different: no longer the 'fermiers-généraux' and financiers of the seventeenth and eighteenth centuries, but bankers and industrialists, rich from the growth of international finance and the burgeoning of the Industrial Revolution and mass-markets. A few historic families, like the La Rochefoucauld ducs de Doudeauville, were able to build up large estates without infiltrations of new money, through a happy combination of good marriages and small families. Others were as happy to cash in on new money as their predecessors, and many a family or château in difficulties, or likely to run into them, was rescued by the infusions of capital which it provided. France was less industrialized than England, and there was accordingly less of this kind of money from French sources available, but there was still no shortage of it, and it was augmented by American money, from both North and South.

To list the families with new or recent money which feature in the period could become wearisome, but the list can perhaps be varied if subdivided into three parts: types of client, the clientele of one particular architect, and a couple of individual families, looked at in more detail.

In the late 1860s Madame de Baritault, whose husband was about to employ Viollet-le-Duc and Duthoit to restore the great medieval château of Roquetaillade, near Bordeaux, commented acidly in her diary that the Gironde was being taken over by Protestants and Jews.[18] One can imagine that similar remarks were being made around Catholic card-tables in upper-class salons all over France, and although

Their share of the Furtado-Heine banking fortune enabled the Murat family to live and entertain in legendary style in their Paris hôtel and their two châteaux, including Chambly (below), where they went for the hunting. In fact, they ultimately over-spent, and Chambly was left uncompleted.

UNE CHASSE AU CHATEAU DE CHAMBLY
Le Départ

– as far as concerned the Gironde as much as anywhere else – they were a gross exaggeration, they did reflect the success and growing wealth of these two groups in the second half of the nineteenth century.

It was probably the purchase by Baron James de Rothschild of the château of Lafite and its vineyards in 1868 which prompted Madame de Baritault's remark. In terms of the buying and building of châteaux, as of so much else, the Rothschilds were the most prominent of the Jewish families, with at least four major new châteaux to their credit, and a number of smaller ones. The best known of the châteaux was the great house at Ferrières, built for Baron James de Rothschild to the designs of the English architects Paxton and Stokes between 1853 and 1863; in England the same firm had just designed the equally imposing Mentmore for Baron Mayer Amschel de Rothschild. In 1878 his daughter and heiress married the Earl of Rosebery. In the same year Margaretha, the niece of Baron James, married the Duc de Gramont; in 1882 her sister married the Prince de Wagram. Within four years, three grand French and British families were happy for their sons to marry a Jewish wife, as long as she was rich enough. The Gramont marriage produced Vallière, a massive neo-Renaissance château in (for France) an enormous park, built with Rothschild money by the Jewish architect A. P. Aldrophe, between 1891 and 1895;[19] the Wagram marriage led to the substantial remodelling of the interiors of the château of Grosbois.

Daughters of at least one of the other rich Jewish banking families made grand Catholic marriages. The heiresses of the Furtado-Heine family married the Duc d'Elchingen in 1866 and the Duc de Richelieu in 1875. The former marriage brought the Elchingens and their heirs the Murats the château of Rocquencourt, just outside Paris, a big new hôtel in Paris, and a large fortune, which enabled them to live and entertain in lavish style, in Paris, at Rocquencourt and at their new-built hunting-seat at Chambly, all through the years of the Belle Époque.

The French Protestants formed another group which became increasingly prosperous in business in the second half of the nineteenth century. They included the banking Hottinguers, Ferays and Mallets; the Havilands, who made china of an attractive 'aesthetic' design at their works in Limoges; Baron Schickler, German by origin but settled in Paris, and an influential group in Bordeaux, owners of vineyards and much else besides, including the Johnsons (whose enormous wealth fascinated and shocked Madame de Baritault) and the Cruses. On the whole these rich Protestants married among themselves or into English, American or German Protestant families, or into the old Alsatian noblesse, most of whom were Protestant. They all built or bought châteaux, and at least two of them employed English architects. In the 1860s Baron Schickler virtually monopolized the services of William White, an English architect who had settled in Paris. White designed him two large châteaux, an Italian palazzo at Bizy, facing the great eighteenth-century stables, and a chunky, highly embellished mansion in English Victorian Gothic at Martinvast.[20] In 1897 Guillaume Mallet gave Edwin Lutyens one of his first important commissions, at Le Bois de Moutiers, at Varengeville, with a Gertrude Jekyll garden to go with it.

In 1980 Mary King Waddington, the American wife of the French (in spite of his English name) politician and diplomat William Waddington, published her *Château and Country Life in France*, a charming account of thirty years spent in and around a château near Villers-Coterêts. North American marriages into French château-owning families were perhaps rather fewer than their English or Scottish equivalents, because American millionaires with social ambitions were mainly Protestant, and preferred Protestant English dukes to Catholic French ones. But there was no shortage of them, none the less. The sewing-machine heiress, Winnaietta Singer, married Prince Edmond de Polignac; the Marquis de Breteuil married an heiress of the Garner family of New York, but the most notorious, and ultimately the most disastrous Franco-American marriage was that between Anna Gould, heiress of the railway tycoon Jay Gould, and the Marquis de Castellane, the notorious 'Boni'. They married in 1895; he used her money to build the famous 'Pink Palace' in the Champs-Élysées (so-called from its pink marble staircase), and to buy, restore and embellish the château of Le Marais, before she divorced him for extravagance and infidelity, and married the future Duc de Talleyrand.

In the last decades of the nineteenth century the architects most employed by the new rich to build, restore or embellish their châteaux were G.-H.-A. Destailleur (1822–96) and his son Walter-André (1867–1940).[21] The elder Destailleur had an

exhaustive knowledge of French architecture, based on a formidable library and collection of prints and drawings; he deployed it to produce heavyweight châteaux in a variety of historic styles, mildly asymmetric in design and increasingly up-to-date in their technological equipment. He and his son worked for families new and old, but more often the former: their work for them included the château of Courances, embellished and internally remodelled for the banker Octave de Béhagu in the 1870s; Waddesdon Manor in England, new-built in 1874–84 for Baron Ferdinand de Rothschild; the château of Vouzeron, new-built for the banker Baron Eugène Roger between 1887 and 1893; the château of Trevarez, new-built between 1894 and 1906 for Octave de Béhague's stepson, the Brest entrepreneur

The modest château of Contenson was enlarged and transformed in the 1880s for Baron Camille de Rochetaillé, who was rich from coal-mines in the Saint Étienne area.

James de Kerjégu; and the châteaux of Vaux and Champs, restored in the 1880s and 1890s for the sugar millionaire Alfred Sommier and the banker Comte Louis Gatien d'Anvers. Courances and Vaux were to pass through heiresses into old families, Courances to the Marquis de Ganay, Vaux, much later, to Comte Patrice de Vogué.

Coal-mines around Saint-Étienne provided the money for the impressive transformation of the château of Contenson in the 1880s for Baron de Rochetaillé, and the marriage of a Rochetaillé daughter to Chateaubriand's great-nephew financed the internal remodelling of the château of Combourg, and the embellishment of every square inch of its interior with heraldic and neo-feudal decoration.[22] The great sugar refineries developed by the Say family in Nantes and Paris seemed a sure source of limitless wealth for the two heiress sisters Jeanne and Marie Say, who became respectively the Marquise de Brissac and Princesse Amadée de Broglie.[23] The latter bought, restored and embellished the Renaissance château of Chaumont. She had seen and fallen for the famous château in 1875, when she was aged seventeen. Her sister had said, 'If you like it, why don't you buy it?' and she did. She then looked for a suitably aristocratic husband to go with the château, and almost immediately found Prince Amadée de Broglie.

The Marquise de Brissac (Vicomtesse de Trédern when she remarried after her husband's early death) restored and refurbished the château of Brissac, installed a private theatre on the top floor and gave her son a new stable block as a Christmas present; she took him to his bedroom window the morning after he arrived from Paris: 'Look, I've got a surprise for you.' But she made no attempt to emulate the lavish lifestyle at Chaumont, where the waywardness, vitality and extravagance of her sister amazed the neighbourhood and her wealth (looked after by her sensible husband) poured over from the château on to the village and estate. The château was restored and modernized by Ernest Sanson, the kitchen moved from the ground floor to a basement which was dug out and vaulted to receive it, enormous stables and a basse-cour were built next door, and an equally large model farm a kilometre or so away. Chaumont was one of the first châteaux in France to be lit by electric light. The estate was increased from 1000 to 2500 hectares (2470–6000 acres), seven cottages for gamekeepers and two pavilions for shooting or hunting lunches were built in the forest, and a new church, a cinema, a school, a free dispensary and a crèche were supplied for the village. The Maharajah of Kapurthala came to stay bringing an enormous suite (the princess had met him on an Indian holiday). As a thank-you present he sent her an elephant, which was installed in stables constructed for it next to the model farm.[24]

The Say sugar business collapsed in 1905, as a result of the extravagance, incompetence and suicide of its managing director, and although both sisters had diversified their capital and survived the crash (Princesse Amadée starting on a disastrous downward path after her husband's death in 1917), this particular source of new money for old families ceased to flow. But the huge steel fortune of the Schneider dynasty continued, from the late nineteenth far into the twentieth century, to pass through heiresses into increasing numbers of old families.[25] The

Schneiders themselves moved between their houses in Paris, the château of La Verrière next to their steelworks at Le Creusot, and their enormous château of Rivaulde in the Sologne. The daughters of Henri Schneider married the Marquis de Chaponay, the Comte de Ganay, the Marquis de Brantes and the Marquis de Joigné; his granddaughters married the Duc de Lévis Mirepoix, the Duc de Brissac, the Comte de Rosanbo, Comte Charles de Breteuil and the Comte de Durfort. Schneider money flowed liberally into all these families and their châteaux. One could draw a similar diagram of marriage alliances and refurbished châteaux for the other great steel dynasty, the Wendels.

Baron de Wismes had talked of the need to modernize châteaux in order to keep their owners from being lured away by the 'seductions of luxury, comfort and elegance' in the towns. But although a few families, when they went back to their estates in the 1840s and 1850s, intended to live on them all the year round, and sometimes carried out their intention, most owners did their best to enjoy luxury, comfort and elegance in both country and town, if they could afford it. They combined a château in the country with a house or an appartement in Paris or one of the big provincial towns. From the 1830s onwards, the spread of the railways made Paris much easier to get to. One can watch, as a result, a slow decay of social prestige in the local capitals, and the gradual selling-off of the handsome 'hôtels particuliers' which lined their streets, as their owners gave them up for an appartement in Paris. It was a slow process; the great efflorescence of château building in Sologne from the mid nineteenth century, for instance, was started by families whose town residences were in Orléans, not Paris, and it was not until the end of the century that Paris-based families began to take over.

A rare late nineteenth-century photograph (below) captures the annual migration from town to country, in this case to a modest château in Anjou.

In the second half of the nineteenth century a rigid social ritual developed for the grander or richer families: six months in Paris, six months in the country. The Paris season ended with the Grand Prix de Paris run on the racecourse at Longchamps, and immediately after it any family with social pretensions went off to its château, and did not return to Paris until the New Year. The country six months were unlikely, however, to be spent just in the one château; the family's stay there was normally varied by a month or so in one of the Normandy or Brittany seaside resorts, where the richer families often owned a villa, sometimes by an expedition abroad, and by visits to other châteaux.

The move from town to country was always a formidable affair, involving an uncommon amount of packing. In the 1840s the Armaillé family's move to a château beyond Fontainebleau involved two carts, hired from Fontainebleau, making their way up to Paris, and being piled high with trunks, boxes and pieces of furniture, including a piano and a complete set of household linen.[26] Horse transport continued to be used until at least the end of the century, but with the spread of the railways the move was increasingly made by train, for luggage, family, servants, and often horses as well, put with their grooms in straw-packed wagons.

Hunting remained as important as it had always been as an occupation for the time spent at châteaux and as an inducement for going there; its medieval origins and former monopoly by the noblesse made it an acceptable affirmation of tradition. Shooting, if more recent in origin, became almost equally important. The decision to restore or rebuild a château was often related to its being in good hunting country, which in France meant in or next to a forest, or forests. The château of Regnières-Écluse, for instance, was rebuilt as early as 1830, predominantly as a hunting-lodge, and carvings of medieval hunting scenes decorated its façades, just as, at

The château of Rivaulde was rebuilt by the Schneider steel family in 1902 as a venue for their huge shooting parties in the Sologne.

the château of Contenson, fifty years later, the staircase was frescoed with a medieval hawking-party, the members of which were in fact portraits of the owner, his family and friends. In the 1860s the Duc de Doudeauville's château of La Gaudinière was built on a virgin site in the middle of the Fôret de Fréteval, entirely for the hunting.

Chantilly, with its vast forests, remained, as it had been for centuries, a great area for hunting, and it was here that the Murats built their château of Chambly, and gave huge hunting parties. But in the late nineteenth century the area most in demand for both hunting and shooting was the Sologne. It was easily accessible by rail from Paris, large estates could be acquired there and it was increasingly colonized by new rich families with social ambitions, who bought old châteaux or built new ones. Building up a hunt or a shoot took over from agricultural improvement as the fashionable activity in the Sologne, and farmland was increasingly replaced by woodlands, not least because owners discovered that they could now get a better return from letting out land for shoots than from farming it.[27]

The Schneiders' château of Rivaulde was in the heart of the Sologne. The family bought the property in 1893, and lived for some years in the existing château, but it was not big enough for their needs, and a large new château was built in 1902. The estate, originally of 1209 hectares (3000 acres), was increased in the next five years to 2750 hectares (6800 acres). It was for shooting, not hunting. Two types of shoot were held: small ones for three to five guns, and big ones, for up to twenty guns, with correspondingly large house-parties. Including members of the family, 233 people came to shoot there between 1897 and 1913, many returning year after year. The guns included neighbouring landowners, business associates and friends from the Faubourg, but the core was always made up of the Schneider clan in all its ramifications, and the château served as the autumn rallying-place of its different branches.[28]

The spread of the railways, followed by the introduction of the motor-car, in general made it much easier to assemble large groups of people together. One result of this was that fashionable weddings, which had mainly been celebrated in Paris, began to take place in the country. An early example was the golden wedding of Baron and Baronne Alfred Renouard de Bussière, at the château of La Robertsau in Alsace in 1875. The celebration of this was little, if any, more lavish than the weddings which occur monthly at French châteaux today, but was then considered sufficiently remarkable to be recorded in a large privately printed folio.[29] A Parisian firm was summoned to Alsace to decorate a large horseshoe-shaped marquee attached to one façade of the château and opening through pillars decorated with flowers and garlands into a garden laid out inside the horseshoe. Twenty-five gentry and forty-two servants were put up in the château, and thirteen bachelors in a chalet in the park; there was a family dinner in the tent on 14 June, but the main festivities were on the fifteenth. A drive through triumphal arches to and from a service in the church was followed by a sit-down meal served to 218 people. Unfortunately the tent failed to protect the festivities from a torrential cloudburst, which delayed service of the meal, caused the cancellation of the procession and made it necessary for servants with sponges on the ends of long sticks to endeavour to mop up the dripping water all through the meal. One of the functions of 'le hall' or of covered concourses in the stables was to provide a more waterproof setting and guard against this kind of débâcle.

A wedding was always the responsibility of the bride's family, but a lavish party could also be given at the groom's château to introduce his bride to the neighbourhood. An article in the magazine *Femina* for 1 October 1906 describes and illustrates such an occasion, a fête at the château of Josselin, following on the marriage of the Duc de Rohan's son, the Prince de Léon. The fête was for the whole neighbourhood, and all classes. The duc came out on to the perron of the château with the bride, to show her to the assembled crowds, and a sit-down dinner for 300 people followed, at tables set out in the open in the garden. Dancing for many more followed, at the family's second château, of Saint-Pierre, on the river just outside Josselin. Illustrations show 'Princesse Murat, the Comtesse of Cardusan, Monsieur François and Monsieur de Talbouet dancing with the peasants', and so on.

One is reminded of Blarenberghe's eighteenth-century depictions of the noblesse dancing at peasant weddings outside the château. At Josselin, when there was a big celebratory dinner in the château, the dining-room windows were opened so that the local people could file by on the lawn and look in at the dinner, a nineteenth- or early-twentieth-century refinement of the onlookers being allowed into the dining-room to crowd round the tables, as at the Duc de Croy's dinner at Condé in 1752, and numerous royal occasions. At Josselin, too, as late as the 1930s, any passing tramps knew they would be supplied with hunks of bread and meat, brought out from the kitchen to feed them.[30] One might think this an appropriately feudal and ducal custom, but Mary King Waddington relates how the Waddington château and all the neighbouring ones along the high road invariably supplied 'good thick slices of bread' and a two-sou piece to any passing tramp who asked for it.[31]

Some of the events may have been the result of a conscious revival of customs that had been discontinued, but even so one is left with a feeling of the intensely traditional nature of French château life – perhaps especially in evidence in poorer or less fashionable châteaux, but by no means confined to them. As in the eighteenth century, all châteaux had their big celebrations and parties, even if these took place more frequently in the richer and more fashionable ones, but the basic rhythm of château life at all levels remained much what it had been in the eighteenth century, unostentatious gatherings of aunts, uncles, cousins and grandchildren, visiting and receiving neighbours, going on excursions, hunting, shooting, amusing themselves with dressing-up or acting, but essentially centring around the life and rituals of the salon; and in châteaux salons all over France the life lived in the 1930s was not all that different from that lived in the 1760s, as descriptions, memoirs and people's own memories make clear.

Madame d'Armaillé recalled with some nostalgia the salon of the château of La Rivière in 1847, the black marble chimney-piece with its Louis-Seize clock, and porcelain and crystal vases on pedestals painted by her mother with scenes from Walter Scott: and to the right of the chimney-piece a Louis-Seize sofa, on which my mother and my elder sister were having a lively conversation. Opposite, my father, ensconced in a deep armchair, sounding off against the weakness of the government; my brother next to him, expressing an exactly opposite point of view. Then my brother-in-law Monsieur de Bonneval, always a dyed-in-the-wool legitimist; the rest of us at our work around the table; my nephews at the far end of the salon, playing billiards or at the games-table. Madame Durosuel … knitting with her little hands pitted and wrinkled like old apples; the tea steaming on the square table; the two old lamps above the billiard-table going out one after the other; the pots of flowers, brought in out of the first frosts in the conservatory. And the cold rain which fell, streaming on the glass, and dripped through the gaps in the corners.[32]

The atmosphere has not changed all that much if one moves on to the old Duchesse d'Uzès at the château of Bonuelles in the 1920s, in her salon with its immense

vases of flowers, clavichord, old billiard-table and tables covered with photographs … There, next to Madame d'Uzès, are six of us, hurriedly lining up the patience cards. Our venerable partner intones 'ten of hearts … knave of clubs … king of diamonds'. 'Oh, not so quick,' softly begs her granddaughter, Mademoiselle Yolande de Luynes. Next to her is her son, the Duc d'Uzès, and her eldest daughter, the Duchesse de Luynes, and then her granddaughter Anne, Comtesse de La Rochefoucauld, and myself. The secretary, a lady as swarthy as a Moor, is always left behind-hand, gasping and despairing … Near the table, reading and day-dreaming, is the very charming Vicomtesse de Luppé, the child of her dear dead friend the Duchesse de Brissac … Against a wall on a sofa dozes the Curé of Bonuelles, his eyes half-closed behind his spectacles with their rusty frame, his arms crossed, his chin on his stock. At the end of the salon the Marquis de Crussal, the grandson of the Dowager Duchess, cannons billiard balls with his cousin the Duc de Luynes. An old man of eighty, with a velvet collar and a monocle attached to a silk ribbon, is talking loudly to himself (no one is listening to him) … Madame d'Uzès has finished her patience. 'We must go up to bed,' she says to the company, 'for we're hunting tomorrow.'[33]

One element is lacking in this description, the ladies sitting round a table, or at an embroidery frame, doing their work. It may be that the company at Bonuelles was just too old, or that by the 1920s this traditional and, for at least 150 years, almost inevitable element of salon life, was beginning to disappear. One meets with it constantly in descriptions ranging from the grandest châteaux to the most modest manoirs. In the nineteenth century it acquired a moral and religious sanction, for the work being done was often for the parish church or the château chapel, the embroidery of altar frontals, or the turning of wedding-dresses into vestments.

Descriptions by Mrs Waddington and others show how old-fashioned and simple the poorer or remoter châteaux still were around 1900. Salons were still uncarpeted, and the chairs lined against the wall, as in the eighteenth century. The serving of tea was only just beginning to come in, as an English-style alternative to the 'goûter', of cake and wine. According to Mrs Waddington, when she first offered tea to visitors from neighbouring châteaux in the 1870s, they would say, 'I'm in good health, thank you!' as though they were being offered a medicine.[34]

But by the early twentieth century, when Ferdinand Bac was staying with the Rohans at Josselin and visiting neighbouring châteaux and manoirs with them, tea had become an established custom. He comments,

Nothing was more curious for me than these visits. One enters into dilapidated châteaux replete with noble misery, gloom, bad taste, resignation, and deplorable mismanagement by earlier generations … at times one could suppose that the denizens had lived in splendour in 1867, but had grown old in unaltered clothes and surroundings … Sometimes one is told of a son who is in some indeterminate office in Paris, and has married his mistress. But if one surprises these excellent people around tea-time, there is always a good cake freshly baked. Outside, the châteaux still have an air of grandeur, a Louis-Quatorze façade most often, approached by a long chestnut avenue … Before the château a labourer in shirt-sleeves is pushing a wheelbarrow full of manure. The moment he hears the jingling of the horses, harnessed in pairs, he abandons his wheelbarrow and rushes towards the front-door to give the alarm. Then he hurls one of his clogs at the hens, who scatter in all directions, and hastily pulls on a shabby livery coat and a red waistcoat. But there is no time either to take off his other clog, or to button up his fancy uniform, for already the Princess has jumped down from the carriage.[35]

The changing life of an upper-class family in eastern France in the last decades of the nineteenth century, and on into the twentieth, is vividly evoked in the three fat volumes of the manuscript autobiography of the Baronne Picot d'Aligny. Madame d'Aligny had considerable skills as an artist. She deployed them, among many ways, in frescoing the little chapel at her husband's château of Montmirey-la-Ville, near Besançon in Franche-Comté, in decorating a set of several hundred plates with pictures of châteaux belonging to her family, relatives or friends, and in illustrating her autobiography.[36]

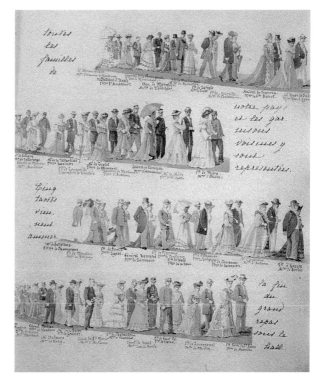

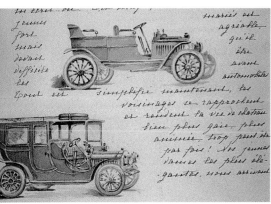

Franche-Comté, although always French-speaking, had only become part of France in 1678, when Louis XIV won it from Spain. Under France it had acquired its own parlement at its capital, Besançon. But the Picots d'Aligny were not a robe family, but old local noblesse, living partly at their château of Montmirey-le-Ville, and partly in a town house in Besançon. When Baron Picot d'Aligny married in 1872, Montmirey was a château of modest size, rebuilt or remodelled in the late eighteenth century as a rather bleak rectangular block, with a small central pediment and a low-pitched roof.

In 1876, after a few years of indecision, the young couple started the routine which they largely kept to until 1892. They spent from the end of December until July in their house in Besançon. Here Madame d'Aligny occupied herself with charitable activities, 'work for the church at the Sacré-Coeur, work for the poor with Madame Dusillet, work at Saint-Michael's distributing good books, work for the "Dames de Charité", visits to help the poor in childbirth'. The rest of the year was mainly spent at Montmirey in 'agreeable family parties' and improvements to the house and park, interspersed with seaside holidays at Dinard in Brittany, visits to other châteaux, trips abroad and excursions to Paris. She and her husband went up to Paris to see the Exposition in 1878, and for the next few years spent a few weeks each spring staying at the Hôtel du Louvre in Paris.

In May 1879 her rich uncle Gluflet died. He was the last of his ancient line, and also a collector. Family portraits, pictures and furniture came to Montmirey, and also money to help in 'improving' it in the taste of the day. The roof was made steeper, a central turret formed, the external façades enriched and the interior largely redecorated; the results were all depicted in the illustrations of the autobiography. More elaborate designs for a total recasting were never carried out, except for one little corner turret.

New purchases or gifts added to what came from their uncle: Louis-Quinze-style tapestries bought in Paris, Arab curios sent from Algeria by their cousin Hubert Lyautey, a fine Louis-Seize ironwork screen from the château of Valay, bought and given to them by Madame d'Aligny's mother, and installed as the entry to a much-extended park. In 1884 a large barn 'in the Russian or Norwegian manner' was built as a very ambitious wood-shed. In 1892 the communs were reconstructed, with stables and accommodation for carriages to either side of a big covered space, in the form now popular for stables, which they called 'le halle'. A familiar complaint follows picture and description: 'The architect who is full of talent and taste made the buildings altogether too fine, and involved us in more expense than we had bargained for.'

In May 1892 a momentous decision was taken. The d'Alignys bought a large appartement on the Quai d'Orsay in Paris. The house in Besançon was ultimately sold. Madame d'Aligny was not good at recording the names of architects, but she did what few of her contemporary châtelaines, or anybody but an architect, would have done: she inserted the plan of the appartement in her autobiography just as, earlier on, she had included the plan of the Besançon house.

Much of the autobiography is a record of improvements and purchases, of social and charitable life, of the inevitable amateur dramatics, and a big party to go with them, of the different stages in the lives of their children, all illustrated – the first haircut, the first bicycle (a reward to André for success in his exams), the first camera – of holidays by the seaside, or in Algeria and Egypt, of summers of lawn-tennis parties for the young, bicycling, hunting and horse-races. Only one unpleasant incident interrupts this gentle chronicle, when her husband collided with the Republican government:

> In March 1881, Henri's commission as a captain in the Territorial Army was suspended for one year, because, when Jules Feroy's decrees came to be executed, he had protested against the expulsion of the Jesuit fathers from Montciel, near Lons-le-Saunier, against the closing of the chapel of Mont-Roland on 2 July 1880, and above all against the expulsion of the Trappist Fathers from the Abbaye of Arey on 4 November 1880, on which occasion Henri had had a lively altercation with the Prefet, Monsieur Jabonville.

The event given most space in the autobiography is the marriage of their daughter Marguerite on 23 October 1895. It was in the new fashion of huge country weddings, and 'le halle' in the communs came into its own as the venue for the wedding dinner. The festivities lasted for three days. Families started arriving on 20 October, when fifty guests were put up at Montmirey and neighbouring châteaux. On the evening of the 21st there was a party for 180 people 'and Marguerite and Henri gaily led an improvised cotillon'. At three o'clock the next day the contract was read in the library. The civil marriage followed, and 'our worthy old mayor gave a charming little address'. In the evening the bishop presided over a 'contract dinner' for sixty people, followed by a firework display on the edge of the lake, a musical performance, and 'a pretty minuet danced with infinite grace by the Countess of Courtivron and the Gouvernant of La Chevainerie' finished the evening.

The marriage took place in the parish church at eleven o'clock, followed by another small reception for friends and relatives in the library, and then 'at one o'clock everyone assembled in the big hall, decorated with hangings and flowers, where dinner was served to 220 people'. The admirable Madame d'Aligny gives the seating plan.

> It really seemed as though all Franche-Comté and Burgundy had come together for this wonderful banquet. At three o'clock, after the usual speeches, according to an old local custom, the young girls presented a white lamb adorned with ribbon to the bride, and the smallest of them sang songs as they offered them doves, corn and rice, placed bunches of lilies and roses at the feet of the young couple.

Tables for fifty to sixty people were set up in the orangery and elsewhere, for 'the political supporters from our villages, the regisseurs and the farmers; our children went to drink healths with them, and were given a delightful welcome'. Finally the company got into their carriages and 'at seven o'clock, filled with the deepest emotion, I saw my beloved daughter climb into the coupé and leave with her husband'.

The wedding of the Alignys' son André followed in 1906. The era of the car had arrived. The wedding itself took place at the bride's family château, and Madame d'Aligny illustrated the long procession from the church, with every individual in it named. Then the young couple arrive at Montmirey in their Dietrich-Lorraine automobile, 'a wedding present'. There was another big dinner for them in le hall. They spent the summer visiting and being fêted at the châteaux of the Auvergne, the bride's country; the Duc de La Salle gave them a dinner for a hundred guests, Monsieur and Madame de Parien a 'big entertainment of music and theatre'.

As the autobiography draws to a close, Madame d'Aligny reflects on the arrival of the motor-car:

This manner of fêting young marrieds is very enjoyable, but would have been difficult without cars. Everything is made easier nowadays, distances close up and country-house life has become much gayer, much more varied

– too much, perhaps, at times. The most elegant young ladies now arrive here concealed behind enormous goggles which give them the appearance of deep-sea divers.

Every day there are stories of accidents, but they do not put off the young. 'Instead of talking about horses and hunting, as in the old days, young men argue about the merits of the different makes, and young women cheerfully sell their diamonds in order to have their own automobile.'

It is likely that the same young people would be reacting against their parents' taste and finding the interiors of their family homes overcrowded and over-heavy. The eighteenth century was coming back into favour, and the result was a gradual clearing out and toning down of châteaux interiors, which has continued to the present day. A pioneer essay, carried out with the greatest sensitivity and panache, was the château of Voisins, as designed by Ernest Sanson for Comte Edmond de Fels in 1902, in a reticent and accomplished Louis-Seize style.[37] It is, in its way, a masterpiece; but rather too often the new nostalgia for the eighteenth century led to a negative good taste which can leave one nostalgic for the full-blooded flavours which it replaced.

The salles basse and haute of the château of Grosbois, run together to form a fashionably overcrowded 'hall' in the late nineteenth century (below), were made into two rooms again and refitted in far more restrained taste in the 1920s (left).

9

INTO THE TWENTIETH CENTURY

A young bridal couple from the neighbourhood pose before the château of Boisset-les-Prévanches, a facility often offered by courtesy of the owners of French châteaux today.

THE DUC DE BRISSAC, looking back from the 1970s, commented ruefully on the attitudes of his class at the beginning of the twentieth century:

an aristocracy, mostly based on land, wasting its gifts and talents, which were real and sometimes remarkable, on continual parties, without taking on any proper and continuous work, without the determination to join up with all those engaged in fighting the battles of the economy and politics, in industry, banking, commerce, research or public life; an aristocracy for the sons of which there was no alternative to the army, the navy or the diplomatic corps (survival of the notion of 'dérogeance'); an aristocracy too often entrusting their affairs to the control of their stewards and agents without taking the trouble to direct and control them … For those who had eyes to see around 1905, it was clear that things were heading for a fall, sooner or later.

The Comte de Chambord, the last Bourbon of the senior line, had died in 1883. Hopes for a monarchy now all centred on the Orléans branch of the Bourbons, but its head, the Comte de Paris, was forced into exile in England and was politically ineffective. The legitimist party had done disastrously badly in the elections of 1889, and by the twentieth century the dynamism of a class that had hoped for an active future under a restored monarchy had evaporated. The Republic seemed unassailable, and although a few families or individuals accepted it and worked with it, as a class the noblesse retreated in on itself. They retained great social prestige; and the lavish and legendary entertainments of the Belle Époque were perhaps a compensation for their virtual loss of political power. In a few families overspending and mismanagement led to financial disaster, and it was perhaps of these that the Duc de Brissac was thinking. But in general the story was a less dramatic one of the slow evaporation of assets and of gradual retrenchment.

The 1914–18 War entailed the destruction of many châteaux in the battle areas of the north of France. The inter-war period was economically a depressed one all over Europe; and the 1939–45 War led to further attrition of châteaux left empty and neglected, destroyed, or suffering from destructive occupation by troops of different nations.

It was not a period conducive to the building or embellishment of châteaux. The main exceptions were the châteaux rebuilt as a result of compensation paid after the 1914–18 War, some on a lavish scale. Some, like the château of Tilleloy in Picardy, were rebuilt as replicas of their destroyed predecessors; at the château of Havrincourt, on the other hand, the Marquis d'Havrincourt chose to erect a facsimile of the seventeenth-century château of Saint-Loup, in a different area of France; and the château of Caulaincourt was rebuilt by a Russian architect as a neoclassical palace. In Lorraine only the ground floor of the eighteenth-century château of Gerbeviller was restored, to produce a single-storey pavilion of manageable size, for which future generations have been grateful.

These post-1918 reconstructions have not been written about and deserve research. But in general what money was available between the wars went into the restoration of historic châteaux; the Sommiers, for instance, continued with the restoration of Vaux-le-Vicomte, culminating in the re-laying-out of the great parterre in the1920s; and between 1906 and his death in 1936 Joachim Carvallo devoted himself to the restoration of the derelict château of Villandry and the creation of its garden. The eighteenth century was back in full favour, and there was a certain amount of reordering and redecorating of nineteenth-century interiors in consequence; but on the whole châteaux were little altered, not least because the money was not there to change them. They simply grew shabbier.

After the further upsets of the 1939–45 War, châteaux entered the post-war decades and a world full of problems for them and the way of life which they encapsulated. In many ways there are parallels to be drawn between country houses in England and châteaux in France, and the struggles for survival in which their owners or supporters in both countries now engaged. Both were faced with houses in bad condition, rising costs of upkeep, rising taxes and dwindling assets. Both were inspired by tradition and family feeling to fight to remain in their houses with all the means at their disposal. Both were able to palliate the burdens of taxation as a result of the grants and concessions given by national and local governments to the owners of historic buildings. Both benefited from the growing interest in, and knowledge of, the history of architecture, as a result of which their houses were recognized as major national assets.

But the owners of English country houses had far greater resources. In the immediate post-war years many English owners, faced with derelict or decaying buildings and the unexpected election of a socialist government, lost heart and confidence, and demolished their houses or handed them over to the National Trust. But although there was a minority of country houses with little or no land attached to them there were many more with very substantial assets in land, contents and house property. The enormous inflation in property values and the art market which took place in the 1960s gave them very large reserves on which to draw. If needs be, a farm, a picture or a block of London houses could be sold, and there was still plenty left.

French châteaux had no equivalent reserve. A few of them have been happily supported on the basis of considerable assets, prudently invested and diversified; and the French seem rather better than their English counterparts today at marrying heiresses; but such châteaux were and are a small minority. Few of them could hope to live off their farms and woods; rather more, perhaps, in the wine-growing districts could live off their vineyards. Properties of under a hundred hectares (247 acres) were a commonplace, and there was no ownership of whole urban districts, such as has brought great wealth to some English families and subsidized their country houses. There was no primogeniture. There was far less in the way of chattels, and the great increase in the value of what there was in the post-war years has in some ways been an embarrassment. In earlier decades, when a property came to be subdivided after a death, a château and its contents could be marked down to a modest valuation, and the younger children were prepared to accept this in order to keep the château together, as the symbol and centre of their family. It is harder for current generations to be magnanimous when very much larger sums are involved. It is all too common today for contents to get split up and dispersed, often to the accompaniment of shattering family rows.

The old pattern of six months in Paris and six months in the château had survived in many families until the 1939–45 War but has all but disappeared in the post-war decades. Today there are an infinite number of variations but two main patterns can be distinguished. In one the owner of a château effectively keeps it afloat by taking a job – no longer just in diplomacy or the armed forces, as in the old days, but in better paying fields, especially as a banker or industrialist, working in Paris, in the bigger provincial towns or, increasingly, out of France, in other European countries or in the Americas. They go to their châteaux in August and

September, or for weekend visits made increasingly easy by autoroutes and fast trains. Only when they retire are they likely to move full time into the château.

The alternative pattern is for owners and their families to live all the year round in their châteaux (with perhaps a pied-à-terre in Paris), and to endeavour to make a financial go of them by developing their assets in every possible way. They open them to the public and try to enhance their attractions by some special extra feature: Goulaine has its butterflies, Thoiry its lions, Vendeuvre its museum of miniature furniture, Meillant its model town, Breteuil its waxworks, and so on. They put on concerts or son-et-lumière shows. They take in paying guests or turn themselves into full-scale hotels. They install a golf-course in the park, with a clubhouse in the communs, or let the house out for conferences. They encourage the creation of groups of 'Friends', who help publicize the château and raise money for it.

Vaux-le-Vicomte – large, world famous, conveniently close to Paris and run with professional skill under an able owner – can draw enormous numbers of visitors and work as a viable commercial proposition. A handful of other châteaux are in a similar position. But for châteaux with less to offer or less advantageously sited there is always the danger that the cost of running a facility can be greater than the income which it brings in (though even so, if the deficit is not too large, such an operation can bring tax advantages which can still make it worthwhile).

The greatest and most reliable standby for châteaux in recent decades has been lettings for weddings. These happen far more in French châteaux than in their English equivalents. They are distinct from the rather charming custom, widespread in France, of allowing bridal couples in full rig to be photographed standing in front of a château. This is a free favour, offered by the proprietor to local residents; it is in the tradition of the alfresco dances held in front of a château to celebrate a peasant wedding, such as feature in a number of eighteenth-century illustrations. The big weddings, in contrast, are commercial ventures which if well run can provide a substantial portion of a château's income. The French middle classes are prepared to spend impressive amounts of money on weddings lasting a couple of days or more and involving a big dinner on the evening before the ceremony and a dance afterwards. A well-organized château can host the whole event, accommodate a selection of the guests overnight and sometimes provide a chapel for the service. Apart from the French, the Japanese are much attracted by the idea of weddings held in the chapels of French châteaux, and are prepared to fly a wedding-party over from Japan for the occasion.

Not all families can survive the strain of trying to keep a château going on inadequate resources. They give up, and put the château up for sale. The more important châteaux may be acquired by the state or the département; France has no equivalent to the National Trust, partly because few owners are in a position to hand over a château with the substantial endowments which are the basis of the National Trust empire, and partly because such an endowment needs the agreement of all the potential heirs, which may not be easy to come by. Other châteaux go to private or company buyers, sometimes French, sometimes foreign; sometimes they are converted into a hotel or an institution, sometimes for occupation as private residences. There are occasional disasters: a much-publicized one was the acquisition by a Japanese development company of a dozen or so French châteaux solely for the purpose of stripping them of their contents and fittings. But on the whole the new owners are solicitous to do their best for their new purchases. Property in France is still cheap by European standards; châteaux or manoirs can be attractive holiday or retirement homes for prosperous foreigners, and they have found Swiss, Dutch, Belgian, English, American and Japanese buyers.

As in England an owner who demolishes or disposes of a château can build himself a more manageable new residence on his propery, as the Duc de Mouchy has done at Mouchy, or Baron Guy de Rothschild at Ferrières. There are so few examples that the tradition of building châteaux can be said to be effectively dead. Any creativity goes into the embellishment of old ones. A notable example is the château of Groussay, where Charles de Beistegui used his visual flair and Central-American fortune in the 1950s to transform a not very interesting early-nineteenth-century château and embellish it with a theatre and a park crowded with follies. At the château of Champs de Bataille, sold by the Duc d'Harcourt, the Spanish decorator Jacques Garcia has made the interiors a series of staggering stage-sets in Louis-Quatorze or neoclassical style. But these are far from typical.

The situation can look different depending on whether it is looked at from the inside or the outside. To the old château-dwelling families, conscious of how much has been or is being sold, of the problems of succession or taxation, of the new wealth tax and the traumatic necessity of filling in returns for it at the beginning of each year, of the burglars to whom châteaux inadequately secured or left empty for large portions of the year are deliciously attractive, it may seem that their world is in dissolution. To an outsider who has any experience of the summer season in French châteaux, of the hospitable networks linked by relationships or old friendships, of the houses crammed to bursting with huge families of children and grandchildren, of the occasional even larger assemblies for a wedding or a family event, it may seem a world still vigorous and alive; though even he or she may reflect that all those charming children bicycling round the courtyard or prostrate in rows in the bedrooms after last night's party have an ultimate claim to their share of the family assets.

But much of the world of the French château is still a hidden one. Below the iceberg tip of those which consciously publicize themselves, or those which hit the news because they run into trouble, are many more which keep a low profile; the French upper classes are secretive by nature, and fear of burglaries or the tax inspector has made them even more so. There are hundreds, perhaps thousands, of châteaux still privately lived in, still surviving without the need for commercialization, a whole hidden world of undiscovered contents and life kept vigorously private behind the barriers of that forbidding phrase which keeps the inquisitive at bay: 'On ne visite pas.'

NOTES

Abbreviations used

AN – Archives Nationales, Paris
MC – Minutier Central (in
Archives Nationales)
BN – Bibliothèque Nationale,
Paris
BN est – Département des Estampes, Bibliothèque Nationale
AD – Archives Départementales
Havard – Havard, *Dictionnaire de
l'ameublement et de la décoration*
(Paris, 4 vol., 1887–90).

CHAPTER 1

1. G. Lenotre, *Le Château de Rambouillet* (Paris, 1930), pp.113–15.

2. The literature on the noblesse is extensive, but a useful survey of its history and legal position is Alain Texier, *Qu'est-ce que la noblesse* (Paris, 1988), with a good glossary and bibliography of terms. A seminal, and in some respects, revisionist study is Guy Chaussinand-Nogaret, *La noblesse au XVIIIième siècle* (Paris, 1976, translated as *The French Nobility in the Eighteenth Century*, Cambridge, 1985). See also Christian de Barbillat, *Histoire de la Noblesse Française 1789–1989* (2 vol., Paris, 1988–91).

3. Chaussinand-Nogaret, *The French Nobility*, pp.28–30 supports Hippolyte Taine's nineteenth-century estimate (*Les Origines de la France Contemporaine, 1876*) of a figure of 130,000, and suggests it may have been even a little lower. Texier, op. cit., pp.78–82, basing himself on Guy Guérin de Masgenet's complex calculations, suggests a figure of 340,000.

4. Clairambault's letter quoted in De Courcelle, *Dictionnaire Universel de la Noblesse* (Paris, 1820), II, p.369.

5. Henri de Boulainvilliers' *Essai sur la Noblesse de France* (Paris, 1732) expounded the theory that the noblesse descended from the invading Teutonic warriors and the Third Estate from the Gallo-Roman population which they conquered. Another book in every eighteenth-century château library, G.A. de La Roque's *Traité de la Noblesse* (1678), expounds the ideal in its preface: 'La noblesse est une qualité qui rend genereux celuy qui la possède … Il y a dans les semences je ne scay quelle force et je ne scay quel principe qui transmet et qui continue les inclinations des pères à leurs descendants: Et tout homme issus de grands et illustres personnages restent necessairement au fond de son coeur un certain mouvement qui le presse de les imiter: et leur memoire le sollicite à la gloire et aux belles actions.'

6. See Chaussinand-Nogaret, op. cit., pp.24–30.

7. From the late seventeenth century the title of 'Sieur' —, originally just a variant of 'Seigneur' —, seems to have been increasingly assumed by the holders of small properties held by swearing fealty to an overlord but without the legal and judicial powers of a full seigneurie. The usage was little, if at all, regulated, and 'sieurs' had a way of becoming 'seigneurs': the process is similar to that by which the title of 'Esquire' or the use of double-barrelled

names worked their way down the social scale in England.

8. Story related by the mid-seventeenth-century writer A. d'Ouville in his *Contes* (1732 ed.), II, pp.86–7.

9. See the list given in Texier, op. cit., p.440. *Un juge d'armes au Jockey Club* (1954), *Le Dictionnaire des Vanités* (1970–72), *L'Encyclopédie de la Fausse Noblesse* (1976–82), etc.

10. D.M.G. Sutherland, *France 1789–1815: Revolution and Counter-Revolution* (London, 1985), pp.386–7 and sources listed on p.468.

CHAPTER 2

1. Chrétien de Troyes, *Eric et Enid* (written *c.*1176, ed. J.-M. Fritz in 'Les Libres de Poche, Lettres Gothiques' series, Paris, 1992), p.172.

2. *Le Roman de Jaufre* (probably late twelfth century). See R. Lavaud and R. Nelli (eds.), *Les Troubadours* (Paris, 1960), I, pp.38–9.

3. J. Beroul, *The Romance of Tristram* (twelfth century, ed. A. Ewart , Oxford, 1939), I, p.21, l.693; *Flamenca*, Lavaud and Nelli, op. cit., I, ll. 292–350.

4. In the late thirteenth century, *La Châtelaine de Vergi*. Printed C.V. Langlois, *La Société Française au Treizième Siècle* (Paris, 1904), pp.222–34.

5. The claim comes in the opening sentences of his *Livre de la Chasse*.

6. Froissart, *Chroniques,* Book III, Ch. XVIII (ed. J.A. Buchon *Collection des Chroniques Nationales Françaises* IX (Paris, 1824), pp.362–4.

7. Ibid.

8. For Coucy see especially Jean Mesqui, 'Les programmes residentiels du château de Coucy du XIIIme au XVme siècle', *Congrès Archéologique de France*, 1989.

9. For the fortified châteaux of the Middle Ages Jean Mesqui's exhaustive and authoritative *Châteaux et Enceintes de la France Médiévale* (2 vol., Paris, 1991–3) is the basic source. For quick reference it can be usefully supplemented by Charles-Laurent Salch, *Dictionnaire des Châteaux et des Fortifications du Moyen Age en France* (Strasbourg, 1979).

10. *Le Jouvencel par Jean de Bueil*, ed. C. Favre and L. Lecestre (Paris, 1887), I, XXXV–VI, pp.24–5, 35. Before Le Jouvencel captures the horses of a neighbouring castle, the garrison had been reduced to going 'two on a horse and the majority on foot' (ibid., p.23).

11. Pierre Charbonnier, 'La vie dans les châteaux auvergnats à la fin du Moyen Age', in J.-M. Poisson (ed.), *Le Château Médiéval, Forteresse habitée* (Documents d'Archéologie Française, no. 32, Paris, 1992), p.32.

12. Charbonnier, loc. cit., quoting Froissart and M. Boudet, *Les Registres consulaires de Saint-Flour* (Saint-Flour, 1900).

13. Quoted Robert Favreau, 'Le Palais de Poitiers au Moyen Age', *Bulletin de la Société des Antiquaires de l'Ouest*, 4th series, XI (1971), p.41.

14. Christine de Pisan, *Le Livre des faits et bonnes moeurs du sage roy Charles V* (ed. S. Solente, Paris 1936–40), 2, pp.112–13.

15. Jean Maillart, *Le Roman du Comte d'Anjou* (ed. Mario Roques, Paris, 1931 and 1974), ll. 193–4.

16. L. de Farcy and P. Piner, *Le Palais Episcopal d'Angers: Histoire et Description* (Angers, 1903), p.76. A contemporary list of who sat where is in AD Maine-et-Loire, G13.

17. The details are among the supplementary material printed in Prosper Tarbé (ed.), *Inventaire après le décès de Richard Picque, Archevêque de Reims, 1389* (Société des Bibliophiles de Reims, 1842), pp.69–74, 129–30.

18. Chrétien de Troyes, *Perceval*, ed. W. Roach (Geneva and Paris, 1959), p.27.

19. View of the Bricquebec *salle* and plan and section of the *salle* at Blois, in Mesqui, op. cit. (n. 9), II, pp.83–4.

20. Pierre-Maxime Relave, *Sur-le-Comtal en Forez, Essai d'Histoire et d'Archéologie* (Montbrisson, 1907).

21. Favreau, op. cit.(n. 13), pp.42–4.

22. J. Mouterde, *La Clayette … de l'Origine jusqu'à la Révolution d'après les archives du château et autres* (Paray-le-Monial, 1931), p.46.

23. Roger Grand, *Une Race, un Château: Anjony* (Paris, 1951), p.83.

24. 'Livre des Faits de Jacques de Lallaing' in *Oeuvres de Georges Chastellain* (ed. Kervyn de Lettenhove, Brussels), vol. 8 (1866), pp.6–9.

25. Texier, op.cit.(ch. 1, n. 2), p.508; R. Favreau, op. cit., p. 41. Favreau refers to similar use of towers at Bourges and Saintes.

26. B. Barbiche, J. Mesqui and others, *Histoire de Sully-sur-Loire* (Roanne, 1986), p.110.

27. Y. Harlé-Sambet, 'Le donjon de Bressieux', *Le Château Médiéval* (see n. 11), p.88.

28. For the donjon at Provins, see J. Mesqui, *Provins. La Fortification d'une ville au Moyen Age* (Paris, 1979), and the cut-away drawing in his *Châteaux et Enceintes*, op. cit. (n. 9) 1, p.112.

29. Inventory of Cornillon printed in *Revue des Sociétés Savantes*, 7th series, I (1880), pp.205–15.

30. Annie Cazenave, 'Châteaux et Castra Pyrénéens – Xe–XIVe siècles', in J.-M. Pastré (ed.), *Château et Societé Castrale au Moyen Age* (University of Rouen, 1998), pp.30–31.

31. AD Gironde, 4J 390, No. 48 (Fonds Lascases). Eighteenth-century copy of a deposition of 1322.

32. Mary Whiteley, 'Le Louvre de Charles V: dispositions et fonctions d'une résidence royale', *Revue de l'Art* (1992), pp.60–71.

33. So Havard, I, p.667, but giving no source.

34. Inventory published in A. Lecoy de la Marche, *Extraits des Comptes et Mémoriaux du Roi René* (Paris, 1873), pp.239 seq. The entry for the 'salle de parement' is on p.247.

35. Aliénor de Poitiers, *Honneurs de la Cour* (*c*. 1485–90), published in de La Curne de Sainte-Palaye *Mémoires sur l'ancienne Chevalerie* (1781 ed.), II, pp.224–5.

36. For the Coucy and Louvre see articles by Mesqui and Whiteley (n. 8 and 32). The description of the 'secret place' at Coucy is by the Duc d'Orleans' secretary, Antoine d'Asti, quoted by Mesqui. The chimney-piece of the Women Worthies is illustrated in Du Cerceau's *Plus Excellents Bastiments*. The suggestion that the 'poele' was the wives' chambre de parement is mine, not Mesqui's.

37. For the donjon at Vincennes see Mary Whiteley, 'La grosse tour de Vincennes, résidence de Charles V', *Bulletin Monumental*, vol. 152–III (1994), pp.313–35.

38. Inventories of Porte Mars and Courville both published by Tarbé (see n. 17).

39. For Septmonts see Thierry Crépin-Leblond, 'Le château de Septmonts', *Congrès de la Société Française d'Archéologie*, 1994 (Aisne méridionale), pp.549–66. Simon de Bucy's will was made on 28th January 1404, at 'Septmonts dans la chambre d'apparat de la maison épiscopale, près de la chapelle' (quoted by Bernard Anclen, *Septmonts: son château, son village* (Septmonts, n.d.), p.10.

40. For the Tours d'Elven at Largoet see 'Le château-fort d'Elven', *Arts de l'Ouest: études et documents* (Université de Haute-Bretagne, Rennes), 1980, 1–2, p.143 et seq., in which the 1481 list of repairs is published.

41. The fireplaces are clearly shown on the pre-Viollet-le-Duc photograph reproduced by Mesqui (op. cit. n. 9).

42. Grand (op. cit. n. 23), p.155.

CHAPTER 3

1. For Villeneuve-Lembron and its builder Rigault d'Oureille see G. Ruprich-Robert, *Rigault d'Oureille Sénéchal de Gascogne et de l'Agenais et son Château de Villeneuve-Lembron* (Clermont-Ferrand, 1935).

2. G. Corrozet op. cit. p. 3.

3. His lifestyle is described in G.-B Nervezé, *Consolations Funèbres sur la mort de ....Albert de Gondy* (Paris, 1602), pp.20–23.

4. For Charles V's Louvre see Whiteley, op. cit. (ch. 2, n. 32).

5. Jacques Coeur's house has been illuminated by the articles of Christian de Mérindol, e.g. 'L'hôtel Jacques-Coeur à Bourges', *Bulletin de la Société nationale des antiquaires de France* (1994) and many others.

6. For the role and importance of governors see R.R. Harding, *Anatomy of a Power Élite. The provincial governors of early modern France* (New Haven, 1978).

7. E. de Robillard de Beaurepaire (ed.), *Le Journal de Sire de Gouberville* (Caen, 1892, 1895), I, p.156 (6 February 1554/5): 'Tout le jour ne cessa de plouvoir … Au soyer, toute la vesprée, nous leusmes en Amadis de Gaulle comme il vainquit Durdan.'

8. La None *Discours politiques et militaires* (Basle, 1587) quoted André Chastel *The Palace of Appolidon* (Zaharoff Lecture, Oxford 1986), p.9.

9. For the gallery at Oiron see Jean Guillaume, *La Galerie du Grand Écuyer: l'histoire de Troie au château d'Oiron* (Chauray, 1996).

10. Philippe Calbo, *Un Château* (Poitiers, 1987) in the 'Regarder et Comprendre' series, although aimed at a popular audience, is a well-researched and lively study of Le Lude, with excellent diagrams.

11. In England, as in France, up to the late sixteenth century one often finds a series of small doors giving access just to the 'lodgings' in subsidiary wings of a large courtyard house, but I am talking about entry or entries to the main building.

12. Information Mary Whiteley.

13. André Mussat, 'La Fin du Gothique: Nantes et Josselin', *L'Escalier dans l'Architecture de la Renaissance* (ed. A. Chastel and J. Guillaume, Paris, 1985), pp.21–6.

14. For Saumur, Châteaudun, Meillant and the later development of the French staircase see articles by Whiteley, Guillaume, Mignot, Boudon and others in *L'Escalier*, op. cit. (n. 12).

15. An especially large donjon-type staircase of *c*. 1520 at the relatively modest Prieuré de Saint-Ouen is illustrated by Guillaume in *L'Escalier*, Fig. 28 and p.29: 'L'escalier hypertrophié fait oublier le château!'

16. Olivier de la Marche, 'Estat du Duc Charles le Hardi', in *Les Mémoires de Messire Olivier de La Marche* (3rd and 4th eds., 1616 and 1645), reprinted in Michaud and Poujolat, *Nouvelle Collection des Mémoires pour servir à l'histoire de France*, 1st series III (1851), pp.579–603; E. Griselle (ed.), 'Henri III et sa maison royale', *Collection de Documents d'Histoire* vol. 3 (1912), pp.382–95.

17. *Journal de Jean Héroard* (ed. E. Soulie and E. de Barthelemy, 2 vol., Paris, 1868), 2, p.174. Heroard was Louis XIII's doctor.

18. 'Mémoires de Vielleville' in Michaud and Poujolat, *Nouvelle Collection*, 1st series IX (1838), p.49; Elie Brackenhoffer, *Voyage en France 1644–6* (1927 ed.), II, p.69.

19. E. de Quinsonas, *Matériaux pour servir à l'histoire de Marguerite d'Autriche* (1860), III, pp.295–315; Bibliothèque Nationale MS NAF 9647/18r–25r.

20. Agrippa d'Aubigné, *Avantures du Baron de Faeneste* (1630), ch. 16, reprinted in *Oeuvres* (ed. H. Weber, Paris, 1969), vol.4.

21. A. d'Ouville, *Contes* (1732 ed.), II, pp.30–32.

22. Memoirs of Thomas Platter, quoted in L. Legre, *La Botanique en Provence au XVme siècle* (Marseille, 1900).

23. Héroard, op.cit. (n.17), I, p.282 (sparrow-hawk), p.289 (marriage of daughter of concièrge), p.291 (marriage dance of falconer), p.296 (ballet des lanternes); duchesse de Montpensier, *Mémoires* (ed. Cheruel, 4 vol., Paris, 1891), I, p.14 (ballet at treasurer's, Montglat).

24. BN, Ms NAF 9647, ff. 23v–24.

25. Platter, op. cit., (n. 22).

26. André Joubert, *Histoire de la Baronnie de Craon de 1382 à 1626* (Angers/Paris, 1888), pp.463–8 (expenses), p.468 et seq. (inventory).

27. BN, Ms 9648, ff.102 et seq.

28. AD Ile-et-Vilaine IF 1225 (nineteenth-century transcript of original inquest), ff. 26–31.

29. Quinsonas, op. cit. (n. 19), III, p.308.

30. The 1542 inventory of Thouars is published in Louis de La Trémoille, *Inventaire de François de la Trémoille et Comptes d'Anne de Laval* (Nantes, 1887).

31. Thomas Artus d'Embry, *Description de l'Isle des Hermaphrodites* (1724 ed., Paris) p.111.

32. A. Deville, *Comptes de dépenses de la construction du château de Gaillon* (1850), pp.533, 542, 545.

33. The dating of the château of Lanquais is discussed in an article by André Chastel, to which I have mislaid the reference.

34. R.F. Le Men, 'Le pillage du manoir de Mezarnou en 1594', in *Études Historiques sur le Finisterre* (Quimper, 1875), pp.153–73. See also *Revue de Bretagne et de Vendée*, vol. for 1860, pp.401–10.

35. Inventory published in *Bulletin Historique et Archéologique de Périgord*, XVIII (1891), pp.366 et seq.

36. The complete set is reproduced in David Thomson, 'France's earliest illustrated architectural pattern book: designs for living "à la française" of the 1540s', *Architecture et Vie Sociale à la Renaissance* (ed. J. Guillaume, Paris, 1994), pp.221–34. The set of designs is for sizeable châteaux, but is confusingly described in the Bibliothèque Nationale and elsewhere as the 'Petites Habitations'.

37. Printed as E35 in the *Inventaire des Archives de la Côte d'Or, Series E*.

38. Noel du Fail, *Contes et Discours d'Eutrapel* (1585), ch. XX, 'Du temps present et passé'.

39. *Journal de Gouberville*, op. cit. (n. 8), II (1895), p.21: honey-straining; p.91: 'nous souppasmes tous ensemble', probably in the salle, since a serviteur was involved, though the location is not mentioned. For Gouberville's chambre at Mesnil being on the first floor see II, p.68, 'au matin quand je descends de ma chambre'. For dining in chambre at Gouberville see e.g. 4th June 1549: 'Le mardy IIIIe à Gouberbille, Harcla le lieutenant de Sct. Saulveur, Beaurepaire, missire Guillaume Le Flamenc, Jehan Fleury, Richard Becquet et plusieurs aultres dinasmes en ma chambre', II, p.15.

40. AD Gard, E657.

41. Olivier de Serres, *Théâtre d'Agriculture* (1605 ed.), I, pp.23–4.

42. Inventory in archives, château of Boisset-les-Prévanches.

43. Agrippa d'Aubigné, op.cit. (n.20), ch.16, pp.819–20.

44. Quoted Havard, I, p.1072.

45. Ibid.

46. Reproduced by Havard, I, Fig. 794, where described as being in the Bibliothèque Nationale, but I have not been able to locate it.

47. Gouberville op. cit. (n. 8), II, pp.135–6.

48. Op. cit. (n. 41).

49. Monique Chatenet in her seminal 'Une demeure royale au milieu du XVIe siècle: la distribution des espaces au château de Saint-Germain-en-Laye', *Revue de l'Art* 1988, p.26, Fig. 9 and n. 46, p.30. She refers also to 'mengeries' in the basement of the château of La Muette.

50. *Ancienne Chevalerie* op. cit. (ch. 2, n. 35), (1795 ed.), II, p.161.

51. See Monique Chatenet in the official guide, *Château de Châteaudun* (Boulogne, *c.* 1998). The evidence for the sallettes comes from the building accounts.

52. Op. cit. (n. 30).

53. H. Jadart, *Louis XIII et Richelieu à Reims* (Paris, 1885), pp.56–7 (inventory of 1621).

54. Héroard, op. cit. (n. 17), I, p.188. 18 May 1606, the dauphin 'fait porter son escritoire à la salle-a-manger pour écrire sous Dumont'.

55. Gouberville, op. cit. (n. 8), II, p.145 (Rouville), p.44 (Tocqueville), p.45 (Trexot), p.83 (Crenays).

56. Saint-Fargeau accounts, AN 90 AP/23.

57. Ménage, *Menagiana* (Amsterdam, 1695), II, p.44, quoted Maximin Deloche, *La Maison du Cardinal de Richelieu* (Paris, 1912), pp.242–3.

58. Montpensier op.cit. (n.23), III, p.4.

59. Saint-Fargeau inventory, AN 90 AP/23.

60. Op. cit. (n. 30).

61. See Jean Boutier, Alain Dewerpe, Daniel Nordman, *Un Tour de France Royal* (Paris, 1984), especially pp.133–4.

62. AD Côte d'Or, E1924 (accounts and note of numbers attending).

63. The division can be deduced from the room arrangement, e.g. plan in J.A. du Cerceau, *Les Plus Excellents Bastiments de France II* (1607).

64. Héroard, op. cit. (n. 17), 2, p. 248; Robert Dauvergne, *Le Château de Brissac au XVIIIme siècle* (Paris, 1945, with full extracts from the inventories of 1732, 1756, 1760 and 1762), pp.39, 41.

65. Montpensier, op.cit. (n.23), I, pp.14–35. The visit to La Motte is on p.35.

66. See n. 36.

67. The pavillon is usually taken to date from the same period as the seventeenth-century main building of the château, which dates from 1614–21 (but was never completed). But in the inventory of 1732 (Dauvergne, p.64), the first floor of the pavillon is described as containing 'l'appartement de la Judicth'. Judith d'Acigné, Duchesse de Brissac, married in 1579 and died in 1598, and the pavillon is more likely to date from the period of the marriage.

CHAPTER 4

1. For French galleries see especially J. Guillaume 'La Galerie dans le château Français: place et ponction', *Reme de l'Art* 102 (1993) pp.32–42.

2. A. Lecoy de La Marche, *Extraits des Comptes et Mémoriaux du Roi René* (Paris, 1873), pp.16–17, 242.

3. See p. 54 n. 36, ch. 2.

4. Anon, *Les Amours, intrigues et caballes des domestiques des grandes maisons de ce temps* (Paris, 1633), pp.68–9.

5. Corrozet, *Les Blasons Domestiques* (1539), p. 33r.

6. *Bulletin Historique et Archéologique de Périgord XVIII* (1891), pp.147, 224.

7. *Mémoriales de la Société Ag. Sc. et Art. d'Angers*, 5th series, XIV (1911).

8. Montpensier, *Mémoires*, I, p.31.

9. Bruno Tollon, 'Ovide dans le "cabinet de quatrains": un décor peint identifié dans le château de Pibrac (Haute-Garonne)', *Mémoires de la Société archéologique du Midi de la France*, 56 (1996), pp. 303–6.

10. Scudéry, *Clélie*, IV, pt.2 (1660 ed.), p.674.

11. Ibid., V, pt.I (1661 ed.), p.483.

12. Scudéry, *Le Grand Cyrus*, IV, pt. 3 (1654), p.419.

13. *Clélie*, V, pt.1 (1661 ed.), p.481.

14. Ibid., III, pt. 3 (1658 ed.), p.1501.

15. Ibid., V, pt. 2 (1661 ed.), p.696 (Cloramiste); V, pt.1 (1661 ed.), p.514.

16. *Mémoires du Maréchal de Bassompierre* (Amsterdam, 1723), I, pp.209–10, 218.

17. G. Tallemant des Réaux, *Historiettes* (ed. G. Montgredien, Paris, 1932–2), II, pp.317–18.

18. Monique Chatenet, *Le château de Madrid* (Paris, 1987), pp.74–5. *Sebastiano Serlio on Domestic Architecture* (ed. M.N. Rosenfeld, New York, 1978), Pls. XLVIII–LII, LX.

19. See Charles Sauze (ed.), 'Inventaires de l'Hôtel de Rambouillet', *Société Archéologique de Rambouillet: Mémoires et documents relatifs au département de Seine-et-Oise*, XX (1894).

20. Somaize, *Grand Dictionnaire Historique des Prétieuses* (Paris, 1661, ed. C.L. Livet, 2 vol, Paris, 1856), 1, p.215.

21. Michel de Pure, *La Prétieuse* (ed. Emil Magne, Paris, 1938), I, pp.66–7.

22. Corrozet, op. cit., pp. 20v–21r.

23. Étienne Pasquier to Pierre Ayrault, *Oeuvres d'Étienne Pasquier* (1723), II, p.897.

24. Scudéry, *Grand Cyrus*, IV, pt.3 (1654 ed.), p.422 et seq.

25. Ibid., *Clélie*, IV, pt.2 (1660 ed.), pp.726–29.

26. *La Prétieuse* (see n. 21), I, p.28.

27. Sauze, 'Inventaires' (n. 19); Tallemant des Réaux, op. cit. (n. 17), II, p.305. 'C'est la première qui s'est avisée de faire peindre une chambre d'autre couleur que de rouge ou de tané; et c'est ce qui à donné à sa grande chambre le nom de la Chambre bleue.'

28. Émile Magne, *Voiture et les origines de l'Hôtel de Rambouillet* (Paris, 1911), I, p.112.

29. Illustrated and accounts quoted in Relave, op.cit. (ch. 2, n. 20). The alcoves in their present form are restorations after a fire in 1937.

30. Le Muet shows alcoves in the Hôtels Davaux and Tubeuf in Paris and the (demolished) château of Pons in Champagne. Plans in Pierre Le Muet, *Manière de Bien Bastir pour toutes sortes de Personnes* and *Augmentations de Nouveaux Bastimens faits en France* (Paris, 1647).

31. Montpensier, op.cit. (ch. 3, n. 23), 2, pp.230, 284. And see Claude Mignot, 'Mademoiselle et son château de Saint-Fargeau', *Papers on French Seventeenth Century Literature* XXII (1995), No. 42, pp.91–101.

CHAPTER 5

1. Inventory in AD Isère, ILJ20/40.

2. Room so described in inventory of 1677, AN MC CXII, 168.

3. For La Raincy see the *Petit Marot* (n.d. 2nd ed. Mariette, c.1738); for Turny the *Grand Marot* (n.d. 2nd ed. Manette, 1727) vol. IV.

4. For Vaux-le-Vicomte see especially J.M. Pérouse de Montclos, *Vaux-le-Vicomte* (Paris, 1997), in which numerous plans and drawings are reproduced.

5. Plans of Plessis-Belleville and Balleroy reproduced, *François Mansart: le génie de l'architecture* (ed. J.-P. Babelon and Claude Mignot, Paris, 1998), pp.116, 120.

6. Daviler, *Cours d'Architecture* (Paris, 1691), II p.815.

7. For Bussy-Rabutin in exile, see *Les Heures Bourguignonnes du Comte de Bussy-Rabutin* (Caisse Nationale des Monuments Historiques et des Sites, Autun 1993).

8. Ibid., p.50. Bussy-Rabutin also owned the château of Claseu (demolished), where, as he wrote in 1675, 'I have one of the finest salons in France.' Ibid., p.22.

9. J.F. Blondel, *Maisons de Plaisance* (Paris, 1737), I, pp. 31, 47. Français Blondel, additions to Louis Savot's *L'Architecture Française* (Paris, 1673).

10. See ch. 4, n. 19.

11. Plans of both floors are still at Kernault and are reproduced in Association du Manoir du Kernault, *Kernault, Manoir Breton* (1994), pp.14–15.

12. Charles-Étienne Briseux, *L'art de batir des Maisons de Campagne* (Paris, 1743), I, p.22.

13. Inventory of 1771 Archives, Château of Merville.

14. For Bagatelle, see Marcus Binney, 'Bagatelle, Picardy', *Country Life*, 12 July 1973, pp.82–5.

15. The inventory was published by W.S. Lewis, *Horace Walpole's correspondence with Madame du Deffand and Wiart* (New Haven and London, 6 vol., 1939), VI, pp.504 (also published as vol. 8 of Lewis's complete edition of the correspondence).

16. Madame de Genlis, *Dictionnaire Critique et Raisonné des étiquettes de la cour, des images du monde, des amusements, des modes, des moeurs, etc., des Français, depuis la mort de Louis XIII jusqu'à nos jours* (Paris, 1818), I, pp.62–3. Voltaire quoted M. Glatz and M. Maire, *Salons du XVIIIme siècle* (Paris, 1949), p.12.

CHAPTER 6

1. Letter of 4 June 1820, kindly communicated to me by Christina Colvin.

2. L.S. Mercier, *Les Tableaux de Paris* (new ed., Amsterdam, 1783), II, p.108.

3. Genlis, *Dictionnaire des Etiquettes* (see ch. 5, n. 16), I, pp.331–2 (entry for 'Logements').

4. Elevation and plans in the first volume of J.A. du Cerceau's *Plus Excellents Bastimens*.

5. Shown on plan of first floor, Berry, AN S2905.

6. Inventory (not quite completely published), Edwin Bonnaffé, *Le Surintendant Foucquet* (Paris, 1882), pp.77 et seq. The original is in BN, Ms Français 7620, f. 106 et seq.

7. Pierre Patte, *Discours sur l'architecture* (Paris, 1754).

8. Pierre Choderlos de Laclos, *Les Liaisons Dangereuses* (1782), Lettre LXXXV.

9. *Lettres de Geneviève de Malboissière* (1925), pp.149–50.

10. Inventaire d.d. M. Lemaistre de La Martinière, AN MC EtXCI/1211.

11. Blondel (op. cit. n.9) I p.29.

12. J. de Crébillon, 'Le Sopha, Conte Moral', *Oeuvres Completes de M. de Crébillon, fils* (Maastricht, 1779), vol. III, pp.11–34.

13. *Manuel des boudoirs* is referred to by Havard (entry under 'boudoirs'), but is not in the catalogue of the Bibliothèque Nationale.

14. Quoted without source by Havard, loc. cit., as written in a letter to Natoir.

15. L.P. de Bachaumont and others, *Mémoires Secrètes*, XV (1781), p.187, quoted Havard, loc. cit.

16. Quoted John Whitehead, *The French Interior in the Eighteenth Century* (1992), pp.73, 76 and footnotes, pp.245–6.

17. J.H.A. de Bonardi du Mesnil, Manuscript memoirs I.I.XXIX in archives, Château of Boisset-les-Prevanches.

18. Anon, 'Aieux tournés en derision', *Correspondance sécrète,* XIV, p.91, quoted Havard, loc. cit.

19. Beaumarchais on 'Dames du jour', *Correspondance sécrète,* XIII, p.43, quoted Havard, loc. cit.

20. Havard, loc. cit.

21. N. Le Camus de Mézieres, *Le Génie d'architecture ou l'analogie de cet art avec nos sensations* (1780), quoted in Bernard Toulier, *Châteaux en Sologne* (Cahiers de l'inventaire, Paris, 1991), p.310, n.65.

22. Genlis, op. cit. (ch. 5, n. 16), I, p.209–10.

23. Inventory published in R. Dauvergne, *Les résidences du Maréchal de Croy 1718–84* (Paris, 1950), p.124. Dauvergne transcribes them as 'bouilloirs', which may be a misreading, but if correct seems likely to be a version of 'boudoirs'.

24. Plan by G.-P.-H. Dumont, 'Nouveau projet de distribution sur l'emplacement entier d'un terrain situé près le Parc au Cerf, Versailles, 1768', reproduced in Monique Eleb-Vidal, *Architectures de la vie privée* (Paris, 1989), p.64.

25. Plan in Bibliothèque Municipale, Bordeaux, reproduced Toulier (op. cit. n. 21), p.157.

26. D Ile-et-Vilaine, E supplément, fond de La Bourdonnaye, Montluc, liasse II, quoted in Jean Meyer *La noblesse Bretonne au XVIIIme siècle* (1972).

27. Plan reproduced J.-L. Baritou and D. Foussard, *Chevotet-Contant-Chaussard: un cabinet d'architectes au siecle des Lumières* (Lyon, 1987), p.223.

28. Archives, Musée Condé, Chantilly.

29. Archives, Marquis de Lastic, château of Parentignat.

30. Antoine Caillot, *Vie Publique des Français,* II, p.99, quoted Havard, loc. cit.

31. *Mémoires du duc de Luynes,* ed. Dussieux and Soulie, VIII (Paris, 1862), p.331.

32. See n. 29.

CHAPTER 7

1. Arthur Young, *Travels in France during the Years 1787, 1788, 1789 and 1790* (ed. H. Betham-Edwards, London, 1889), p.84. (The first edition published in two volumes, 1792–4).

2. Stéphanie-Felicité de Genlis, *Les Veillées du Château* (Paris, 1784), I, p.8.

3. J.-L. Adam, *Étude sur la ville de Valognes* (Valognes, 1912), pp.89–94.

4. Letters from James Coltee Ducarel to his brother, Doctor Andrew Ducarel, in the archives of Mr Gerard de Lisle at Quenby Hall, Leicestershire, kindly communicated to me by M. Pierre Salmon-Legagneur, the present proprietor of the château of Bonnemare. In the mid eighteenth century it belonged to Ducarel's uncle, Pierre Cromelin de Villette.

5. Quoted in Jean-Jacques Rioult, 'L'Hôtel de Blossac à Rennes. Résidence du Commandant-en-Chef pour la Bretagne', *Mémoires de la Société d'Histoire et d'Archéologie de Bretagne,* LXVIII (Rennes, 1991), p.317.

6. There is a good description of the annual visit to Montpellier of Arthur Dillon, Archbishop of Narbonne and Président des États du Languedoc in Chapter III of Henriette-Lucie Dillon, Marquise de la Tour du Pin, *Journal d'une Femme de 50 ans, 1778–1815.* She was his great-niece.

7. E.g. J.-F. Blondel, *Cours d'architecture civile* (Paris, 1771–3). 'De la science de l'agriculture ... il n'est l'art du jardinage. ... Ce sont ces deux arts qui font que le Prélat, l'homme de guerre et le magistrat trouvent une douceur infinie dans la vie champêtre, qu'ils quittent leurs travaux pour aller dans leurs domaines jouir tranquillement de la fertilité et de l'abondance que produit l'Agriculture et de la beauté qu'offre le jardinage.'

8. Jean-Marie Constant, *La Noblesse Française aux XVIe–XVIIe siècles* (2nd ed., Paris, 1994), pp.54–5.

9. AN, AP1 1059 (Thouars), AP1 470 (Gennevilliers).

10. Gérard Sabatier, *Le Vicomte Assailli: économie rurale, seigneurie et affrontements sociaux en Languedoc des montagnes* (Saint-Vidal, 1988), pp.173–228.

11. Daniel Morvan, *L'oeil du Maître: Rosanbo, une seigneurie au quotidien 1776–1806* (Skol Vreizh, L'école Bretonne, No. 24, Montroules/Morlaix, May 1992).

12. Christian Trezin, *Le 'Château Royal de Grignan': décor et mobilier au temps de Madame de Sévigné* (Grignan, 1989).

13. Saint-Simon, *Mémoires,* (ed. Yves Coirault, Paris, 1983–8) VIII, p.1705 (index entry for 'voyages et séjours à La Ferté').

14. Voltaire, *Correspondance* (ed. Theodore Besterman, 1968), I, pp.54–5, 58 (vol. 86 of *Collected Works*).

15. Manuscript in the archives of Olivier, Vicomte de Rohan-Chabot, kindly communicated by him to me.

16. See Louis Le Guennec, *Les Barbier de Lescoët* (Quimper, 1991), especially pp.455–63, 535–7.

17. Ibid., p.459–60.

18. The mss of the Duc de Croy's journals are bound up in many volumes in the library of the Institut de France in Paris (Mss 1640 et seq.). They were published in part in four volumes as *Journal Inédit* (Paris, 1906–7), but these volumes are mainly concerned with his public and military life, and his life in Paris, and omit almost all the portions dealing with his life and work at Condé and l'Hermitage.

19. Institut de France, Ms 1650, f.23v.

20. Ibid.

21. Ibid. f.117 et seq.

22. Ibid.

23. Ibid. f. 115r.

24. J.N. Dufort de Cheverny, *Mémoires* (Paris, 1886), I, pp.338–47, 381, 431.

25. A.-F.F. de Frenilly, *Souvenirs* (Paris, 1908), p.103.

26. *Mémoires du Général d'Andigné* (ed. E. Biré, Paris, 1900–1901), pp.51, 53.

27. AD Haute-Garonne (Toulouse), 4J21/88.

28. Ibid., 6J41, quoted in R. Forster, *The Nobility of Toulouse in the 18th century: a social and economic study* (Baltimore, 1960), p.155.

29. R. Shackleton *Montesquieu: a critical biography* (London, 1961).

30. Detailed designs for the dress and accoutrements of all the Condé servants in livery are presented in a splendid folio volume, *Les Dessins des Livrées, 1776* (Musée Condé, Chantilly), Ms 1262.

31. Young, op. cit. (n. 1), p.77. (Entry for 10 Sept. 1787.)

32. *Mémorial de J. de Norvins* (ed. L. de Lanzac de Labone, Paris, 1896–7), I, pp.101, 115; article on Brienne, *Fermes et Châteaux,* vol. I (1905), No. 5, p.18.

33. Norvins, op. cit., p.108.

34. Frenilly, op. cit. (n. 25), p.116 et seq.

35. Ibid., p.117.

36. Bonardi du Mesnil, op. cit. (ch. 6, n. 17), I.I.24 (and typescript I, pp.36–8).

37. Ibid., I.I.30, II.III.I (typescript I, pp.43–4, 130).

38. Ibid., I.III.9 (typescript I, p.51).

39. For life at Le Marais see especially Pierre de Zurich, *Une Femme Heureuse, Madame de La Briche, sa famille, son salon, le château du Marais* (Paris, 1934).

40. Frenilly, op. cit. (n. 25), p.242; Norvins, op. cit. (n. 32), I, pp.70–71.

41. Zurich, op. cit., p.172.

42. *Les Barbier de Lescoët* op. cit. (n. 16), pp.193–4.

43. Ibid., n. 15.

44. Institut de France, Ms 1649, f.185.

45. See ch. 5, p.139 and n. 11.

46. Plan reproduced in J.M. Pérousse de Montclos, *Vaux-le-Vicomte* (Paris, 1997), p.78.

47. See Marcus Binney, 'Château de Moncley, Franche-Comté', *Country Life*, 21 and 28 September 1972.

48. Inventaire a.d. M.-F. de Poule d'Ormesson, 1775. AN, 144 AP/96 (Microfiche 156 mi59). Inventaire a.d.. M. Lemaistre de La Martinière, AN, MC XCI 1211.

49. Extracts from *La Garçonnière* are published in Abbé Larrondo, *Une Commune Rurale* (1891). The original copy seems no longer to be at Merville.

50. Loc. cit., n. 44.

51. Contents as listed in the inventories of Beauregard, AD Haute-Loire, 24J184. The Inventory of Flines is in the archives of the château, but a photocopy is in the library of Conservation des Antiquités et Objets d'Art, Département de Maine-et-Loire, Angers.

52. Frenilly, op. cit. (n. 25), p.242. Zurich, op. cit. (n.39), pp. 231–2.

53. Dufort, op. cit. (n. 24), I, pp. 391, 394.

54. Marguerite Glotz and Madelaine Maire, *Salons du XVIIIème siècle* (Paris, 1949), pp.264–5.

55. For life at Chaville see Howard C. Rice, *Thomas Jefferson's Paris* (Princeton, 1976), pp.96–8.

56. Both inventories in archives, château de Merville.

INTERLUDE I

1. There is a list of theatres at châteaux in Françoise Teynac, *Théâtres de Châteaux* (Paris, 1996), pp.146–7, but it deals only with existing theatres, and does not claim to be exhaustive. I made my own list on an ad hoc basis, from a variety of sources, and it is certainly incomplete.

2. *Il Luogo Teatrale a Firenze* (Spettacolo e Musica nella Firenze Medicea: Documentie restituzioni I (Florence, *c.*1980), with reconstruction of proscenium stage plan on p.95.

3. Baltasar de Beaujoyeux *Ballet comique de la Reine*, Paris, 1581 (and facsimile Binghampton, N, 1982).

4. Tallemant des Réaux, *Historiettes* I, p.73; *Gazette de France*, 28 November 1634; Sauvel, *History of Paris*.

5. The salle de spectacle at the Palais Cardinal was engraved at the time of the first performance and the engraving has often been reproduced, e.g. O.G. Brockett *History of the Theatre* (3d ed., 1977), p.221.

6. Emil Magne, *Voiture de les Années de Gloire de l'Hôtel de Rambouillet* (Paris, 1912), pp.250–55, quoting *Gazette de France* and other sources.

7. Godefroy *Le Cerémonial Français* (1649) vol. II.

8. See ch. 3, p.88–9.

9. *Mémoires de Nicolas Goulas* (Soc. Hist. de France, Paris, 1879), pp.100–101.

10. Montpensier, op. cit. (ch. 3, n. 23), II, pp.249-50.

11. *Clélie,* vol.V, pt. 2 (1662 ed.), p.758.

12. The entry in the joiner's accounts is to 'avoir dressé le théâtre et les portiques des décorations dans l'une des grandes chambres'. Quoted Jean Cordey, Vaux-le-Vicomte (Paris, 1924), p.204.

13. *Historiettes,* II, p.307.

14. Archives, château of Maille.

15. G. Macon, *Les Arts dans la Maison de Condé* (Paris, 1903), pp.104–8.

16. *La Vie de Voltaire* (anon, Paris, 1786), pp.52–3.

17. Quoted in Teynac, op. cit. (n. 1), pp.25–6.

18. Quoted in Larrondo, op. cit. (ch. 7, n. 49), p.287.

19. *Journal Inédit* (ch. 7, n. 18), II, pp.384–5.

20. Archives, château of Parentignat.

21. Designs illustrated in Macon, op. cit. (n. 15).

22. Nancy Mitford, *Madame de Pompadour* (London, 1954), p.24.

23. Dufort, op. cit. (ch. 7, n.24), pp.86–7.

24. Ibid.,I, p.334.

25. Young, *Travels in France*, September 1787; Dufort, op. cit., I, pp.132, 433.

26. The date is inscribed on the theatre.

27. Institut de France, Ms 1661, f. 90.

28. Ibid., Ms 1667, f. 182 et seq.

29. Norvins, op. cit. (ch. 7, n. 32), I, pp.105–8. The château is now a hospital, and most of its fittings have been sold.

30. Zurich, op. cit. (ch. 7, n. 39), p.194.

31. Ibid., pp.384–5.

32. Teynac, op. cit. (n. 1), pp.46–55.

33. Ibid., pp. 72–9.

34. Ibid., pp. 108–119.

35. Ibid., pp.124–9. *Les Schneider, Le Creusot: une famille, une entreprise, une ville 1836–1960* (Catalogue of exhibition, Musée D'Orsay, Paris, and Écomusée, Le Creusot, 1995), pp.98–101.

36. Undated press cutting, archives Olivier, Vicomte de Rohan-Chabot.

37. Livre d'Or in archives, château of Brissac.

38. Photographs and other material, archives, château of Boisset-les-Prévanches, kindly communicated by Comte Hugues de Bonardi du Mesnil.

39. Teynac, op. cit. (n. 1), pp.130-45.

INTERLUDE 2

1. Shown on the plan of the château in the Ms treaty of architecture by Jean Cherau, Public Archives, Gdansk.

2. Lecoy de La Marche, op. cit. (ch. 4, n. 2), p.248.

3. Mesqui, op. cit. (ch. 2, n. 9), II, pp.182–6, part of a comprehensive section on 'l'Hygiène'.

4. Corrozet, op. cit. (ch. 3, n. 2), p.36r.

5. Chatenet, op. cit. (ch. 3, n. 51), p. 29, p. 31 n.60 and annotated plans.

6. AD Maine-et-Loire, E2099.

7. Brantôme, *Des Dames* (*Oeuvres Complètes,* IX, Paris, 1876), pp.203-4.

8. Bassompierre, op. cit. (ch. 4, n. 16), pp.1, 155; Piganiol de la Force, *Description de Paris,* IX, p.228; Havard, under 'bains', quoting Saint-Foix, *Essais historiques sur Paris* III, p.38.

9. Savot, *L'Architecture Française* (1624, new ed. Paris, 1685), I, pp.102–8.

10. There is a long description of the Versailles salle de bains in Havard, IV, pp.900-901.

11. Article on Pibrac by Bruno Tollon, quoting the inventories, in *Châteaux en Haute-Garonne* (ed. Daniel Briand, Paris, 1995). A small terracotta model of the plan as revealed by the excavations is preserved in the château.

12. Shown on Mariette's plan (reproduced, p. 131).

13. Plans and exterior views published by Marot in *Le Magnifique Chasteau de Richelieu* (Paris, n.d.).

14. Mariette, *Grand Marot* (op. cit. ch. 5 n.3) vol. I.

15. J.-F. Blondel, *Maisons de Plaisance* (1737), I, p.71–5.

16. Briseux, *Maisons de Campagne* (Paris, 1743), I, pp.7–8.

17. Blondel, op. cit., I, pp.71–7; II, pp.129 et seq.

18. Voltaire, *Correspondance* op.cit. (ch.7 n.i4), 5, p.414.

19. Plan in the Cotte collection in BN est, reproduced in the published catalogue 290, nos. 22–4.

20. Described in inventory of 1741, AN 1AP 470, f. 244v.

21. Malboissière, op cit. (ch. 6, n. 9).

22. As listed in the inventory a.d. of M. Lemaistre de La Martinière. AN, MC XCI, 1211.

23. As quoted for 1765, 1773 and 1779 by Havard, IV, p.902.

24. Photograph in Bibliothèque des Arts Décoratifs, Paris. The room is shown in Clérisseau's plan of château Borély, reproduced Jean-Luc Massot, *Architecture et Décoration du XVIme au XIXme siècle* (Aix-en-Provence, 1992), p.231.

25. German Boffrand, *Livre d'Architecture* (1745).

26. Illustrated pls. 43 and 44, Jean Chavigny, *Le château de Ménars* (Paris, 1954). Marigny talked about it to Joseph Jekyll, when he visited in 1775: 'Don't overlook the hydraulique machine I have lately constructed on an improved plan of your affair at Chelsea. The first agent in mine is water, and it is a masterpiece of mechanics that would do honour even to an English artist.' *Correspondence of Mr Joseph Jekyll*, quoted in N. Mitford, *Madame de Pompadour* (London, 1954), pp.150-51.

27. Information Comte Patrice de Feuillade de Chauvin.

28. BN est Va 27 (Eure) T7.

29. Archives, château de Barbentane. The design is based on an unidentified engraving, also in the archives.

30. Information Marquis de Contades.

31. Information Comte Geoffroy d'Anthenaise.

32. AD Maine-et-Loire, Angers, 90J.

33. Information Comte Geoffroy d'Anthenaise.

34. Dominique Letellier, *Le château de Montgeoffroy : architecture et mode de vie* (Angers, 1991), p.140.

35. Information Vicomte de La Panouse.

36. Plans, etc. AN 143AP (cartes et plans) 527–8.

37. Information Comte Hugues de Bonardi du Mesnil.

38. Information Vicomtesse Jean-Pierre de Baritault du Carpia.

39. Christiane Mazery and Jean de Nicolay (eds.), *Lettres de Famille* (privately printed, 1989), p.275.

40. Plans in AN 143AP (cartes et plans), 29 (Mennetou), 4 (Chaumont).

41. Pauline Prevost-Marcilhacy, *Les Rothschild, bâtisseurs et mécènes* (Paris, 1995), p.212 (Armainvilliers plan), p.273 (Ferrières, with illustration).

INTERLUDE 3

1. La Marche, op. cit. (ch. 3, n. 16), p.583.

2. Lists printed in Tarbé, op. cit. (ch. 2, n. 17), pp.76–87.

3. Published Joubert, op. cit. (ch. 3, n. 26), p.60.

4. La Tremoille, op. cit. (see ch. 3, n. 30).

5. There is no simple household list in Gouberville's *Journal* (see ch. 3, n. 8), but its approximate size can be gathered by scattered references to payment of wages, etc.

6. A. Join-Lambert *Le château de Quermelin* (Évreux, 1886).

7. Longueville, BN Ms NAF9647/18, f. 26 et seq.; Thouars, see n. 3; Le Lude, 'Une livre de gages', *Province du Maine* XLII (1897), quoted Calbo, op. cit. (ch. 3, n. 10), pp.46–7; Richelieu, Deloche, *Maison de Richelieu* (ch. 3, n. 57); Epernon, Bridon agreement published Henri Ribadieu, *Les Châteaux de Gironde* (2nd ed., Paris, 1856), pp.294–7.

8. Antoine Aubery, *L'Histoire du Cardinal Duc de Richelieu* (new ed., Cologne, 1666), II, p.437.

9. J. de Callière, *Traité de la fortune des Gens de Qualité* (Paris, 1661), p.104.

10. Audiger, *La Maison Reglée*, printed in Franklin, *La Vie Privée* (Paris 1887–1901) vol. 23, pp.11–12, 68–9.

11. Musée Condé, château de Chantilly, Ms 1260.

12. Chaussinand-Nogaret, op. cit. (ch. 1, n.2), p.57.

13. Genlis, op. cit. (ch. 5, n. 16), p.126.

14. J. Sabattier, *Figaro et son maître: domestiques à Paris* (Paris, 1984) is a comprehensive and thoroughly documented study. Although concerned primarily with Paris, ch.VI ('Madame Bertier de Sauvigny et ses domestiques') deals with a household in both town and country.

15. The many later eighteenth-century plans, executed and unexecuted, of the Britanny amateur architect the Commandeur de Brilhac (AD Ile-et-Vilaine, 13J 52) show kitchen arrangements in some detail.

16. As listed in inventory (see ch.7, n.48).

17. Plan in archives, château of Le Touvet.

18. Olivier Meslay, 'Un inventaire du château de Mazères en 1776', *Bulletin de la Société archéologique du Gers*, 1997.

19. Archives, château of Commarin.

20. Norvins, op. cit. (ch. 7, n. 32), I, pp.116-17.

21. Forster, op. cit. (ch. 7, n. 28), pp.170-72.

22. P. Meyer, *Noblesse de Bretagne* II, pp. 1188–91. For similar figures for Bordeaux see W. Doyle, *Parlement of Bordeaux* (1974), p.127.

23. Chateaubriand, *Mémoires d'Outre Tombe*.

24. Archives, château of Longpra.

25. Mazery and Nicolay, op. cit. (int.2, n.39), p.417.

26. Paul Chabot, *Jean et Yvonne domestiques en 1900* (Paris, 1977), p.33, etc.; Pauline de Pange, *Comment j'ai vu 1901* (Paris, 1975), p.16.

27. Inventaire, AN 14 AP 1 doss. 4.

28. Inventaires, archives châteaux of Longpra and Flines (for Flines see also ch.7, n.51).

29. Christian de Nicolay, *Aux jours d'autrefois* (1980), quoted in Christiane de Nicolay-Mazery, *La vie de château* (Paris, 1991) pp. 78–9.

30. The household and social life of the Murats is copiously documented in their archive, now AN, 31 AP. The lists of household in 1906–20, 31AP 293; extra staff for entertainments, 31AP 92.

31. Inventory, AN, 31AP 537.

32. Inventory, AD Finisterre 109J43.

33. Pange, op cit. (n. 26), pp.16–17.

34. Manuscript memoirs, archives, château of Montfort. Photocopy kindly supplied by Christiane de Nicolay-Mazery.

35. Pange, op. cit., (n. 26), pp.303-4.

36. Chabot, op. cit. (n. 26), pp.94-118.

INTERLUDE 4

1. The relationship of basse-cour to main château is vividly shown in many of the views of towns, and châteaux in the 'Armorial de Revel' (BN Ms FR22297), a survey of the seigneurie of Louis de Bourbon, Comte d'Auvergne, in central France (part published by G. Fournier, *Châteaux, villages et villes d'Auvergne au XVe siècle d'après l'Armorial de G. Revel*, Geneva, 1973). It is interesting to see how many of the basse-cours are filling up with housing and in the process of becoming villages or even towns, a process accentuated in succeeding centuries.

2. *Revue des Sociétés Savantes*, 7th series V (1882), p.259 et seq.

3. Sylvia Pressouyre, *Le château de Tarascon* (official guide, Paris, 1982), p.33.

4. D. Hervier, *Pierre le Gendre et son inventaire après décès 1524*, (Paris, 1977) pp.678–80.

5. From his description of the château of Bury, vol. I of *Les Plus Excellents Bastimens*.

6. Héroard, op. cit. (ch.3, n.23), II, p.194.

7. Montpensier, op. cit. (ch.3, n.23) II, p.214.

8. E. Tambour, *Les Gondi et le Château de Noisy* (Paris, 1925).

9. See ch.6, n. 6.

10. Liger, *Nouvelle Maison Rustique* (1721 ed.), p.33–4.

11. Young, op. cit. (ch. 7, n. 1), p.77 (entry for 10 September 1787).

12. Inventory, 1844, archives, château de Longpra.

13. Armaillé, *Quand on savait vivre heureux* (Paris, 1934), p.145.

14. Mazery and Nicolay, op. cit. (int. 2, n.39), p.53.

15. AN, 31AP 528.

16. Ibid.

17. AN 31 AP 524.

INTERLUDE 5

1. For Noisy, see ch.4, n.8; for Richelieu, int. 2, n.13, and bird's-eye view reproduced on p. 271; for Fleury, J.-M. Pérouse de Montclos (ed.) *Le Garde du Patrimoine: Ile-de-France* (Paris, 1994), pp. 265–8.

2. J.-P. Babelon and Claude Mignot (eds.), *François Mansart: le génie de l'architecture*, pp.118–22, with a good eighteenth-century plan of the lay-out.

3. Ibid., p. 179, n. 18; Ile de France (n. 1), pp.382–3.

4. Françoise Vignier, *Bourgogne Nivernais* (Paris, 1980, one of the three volumes of the discontinued *Dictionnaire des châteaux de France*), pp.262–3. The original plan, or a photocopy, is on show in a useful small exhibition in the stables.

5. Baritou and Foussard, op. cit. (ch.6, n.27), pp.115–19.

6. Ibid., pp. 57, 61.

7. Plans, etc., AN, 143AP 189 and AP4 (cartes et plans)123, 130.

8. In addition to the covered court at Gatines, illustrated in this book, there is a good example (with an iron and glass roof) at the château of Beaumanoir, also at the châteaux of Meillant, Vauboisseau, Montmirey-la-Ville (see p.327), and no doubt many others.

9. Plans, AN, 143AP 4 (cartes et plans), 172.

10. A. Johannet, *Vérités Sociales* (Paris, 1850), quoted in Toulier, op. cit. (ch. 6, n. 21), p.16.

CHAPTER 8

1. E.g. the pioneering *Architecture d'hier* (n. 5), Bernard Toulier *Châteaux en Sologne* (Paris, 1992), Pauline Prevost-Marcilhacy, *Les Rothschild* (Paris, 1995, English ed. 1996) and articles by Vincent Bouvet, Guy Le Goff, Claude d'Anthenaise and others.

2. Toulier, op. cit. (ch. 6, n. 21), p.179.

3. Archives, château of Parentignat.

4. Abbé Methivier, *Études rurales* (Paris, 1861), p.9, quoted in Toulier, p.163.

5. Baron Olivier de Wismes, *Le Maine et l'Anjou historiques, archéologiques et pittoresques* (Paris, 1862), 45e notice. Le Bourg d'Iré quoted in *Architecture d'hier: Grandes demeures angevines au XIXe siècle: l'oeuvre de René Hodé* (Édition de la Caisse Nationale des Monuments Historiques, Paris, n.d.).

6. Prevost-Marcilhacy, op. cit. (n. 1), pp.104–5, 308–10.

7. The rooms are so described in contemporary articles in *Fermes et Châteaux* and elsewhere.

8. *Fermes et Châteaux*, I, no. 4 (December 1905), pp.15–19.

9. Pange, op. cit. (int.3, n.26), p.181.

10. In the inventory of 1901 (AN, 31AP 537) the room described as 'hall' on the plan (AN, 31AP550) is called 'salle de billard'.

11. Mary King Waddington, *Châteaux and Country Life in France* (London, 1908, illustrated), pp.90–91.

12. There was a 'fumoir' at Trevarez, in a corner tower leading off the bibliothèque (plan AD Finisterre, 109J13). And e.g. article on 'le cabinet de travail' in *Fermes et Châteaux* IX (1908–9), p.217. 'Beaucoup de cabinets de travail sont en même temps le fumoir, et les quelques cigares qu'on y consomme après diner sont prétexte pour l'hôte à montrer les belles reliures que recèle sa bibliothèque'.

13. The enormously rambling and irregular Rothschild château of Armainvilliers (Prevost-Marcilhacy, p.212) is quite untypical and clearly influenced by the plans of George Devey, who worked for the Rothschilds in England.

14. John Bateman, *The Great Landowners of Britain and Ireland* (London, 1971, a reprint of the 1883, and last edition).

15. 'Les réalisations rurales des propriétaires terriens entre 1840 et 1870', in *Grands Demeures*, op.cit. (n. 5).

16. Toulier op.cit. (n.1), pp.170–71.

17. Pange op.cit. (int.3, n.26), pp. 45–7, 207.

18. Archives, château of Roquetaillade.

19. Prevost-Marcilhacy, op.cit. (n.1), p.326.

20. A sizeable collection of White's designs for Schickler are now in the RIBA Drawings Collection, London.

21. The architectural drawings of the Destailleurs are now mainly divided between Paris (AN [cartes et plans] 536AP) and Berlin (Kunstbibliothek OZ 107, vol. I–XX).

22. There is a useful article on Combourg in the periodical *La vie à la campagne*, 1 (1906), pp.140–47. Some good contemporary watercolours of the interiors are preserved in the château.

23. Biographical entries in J. Valynseele *Les Say et leurs alliances* (Paris, 1971).

24. Jacques de Broglie, *Histoire du château de Chaumont* (1944), especially pp.212–26. Plans in AN, 143AP (cartes et plans), 4.

25. Family tree and much else in *Les Schneider*, op.cit. (int.1, n.35).

26. Armaillé, op.cit. (int.4, n.14), p.38.

27. Toulier op.cit. (n.1), pp.173,177.

28. B. Heudé and B. Toulier,' Chasse, famille et mondanités: Rivaulde à la Belle Époque', *Les Schneider*, pp.114–29.

29. Copy in the library of château of Schoppenwihr.

30. Typescript recollections of de Rohan-Chabot, archives, Olivier, Vicomte de Rohan.

31. Waddington op.cit. (n.11), p.39.

32. Armaillé op.cit. (int.4, n.14) pp.93–4.

33. Jean Puget, *La duchesse d'Uzès née Mortemart* (Paris, 1937), pp.10–16.

34. Waddington, op.cit., p.39.

35. Ms. description, archives Olivier, Vicomte de Rohan.

36. I am grateful to the Baron d'Aligny for showing me the memoirs and allowing me to take photographs.

37. Vincent Bouvet, 'Le château de Voisins', *Monuments Historiques* No.142, Dec/Jan 1986, pp.81–96.

CHAPTER 9

1. Pierre de Brissac, *En d'autres temps* (Paris, 1972) pp. 56–7.

INDEX

Malouinières (St Malo merchants' houses) 137, *137*
mangeoir 102
manoirs 27, 83, 95–6
Mansart, François *119*, 126–7, 134–5, 150, 283–4, *283*, *284*
Mansart, Jules Hardouin 21–2
Marais, château of 152
Marchand (treasurer of Grande Demoiselle) 89, 107
Marchès, Aymerigot 41
Maretz, Hubert de 101
Mareuil, château of 266
Maréchal, Sylvain 154
Margaret of Austria 87, 92
Marguerite de Navarre; *Heptameron* 72–3, 88
Marguerite de Vienne 125–6
Marie de Medici, Queen of France 107, 108
Marie-Antoinette, Queen of France 155, 170, 275–6
Mariette, Jean 225, *227*
Marigny, Abel François, Marquis de 153, 177–8, 229
marionettes 206
Marivaux, Pierre Carlet de Chamblin de 216
Marly, château of (Yvelines) 135
Marseille 88, 90
★Martainville, château of (Seine-Maritime) 65, *65*
Martel, François, of Charolles 285
Martinvast, château of (Manche) 317, 318
masques 88–9, 130, 200
Maulnes, château of (Yonne) 223
Mazarin, Jules, Cardinal 131
★Mazères, château of (Gers) 254
meals 91–2, 96, *97*, 124, 141–2, 200
see also dinners
medieval style 28, 300, *301*, 308, *310*, 322–3
Mehun-sur-Yèvre, château of (Cher) *51*, 51
★Meillant, château of (Cher) *15*, 16, 336, 345 n.8
staircase towers *80*–1, 81–2, 83
Ménars, château of (Loir-et-Cher) 177–8, 229
Menetou-Salon, château of (Cher) 238
Mentmore, England 308, 317
merchants' houses, St Malo 137, *137*
Mercier, L.-S. 148–9
Mercier de Compiègne, Claude François Xavier 153
★Merville, château of (Haute-Garonne) 140, *140*, *141*, 195, 206
'La Garçonnière' *162*, 190, 206

Mesarnou, manoir of (Finistère) 96
Mesnil-au-Val, manoir of (Manche) 98, 102, 248
Methivier, Abbé 298–9
métayage (shared-profit lettings) 276
Michou (game) 87
Middle Ages 30–65
households 240–6
later imitation 28
logis 52–7
towers 54–64
see also feudal system
migration, town/country 166, 179–80, 261–2, 321–2, 335–6
Millement, château of (Yvelines) 156, *157*
minstrels 33, 34, 35, 36
mirrors *119*, 153, 154
Missery, château of (Côte d'Or) 22, *23*, 224, *225*
moats 78, 129, 266, *266*, *267*
Molé, Mathieu-François 287
Molière, Jean Baptiste Poquelin 130, 201–2
Monbrun, chartreuse of (Dordogne) 24–5
Moncley, château of (Doubs) 22, *146*, 156, *188*, 188–9, 288
Monet, Paul; dictionary 118
money economy 38
★Montaner, château of (Pyrenées-Atlantiques) 34, *36*, 37, 55
Montargis, château of (Loiret) 44, *46*, 282
Montesquieu, Charles de Secondat, Baron de la Brède et de 180
Montfort, château of 237, 257, 261, 278
★Montgeoffroy, château of (Maine-et-Loir) *6*–7, 22, *23*, 189, *194*, 231, *234*
harness room *280*, 293
household *255*, *256*
stables 286, *287*
water supply 231, *234*, 235, *236*
Montglat, château of 89, 107
Montmirey-la-Ville, château of (Jura) 326, *326*–7, 328, 329–30, 345 n.8
Montmorency, Anne de, Constable of France 101, 106–7, 112, 120
Montorgueil, seigneury of 11–12
Montpensier, Anne Marie Louise d'Orléans, Duchesse de (Grande Mademoiselle) 105, 115–16
châteaux 127, 135, 200
in Fronde 127, 270
journey to Blois 87, 89, 107, 270
★Montreuil-Bellay, château of (Maine-et-Loire) 38
★Montréal, château of (Dordogne) 74, 96–8

Monts, château of (near Poitiers) 182
More, Clément 239
motor cars *292*, *293*, 293–4, 323, *327*, 330–1
staff 259, 263
Mouchy, château of (Oise) 337
mourning 115–16
Moustier, Marquis Leonel de *28*–9
Murat family 258–9, *262*, 279, *316*, 318
musical instruments 138, 195

names of noblesse 18–19, 22
★Nancy, château or Palais Ducal of (Meurthe-et-Moselle) 91, *91*
nannies 263, 307
★Nantes, château of (Loire-Atlantique) 81
Napoleon I, Emperor of France 24, 26, 55, 211
see also Code Napoléon
Napoleon III, Emperor of France 26, 299
needlework 325–6
new rich 212–13, 216, 235, 237–9, 315–21
Nicolay family 184, 237, 257, 258, 261, 278
noblesse 10–29
buying of 17, 18, 65
connotations of term 12
and crown 74, 130–1, 250
de robe and d'épée 17–19, 20–1, 166
inner core 21, 26, 27
legal status 14, 16, 18
medieval system 12–16
myth of 20, 21
and non-nobles 27, 79, 336–7
numbers 14, 20
post-medieval development 16–22
privileges 14, 17–18
provincial 166, 195, 298, 321
and Revolution 12, 24, 26–7, 299, 314
towers symbolic for 21–2, 22–3
see also inheritance; names; seigneuries; taxation; titles
Noilly-Prat family 235
Noisy, château of (Yvelines) 88–9, 200, 271, 282
Nonette, château of (Puy-de-Dôme) 41
noria (pump) 231, *233*, 235, *236*
novels 87–8
nurses 247, *261*

office 252, 254, 257, 263
★Oiron, château of (Deux-Sèvres) 106, 116, *117*
frescoes 77, 112, 113, *113*
★Olhain, château of (Pas-de-Calais) 266, *266*–7

orangeries 176, 203, 206
oratories 52, 59, *59* 113, 150
Orléans, Gaston, Duc d' 200
Orléans, Louis, Duc d' 54, 63
Ormesson, château of (Val-de-Marne) 189
Orthez, château of (Pyrenées-Atlantiques) 34, 37, 111
★Oudon, château of (Loire-Atlantique) 62, *62*
Oureille, Rigault d' 68, *69*, 72, 75–6
Ouville, Antoine le Metel d'; *Contes* 87–8, 101
ovens 101–2, 252
see also bakehouses
Ovid, scenes from *117*

pages 244
paint, scented 153–4
paintings
in cabinets *110*, 116
in chambres *124*–5
in galleries 112, 113, *113*, 116, 127
of Merville garçonnerie *162*
in salons *128*, 132, *133*
see also frescoes
palaces
bishops' 42–4, 55–60, 92, 245
ceilings 57
grandes salles 44, *49*, 51, 79
see also under Avignon; Paris; Poitiers; Versailles
palfreniers 244
paneterie 243
★Pange, château of (Moselle) 261
Pange, Pauline Comtesse Jean de 257 n.26, 261, 262 n.35, 308, 315 n.17
papacy 13, 17, 26, 220
see also under Avignon
Paris
Arsenal 199
Bastille 136, 270
boudoirs 154, 155
Comédie Française 200
courtesans 154, 155, 228
Galerie des Merciers 112
Hôtel de Petit-Bourbon 198, *199*
Hôtel de Soubise 225, *227*, 286
Louvre 46, 48, 53, 71–2, 108, 223
Marais 120
Palais Bourbon 206, 250, 228
Palais de Justice 46
Palais de la Cité 41, 44, 46, 112
Palais-Royal 199–200
Parlement 18, 19, 46, 71, 74; ennoblement of members 17, 170
'Pink Palace', Champs-Élysées 318

provincial noblesse in 321, 328
royal government 44, 71
salles à manger 104
salon culture 120, 121–5
town houses of nobility 127, 155, 166, 169, 227, 321, 328;
see also individual houses above
Tuileries 198
Paris, Comte de 334
parlements 12, 22
see also under Paris
Parliament, British 167, 313, 314
Passy, château of (Paris) 207
Patte, Pierre 150
★Pau, château of (Pyrenées-Atlantiques) 34, 37, 55
pavillons 108, 135, 251
des bains 223
Paxton, Sir Joseph 308, 317
Perceval romances 44, 76
Perelles (engravers) 283
personalization of logis 108, 114, 116, 117
Petit-Trianon 275–6
photography 307, *332*, 336
Pibrac, château of (Haute-Garonne) *117*, 223
Picot, Gille, *see* Gouberville, sire de
Picque, Richard, Archbishop of Reims 43, 245
★Pierrefonds, château of (Oise) 63, 220
Pignerol 130
Pinsaguel, château of (Haute-Garonne) 180
Pisan, Christine de 41, *112*
Platter, Thomas 88, 90
Plessis-Belleville, château of (Oise) 134–5
plumbing *see* sanitation
poêles (stoves) 54, 223
Poisson de Bourvallais, Paul 137
Poitiers 46, 179
Palais des Comtes 39, 41, 44, 48, *49*, 51, 57
★Polignac, château of (Haute-Loire) 169, *170*
Polignac family 169–70, 178, 207, 300, 318
Pompadour, château of (Corrèze) 258
Pompadour, Jeanne Antoinette Poisson, Marquise de 147–8, *156*, 156, 207
Pont, château of (Aube) *126*, 270
Pont d'Ain (Ain) 87, 92
Porte-Mars, château of, Reims 56, 245–6
porters 245, 251–2, *252*
post-war years 334–7
potager (stewing stove) 252, *253*
presses in basse-cour 263, 269, 276
Prétieuses 119–20, 137
primogeniture 26, 315, 335

ACKNOWLEDGEMENTS

Archives Nationales, Paris:
  236 (above), 278, 312
Michel Berger: 85, 302
  (above)
Bibliothèque de l'Arsenal,
  Paris: 34
Bibliothèque des Arts
  Decoratifs, Paris: 226, 227
  (above and below)
Bibliothèque Mejanes, Aix-
  en-Provence: 22
Bibliothèque Nationale de
  France, Paris: 36, 57 (below
  right), 91, 115, 121, 126
  (below), 134, 169, 199, 209,
  224, 233, 249, 252, 271,
  272, 279, 309, 310
Bibliothèque Publique et
  Universitaire, Geneva: 54
Caisse nationale des
  monuments historiques et
  des sites, Paris: 24, 37
  (below, left and right), 39,
  49, 66, 68, 69 (above left
  and right), 74, 75, 106, 116,
  117 (below), 119, 133, 156,
  229, 266
Castelet, Boulogne: 288
Château de Longpra: 189
Château du Plessis-Bourré: 69
  (below), 73
Collection Thyssen-
  Bornemisza: 152
Conservation des antiquités et
  objets d'art, Departement
  de Maine-et-Loire: 259,
  304, 308
Country Life, London: 64,
  110, 114, 128, 145
Direction Regional de affaires
  cultural du pays de la Loire:
  62 (right), 291
Ecomusée du Creusot: 214
Georges Fessy: 127, 150
Photo Marc Garanger: 181
Mark Girouard: 15 (below),
  29, 56, 57 (above), 58, 59,
  62 (left), 65, 137, 231, 235,
  236 (below), 237, 253, 260,
  264, 267 (above and below),
  269, 276, 277 (above and
  below), 282, 285 (above and
  below), 286, 287, 295
  (below), 314
Jean Guillaume: 113
Philip Hawkes: 23 (below),
  143, 157
Inventaire général,
  A.D.A.G.P.: 197, 215
  (photos. Michel Rosso),
  313, 322 (photos. R.
  Malnoury)
A.F. Kersting: 130 (below)
Mairie de La Ferté-Vidame:
  171
Mairie de Raon l'Etape: 2
Manoir de Kernault: 138,
  261

Rosine Mazine: 142 (above
  and below)
Musée de Beaux-Arts de
  Tours: 103
Musée de la Chasse et de la
  Nature, Paris: 164
Musée Condé, Chantilly
  (photo Giraudon): 30, 50,
  51, 112, 148, 149, 240, 242
Nationalbibliothek, Vienna: 52
Jean-Bernard Naudin: 258
Thomas Pakenham: 15
  (above), 80, 125, 151
  (above, below and right),
  225, 238, 290
Photo RMN (Réunion des
  Musées Nationaux): 97, 274
Private collections: 3, 14 (left),
  18, 23, 162, 185 (above and
  below), 186, 188 (photo.
  Jean-Michel Tardy), 195,
  208, 213, 216 (above and
  below), 217 (above), 233
  (above), 255, 256 (above
  and below), 257, 262, 263,
  289 (above and below), 292,
  293, 294, 295, 300, 306
  (photos. Caroline Rose),
  316, 317, 319, 321, 326–7,
  330, 331, 332
Bernard Renoux: 42, 45, 63,
  77, 82, 84, 94, 95, 109, 191,
  194, 212, 218, 234 (above,
  left and right, below), 244,
  280, 302 (below), 303, 305
Caroline Rose: 284
Royal Institute of British
  Architects, London: 139,
  283
Service départemental de
  l'inventaire, Maine-et-Loire
  (photos. Bruno Rousseau):
  7, 193
Sotheby's: 217 (below)
Jean-Michel Tardy: 10, 14
  (right), 25 (above and
  below), 32, 60, 61, 89, 96,
  99, 117 (above), 141 (above
  and below), 146, 158, 159,
  160 (above, below left and
  right), 161 (above), 177,
  201, 202, 203 (left and
  right), 205 (above and
  below), 232, 250, 275, 296,
  301

Most of the plans have been
drawn for this edition by
Chris Orr Associates. The
plans of Montgeoffroy (p.192)
are based on those in
Dominique Letellier's *Le
château de Montgeoffroy*
(Angers, 1991).